Books by J. Frank Dobie

A VAQUERO OF THE BRUSH COUNTRY

CORONADO'S CHILDREN

ON THE OPEN RANGE

TONGUES OF THE MONTE

TALES OF THE MUSTANG

THE FLAVOR OF TEXAS

APACHE GOLD AND YAQUI SILVER

JOHN C. DUVAL: FIRST TEXAS MAN OF LETTERS

THE LONGHORNS

GUIDE TO LIFE AND LITERATURE OF THE SOUTHWEST

A TEXAN IN ENGLAND

THE VOICE OF THE COYOTE

THE BEN LILLY LEGEND

THE LONGHORNS

THE STAMPEDE

Original mural is in the U. S. Post Office, Odessa, Texas

THE LONGHORNS

BY J. FRANK DOBIE

ILLUSTRATED BY TOM LEA

LITTLE, BROWN AND COMPANY · BOSTON

English.

Published March 1941
Reprinted March 1941
Reprinted May 1942
Reprinted August 1943
Reprinted February 1944
Reprinted August 1944
Reprinted April 1945
Reprinted September 1945
Reprinted June 1947
Reprinted April 1949
Reprinted December 1950

41-51625
6/9/51

CONTENTS

INTRODUCTORY: MAKERS OF HISTORY

THE TEXAS LONGHORN made more history than any
other breed of cattle the civilized world has known. As an
animal in the realm of natural history, he was the peer of bison
or grizzly bear. As a social factor, his influence on men was
extraordinary. An economic agent in determining the character
and occupation of a territory continental in its vastness, he
moved elementally with drouth, grass, blizzards out of the Arctic
and the wind from the south. However supplanted or however
disparaged by evolving standards and generations, he will remain the bedrock on which the history of the cow country of
America is founded. In picturesqueness and romantic realism his
name is destined for remembrance as long as the memory of
man travels back to those pristine times when waters ran clear,
when free grass waved a carpet over the face of the earth, and

America's Man on Horseback — not a helmeted soldier, but a booted cowboy — rode over the rim with all the abandon, energy, insolence, pride, carelessness and confidence epitomizing the booming West.

The Longhorn was, as will be detailed, basically Spanish. Yet, when he entered upon the epoch of his continent-marking history, he was as Texan as his counterpart, the Texas cowboy. *Cavalier* means "horseman." The Texan had behind him the horse-riding tradition of the more literal than figurative "cavalier South." In the lower part of Texas he met the herd-owning Spanish *caballero* — which word also means "horseman." He met the Spaniard's *vaquero*, the mounted worker with cows. He met the ranching industry of the open range, appropriated it, and shortly thereafter began extending it beyond the limits of the wildest initial dream. The coming together, not in blood but in place and occupation, of this Anglo-American, this Spanish owner, and this Mexican vaquero produced the Texas cowboy — a blend, a type, new to the world. The cow that called forth both him and the industry he represented was the mother of the Texas Longhorn.

The same cow was in California. The Anglo-Americans that towards high noon of the last century suddenly rushed into that land and took it over were all gold-mad. They went to eating up the cow. With gold to buy with and the cow almost consumed, the price of meat rose to such heights that early in the 1850's Texas cowboys, ready to fight Comanche or Apache, began driving herds to California. Geology, geography and the character of Texas cows, cowboys and cowmen, together with movements of population and with economic conditions, conspired to put the Texan stamp upon the range industry of all Western America.

When it had nothing else, Texas had more and more land for the raising of cattle and more and more cattle for the world beyond. At the very hour of the battle of San Jacinto, which gave Texas her independence, a herd of Texas cattle was being trailed to New Orleans, which for decades continued as a market, cattle being shipped thence north by boat. Shreveport and Vidalia (opposite Natchez on the Mississippi) and New Iberia were other loading points. A good many cattle were shipped from Texas ports. Before the Civil War thousands had been trailed to Chicago. During the forties and fifties, Missouri and other states of the Middle West received many small herds. At least one went to New York.

Meanwhile ranches were expanding. If a range became crowded, all the owner or the self-dependent cattle had to do was to push on. The depredating Indians were a hundred times more avid for horses than for cattle: they raided down from lands swarming with buffaloes, and generally they preferred buffalo meat to cow meat. A reserve of cattle was mounting from which the exports and the negligible home consumption amounted to hardly a tithe. Beef for eating was virtually free to whoever wanted to go out and kill.

According to Department of Agriculture figures, in 1860 the United States (including Texas) had 31,417,331 people and 25,640,337 cattle; in 1870, more than 40,000,000 people and a decrease in cattle to the number of 21,633,069. Yet during the first half of this period the Texas cattle had probably doubled in number. Here in Texas was a population so sparse that half the state's area still belonged to the Indian and the buffalo. At the same time, cattle were so plentiful and capital so utterly lacking that at the end of the War they could not be sold for a dollar apiece. As late as 1874, "Fine fat beef sells at three cents per lb. in San Marcos market stalls." Before the Texans put a single branded cow on the luxuriant grass of their own Panhandle-Plains territory — which began to be stocked in 1876 — they had driven millions of Longhorns up the trail.

The Chisholm Trail was a canal out of the mighty dammed-up reservoir of Texas beef to meat-lacking consumers with money

[xv]

to buy. That Trail became a fact when in 1867 Abilene, Kansas, with a railroad carrying stock-cars eastward — and with construction pushing rails on towards the Pacific — established a definite, dependable market for Texas cattle. The year before this, it is true, more than a quarter of a million of Longhorns had been trailed northward without specific destinations — like the boll weevil, "just looking for a home," and with results generally disastrous.

The Chisholm Trail was a lane opening out of a vast breeding ground swarming with cattle life to a vacant, virgin range of seemingly illimitable expanse. It initiated the greatest, the most extraordinary, the most stupendous, the most fantastic and fabulous migration of animals controlled by man that the world has ever known or can ever know. During the seventies the Plains Indians were all being killed off or rounded up; at the same time the buffalo were all but annihilated. An empire of vacated grass awaited occupation — an empire fringed with population far to the east — being traversed, but not halted in, by streams of human beings migrating to the Pacific slope.

Governor O. M. Roberts, the "Old Alcalde" of Texas, said "Civilization follows the plow." Over a great part of Texas and west of the Missouri River, the plow followed riders of cow ponies; and these riders followed Texas Longhorns. During a swift, dramatic, sweeping generation, the Longhorns, their trails crossing at right angles the trails of population, occupied the world being left empty by the buffaloes. The Chisholm Trail, with many prongs flowing into it from the south, was pushed farther and farther west, taking on other names and sprangling out with many extensions. These trails became rivers of Longhorns, surging and flowing to locate themselves and to establish the ranching industry — in the Indian Territory; on the high Plains of Texas; over New Mexico, Arizona, Kansas, Nebraska, the Dakotas, Wyoming, Montana; in parts of Colorado, Nevada, Utah, Idaho, and away on into Canada.

By the hundreds of thousands these Longhorns were dispensed at agencies to Indians whose natural supply of meat had vanished. Their frozen carcasses, in the seventies, were being shipped in such quantities from the Atlantic seaboard that the economy of the British Isles was disturbed. To Texas they brought financial recovery from war and reconstruction far in advance of the other Southern States, laying foundations for fortunes now hardly computable. They were the makers and shakers of a ranching boom into which syndicates from across the Atlantic and capitalists of New England frenziedly pitched millions.

After 1888 the north-flowing stream of Longhorns became a dribble. By 1895, the trails out of Texas were all fenced across or plowed under. Ten million cattle, it has been authoritatively estimated, were driven over them between 1866 and 1890.

Emphasis on the great number of Texas cattle, and on their low values at times, is likely to be misleading. Prices, as of all produce, fluctuated. Even before 1836 mature steers sold for ten dollars a head in Texas, though cash buyers were scarce. This was far more than they brought in 1866. But ten years later they were worth twenty dollars, other classes of cattle advancing accordingly. In the early eighties, prices went out of sight and the demand for stock cattle was so great that some ranges in South Texas were virtually denuded of cattle. In 1893, Texas cows — "calves throwed in" — that had sold for twenty-five dollars in 1884 brought six dollars.

It cost about a dollar a head to drive an average herd from Southern Texas to the far Northwest. At the same time, the spread in prices between the two regions was from three to five dollars a head. In some years the big trail operators made "barrels of money." Most of them, however, died broke. A common range term for cattle trader was "speculator." A man who in January contracted for June delivery of big steers might make or lose from five to twenty dollars a head. Uncertainty of rain and grass and certainty of price fluctuation have made the cattle industry the most speculative of businesses.

But this book is not a history of the cattle industry, least of all of economic development over the cow country. It is about the animal itself that generated cowboys, brought ranches into existence, gave character to the grazing world of America, and furnished material for political economy.

It attempts to show the animal's wild beginnings and his life during the times when he walked up the greatest cattle trails of history and dominated an ocean of grass, brush and mountain, before he suffered a displacement as absolute as that he was employed to make of the buffalo. His horns, hide, and hardihood will loom large in the picture. Not a psychologist, I have attempted to master cow psychology and to picture its manifestations in stampedes and silent thickets. With no claim to being a naturalist, I have gone into the habits and instincts of the animal. I am a teller of folk tales, and as a historian I have not hesitated to use scraps of folklore to enforce truth and reality.

While this book is not about the men of the range, necessarily they come into it many times, in many ways, in many episodes. They come into it as men of cattle. The psychological impact — of which they were as unconscious as the impactors — upon them by their iron-sinewed, wild-living cattle, creatures primordially harmonized to a nature that they at times defied, is a part of the Longhorn record.

"How can they be wise whose talk is of oxen?" the son of Sirach asked. John Lockwood Kipling, who begat not only the author of the Jungle Books but a very interesting book of his own entitled *Beast and Man in India*, calls the ox "the chief pillar of the Indian empire." The "close association of the ploughman with his cattle," he says, "the slow steady tramp at their heels over the field and over again in infinite turns, has given a bovine quality to the mind of those who follow the plough all round the world. Perhaps the Irish potato-digging cottier, the English market-gardener, the French vine-dresser and spade cultivators generally are smarter and more alert. The lagging, measured step may compel the mind to its cadence, and the anodyne of monotony may soothe and still the temper. However this may be, it is certain that the Indian cultivator is very like the ox. He is patient, and bears all that drouth, flood, storm and murrain can do with the same equanimity with which the ox bears blows. When the oxen chew the cud and their masters take their nooning, the jaws of man and beast move in exactly the same manner."

But no "brother to the ox" was the cowboy of the Longhorn range. The men that have ridden down the dawn have never been fat and scant of breath. They often rode into camp and drank coffee sitting in the saddle, ready to spring forward. At pools they dipped up water with the hand, in the manner of the chosen fighters under Gideon, with eyes averted, made ceaselessly alert by the alert animals they watered with. Many a night they slept booted and spurred and ready to ride. They knew how to linger; they had "ample time"; but their repose was the repose of strength capable of steel-spring action and not that of constitutional lethargy.

I myself have ridden a few good horses, not only on the range but as a mounted artilleryman. Directing a battery of field artillery in a hot gallop, the caissons rumbling and rattling, the harness jingling, the eager horses pounding the earth into a tremble, gives a wonderful exhilaration. It must be a fine feeling that some men get from riding a proud and beautiful horse on exhibition before admiring spectators. The chase of cat or wolf to the music of hounds and horn is dawn itself. But I do not believe that any kind of riding will pump *virtue* into a man like that in pursuit of wild, strong, mighty-horned cattle plunging for liberty or just walking like phalanxes of destiny towards the tail end of the world. In any just comprehension of the Longhorn, his effect on men emanates constantly — like the effect of sailing ships and oceans upon "the Children of the Sea."

I appeared on this spinning globe just as the Texas Longhorn was being whirled off it. But it was my fortune — good fortune, I have always regarded it for myself — to be born in that part of Texas where the Longhorn was most at home and where he made his last stand. I was born on a ranch in the brush country, to a father who had gone up the trail with his brothers, sons of ranch parents, and to a mother whose father and brothers were range men and trail drivers also. Until I was a young man the only people I knew were people of the Longhorn and vaquero tradition.

Seventeen years ago I began making notes from reading and from the talk of men who had lived with Longhorns. For years I sought these men in widely divergent places, interviewing them, drawing them out. Often and often I have wished that I had been born earlier with opportunities for more firsthand observation and experience. I have back-trailed the Longhorn into Mexico, whence he came, and Mexican vaqueros on both sides of the Rio Grande have told me much. Many of these men who "learned me their lore" are dead now. In places through this book, mention is made of some of their names, as well as of others who still make the earth a saner place by living on it. By the time the grass greens and this book is published, some of these will be lying still in the earth they belong to. A long list, still incomplete, of men to whom I am indebted appears in the Notes.

Parts of some of the chapters of the book have appeared in the *Southwest Review*, *Saturday Evening Post*, *Southwestern Historical Quarterly*, the *Southwestern Sheep and Goat Raiser*, *The Cattleman*, the *New York Herald-Tribune Magazine* (which syndicated), *Frontier Stories*, and elsewhere. I here acknowledge the courtesy of various editors concerned. The Section of Fine Arts, Federal Works Agency, Washington, District of Columbia, has graciously given permission to reproduce the design of "The Stampede," by Tom Lea, in the post office at Odessa, Texas. My wife, Bertha McKee Dobie, has not only read proof but given me the benefit of her acute criticism.

Since Joel A. Allen's noble work on the American bison appeared in 1876, there has been a succession of books and studies on *Bos bison*, the work of Hornaday and Martin S. Garretson's recent *The American Bison* being outstanding. No book on the Longhorn (*Bos texanus*) has ever before this been attempted. Scattered facts about him may be found in Evetts Haley's *History of the X I T Ranch* and in his life of Charles Goodnight, in Oscar Rush's little-known but excellent *The Open Range and Bunk House Philosophy*, in J. L. Hill's pamphlet on *The End of the Cattle Trail*, in Jack Potter's two booklets, *Cattle Trails of the Old West* and *Lead Steer*, in Sam P. Ridings' monumental *The Chisholm Trail*, in R. B. Townshend's *A Tenderfoot in Colorado*, in that rare and information-packed volume entitled *Prose and Poetry of the Livestock Industry of the United States*, and in a few other books I might mention; but generally in range histories and reminiscences of old-time cowboys facts about cows are as meager as facts about bears in the autobiography of America's best-known bear hunter, David Crockett. I believe that I have virtually exhausted all printed and all available manuscript sources in the search for facts.

The Longhorn has been more essayed by art than by history. He bellowed to the stars in a call for the color and form and swiftness of art. About 1879 Frank Reaugh began painting the Longhorn from life. Although lacking in the barbaric virtue necessary to a realization of such primitive strength, he has nicely expressed the color harmony between grassland, sky and cattle. His contemporary in Texas, Harvey Wallace Caylor (1867–1932), less schooled and more rangy, caught something of the animal's elemental vigor and pride in life, but violated its anatomy.

The greatest artist of the West was Charles M. Russell. He knew the range from working on it and yearned towards it with primal gusto. He had a genius burning inside him that hardly another American artist has felt. He painted magnificently the Longhorn's fire, muscle and movement. Frederic Remington needs no adjective. He painted stampede and trail herd too. The etchings of Ed Borein (Santa Barbara, California) are authentic. Boyd Smith, who illustrated the books of Andy Adams, was faithful with the fidelity that *The Log of a Cowboy* and other works by Andy Adams stand for. Maynard Dixon and Will James — poles apart, for Dixon is finished, exact and historical, while James is sensational — belong in the gallery of Longhorn translators through art. The names of artists who have depicted or tried to depict the Longhorn are as numerous as the titles of Wild West magazines.

I wish it were possible to reproduce in a folio the best of the good Longhorn pictures. Some day, many of them will be gathered into the RANGE MUSEUM that is inevitable for Western America and that should, above all other places, be built where the Longhorn originated.

In 1886 Doctor William T. Hornaday, then chief taxidermist of the National Museum in Washington, realizing that the buffaloes — of which not a quarter of a century preceding perhaps sixty million, and possibly as many as one hundred million, blackened the Plains — were in imminent danger of extinction and that the great museum he represented did not have a single specimen, undertook to secure a few individuals for mounting. He was successful, and now there are magnificent habitat groups of the buffalo, magnificently mounted, in Washington, New York, Los Angeles, Denver, and perhaps elsewhere.

There is not in all America a properly mounted example of the Longhorn.

In 1905 the American Bison Society was organized to preserve for the American people not merely mounted specimens of dead buffalo but living examples on their native ranges. At that time there were probably 2000 specimens in the world. Today there are over 25,000.

Since about 1922, the Texas Longhorn has been nearer extinction than the buffalo ever was. The Federal Government has a herd on the Wichita Mountains Wildlife Refuge in Oklahoma. They are doing well and are being intelligently handled, but they will never become the counterparts of the wild-antlered creatures that ranged over southern Texas.

Except for a limited rescue, mostly of steers alone, by a few individuals, no effort at all is being made to preserve the Longhorn in the Texas that marked him and that he marked no less.

We turn to the past. Readers who object to facts will do well to skip the first three chapters — and then merely to skim all the others. Like Mark Twain, I "seem to exude facts."

J. FRANK DOBIE

Austin, Texas
When the work's all done this fall, of 1940

THE LONGHORNS

I · THE FIRST SPANISH CATTLE

To Marcus Snyder. His just father trailed Longhorns marked by the "mustang" blood, and he himself has carried the Texas range tradition from the tropics to the Big Horn.

ON HIS second voyage, the year following his discovery of America, Columbus landed cattle in Santo Domingo. In 1521, two years after Cortés began the Conquest of Mexico, Gregorio de Villalobos brought over from Santo Domingo to the mainland "a number of calves, so that there might be cattle, he being the first to bring them to New Spain."[1] Other importations followed. Cortés himself had developed a hacienda in Cuba, and the great estate in Mexico that he stocked from it was significantly named Cow Horn (Cuernavaca).

The English sparrow that came to the United States centuries later and the boll weevil of the Mexican tropics that only a generation ago settled down on an Alabama plantation did not find conditions for propagation more favorable than those the domestic animals of Spain found in America. The continents supplied no enemies that the hardy importations from the Spanish Peninsula could not, unaided by man, readily overcome. At the same time, the Mexican Government from the very beginning favored the grazing industry.[2] In 1540, only nineteen years after the initial introduction of seed stock, Coronado, without any effort worthy of note, gathered at least five hundred head of cattle, besides thousands of sheep, goats and hogs, to supply food for his great expedition in search of the golden Seven Cities of Cíbola.

These were the first cattle to enter what is now the United States. On his way north, Coronado left a number of exhausted animals in the lower part of Sinaloa. When Francisco de Ibarra arrived in that territory twenty-five years later, he found cattle running wild by the thousands.[3] Before the century was spent, a single owner in the province of Jalisco was branding 30,000 calves a year, and in Durango and southern Chihuahua there were individual herds numbering tens of thousands.[4] Ships loaded with hides plowed the same waves eastward that the fleets of silver plowed, to enrich Spain. At the inauguration of a viceroy in Mexico City in 1555, seventy or eighty bulls were brought in — for the bullfight — from lands beyond all settlements, "some of them twenty years old without ever having seen a man, *cimarrones*, outlaws fierce and desperate for liberty."[5]

Wherever the Spanish went, they took horses and cattle. It was their custom in colonial times to leave most of the males uncastrated, and the sterilizing of females was unknown. In consequence, any animals lost or dropped out were fertile to breed. As late as 1823 it was against the law in Mexico to kill calves for meat, and veal could not be purchased in the markets of the capital city.[6] Bull meat was supposed to be more invigorating and life-prolonging, anyhow, as the hero of *The Journey of the Flame* has so delightfully emphasized.

We shall meet later on the herds of cattle that the Spanish in 1790 began building up along the valleys of the Santa Cruz, the San Pedro and the Sonoita rivers in what is now southern Arizona, and that were, about 1822, abandoned to run wilder than the Apache Indians who killed and extirpated the owners.[7] Probably none of the cattle that Coronado took into New Mexico survived. Those introduced by colonists sixty years later did not increase extensively. Under both Spanish and Mexican rule, New Mexico was more of a sheep country than a cattle country. There was no significant development of the range cattle industry in Arizona and New Mexico until after the Civil War.

The Spanish cattle of California, however productive of hides, had small part in the conquest of the West by the Longhorns. Certain facts out of their record, however, contribute to the establishment of the character of the breed.

In 1769 the *San Carlos*, called "the *Mayflower* of the West," landed at San Diego with six or seven head of cattle — along with colonists, hens, red pepper, garlic and other requisites for a settlement. Other stock followed, and before the close of the century there were probably a million head of cattle in the province.[8] At first the herds belonged largely to mission ranches, but in time anybody willing to put up a house and locate a hundred head of cattle could procure from the Government a grant to a league (about 4438 acres) or more of land. The breeding of cattle was the only remunerative occupation of California before its annexation to the United States, and the ranching industry determined the whole structure of the land's society.

The value of the cattle lay almost solely in the worth of their hides and tallow. The hide trade became quite active about 1826. Ships brought cloth, cutlery, brass kettles for rendering tallow

[5]

in, a great variety of articles, to sell and to barter for the hides and tallow. One competent authority estimates that from 1800 to 1848 five million hides were exported.[9]

Sometimes vaqueros rode the cattle down, out on the prairies, and lanced them, Indian followers skinning the dead animals and wrapping the tallow up in the hides. The diet of the inhabitants was chiefly meat, with tortillas. Often only a single mess of meat was cut from the carcass of a freshly killed animal. The killing season for commercial purposes having arrived, cattle were driven from the rodeo ground to some spot near wood and water. Although bulls were eaten, mostly mature steers were slaughtered, the cows and bulls being left for breeding. The custom was to cut out fifty beeves at a time, roping and dragging them one by one to the butchers, who stuck them. Two days were allowed for skinning, stretching the hides, trying out the tallow, packing it into rawhide bags or into bladders and entrails, and drying the meat to be saved. Then another fifty beeves would be brought up. The slaughtering process was called the *matanza*. Especial care was taken of the *manteca*, the fat lying between the hide and the flesh. It afforded the ranchero's only lard.

The *matanza* grounds were paradise for buzzards, flies, coyotes, and bears. One night in 1835, it is recorded, eleven vaqueros roped forty grizzly bears on a *matanza* ground near San Francisco. So that grizzly roping might be enjoyed, the *matanza* was held in the light of the moon. Often the fiercest grizzlies caught were kept to match against the fiercest bulls the rodeo could furnish. It was a time when work was play, a time of plenty, of room, of cattle, horses and horsemen. "Don't be in a hurry," a ranchero gently urged his guest. "Let's take a ride out this beautiful April morning. The cattle and horses are beginning to change their coats, and everything is fresh and new. Let's ride and enjoy the day." [10]

The first civilized man to plant his feet on, and draw sustenance from, the soil of Texas (1528) bore prophetically the name of Cabeza de Vaca; but more than a century and a half passed before cattle crossed the trail made north of the Rio Grande by this wandering Cow's Head. Unlike California, Texas had the Comanche, the Apache and the Lipan Indians. They were magnificent riders, but they never submitted to baptism or rode as obedient herdsmen for Spanish-tongued masters, as did the Indians of California. The harbors of Texas were well known, but missions and *hidalgos* never exported hides and tallow from them. Although the Spaniards stocked wide ranges in Texas, not until the "North Americans" came, subdued the fiercely marauding Indians and developed markets did the ranch industry here really fruit.

Excepting the nonpropagating cattle that Coronado drove over the Llano Estacado in 1541, probably the first to enter what is now Texas, and certainly the first cattle of any consequence, came with the establishment of the first mission,[11] located near the Louisiana line, in 1690. Its seed stock of two hundred head of cattle came from far south of the Rio Grande. Seventy-five years later a report (often repeated and denied) arose that in conducting the expedition to found this mission Captain Alonso de León left "a bull and a cow, a stallion and a mare" at each of the various rivers crossed,[12] thus accounting for "many Spanish cattle, unbranded and ownerless," to be seen throughout the land.

Whether deliberately left to propagate or not, animals would escape from traveling herds; they would stray from the unfenced ranges on which they were located. From the first, Indians dispersed as well as killed them. The seed were certainly being sown for a stock to become in time far more numerous than the famous wild cattle of Chillingham and wilder and fiercer than those "strong bulls of Bashan" that, in vague lands somewhere beyond Jordan's stormy banks, roared among giants. Within three years the missionaries on the Neches River were

[7]

reduced to eating crows.[13] Yet only a quarter-century later, "thousands of cows, bulls, horses and mares" were reported as using over the country around the mission.[14]

In 1716, the year that the Spanish seriously began the establishment of missions and colonists in Texas, two men reported having seen, in thick underbrush of the Trinity River bottoms, "wild cattle lost by the Spaniards on their first expedition into Texas. They killed a fat cow and some turkeys." [15]

It would be tedious to list the stocks of cattle, always accompanied by stocks of horses, brought up into Texas from Mexico, and to note this or that "black Castilian bull" sighted in one place or another.[16] By the time fifteen favored families from the Canary Islands reached San Antonio, in 1731, the mission ranches there already had numerous cattle. Yet each family came provided with a yoke of broken oxen, ten nanny goats and a buck, ten ewes and a ram, five sows and a boar, five mares and a stallion, and five cows and a bull.[17] Stock-raising became almost the only civilian occupation, despite governmental attempts to enforce farming.

Meanwhile, the most prolific ranches in Texas were raising cattle around the Goliad missions farther down the San Antonio River.[18] Around 1770, the Mission of Espíritu Santo, near Goliad, claimed 40,000 head of cattle, branded and unbranded, that ranged between the Guadalupe and San Antonio rivers, while the neighboring Mission of Rosario claimed 10,000 branded cattle and 20,000 unbranded cattle, ranging westward. The unbranded cattle were called *mesteñas* (mustangs). Theoretically at least, they could be rounded up with the branded cattle, in contrast with the utterly uncontrollable *cimarrones*.

Following 1770, ranching all up and down the San Antonio River declined rapidly. During the seven years preceding 1778 the vast herds of the Mission of Espíritu Santo were rounded up only three times. The Comanches, Apaches and Lipanes slaughtered cattle in "unbelievable" quantities. The Lipan Indians, it was claimed by owners, at one time killed and ran off 22,000 head from the San Antonio territory. There were times when the Comanches left hardly a broken horse for the town's population to ride, and men were afraid to venture beyond the immediate protection of the fort.[19]

With no demand for hides and with exports to French-owned Louisiana interdicted, cattle were usually worth very little. Occasionally a herd of a hundred or so — horses more than cattle — was smuggled across the Sabine.[20] The small amount of dried beef carried in bales on pack animals to cities in Coahuila added little to the demand for cattle. There was no money in the country. While Louisiana was under Spanish dominion (1763–1800), herds of cattle numbering as high as 2000 head each were driven from the mission ranges down the San Antonio River to stock Louisiana territory. This trade, sporadic and short-lived, was largely the result of the Government's claim to all unbranded cattle and to the policy of issuing permits to kill or drive them away for four-bits a head — a license in many instances for downright theft. For years, there was wrangling between representatives of the Government and citizens of San Antonio as to who owned the *orejanos* — "eared," unmarked, animals.[21]

The populations of the missions Espíritu Santo and Rosario prized bulls more for *fiestas* than for breeding. Matadors and bull-rings may have been wanting, but on the "days of the bulls" there were bull-tailing, bull-riding and bull-roping. If a bull was to be turned into a steer, it was more fun to rope him on the range after he was grown than to twist him down as a calf. The way the cattle were handled or not handled, as well as the open range itself, produced countless runaway *cimarrones*.

A Frenchman who crossed Texas in 1767 began noticing west of the Brazos River "horned cattle, originally tame, that long since became wild and now roam in large herds all over the plain." "Hunting the wild bull" was an established sport, and

[9]

he took part in one such hunt with accompanying Spanish cavalrymen. They ran down the slowest of a bunch of the cattle — leaving the fleetest and wildest to propagate their kind. A decade later that observant traveler and reporter, De Mézières, another Frenchman, had no other adjective to describe the "Castilian cattle" and mustang horses he saw on the Colorado and Brazos rivers than "incredible in number." He noted that the wild cattle ranged far away from settlements, the inhabitants of which hunted them.[22]

A typical illustration of how cattle, hardly to be called "domesticated," escaped and reverted to primordial nature is found in the record of two herds in one particular locality. Early in the last century Don Felipe Partilleas established a ranch on the San Marcos River. Owing to the continued raids of the Comanches, he had to abandon it, and there left various cattle he could not gather. The remnant multiplied so thriftily that "when the Anglo-American settlers penetrated that country in 1833–1835, they found the region stocked with wild cattle entirely free of all marks or other indices of ownership. But so wild were they that only the expert hunters might hope to come up with them." [23]

In 1851 Captain Richard Ware on his way farther west with a drove of cattle decided to winter on the San Marcos River, in the region of the abandoned Partilleas ranch. "Grass was fine and the stock did well, but many of them were lost on account of their mixing with wild cattle in the big thickets. These wild cattle" — and here the chronicler expresses an erroneous belief once common — "were not domestic gone estray, but original wild cattle, smaller than the common breeds of home cattle, and all one color — brown. . . . They were wilder than the deer." [24]

What became of the 1400 head of cattle that the Spaniards in 1757 drove from the San Antonio River to their mission on the San Saba,[25] no one can say. Comanches promptly annihilated the mission, and the *presidio* three miles away from it was short-

[10]

lived. One of the last stands of the wild Spanish cattle in Texas was in the rough breaks, densely timbered and abundantly watered, down the San Saba River and below its junction with the Colorado. As late as 1880 some survivors were killed in this region.

Not until Texas achieved its independence from Mexico was the territory between the Nueces River and the Rio Grande considered a part of the state. But it became the primary nursery and stronghold of the Longhorn. Ranching on the Rio Grande began about 1700. Sixty years later cattle owned by ranches on both sides the river, from Laredo to its mouth, were ranging clear to the Nueces.[26] According to alleged records, three million head of stock, including goats, sheep and horses as well as cattle, occupied the area in 1835,[27] but this account must take in the Mexican side of the Rio Grande as well as the Texas side. When, in the middle of the century, Major William H. Emory, representing the Boundary Survey, made a reconnaissance of the border country, he reported: "The numbers of horses and cattle that ranged here under Spanish rule are incredible. To this day remnants of this immense stock are running wild on the prairies" — and, he should have added, *in the thickets* — "between the two rivers. Hunting the wild horses and cattle is the regular business of the inhabitants of Laredo and other towns along the Rio Grande."[28]

After the English-speaking colonists began to spread over Texas, the wild cattle were to be found from the Red River on the north to the Rio Grande on the south, as attested by many witnesses,[29] and from the Louisiana line on the east to the uppermost breaks of the Brazos on the west. They did not get out on the Great Plains. They did not run in the great herds sometimes reported, but kept in little bunches, staying in cover during the day and venturing out on the prairie only at night, grazing against the wind. A rider seldom saw one in daytime unless he happened upon it in a thicket. As watchful as wild turkeys, as alert in the nostrils as deer, they came, after being hunted, to flee the approach of any human being.

Bob Routh told me that after he went up into the broken, brushed country of Brown County in 1872, the range men shot many of them, letting their carcasses lie, because they tolled off branded cattle. Mixed with the black and brown *cimarrones* were whites with blue heads. An old outlaw steer that took up with them was roped and belled and turned loose. His bell betrayed the location of several bunches of the wild cattle. Routh was once running a cow in the rocks when she caught her foot in a crevice and pulled a hoof off. She went on for a while and then stopped with her head hidden in a bush, her body exposed. If captured and herded with other cattle, one of these animals would wilt and shrink like a caged eagle.

Many of the early colonists, ignorant of natural history, considered the cattle — almost as foreign to their own domesticated stock as the buffaloes — indigenous to the land. Translating the Spanish *mesteñas*, old-timers called them "mustang cattle," a name yet heard; others called them "Spanish cattle." A common description was simply "wild cattle." It was after the Civil War that some range men took to calling the surviving remnants "Texas cattle," which in time came to mean Longhorns.

They were considered as game animals, along with deer, antelope, buffaloes, and were so classed by writers treating of sport in the Southwest. As late as 1876, Colonel R. I. Dodge, whose *Plains of the Great West* remains a standard treatment of Western wild life, wrote: "I should be doing injustice to a cousin-german of the buffalo did I fail to mention as game the wild cattle of Texas, . . . animals miscalled tame, fifty times more dangerous to footmen than the fiercest buffalo." Another military man, whose experiences were confined to the decade following the Civil War, testified, "It is much more difficult to get a shot at a wild Texas cow than it would be at the most cautious and wary old buck. To kill a buffalo is but child's play compared with it." [30]

The early colonists, who had to make their living entirely off the land and who could seldom kill buffaloes, never abundant in eastern Texas, hunted the mustang cattle relentlessly. Their number must not be exaggerated, however. The colonists at times resorted to eating the flesh of mustangs, which they would not have done had beef been available. Yet one wonders why they ate horseflesh amid the general plenitude of deer. The wild cattle were harder to shoot than either mustangs or deer.

The noted Indian fighter Buck Barry "put in all of a month," in the year 1841, "hunting deer, turkeys and wild cattle" in the Red River country. "We have only to go out a few miles into a swamp between the Big and Little Brazos to find as many wild cattle as one could wish," a chronicler going back to 1822 wrote. He and some other hunters on an expedition after buffalo tongues "amused themselves by shooting wild cattle." It was dangerous, however, to camp on the east side of Little River, "on account of the cattle coming in for water, the night being the only time they drink." [31]

They were hunted in the swamps of western Louisiana too, where great numbers of "the Spanish breed, small and spike-horned," ran, the chief graziers being Acadians. Before James Bowie came over the line into Texas — there to achieve fame with his knife, his search for a lost mine that took his name, and his death in the Alamo — he chased these cattle on horseback, knifing them down in the manner that Plains Indians lanced the buffalo. Bayou Boeuf (Beef) took its name from their presence. On Attakapas prairie, John McHenry, who had been a filibuster in the Spanish days and who years later set out afoot from a settlement on the Lavaca River in Texas for New Orleans, was suddenly charged upon by the little Louisiana cattle. "Tossing their heads high in the air, bellowing, switching their tails," they chased McHenry up a tree, whence he accidentally dropped his bundle of clothes. Sharp horns immediately tore them into ribbons — but the soldier of fortune had saved his bacon.[32]

Plantation owners in colonial Texas sometimes kept a professional hunter employed to bring in meat, also eggs from the wild fowls. These hired hunters were generally Indians or Mexicans, but white frontiersmen served. "Captain" Flack, a hunter-naturalist that Theodore Roosevelt would have approved of, spent several years before the Civil War in the canebrake and Spanish-moss parts of Texas, and after returning to England wrote books that give full details about hunting wild cattle.

He roped them — to "beef" — on moonlit prairies. In the early dawn he slipped up to the edge of timber to catch them as they returned to cover from grazing and watering in the darkness. He ran them through the thickets with dogs, and, thus following the wild-bellowing animals, the horses of the pursuers quivering with excitement, experienced a sport beside which all English hunting was "tame indeed." But as a mere meat-getter, with hundreds of the animals — so he claimed — to his credit, he seems to have mostly still-hunted, sniffing the air for their strong scent and guarding against allowing his own scent or the sound of a twig trodden on being carried to the animals.

"A good hunter can in this way," he says, "kill three or four cows or bulls in a morning. Having killed as many as he thinks necessary, he returns to the plantation and informs the owner or overseer what he has done; the overseer then calls up three or four negroes. A wagon and some mules are made ready, a couple of axes are put into it, and some butcher-knives, a whetstone, and perhaps a hatchet. When all is ready, the hunter leads the way to where he has left his slaughtered game."

An animal merely wounded would charge the hunter with great fury. Once, Captain Flack narrates: "I had my hunting shirt stripped from my back by a wild red bull I had wounded. Fortunately his fierce rush carried him some distance beyond me; and before he could turn round to renew his attack, I had climbed a tree. He kept me a prisoner until he bled to death from his wounds." [33]

Colonel Dodge relates the incidents of a wild bull hunt that a doctor visiting an army post in Texas about 1850 had reason to remember. A bull the doctor had wounded turned on him and was winning the race across a small opening, when an army officer dashed up on a fine "American horse" and fired his pistol at the bull. Instantly the brute wheeled to attack the new foe. The big American horse, too slow in turning, was met full in the side by the bull's horns.

"Both horse and rider were lifted for one instant into the air, and then came down in a heap together. The horse was dead without a struggle, one horn being completely through his body, the other caught in the bones of the chest. One leg of the rider was between the horns of the bull, pinned fast between his head and the body of the horse. When heaped together, the horse's body was on the bull's head, fastening it to the ground; and the rider was lying on the bull's back. The whole hunting party was soon assembled. They were afraid to shoot the bull, lest his struggles might further injure the man pinned to him. At last the bull's jugular vein was opened, and he slowly bled to death. His horns were then cut off, the horse lifted off, and the now nearly dead man carried in a litter to the post."

When General Taylor's army was on the march from Corpus Christi to the Rio Grande, an infantry man saw a bull to one side and fired at him. He immediately charged, the soldier taking refuge in the column. The bull came on, "scattering regiments like chaff," the men so mixed with each other and the bull so mixed with everything that they could not fire without danger to human life. The bull finally escaped unhurt. He had done what Santa Anna's army could not do.

But the historic engagement between wild bulls and the military was a short distance below the Arizona line. In 1846 Colonel

Philip Saint George Cooke was leading the so-called Mormon Battalion, of around 400 people, from Santa Fe to California over the southern route. Long before arriving at the great San Bernardino hacienda east of the San Pedro River, the troopers began noticing cattle trails and cattle. The Apaches had killed and run off all the inhabitants of this region a quarter of a century back, and now the descendants of their herds abounded over a vast range as wild and primitive as the *urus* of prehistoric Europe, thought to be the originator of most of the domestic cattle of the world and immortalized in the Sign of Taurus in the zodiac. Several of the bulls were killed for meat; several men narrowly escaped horns; the Battalion was learning caution. Then, in a wide, grassy canyon, came the "engagement."

Colonel Philip Saint George Cooke reports with military precision: "I had to direct the men to load their muskets to defend themselves. The animals attacked in some instances without provocation, and tall grass in some places made the danger greater; one ran on a man, caught him in the thigh, and threw him clear over his body lengthwise; then it charged on a team, ran its head into the first mule and tore out the entrails of the one beyond. Another ran against a sergeant, who escaped with severe bruises, as the horns passed at each side of him; one ran at a horse tied behind a wagon, and as it escaped, the bull struck the wagon with a momentum that forced the hind part of it out of the road. I saw one rush at some pack mules and kill one of them. I was very near Corporal Frost when an immense coal-black bull, a hundred yards away, came charging at us. Frost aimed his musket, flintlock, very deliberately, and only fired when the beast was within six paces; it fell headlong, almost at our feet. One man, charged on, threw himself flat, and the bull jumped over him and passed on.

"A bull, after receiving two balls through its heart and two through its lungs, ran on a man. I have seen the heart. Lieutenant Stoneman was accidentally wounded in the thumb. We crossed a pretty stream that I have named 'Bull Run.' " [34]

The Battalion of 400 stomachs lived off bull meat for two weeks. "Cows and calves were scarcely seen, and none killed." The bulls, in the manner of buffaloes during certain seasons, were separated from the cows, running together. They seem to have been black, brown and red in color, blacks predominating. This was in December, 1846. Emigrants following Cooke's route in the years that followed replenished their stores from the wild meat. In May, 1851, United States Boundary Commissioner John R. Bartlett came to the region and saw the wild cattle ranging in bunches of five or six head, each "led by a stately bull." It was spring and the bulls were with the cows.

In Texas, Colonel Dodge almost always found the wild bulls apart from the cows and greatly disproportioned in numbers. He saw the wild cattle after they had been much hunted and attributed the scarcity of males to "the fact that it seems impossible for the bull to keep his mouth shut. When not actually eating he is bellowing, or moaning, or making some other hideous noise which indicates his whereabouts to the hunter."

The animals, as has been seen, had an astonishing vitality. Along in the forties the noted guide José Policarpo Rodríguez went up to Bandera County with a man named Lynn to hunt. "We had," Policarpo remembered,[35] "four horses and six dogs. We killed several deer, a number of turkeys, one bear, and cut several bee trees. We found a bunch of wild cattle, most of them black or brown. We got after a cow and had to empty our guns into her before we killed her. Lynn had an eight-shooting pistol he had made himself, a rifle, and a pair of holsters; I had a rifle, a six-shooter, and a pair of holsters. Twenty shots went into the body of that black cow before we killed her."

It may be asked why the Texas colonists did not capture and domesticate these wild cattle. The mustang horses were far easier to capture and tame than the mustang cattle. Neither bull

[17]

nor cow bent on a certain direction could be turned by a horseman, and if roped, nothing could be done with it unless it was
necked to a gentle ox, and then it was likely to "sull" and die.
W. W. Burton, an old Texian whose memory went back to the
days of the Republic, told me years ago of a man named Dunn
who built a big pen with wings to it on the Navasota River for
the purpose of capturing wild cattle. He caught a considerable
number of calves, maybe fifty, and raised them by hand, letting
them suck gentle cows, but the instinct of the wild was too
strong for them ever to become of the "old Bossy" character.

One instance of semi-domestication, and also of infiltration
of the breed, is given by meaty and juicy old Noah Smithwick.
When, about 1850, he located on Brushy Creek, east of the
Colorado River, he found himself and his animals among numerous "descendants of the Spanish cattle brought to the Mission San Gabriel away back in the eighteenth century. Some
were very handsome brutes, coal black and clean-limbed, their
white horns glistening as if polished." Two of the bulls took
up with Smithwick's cattle and became "quite domesticated."
About the same time lobo wolves began to depredate. When
the milch cows and other gentle stock were attacked, they
would try to get to the house. The wild cattle, on the other
hand, "would form a ring around their calves and, presenting a
line of horns, fight the lobos off." [36]

We may be sure that whatever offspring Smithwick got from
the two coal-black bulls knew better than their mothers how
to take care of themselves. Here in a nutshell is why the cattle
that endured and throve in the wild lands of Texas, before man
fenced, watered and cleaned them of predatory animals, either
had the blood or generated the instincts of the Spanish cattle.

One fine spring day in the year 1831 a visitor to Austin's
colonies on the Gulf Coast was looking out over the vast prairie
watching cattle graze near at hand and picking out faraway dark
specks. Suddenly he heard a bellowing near the edge of some

woods. Every animal within sight raised head and listened. Immediately they began making for the sound, "not at a slow and leisurely gait, but with a rapid motion, a wild and angry look, and occasionally with a loud bellowing." The specks rushing in from two and three miles away became cow brutes with tossing horns. The cattle converged from every direction until hundreds had assembled at the edge of the woods, where they milled, bawling and bellowing with extreme vigor. What brought them was the bawl of a calf attacked by a lobo. The lobo escaped — and so did the calf.[37]

When the wild cattle, "black with brown backs and bellies, in time became mixed with the domestic cattle, their calves took on mixed colors." [38] But often they would have nothing to do with domestic stock, probably repelled by the human taint they bore. On the other hand, the settlers' cattle showed a strong disposition to take up with the wild ones. After all, such stock as the colonists brought to Texas were not generally too "fine-haired" for the wilderness. A fine-haired bull could hardly survive the native range bulls. Towards the beginning of the present century General Manuel Treviño, owner of the great La Babía hacienda in northern Coahuila, was siring his herds with bulls famous among patrons of bullfights in Mexico City and elsewhere as "Piedras Negras toros." He castrated his calves only every other year, in alternate years leaving all the males to breed and fight. Finally, however, having listened to the preachers of progress, he bought a wholesale quantity of Hereford bull yearlings and scattered them over his ranges. Before they had a chance to mix with the cows, the native bulls killed all of them.

Not all — probably not a majority — of the Spanish cattle in colonial Texas ran wild. Many of the original ranchos, despite Indian depredations, had great numbers of cattle under control [39] between the Nueces and the Rio Grande. Yet the rancheros and their Indian vaqueros — whether in Texas, Mexico or California — handled the branded stock in a way to make them as feral in instincts as the mustangs. The owners wanted them wild, as a protection against raiding Indians. They followed the principle on which the Arkansas stock judges awarded the prize, over Poland China sows and Duroc–Jersey boars, to a varicolored bunch of long-snouted, long-tusked, long-legged, long-tailed native razorbacks. "A hawg in this country," the judges announced, "ain't no 'count 'less he can outrun a nigger and outfight a b'ar." In California, as in Texas, the cattle had a reputation for being "more dangerous to footmen than grizzly bears." [40]

The Spanish chroniclers consistently neglected to describe their cattle. When Juan de Oñate and Pedro Ponce de León were bidding against each other, in 1595, for the privilege of leading a colony into New Mexico and becoming captain-general of that province, Oñate promised to take — along with 500 pesos' worth of jerked beef, 3000 sheep for wool, 1000 sheep for mutton, 1000 goats, and a great number of mares, colts and horses — "1000 head of cattle" (*ganado mayor*) and "100 head of black cattle" (*ganado prieto*). Ponce de León, raising the ante in every particular, said he would take 2000 head of "cattle" and 400 head of "black cattle." [41] Evidently black cattle were scarcer and more expensive at the time. They were to raise fighting bulls.

The Spanish ranchers often set a higher value on color than on any other characteristic. The old-time *hacendados* would keep their *manadas* — a *manada* being a bunch of mares, with their colts, dominated by a stallion — of duns, bays, browns, *grullas*, sorrels, greys, pintos, and so on, all absolutely separated. To this day, country Mexicans consider milk from a black cow more healthful than that from a cow of any other color and seek it for ailing children. In the seventeenth and eighteenth centuries, the breeding of black cattle in Mexico was much encouraged. The seed cattle brought into Texas, California and

[21]

Arizona — from one to two hundred years after Oñate and Ponce de León bid against each other on "cattle" and "black cattle" — seem to have been mostly of the black kind.

Early in the nineteenth century "black cattle" became almost a generic name [42] — analogous to the present-day use of "white faces." For instance, Thomas Jefferson Green of the Texan Mier Expedition, while being marched south as a prisoner, came to a hacienda between Saltillo and San Luís Potosí that ranged "ten thousand black cattle and forty thousand sheep." In the very first book on Texas to be published in English — *Texas . . . in a Series of Letters*, 1833 — Mary Austin Holley noted that the principal occupation of the settlers was "farming and raising black cattle," and she could not recommend too highly the prairie lands for pasturing "black cattle." The color seems to have been common in Florida. Major Howell Tatum, who was with General Andrew Jackson on his march to New Orleans and kept a diary, made an entry concerning "200 head of Black-Cattle taken" near Pensacola.[43]

Solid blacks were not uncommon, but line-backs were very characteristic — a stripe white, yellow or brown in color going down the back to the tail and up the top of the neck. Sometimes the line forked at the shoulders, running down on either side like the lines that make "the cross" on the burro. This line-back was remarkable on not only Spanish cattle, burros and mules but on Spanish horses of dun shades. Texans called it a "lobo stripe" — a parallel to the *bayo coyote* name for a dun horse with the stripe down his back. Often, however, the stripe was not distinct, the hair along the back being merely of a lighter color than that on the remainder of the body. Because the cattle were frequently splotched beneath — or perhaps because they were recognized as Mexicans — they were sometimes called "yellow bellies." There were reds, browns and blues and occasionally a pinto, but the brindles and duns so common among the Longhorns seem to have been lacking.

[22]

The face was covered with shaggy hair inclining to look sun-browned. Lines of lighter hue circled the eyes and muzzle. "Mealy-nosed" was the old Texas description. Sharp, neat, polished hoofs made tracks that good trailers could distinguish from those printed by other cattle.

The mustang cattle were, perhaps accurately, called Moorish. Their type is yet to be seen in bull-rings. They afforded the basis of comparison for the first Spanish descriptions of the American bison. The captive buffalo that Cortés and his followers gazed in wonder upon in Montezuma's menagerie had a "head armed like that of a bull, resembling it in fierceness, with no less strength and agility." Cabeza de Vaca, who saw herds of the "native cows" on the Texas prairies, described their horns as "small like those of the Moorish cattle."

Obversely, plainsmen described the black cattle as having horns, "set forward to kill," like the buffalo's. "The horns came out of the head close together and the skull between them was as thick as a buffalo's." In fact, there were men who argued that some of the cattle must have buffalo blood in them, especially certain big bulls with humpish shoulders and heavy curly hair. James Capen Adams, the California hunter and tamer of grizzly bears, saw fifteen or twenty of the cattle running wild in mountains far removed from any ranches and was half of that opinion. "Their hides are thicker," he told his biographer,[44] "their hair longer and shaggier, and their eyes more like those of the buffalo than those of any domestic cattle." Furthermore, the frontal bone between the horns was often high-ridged, covered with long, coarse hair.

In many ways, however, these cattle were more like deer than buffaloes — quick, uneasy, restless, constantly on the lookout for danger, snuffing the air, and moving with a light, elastic step. In their sense of smell they were fully the equal of deer. A wounded bull has been known to hunt for his enemy by scent, trailing him on the ground like a bear.

The horns were long, compared with the horns of cattle of New England and Missouri, but probably never the equal in length of those that gave a name to the breed we are progressing towards. The horns were generally trim, the horny substance itself so thin at times as to be translucent when the bone was removed. This thinness of the cornuous substance was in marked contrast to the thickness generally characteristic of the wide-horned Mexican cattle. White horns, jetted at the tips, on coal-black bulls made a striking sight. There were black horns too. A few of the cattle were muleys, hornless. I am not convinced that the muleys could cut with their hoofs, in the manner of deer or antelopes, as has been claimed.[45] However, the Texas cattle could use their hoofs in one way so effectively that, instead of saying "kick like a mule," the Texans said "kick like a bay steer."

In attempting to revive the extinct wild aurochs or urus by breeding selected individuals of the most primitive types extant, German scientists some years ago picked out a breed surviving on the island of Corsica.[46] These cattle have a ring around the nose, a stripe down the back, and a high crown surmounted by coarse hair. The wild Spanish cattle had these characteristics also, and were probably as near their "wild ox" progenitors as the Corsicans. The characteristics noted have been exceedingly persistent. If Brahma and Hereford bulls were entirely removed from the herds along the Texas coast from Matagorda Bay to the mouth of the Sabine River, and if those herds were left free to breed without man's interference, it would not be a great many cow-generations before the line-backs and mealy noses reappeared.

Into the stock that emerged as Texas Longhorns the "black cattle" stamped their stamina, fierceness, keen senses and staglike muscles. Mustang and branded alike, through long years they went on merging with other cattle. As long as the Longhorns remained dominant on the ranges of southern Texas, until in the

1880's, many alert *zorrillas* — "polecats," as the borderers used to term the line-backed blacks — preserved their identity among them.

I have dwelt long and minutely on the *ganado prieto* called Moorish. Whereas these "black cattle" were in the old days called "Spanish," the broad- and heavy-horned type — just "cattle" — were nearly always called "Mexican." They came also from Spain, where their dun prototypes may be seen today, more common as oxen than in the bull-ring. I cannot adduce figures to back up the assertion, but I am sure that a high percentage of the cattle that before the Texas Revolution ranged between the Nueces River and the Rio Grande, and also southward from the Rio Grande, were of the many-colored type. This territory, as we shall see, was heavily drawn on for stocking the Republic of Texas.

As the nineteenth century advanced, no chronicler used the adjective "black" to describe Texas cattle in general. The horns grew longer, the bodies heavier and rangier, the variations in color unlimited. At the same time, remnants of the wild cattle were found up the Nueces and elsewhere until the country was fenced.

In the popular mind buffaloes by the multiplied millions are indelibly associated with the Great Plains, but the plentiful herds that once roamed between Buffalo on Lake Erie and Buffalo Mills on the southern line of Pennsylvania have long been forgotten. The Moorish cattle, wild and black, have been forgotten in the remembrance of a vaster and more history-compelling breed. But a hundred years ago they were far more numerous than has been generally supposed. They too projected themselves into history.

II · THE TEXAS BREED

To Walter Billingsley. His blood raised the cry of
"Remember the Alamo" at San Jacinto, and he's a
straight Longhorn. He has made mine many of his
experiences with cows and cow people.

THE MAP of Texas looks somewhat like a roughly skinned
cowhide spread out on the ground, the tail represented by
the tapering peninsula at the mouth of the Rio Grande, the broad
head by the Panhandle. But "Cattle," by Berta Hart Nance,
goes deeper than the map.

> Other states were carved or born;
> Texas grew from hide and horn.
>
> Other states are long or wide;
> Texas is a shaggy hide.

Dripping blood and crumpled hair,
Some gory giant flung it there,

Laid the head where valleys drain,
Stretched its rump along the plain.

Other soil is full of stones;
Texans plow up cattle bones.

Herds are buried on the trail,
Underneath the powdered shale,

Herds that stiffened like the snow,
Where the icy northers go.

Other states have built their halls,
Humming tunes along the walls;

Texans watched the mortar stirred,
While they kept the lowing herd.

Stamped on Texan wall and roof
Gleams the sharp and crescent hoof.

High above the hum and stir,
Jingle bridle-rein and spur.

Other states were made or born;
Texas grew from hide and horn.

Up to the time of the establishment of the Republic of Texas, in 1836, the word "cowboy" was unknown in the sense that the American language has long since made common. Then bold, adventurous and not at all squeamish-stomached Texians began raiding Mexican-held ranges. The raiders were nearly all young men, mostly out of that nondescript, un-uniformed, undisciplined, self-willed, ready-to-die aggregation of game-spirited recruits from the States and from home-defending settlers making up the Texas army.

They were called "cowboys." [1] For years the new word — actually a very old word given a new meaning — was, when printed, enclosed by quotation marks, and the initial odium attached to it has never been entirely removed. Many of these first cowboys thought no more of killing a Mexican than of "upping" an Indian or using the double of a rope on a rattlesnake. Some of them allied with Mexican filibusters in making a *pronunciamiento* for "the Republic of the Rio Grande." A few were out strictly for gain. Certain of their associates, like the brave ranger and gentleman Ben McCulloch, would have no part in driving off the Mexican cattle because the business too patently "violated the Ten Commandments." The raiders not only re-enacted, but, on a wilder and more extraordinary stage, added climactical daring and incident to each scene of the drama of cattle-lifting played by Sir Walter Scott's borderers in *Rob Roy*.

They found many cattle along the Guadalupe and San Antonio rivers — some of them the property of Mexicans who had fought loyally on the Texas side. But to the raiders all Mexicans had the same color. Their great hunting grounds were between the Nueces River and the Rio Grande. They even crossed the Rio Bravo and chased back to this side cattle that harrying Indians and Indianized *vaqueros* had for generations been developing into race stock. Generally timing their forays with moonlight, a band of ten or fifteen cowboys would rush from two to six hundred cattle together and head them northeast in a long run, which they would more or less keep up for twenty-four hours, after that merely walking or trotting. The country, now densely brushed, was then mostly open, and they knew how to get over it. "At the end of two or three days," historian John Henry Brown says, the herd "could be managed somewhat like domesticated cattle."

Some of the cattle thus lifted were driven to the New Orleans market. The majority were used to stock the coastal ranges [2] — Goliad, of mission and massacre tradition, becoming a kind of trading center. How the Mexicans, in time, counter-raided, and how for forty years the Bloody Border and its cattle knew no peace, I have told in *A Vaquero of the Brush Country*. The way to make cattle wild is to turn them out in the wilderness and chase them.

Away across the state from the old Spanish-Mexican ranches supplying seed stock — so far east as to be beyond contact with the original Texas colonists — three or four French ranches in the Trinity River country, against Louisiana, were producing cattle even before the land was opened to settlement. One of the ranchers, Taylor White (originally Leblanc), was driving cattle to New Orleans years before the Texans had cattle to drive.[3] All these French-Texas cattle seem to have been of "the pure Spanish breed." In becoming assimilated in the general Texas mixture they afforded an ingredient neither important nor foreign.

Although the colonists were largely from the South and, therefore, as a rule knew how to ride and shoot, they had come to Texas without any conception of ranching. After Austin, "the Father of Texas," had drawn up what he considered a full code of civil and criminal regulations to govern his colonists, the representative of the Mexican Government at San Antonio added only two articles. Both pertained to an occupation foreign to the newly-arrived Americans. One provided for the registration of brands and the other for the disposition of estrayed stock.[4] The Texians were familiar with livestock; David Crockett, who came only to die, had driven cattle afoot across the Tennessee mountains; but handling wild cattle on the open range was something new.

The colonists found that by declaring an intention to raise cattle, they could procure a grant for ten times as much land as if they merely declared an intention to farm. They all avowed the intention to ranch. During the 1820's and 1830's they became landholders looking for cattle to eat their grass — the reverse of conditions a generation later, when owners of great herds pushed out looking for grass. Although the colonials raised cattle from the beginning, some of them developing herds of considerable size, the ranching industry, symbolized by the head of a Texas steer, did not burgeon among them until they achieved a nation for themselves.

Into the stock of this industry went a strain of the mustang cattle already described at length. They, the wide-horned "Mexican" cattle, and the mixture of these two kinds that the Texians gradually traded for and then summarily took from the Mexicans, provided the basic strain.[5] An infiltration of mongrel American blood modified to a limited extent the bodies, though not the natures, of the resultant blend — the Texas Longhorns.

The early importations from the States are not determinable either in quantity or character. There were Missouri cattle, noted for their prowess as oxen; Arkansas travelers, nothing to boast of; Louisiana canebrake splitters, thoroughly adapted to the coast against which Austin's "First Three Hundred" made their homes. A great many of the colonists, Americans as well as Irish, came by boat and brought no cattle. Frequently a cow and less often a bull helped pull a family coming overland. "Old Cherry" may be considered typical of the stock accompanying homeseekers. She was a favorite milk cow that the Anderson family, traveling in two ox wagons and a buggy drawn by an old mule, set out with from Mississippi. The older children and several slaves walked most of the way to keep Cherry company. As she progressed westward, "she had a growing hatred of dogs and never failed to lunge at one that came near her. One evening about dusk," a child of the family long afterward wrote,[6] "as we were driving her along the way, we came to a large black stump by the roadside, and Old Cherry, evidently thinking it was a dog, made a lunge at it and knocked herself senseless."

Yet when the Tumlinson clan came from North Carolina in 1821, their goods loaded on pack horses, they brought two

MAKINGS OF THE TEXAS BREED

hundred head of cattle and the same number of hogs.[7] More representative were the family milk cows, from Arkansas, that Abner Kuykendall on January the first, 1822, turned loose on the creek he christened "New Year's."[8]

In eastern Texas, the Cherokee Indians had a special breed of cattle that they were forced to abandon when they were driven from the land. For years some of them propagated mustang stock.[9] Others of their kind were brought down from the Cherokee Nation.

More cattle were brought in from western Louisiana than from any other state.[10] These canebrake splitters were themselves predominantly Spanish. The noted Randall Jones took a Negro boy and swapped him for sixty head.[11] Other men drove horses across the Sabine and exchanged them for cows.[12] A few old-timers contend that both the horns and bodies of the Texas cattle were derived from importations from the States out of the Longhorn Herefords of England. If there was a strain of this stock, it was minor.

We may be sure that the "Spanish fever" overtook most of the bulls and cows of "the improved breed of teewater Durham cattle" that an English settler at Matagorda proudly wrote to the President of the Republic, in 1841, he was importing.[13] The ticks carried by Southern cattle, against the virus of which native-born animals were immune, guaranteed that the Longhorn blood would not be too much contaminated before science took matters in hand.

For a long time the Texians did not generally want fine cattle. When Colonel Thomas Jefferson Shannon in 1848 received as a gift from Queen Victoria two young cows and a bull out of her own Durham herd, the animals being landed free in New Orleans and hauled thence in crates on ox wagons to north Texas — beyond the tick zone — he found neighbors indignant at the introduction of such stock. Their legs were too short to cover ground that a good grazer and rustler must cover! They were not as tall as the Longhorns either! Actually, it is claimed,[14] some of Colonel Thomas Jefferson Shannon's bulls — for the Queen Victoria stock throve — were shot dead on the open range by men who wanted none of that squatty build in their brands.

The number of cattle in Texas when it became a Republic and for decades to follow must remain as estimates, for there are no accurate figures. One estimate places the number in 1830 as 100,000, one fifth of them American importations and the remainder Spanish.[15]

The Longhorn became what he was with only a limited influence beyond Mexico. The characteristics of this basic stock were so persistent that, without fences to control breeding, any imported strain tended to be absorbed. The superiority of the Texas cattle to those below the Rio Grande was due primarily to the selection of calves to be left for bulls. On the other hand, the point of view of the Mexican exercising any judgment at all was expressed by an old ranchero on the Frio River. "That calf," he would say at a branding, "looks like it would not make much of a steer. Just leave him for a bull." The early Spanish custom of castrating nothing is observed in some sections of Mexico to this day.

Selective breeding, some outside blood, a difference in range, and perhaps other factors — unknown to me — made the Texan a rangier, mightier-horned and heavier animal than the straight Mexican.

Of tails that often dragged the ground and of race-horse legs, I shall speak extendedly. Next to the horns, which require a separate chapter, the most striking quality in appearance of the Texas cattle was their coloration. It is incorrect to say that they represented all the colors of the rainbow. Their colors were more varied than those of the rainbow, but they were generally dull, earthlike. There were brindles; blues — mulberry blue, ring-streaked blue, speckled blue; *grullas* — so-named because they had the hue of the sand-hill crane, called also mouse-colored, or slate; duns, dark, washed-out and Jersey creams — all hues of "yellow"; browns with bay points and bays with brown points; blacks, solid and splotched with white, brown and red; whites, both cleanly bright and dirty speckled; many *sabinas*, red-and-white peppered; reds of all shades except the dark richness characteristic of Herefords, pale reds being very common; paints of many combinations. The line along the back was common, as in the mustang breed. Coarse brown hairs around the ears were characteristic. The shadings and combinations of colors were so various that no two were alike.

The cattle were at home on the coastal prairies. They seemed even more at home in brushy or rough country — no matter how arid. They adapted themselves to swamps. They attained maximum size on high land to the north and west. Yet, even there, they never became uniform in the manner of characteristic Plains fauna, such as antelopes, buffaloes and prairie dogs — millions upon millions of individuals of each species almost exactly alike in appearance. They did not originate on the plains any more than the Texas cowboy did. At least four different regions of Texas — coastal prairie, timbered areas of the east, brush of the southwest, and widely differing uplands — produced divergent types of this Longhorn breed. Yet the "mountain boomer" in the high hills above the headwaters of the Guadalupe River and the "coasters" were essentially the same animal.

The Longhorn was exceedingly slow in development, not reaching the maximum of weight until eight or ten years old. He was not considered mature until past four years old. Steers from four to eight years old averaged around eight hundred pounds, while ten-year-olds and up weighed a thousand pounds or better, sometimes going to sixteen hundred pounds. In 1868 a herd of 224 picked Texas steers that were weighed in Abilene, Kansas, averaged, after standing in the pens twelve hours, 1238 pounds each.[16] The present always patronizes the past; moderns of every age suppose that all preceding them was in a molluscan state. Yet to suppose that the Longhorns were scrubs is like presuming that George Washington's soldiers, merely because they had no tanks, could not fight.

A mass of evidence might be adduced to corroborate a statement made by Judge Joseph Eve, of Kentucky, United States Chargé d'Affaires to the Republic of Texas. He came to this country, in 1841, "prepared to be dissatisfied with it," but found "the best stock country in the world, covered with grass, the cattle equal to our best Kentucky cattle in size and appearance. It is not uncommon for a planter here to own a thousand head, which they tell me are good beef upon the grass in winter as well as in summer, and which they say cost them nothing but the trouble of marking and branding them." [17]

It is true, however, that for all his heroic stature, the Texas steer stood with his body tucked up in the flanks, his high shoulder-top sometimes thin enough to split a hailstone, his ribs flat, his length frequently so extended that his back swayed. Viewed from the side, his big frame would fool a novice into a ridiculous overestimate of his weight, but a rear view was likely to show cat hams, narrow hips, and a ridgepole kind of backbone. His bones appeared to be heavier than they actually were. The bones of running stock are never ponderous. He could get "seal fat" and "carry plenty of tallow," which was well disposed and not wadded up in his belly and on his legs. "He looked more natural to me," Walter Billingsley said, "when in good living condition than when fat." As a quick converter of feed into beef and as a producer of heavy cuts clean down to the hock, he was notably defective. Yet carcasses "dressed out" surprisingly well, disproving the saying that Texas cattle were "all legs and horns." [18]

One cannot get away from the fact that the Longhorn suited the men to whom he gave his name and for whom he became a symbol. There have always been ranchmen, like Tennyson's

"Northern Farmer," hearing in hoofbeats only the syllables, "Pro-put-ty, pro-put-ty, pro-put-ty." Their kind today see in sheer avoirdupois something beautiful — like a sack lumpy with stuffed bank notes. But many men of the open range would have agreed with what Charles M. Russell wrote in *Good Medicine:* "When it comes to making the beautiful Ma Nature has man beat all ways from the ace. . . . I have made a living painting the horned animal that the old lady I'm talking about made. . . . I would starve to death painting the hornless deformity that man has made."

Sheer avoirdupois and animation do not go together, and in animate things it is animation, alertness, vitality that arrest and delight us. "One of the prettiest sights I ever saw," wrote an old-time Texas cowman, "was on a cool September morning when a bunch of wild cattle, led by three or four big old mossbacks, raised their heads as they saw us coming and made a dash for the cañon breaks. When a real cow horse sees the sun flashing on the horns of cattle like these as they break to run, he will straighten out his neck, grab the bit in his teeth, and light out after them. And the man on such a horse after such cattle will have a dose of life injected into him stronger than any goat serum ever invented."

These were the cattle that caused a German traveler in 1848 to remark on "the old tried Texan saying, 'In Texas cattle live for the sake of man, but in all other countries man lives for the sake of his cattle.' " [19] That is to say, here the cattle had to live absolutely independent of man's help. Feeding them, sheltering them, salting them, doctoring them, doing anything for them in any way was unthought-of. As the range was all free and as the cattle were worth little, their survival was left entirely to the wholesome winnowing processes of nature. "It will cost more to raise a brood of chickens in Texas than an equal number of cattle," an agent for immigration wrote. [20]

Cattle were so common and money was so scarce that a "cow

and calf" represented the medium of exchange.²¹ Stephen F. Austin wrote that he could "always get Cows and Calves but money was out of the question." By tacit understanding a cow and calf passed for ten dollars, although selling them for actual money was often beyond possibility. The custom was for an individual to give a promise to pay one cow and calf, three cows and calves, or any other number. This piece of "cow paper" was passed on from person to person just as bank notes or checks are now, somebody finally presenting the claim and receiving the cattle. Thus, on Matagorda Bay, about 1829, Mary S. Helm and her husband traded "an order of five cows and calves for hewed logs sixteen feet long to build one room." "Sam Slick," the Yankee peddler, went over the country trading off wooden clocks and other notions — "most of 'em things you couldn't sell or give away" — for cows and calves until he had "a very large drove."

The Texas cow and calf represented the principle behind the world's first coined money, in Greece — the image of an ox roughly stamped on metal. The Latin word for money, *pecunia*, goes back to that Grecian ox, *pecus* meaning "cattle." In Texas, an "impecunious" man was literally "without cattle," pecunious and impecunious alike being without money. "Many good citizens — very good livers — men of property," an alcalde wrote Stephen F. Austin, "do not handle five dollars a year." A man's chattels came to be, in the root meaning of that word, cattle. To go further into the history of cow linguistics, the Sanskrit word for soldier means "one who fights about cows"; in Texas for many decades much of the fighting was "about cows," though the fighters were anything but soldierly. On one of the bank notes issued by the Republic of Texas a Longhorn steer races ahead of a rider. The fact that a hundred-dollar note came to be worth less than a fraction of some illiterate settler's scrawled promise to pay "A cow & Caf" was no reflection on the fitness of the beautifully engraved design.

As money, as furnisher of rawhide that had illimitable uses, as the material of a people's occupation, and as food, the Longhorn became to ranch Texans, who "lived at home," almost what the buffalo was to the Plains Indians. Even in the Age of Horse Culture, he made "cow sense" a synonym for "horse sense." His flesh was the staff of life, affording the only genuine breakfast food known. In the fight against General Woll's army of Mexicans that invaded San Antonio in 1842, one Texan who had that morning eaten a very heavy bait of beef was shot in the stomach. After the doctor had examined him he said it was the most fortunate shot he had ever seen. "If it had not been for the beef," he explained, "the bullet would have killed the man, and if it had not been for the bullet, the beef would have killed him." [22]

The Longhorn men did not exactly have Sir Roger de Coverley's "roast beef stomach," but as beef-eaters, who had never tasted a leg of mutton, they surpassed the beef-eating for which Britons centuries ago became famous. They fried their steaks. They roasted ribs and joints on the open fire. They jerked quantities of meat and ate the sun-dried — often sun-baked — jerky raw, cooked it a little more on coals, or stewed it. Onions or garlic and — when possible to obtain — Irish potatoes helped the stew; native red peppers made it just right. If dried properly, *carne seca* will keep indefinitely. Like parched corn, it is the very essence of food. If it gets too dry, it can be beaten into pemmican — though that word was unknown to the lean eaters of lean jerky.

Inside houses, more beef was eaten fried than any other way. Some flour, fried in melted tallow, peppered and diluted with water, resulted in a gravy good enough to make a fellow want to whip his own grandmammy. Isom Like was representative.[23]

After fighting his way out of Texas, Isom Like continued to fight Indians in New Mexico a while, and then, with his horse stock, settled down near the Colorado line. He had six sons, and when he was in his seventies he and they would have a riding contest annually. Old Isom always won, his wife usually acting as judge. He lived strictly at home, but along in the nineties buyers quit coming for his horses and he decided to drive a bunch east and peddle them out. Arriving in a town, he would go to the hotel to eat. When the waiter set dessert before him, he would shove it aside, saying, "Oh, that's children's food." Or, if toast was offered him for breakfast, he would calmly state, "I ain't sick."

After he had celebrated his hundredth birthday, Jack Potter paid him a visit and asked his *remedio* for long life. He got it: "Live temperately in food and drinks. Try to get your beefsteaks three times a day, fried in taller. Taller is mighty healing, and there's nothing like it to keep your stumich greased-up and in good working order."

Tallow was a substitute for both lard and butter. Melted and poured sizzling hot into a tin plate of blackstrap — black sorghum molasses — it helped end a meal with a dessert as good as a hungry man ever flopped his lip over. But melted tallow will quickly congeal in the mouth and stick to the roof of it. My grandfather, Rufus Byler, who was murdered in south Texas immediately after he came home from the Civil War, was baldheaded. "When I was a boy," he would explain, "I complained once about tallow that glued-up in the top of my mouth. They put a hot skillet on top of my head so's to drive the heat down and melt the tallow, and in that way burned all my hair out at the roots."

Charles Goodnight was Indian enough to consider buffalo meat even more conducive to longevity than Texas beef. He kept a herd of buffaloes almost to the end of his life. When he was past ninety he told me that the best tonic he had ever been able to find was a mixture of the extract of buffalo meat with whisky.

But for ranch people in general, "meat" meant beef and nothing else. "Boys," a mother down in the lower part of Texas would say, "we are about out of meat." "All right, Mama!" — and before supper a yearling would be hanging up. Along in the seventies, the McWhorters, of Live Oak County, sold out their brand to Henderson Williams. Not long afterwards Cal Wright came along about dinner time. "What," he exclaimed, as he looked at the table, "no meat! How's this, living in a cow country and no meat?"

"We've sold out our brand and have no range rights now," answered Mr. McWhorter, a notably honest man, though many other ranchmen regarded the difference between *mine* and *thine* in the same way.

"Well, I'll give you range rights to meat right now," Cal Wright thundered. "I represent my own brands and the Bluntzer brands and Henderson Williams' brands. If you can't find any of them handy, take from any other brand. The idea of living here where all these wild cattle are and not having meat! Why, damn it, Nick Bluntzer has actually advertised that anybody hungry can eat his beef, provided it's not wasted and the hide's saved. That's the way we all feel."

As for game, plenty of ranch people are yet willing to leave venison for city hunters. Back in the early eighties, while the custom of beefing any heifer calf found on the range at a convenient hour and place was not generally considered exactly as stealing, and while Sam Blalock was roping outlaws in the brush, two "fellers," as he tells, came to his part of the country, west of the Nueces, to kill deer and ship them east for the Christmas market. "One day one of them killed seventeen and the other sixteen. The deer ran in bunches. You could kill all of them things you wanted. But we ranch people didn't think much of their meat. We preferred fat beef and had plenty of it." [24]

These beef-eaters never hung a carcass up to skin it and butcher it out. They let it lie flat on the ground. Thus, "the meat was sweeter and more nutritious than if the blood had been drained as much as possible out of it." [25]

But on account of the disease the cattle from lower Texas spread through ticks, which they dropped and which hatched little ticks that crawled up on Northern cattle and gave them a fever often fatal, the Longhorns came to be regarded by many people as diseased. The result, only temporary, was a strong prejudice against Texas beef. Some trail men thought that traveling gave cattle a kind of disease, and after they set out with a herd were so leery of "trail fever," or "traveling fever," that they would not eat one of their own animals. Many of them, however, had no prejudice against the meat of a fat stray that got too close to the herd.

The Northern prejudice is exemplified in the diary entry of a Texas-bound traveler crossing the Indian Nation south of Baxter Springs, Kansas: "*Nov. 4, 1870.* Halted at a rocky branch for lunch. Here an old Indian had half a beef dressed and hung up on some saplings. The boys were afraid to buy any of his beef for fear it was a diseased Texas beef out of some of the droves passing." [26] In the same way many people of the North and East were for a time afraid of Texas beef in butcher shops.[27]

Regard now some herd among the millions of these cattle that for approximately a quarter of a century flowed north over the long trails. Tall, bony, coarse-headed, coarse-haired, flat-sided, thin-flanked, some of them grotesquely narrow-hipped, some with bodies so long that their backs swayed, big ears carved into outlandish designs, dewlaps hanging and swinging in rhythm with their energetic steps, their motley-colored sides as bold with brands as a relief map of the Grand Canyon — mightily antlered, wild-eyed, this herd of full-grown Texas steers might appear to a stranger seeing them for the first time as a parody of their kind. But however they appeared, with their steel hoofs, their long legs, their staglike muscles, their thick skins, their power-

[41]

ful horns, they could walk the roughest ground, cross the widest deserts, climb the highest mountains, swim the widest rivers, fight off the fiercest bands of wolves, endure hunger, cold, thirst and punishment as few beasts of the earth have ever shown themselves capable of enduring. On the prairies they could run like antelopes; in the thickets of thorn and tangle they could break their way with the agility of panthers. They could rustle in drouth or snow, smell out pasturage leagues away, live — without talking about the matter — like true captains of their own souls and bodies.

They were the cow brutes for the open range, the cattle of the hour. They suited the wide, untamed land and the men that ranged it. Although of Spanish origin, they were marked by Texas suns, magnified by Texas grasses and scarred by Texas brush. The Mexican cattle that they came from and resembled were long-horned, but Longhorn as a generic name seems not to have been much used until after the Civil War. By then, they had assumed distinct characteristics and had entered upon a history entitling them to be called a "breed," in the strictest sense of that word, even though not one of all their progenitors ever had his name enrolled in a herd book or his ears tagged with a brass number. Had they been registered and regulated, restrained and provided for by man, they would not have been what they were.

III · MAVERICKS AND MAVERICKERS

*To Asa Jones. I have eaten his frijoles in both Texas
and Arizona. Maverickers were eating the beef — but
nobody ever heard of a calf in his brand sucking
the wrong cow.*

Old Diamond Joe was a rich old jay,
With lots of cowboys in his pay;
He rode the range with his cowboy band,
And many a mav'rick got his brand.
   — "Diamond Joe," in LOMAX's *Cowboy Songs.*

WHEREVER the Spanish introduced cattle some of the
offspring soon ran wild and unbranded. While these
cimarrones — the original cattle of Texas — were being caught
and killed by the colonists or absorbed into their small herds,

[43]

the ranching industry advanced. Meanwhile cattle were constantly escaping the cow works, taking refuge in remote coverts, and breeding a progeny to mature with ears unmarked and sides unburned. At no time in the history of ranching, until barbed wire brought the range under control, was there a dearth of mavericks in Texas. Their great era was right after the Civil War, about which time the word "maverick" passed from local into wide popular use.

The word and its derivatives took on varying meanings. The simple facts of its origin were expanded by dictionaries, range talk, and books concerned with cowboy life into a cycle of legends. Despite Mr. Webster and other New England authorities on Southern speech, there are only two syllables in the word (mav-rick) as pronounced by any genuine Texan.

Charlie Siringo, who mavericked on the Texas coast and in 1885 published the first cowboy autobiography known, elaborates on how Samuel Maverick, "being a chickenhearted old rooster, wouldn't brand or earmark any of his cattle." All his neighbors branded theirs — and his too. Nevertheless, the "old rooster went on claiming everything that wore slick ears. . . . At first people said, 'Yonder goes one of Mr. Maverick's animals.' Then, upon seeing any unbranded animal anywhere, they got to saying, 'Yonder goes a maverick.' "

According to another source, at a great meeting of stock-raisers in southern Texas each man declared publicly what brand and earmark he would use. Finally, after everybody but an "old Longhorn named Maverick" had recorded his brand, he allowed he wouldn't use any brand at all; and then when range people saw anything unbranded they would know it belonged to him — and would please not claim it. As he was known to possess only "a triflin' bunch of Mexican steers" and not a single cow, the other cattlemen agreed.

Samuel Maverick, the legend goes on, was in 1861 the largest landholder in the United States and owned more cattle than any other man in Texas. His ambition was to travel on his own land all the six hundred miles from San Antonio to El Paso and to stock it. After the Civil War he had a logical claim to tens of thousands of the unbranded cattle — "Maverick stuff" — though little good it did him.

But, no, another form of the legend persists: In the beginning Maverick had nothing except "an old stag, a branding iron, a tireless perseverance, and a morality that was blind in one eye." The stag was more prolific than Tommy Simpson's Scotch cows, which always brought quintuplets, and the branding iron worked faster than a billy goat. A man had to get up early and ride late to do even a small share of the mavericking business when Maverick was on the range. He became "one of the cattle kings" and was the bull of the woods in "bovine aristocracy."

The word "maverick," says one writer, comes from the name of a great cattle driver whose herd, consisting of many thousands, stampeded in a snowstorm at a mountain pass ten thousand feet above the sea and were so scattered that he could not regather them. Their offspring came to be known as "Maverick's cattle," though he had no more power over them than Mother Carey had over Mother Carey's chickens.

Another "authority" tells how Maverick had his cattle on an island off the coast of Texas. As they were entirely cut off from all other cattle, he did not have to brand them to maintain ownership. But one night a tropical storm blew all the water out of the pass between the island and the mainland; the cattle rushed across, mixed with other cattle, and were dispersed beyond recovery. A variant of this story is that some fishermen sent Maverick word that his cattle had overpopulated the island. He had forgotten all about them. Now he ordered a big cow hunt to brand the cattle and move a portion of them to the mainland. Then, a herd of thousands having been assembled, they stampeded, swam the bay, scattered like quail, and became the quarry of whoever could rope and brand them.

Eight hundred bulls, however, the legend concludes, were salvaged by Maverick's men and driven to the Salado above San Antonio. Just bulls and nothing else, and they were fiercer than fierce. Stockmen from all over the country got to "rawhiding" Maverick unmercifully. They would ask him about the price of bull meat, whether he threw in the hide and horns, how many ranches he intended to start, and "otherwise nearly ran the old gentleman to the verge of distraction." Finally, in answer to any allusion to the subject, he would say, "For God's sake help yourself to whatever bulls you want."

There was, in truth, an island. The facts have long been available.[1] Samuel A. Maverick, a lawyer, one of the signers of the Texas Declaration of Independence against Mexico, and an extensive speculator in lands, was the leading English-speaking citizen of San Antonio in 1842 when an invading Mexican army captured him and took him prisoner to Mexico City, where he was in time released.

In 1845 he was living temporarily at Decrow's Point on Matagorda Bay. A neighbor named Tilton owed him $1200, could not raise the money, and persuaded Maverick to take four hundred head of cattle running on Matagorda Island in cancellation of the debt. Maverick did not want the cattle; he knew almost nothing about cattle and had no ambition to learn. Soon after receiving them, he left the four hundred head thus forced upon him, along with a few ponies, under the care of a Negro family nominally slave but essentially free — especially, free to be shiftless.

Matagorda Island, with its southern appendage Saint Joseph's Island, is a great sand bar more than seventy miles long, in places less than a mile wide and in other places spreading out four or five miles. It is beached rather evenly on the outer side by the Gulf of Mexico and indented on the other by scores of inlets from Espíritu Santo, Mesquite, Aransas, and other bays. At shallow places like Dagger Point, the Karankawa Indians

[46]

used to wade across from the mainland at low tide, and until recent times cattle were driven from the island to the mainland in the same way, though barges now take them across.

High sand dunes, some of them grassed over and some of them so loose that they shift constantly with the constant winds, parallel the Gulf shore. Running down the center of the island is an irregular prairie carpeted with coastal grasses. There are fresh water lakes, though wells and windmills nowadays supply most of the stock water. Three or four times a century hurricanes sweep Gulf water over the land. Far in from the bearded salt rye of the dunes one can see occasionally a great drift log, under which deer and even cattle shade. Ranching is the only occupation, and four or five ranches occupy the whole land. Prickly pear, Spanish dagger, mesquite, huisache, catclaw and other low growth are to be found in places. Coons, which live on water life, coyotes, sand crabs, deer, jack rabbits that look almost as big as the deer, rattlesnakes, an infinite variety of shore birds and, in winter, migratory fowls by the hundreds of thousands, give a profusion of life to a land seemingly empty.

Here Maverick's cattle could roam as free as any other creatures of nature. They could scatter not only up and down the long island, but could, if the notion struck them, wade across to the mainland when the tide was low and the wind was blowing the water out of the bay. Perhaps some of them, like the deer, now and then passed to the mainland. Modern Herefords on the island will not make such a venture. When drouths dried up the little fresh water lakes, some perhaps died of thirst, the more thrifty standing in salt water for hours a day absorbing moisture.

The Mexican War was being fought; Texas was ceasing to be a Republic and becoming a state. Maverick was in the stir of the times. Now and then he heard something about the cattle and heard that the calves were not being branded. In 1853 he had his entire stock, in so far as it could be gathered, crossed to the mainland and driven to a range up the San Antonio River. His visible stock still numbered about four hundred head.

The Negro family came with the herd and continued to be the official caretakers. They became energetic enough to brand about a third of the calves. Owners of other cattle in the country were keeping their own calves branded up, and were hunting down older unclaimed animals. Surmising that at least some of the unbranded animals they saw were Maverick's, they got to calling all of them "mavericks" — and they "mavericked" them.

This was not thought of as stealing — it was not stealing; it was the custom of the range at the time. There was comparatively little stealing of cattle before the Civil War. All calves caught in the "cow hunts" were branded in the brands of their mothers, whether the branders knew who the owner of the cow was or not. The old-time cowman was a patriarch, but the range has always been matriarchal. Unbranded cattle of a year old and up went to whoever caught them.

But to get back to Samuel Maverick. In 1856 he sold out his stock of cattle, estimated at the original number, four hundred head, at six dollars around, range delivery. That is, the purchaser, one Toutant Beauregard, took the stock "as they ran." If there were more than four hundred head, he was the gainer; if less, the loser. He hoped to find a considerable number of mavericks on Maverick's range.

These were the last and only cattle that Samuel A. Maverick ever owned. His unintentional contribution to the American language was more important, perhaps, than his honorable and useful part in Texas affairs; at least it has done far more to keep his name green, and it has made him a notable factor in the history of a business he really never entered. One of his descendants, Maury Maverick, recently published a book with the punning title, *A Maverick American*. The word in time came to mean, as applied to persons, one who has separated himself from the herd, or a mere stray.

A "maverick brand" was an unrecorded brand. Theoretically it would "hold" an animal on the range against being driven off, but in case theft was suspected the brand could not be fixed — by any records — on the thief. "Mavericking" graduated into a soft synonym for stealing. The illegitimate "mavericters" would sometimes slit the tongue of a sucking calf so that it could no longer suck and would soon stop following its mother. If a calf with a slit tongue were put in a pen with other calves, it could not bawl and betray its strangeness to the place. Mavericters at times killed the mother cows and hid the carcasses, thus destroying evidence of theft, for a healthy cow with a swollen bag and no calf says that some thief has stolen her baby. Again the mavericters would cut the calves off, drive them to some canyon and rasp their feet so that they could not walk back hunting their mothers. Or the feet of the cows might be rasped so that they could not follow the calves.

Just as some men fudged on the age of calves, anticipating the time when they might become true mavericks, others would brand nothing they did not absolutely know to be their own, though they would fight to the finish in holding that. Jack Potter tells how one day on a New Mexico range he roped a bull maverick that looked to be past a year old and was about to brand it when a notoriously honest cowpuncher loped up yelling for him to wait. The puncher jumped down off his horse, grabbed the young bull's head, and went to smelling its breath. "That yearlin' has a ma," he said, untying the rope. "He had his liquid diet this morning." And sure enough, the very next day, the bull yearling, who had ranged away from his ma only temporarily, was found butting her bag for more milk.

Of the millions of cattle in Texas at the close of the Civil War, none were yet out on the Great Plains; all of them were far east of the Pecos River. Perhaps a third or a fourth of these millions were unbranded. Nearly all able-bodied men, many of whom were killed, had been occupied in warfare, either in the Confederate Army or against Indians. The slave population, very sparse in all but the eastern part of the cow country, had raised cotton and grain — and rested. The women and children and old men could brand calves that stayed around the homesteads. There was nobody to ride the far ranges and work the wilder-growing cattle. During the more than four years of war, calves by the multiplied thousands had grown into twisty-horned cows and fighting bulls without having felt the rope, many of them without having seen a rider, unless perhaps a Comanche. With peace established, the catching and branding of these cattle became in some regions almost the sole occupation of the returned men and developing youth. Even then, on some of the brushy and broken frontiers, for a decade mavericks developed almost as fast as they were caught out.

They were unbelievably numerous, and, therefore, cheap. Once, in a lull of Indian raids, Andrew Gatluf Jones and some other rangers took time off in the Nueces River country and caught four hundred head of mavericks, which they drove to Bandera and sold for two dollars a head — and as a result were fired from the ranger service. They were lucky to get that two dollars a head. Kil Vickers gathered up two hundred head of mavericks and big steers without visible owners, drove them to Rockport, shipped them by boat to New Orleans — and lost $2.50 a head on the deal.

Beyond the settlements there was a wilderness of mavericks. Not long after the war closed, a boy named Vinton James (who had just been cured of chills and fever by a tumbler of whisky mixed with the fire of an even one hundred Mexican peppers) went out with some men on the big divide above the headwaters of the Llano River. The first morning of the hunt, he says, "We succeeded, after a great deal of trouble, in gathering quite a bunch of all kinds of cattle. . . . There were many mavericks, among them a number of old bulls. These bulls absolutely refused to be driven or to leave the herd. They fought so viciously when we tried to cut them out, that the men drew their pistols and guns and killed several. Then a corral was built out of cedar and the captured cattle were driven into it. That night, and every night afterwards, so long as we remained at this place, we kept large fires burning around the corral so as to keep the cattle from stampeding." [2]

According to an old saying representing a common belief, all it took to make a cowman — an owner — was "a rope, nerve to use it and a branding iron." It took more than that. When mavericks were thickest, markets were remote and uncertain. Any man who developed a fortune on the open range was masterful enough to control his part of it and to maintain ownership of stock widely scattered and always being further scattered unless the scatterers were held down.

In the fall of 1876 Adolph Huffmeyer, twenty years old, was drawing thirty dollars a month branding mavericks for his employers and doing cow work generally. He had seen a man brand as many as eighteen mavericks a day; he himself had tied down and run the iron on a dozen in one day — for the men who had him hired. Some maverickers got paid by the head, fifty cents or a dollar being the standard price. Young Huffmeyer decided that if he mavericked on his own hook he could average at least six long-ears a day and in the course of a few months have a herd of his own. He had saved a little money. He bought three cow ponies, took a supply of coffee, salt and meal, a can for boiling coffee in, a skillet for making corn bread in, his overcoat, which would not shed water, two blankets, a running iron and an extra rope, and went to "laying out with the dry cattle."

He was going to be a great cowman, and he decided to make his brand commemorate the year in which he began as an owner. Onto the left side of the first maverick that he roped, he burned **7 T 6** –"Seventy-six." His mark was a smooth crop on the right ear and under halfcrop on the left. After he had roped for six weeks, his tally showed around 250 head of cattle in the **7 T 6** brand. He was averaging the six mavericks a day.

Then one morning a young cowboy friend rode up on him.

"Of course, you've got that brand and mark recorded," the friend said when Huffmeyer told of his success.

The mavericker didn't know much about records, had not thought of the matter. At daylight next morning he was sitting on the courthouse steps in Frio Town waiting for the county clerk.

"What brand do you want to record?" the clerk asked.

"**7 T 6**," and Huffmeyer scrawled it on a piece of paper.

In Texas brands are recorded by counties, not by the state. The law is that no brand may be duplicated in any county, and a brand cannot be legally claimed unless it is legally recorded. The clerk opened his brand book and scanned the pages on which brands beginning with the figure 7 were recorded.

"Why, just the other day," he said, "So-and-so recorded **7 T 6** as his brand with the very earmark you give."

That settled the matter. Adolph Huffmeyer did not have any cattle. He had branded 250 head for another man.

For all the good that the other man derived from his shoddy trick, he might as well not have played it. Two hundred and fifty head of jack rabbits in the chaparral, all branded in his name, would have been of just about as much worth to him as those two hundred and fifty wild cattle, scattered from hell to breakfast in a broken, brushy country as wild as they were. Unless the owner could be represented in many cow hunts, he would never get a tenth of the animals. It took far more power to gather, sell and collect the increase from a bunch of scattered mavericks than it did to merely rope and brand them. That was just the start. The open range was for the strong, for those who could hold as well as take.

[52]

Theoretically a man had no right to start a brand unless he had some seed cows to contribute to the general crop of calves, but in an enormous country of few people and many cattle this theory was often overlooked.

Young L. T. Harmon was working for a ranchman, branding mavericks, in Live Oak County, down in the brush country.

"Why don't you brand a few for yourself?" the ranchman generously suggested.

"Why, I don't have a stock of cattle and have no brand," Harmon replied.

"Start a brand."

Harmon started a brand. He became very energetic in applying it — **X X X L**. After he had worked on his own hook for several months, the man who had started him off bought him out, range delivery, for a thousand dollars. "You are not leaving me enough mavericks," he said. Having a range of his own, and being potent enough to control his own brand, he could along with it take care of the **X X X L** brand. One cowman often gave a dozen brands concurrently.

The average cowman did not encourage cowless cowboys to "start a brand." In the early seventies four brothers by the name of Dunn and young Ike Hewitt were branding mavericks at four-bits a head for cowmen operating on the Gulf coast. They figured their wages against the price of cattle and decided to start a brand of their own, which they recorded and went energetically to putting on what they could rope.

The cowmen who had employed these young men to maverick now looked upon mavericking in an entirely new light. One night a small posse captured the five, led them into a thicket, strung them up, and said *adiós* with a volley of bullets at the swinging forms.

One bullet entered Ike Hewitt's body; another severed the rope by which he hung. It was a cold, cold night. Hours later he came to life. Dazed, he felt the bodies of his comrades. They were as stiff as frozen fish. Hewitt made his way to a friendly family, was nursed back to health, and became a coast freighter. He wore a coonskin cap and was known as "Coonskin Ike." He never used his full name, and he never rode a horse after that night in the thicket.

Many little owners kept their stocks of cattle under day herd, penning them at night. When spring came, they would sell off their steers and keep the calves penned by day so that the mother cows would come to them each evening. Then while the cows stayed in the pen at night, the calves would be turned out to graze.

In 1871 Dan Waggoner, who ranched in northern Texas, made a trade with Joe Loving to handle a bunch of stock cattle for him for five years on shares. A partnership brand was put on them. Of course the more increase Loving could produce, the higher would be his portion. That fall he took an outfit of men and made a raid on counties to the south.

"We gathered," says Dot Babb, who was working for Loving, "all the big early calves we could find that were not marked or branded. We took in the mothers of some of the calves and some we did not. When we did not want the mother cows, we cut them back, and if they returned we shot them in the nose or punched them. In this way we gathered about five hundred 'mavericks' and branded them, turning them loose on the Waggoner range. Then Joe Loving took his outfit in another direction and brought back all the big calves he could see or get, regardless of who owned them. The citizens very soon discovered what was going on, and there was talk of mobbing Mr. Waggoner. He knew nothing of the stealing — the 'mavericking.' As soon as he learned the facts, he bought out Joe Loving's interest and made a satisfactory settlement with the rightful owners" — that is, the assertive owners who could get to him and prove their rights. "In those days," Dot Babb continues, "unbranded cattle belonged to the outfits who could get to them first and then had enough fighting men to hold and keep them." [3]

The cattlemen were forced to make rules fixing dates for the beginning and ending of range work. Then every owner would have an even break, and the cattle would not be continually "choused to death." "Sooners," as men who rushed the branding season came to be called, violated the rules of course, but still the rules helped. In the fall of 1870 the cattlemen of Palo Pinto County assembled and fixed February first of the following year as the date on which branding should begin. One cold rainy day not long afterwards W. C. Cochran was deer-hunting when he came upon a rancher named Will Allen hunting mavericks — legitimate mavericks this time — with dogs. There were not then any matches in the country, and the wood was too wet for Allen to start a fire with the flint, steel and punk that every man carried. He was carrying a chunk of fire from one bunch of cattle to another. He said he had caught and branded fifteen mavericks that day.

On the twentieth of January following he and his men appeared one evening at the pens of West Edwards' ranch with about a hundred mavericks they had brazenly gathered on the Edwards range. He went to branding them under Edwards' eyes. Edwards rode most of the night. By four o'clock next morning he had three hands, each with a blanket, some grub in a *morral*, a Winchester and two six-shooters each. They were "in good shape to work cattle." They rode to Will Allen's range and in two days branded two hundred and fifty mavericks. [4]

In Hood County about the same time an enterprising rancher named Haley had a pen full of big calves and yearlings ready for branding just a day ahead of the date agreed upon for the community work to start. That night an indignant owner took some men, turned the mavericks out of Haley's pen, drove them to his own, and then notified surrounding cowmen to come. They came, the percentage of calves going to each man being based on the number of cows he was supposed to own. There was no way of telling what calf belonged to what cow, but the aggregate of branded cows had produced the aggregate of unbranded calves.[5] The operator on the open range kept tally of the calves he branded and of whatever he sold; he estimated the annual per cent of losses; and then he had a rough idea — sometimes very rough indeed — of the number of cattle he owned.

Mavericking was a sport in which the majority of ropers prized the game more highly than the property.

"We had no wagon," [6] a mavericker of 1866 wrote fifty-seven years later. "Every man carried his grub in a wallet behind his saddle and his bed under his saddle. A wallet is a sack with both ends sewed up and a slit in the middle. As a boy I had to stay on herd. I carried a lot of extra wallets on behind my saddle and a string of tin cups on a rawhide hobble around my pony's neck. Whenever the boss herder couldn't hear those cups jingling, he would come around and wake me up. We would corral the cattle every night at some one of the owners' homes and stand guard around the corral. I didn't stand any guard, but I carried brush and corn-stalks and anything I could get to make a light for those who were not on guard to play poker by. They played for unbranded cattle, yearlings at fifty cents a head, and the top price for any class was five dollars a head. If a man ran out of cattle and had a little money, he could get back in the game. For ten dollars, say, he could get a stack of yearlings. My compensation for light was two-bits a night, or as long as the game lasted. Every few days they would divide up and brand the mavericks and each owner would take his cattle home" — perhaps to day-herd them, penning them every night so that they would get gentle and locate permanently on his range — perhaps never to see them again.

The year 1869 was exceptionally wet in southern Texas. "You could almost travel in a skiff across the prairies from

Houston to Corpus Christi." It was also a fine year for mavericks. That fall Jim (J. N.) Jones, who ranched on the San Miguel Creek in Frio County, threw in with five other men for a maverick hunt. They took along a nest egg of gentle cattle and were able to "ease" many mavericks into the herd without having to rope them. They held what they caught, intending to brand them at the end of the work. A lone mavericker or a pair of maverickers could not operate in this way, but a cow crowd could. After having hunted for a week or ten days, Jones and his companions got back to the San Miguel late one drizzly evening with 260 mavericks, and shut them in the muddy pens.

As the hungry and wet maverickers sat down in the warm kitchen to a supper of hot biscuits, fried steak, and beans and bacon with plenty of black coffee, the rain began to pour. After supper they started playing poker, mavericks making the stakes. Each of the six men was provided with forty-three frijoles, each bean representing a maverick, the two undividable animals being left for future disposition. The game of freeze-out to see who should have all the 260 mavericks began to get warm.

After it had gone on for some time and Mrs. Jones was through washing the dishes, she came to the table and called attention to the rain. "It is a regular waterspout," she said. "With the ground already soaked, the San Miguel is getting up into the pens. I know it is."

There was no move on the part of the gamblers. The woman's eagerness to break the game up, and thus forestall the chance of her husband's losing his share of the property, was plain. "The cattle are all in danger of being drowned," she went on.

The men continued playing. Here was something, for the moment, more interesting than rain or cattle. An hour passed. The rain was still falling in sheets. Again Mrs. Jones went to the gamblers. "Don't you hear those cattle bawling?" she said, her voice high. "They are in distress. I know they are. You had

[57]

better stop and see about them. Those pens are in low ground."

"The water will never get up into the pens," Jim Jones answered. "I built them above the high-water mark. Let the cows low and the bulls beller. . . . Raise you a maverick."

More time passed. Then suddenly Mrs. Jones exclaimed, "Look, the water is coming up into the floor. The San Miguel is raging like the Mississippi."

Now the men stopped, each making count of the beans he had left. The deluge had slacked a little. Peering out, they were aware of a vast expanse of raging waters. They went to the pens, which were made of mesquite logs, the gates being barred with poles. The cattle were moaning and bawling. As the men approached, they heard that clicking of horns and snuffing that told them the mavericks were packed in a mill — were circling like a whirlpool. Flashes of lightning revealed a crazy mass of cattle wound into such a tight ball that a rabbit could not have squeezed to the center from the outside. Doubtless some of the cattle in the center were already down and being smothered and trampled to death. The men tried to break the mill but they simply could not. The only way to break it was to open the gate and get the cattle headed out. The waters of the San Miguel were already a foot deep in the pen.

Turning a maverick, not yet branded, out on the open range was like throwing a dollar into the open sea. The men hastily saddled horses, pulled down the bars, and prepared to do the best they could to hold them when the mavericks should bolt for freedom. The water had risen perceptibly. Not an animal would notice the open gateway. The horsemen rode against the mass. They could not budge it. Again the heavens opened. The flooded creek was rising fast. Jones and his friends now became alarmed for the household. They found Mrs. Jones and her children on the table, water two feet deep on the floor. They were carried to high land. By daylight the water had taken the roof off the house.

[58]

When the San Miguel subsided, a few of the 260 drowned mavericks were about the remains of the pen. Most of them had been washed away. The game of freeze-out poker was never finished.

There were other ways of seeing who should take "the whole caboodle."

When Seco Smith built his cabin on the creek in Medina County that still bears his name — the Seco — he had been a forty-niner. Once, on a scout out from San Antonio, he had lost the tracks of the Indians, though he was a noted trailer, because bears hunting Mexican persimmons were so thick they covered up all sign. Soon after building his cabin he married a young woman whom the Comanches had lanced, scalped and left for dead but who recovered sufficiently to help Seco raise a considerable family of children. At the age of eighty-six he had his third wife and fifteen living children, three or four of them still in the yearling age. When, in his palmy days, he came in occasionally to San Antonio, he'd give a warwhoop on Alamo Plaza that echoed against the cathedral walls on Military Plaza half a mile away. He was strong, wiry and untamed like the country — the country of mavericks.

One time Seco, George Redus, Lon Moore and perhaps another rancher or two went on a maverick hunt in the Frio Canyon country. At the conclusion of the hunt George Redus and Lon Moore, each of whom had thirty animals coming to him, decided to shoot at a mark with six-shooters to see which would take the other's booty. Redus won. Seco Smith then bantered him to shoot for thirty mavericks — and won. Characteristically, he gave the thirty back to his boon *compadre* Moore.[7]

If it had not been for the Indians, the mavericks, which went on breeding more mavericks, would have been more quickly branded up. In the Palo Pinto country Indians kept ranchers afoot most of the time. Five of the Cowden boys and three neighboring Bradford boys began their mavericking operations

[59]

barefooted and afoot. This was in 1867. These eight boys, with a man to bring up the drags, would get around a bunch of cows and manage them into a pen. What they could not pen they would catch with two dogs named Buck and Tige. Jeff Cowden could run the fastest, and he always took the lead. He was the only one of the brothers that did not make a fortune. After the Indians were cleared out and he had all the horses he could ride, he kept on running. He roped the smokestack of the first steam engine run over the railroad built into his country.

A good "catch dog" was prized as highly as a good horse. There were dogs so well trained and so intelligent that upon sighting a bunch of cattle they would single out the only maverick in it and hold it by the nose until a man arrived and roped it. Some maverickers, instead of roping, tailed their quarry down. To run up on a flying cow so that the rider could catch her tail, wrap it around his leg or the horn of his saddle, and then swerve with a jerk in such a way that she would have the "wind busted out of her" required a good horse, well trained.

After cattle became valuable and a pushing population afforded contenders, mavericks in the long run meant more trouble than prosperity.

In the seventies, Jake and Joel English with a hired Mexican vaquero were mavericking in the Carrizo Springs country west of the Nueces River. Population was not pushing very strong in that neck of the brush country at the time.

"One day," Jake English remembered, "we rode down a white-brush draw hoping to scare out something, when all of a sudden my horse, which was in the lead, gave a snort and a lunge to one side. There, swelled up on the ground bigger'n a skinned mule, was a dead sorrel horse.

"He had a bullet hole in his forehead. A few steps off was a two-year-old brown maverick bull with a lobo stripe down his back shot through the head also. On the other side of the horse from the bull was a new saddle hanging from the limb of a mesquite tree. Near it a new saddle blanket, grey with red stripes, was spread over two or three limbs so as to make a shade. Lying on his back under this blanket, was a man. A good hat covered his face. On his feet were a pair of fine shopmade boots, the Petmecky spurs still on the heels. He was dead with a bullet through his heart. He was a white man. We didn't know him. We didn't know who had killed him. The maverick bull explained in a general way. Whoever did the killing had made a neat job of arranging the corpse. Then he had ridden on. It wasn't any of our business. We rode on also, after mavericks."

John Champion, while mavericking on the Arroyo Tortuga in the same region, roped a dun maverick bull, only to discover that the thick brush he had been running through had grabbed his little branding iron. He tied the bull securely. The next day when he came back to brand it, the bull was gone. Near by Champion saw fresh horse tracks. After he had followed them a short distance, he heard brush popping and raking leather. He went to the sound.

A Mexican was leading the dun bull, though he had his own rawhide reata and not Champion's on it. The Mexican said he had found the bull running free on the range. Champion, with six-shooter drawn, called him a liar and several other things, told him he had stolen the bull from the tree, and made a dead shot. Then he put a bullet into the bull at the base of the ear. There was a kind of prejudice against a maverick that had brought on a killing. The most famous example in Texas and the whole West was the maverick branded **M U R D E R.**

In 1890 most of the trans-Pecos country was still unfenced, and in the timbered and brushed roughs plenty of Longhorn blood still ran wild. On January 28 of that year the small cattle owners operating around the Leoncita waterholes in northern Brewster County — which is as large as some states, taking in most of the proposed Big Bend National Park — held a roundup to brand what calves had escaped the fall work. Between two and three thousand cattle were thrown together in the herd.

The chief operators in this part of the country were Dubois and Wentworth. They did not approve of such early work and were taking no part in it, but one of their riders named Fine Gilleland was present to represent their interests.

Among the "little men" was Henry Harrison Powe. He was a Mississippian who had left college to fight in the Confederate Army and was one-armed as a result. He had come to Texas during the hard-handed Reconstruction days. Not many miles from the roundup grounds he had buried the body — eleven bullet holes in it — of a murdered nephew. He was considered an honest man, not at all contentious. His brand was **H H P.**

In the roundup, among other unbranded animals, was a brindle yearling bull. It was not following any cow, but the roundup boss and another range man informed Powe that the bull belonged to a certain **H H P** cow. They had seen him with the cow and knew both animals well by flesh marks. "Are you positive?" Powe asked. They said they would swear to the brindle's identity. Then Powe rode into the herd and cut the brindle out, heading him into a small cut of cows and calves being held by his own son.

Very soon after this, Fine Gilleland galloped up to the cut. "Does that brindle bull have a mother here?" he asked the boy sharply.

"No," the boy replied, "but the boss told Father it belongs to an **H H P** cow."

"He'll play hell taking it unless he produces the cow," Gilleland retorted. Then, without another word, he separated the brindle and ran him back to the main herd.

Powe saw the bull coming, followed by Gilleland. He rode

out and the two men passed some words not heard by others. Then Powe turned back into the roundup and started to cut the brindle out again. Gilleland made straight towards him. Halted in the middle of the herd, the two men had some more words. They were very brief. Powe was unarmed. He rode to the far side of the herd and borrowed a six-shooter out of a friend's saddle pocket.

Back into the herd Powe now rode, found the brindle bull and started him for the **H H P** cut, following him out. Midway between the cut and the big herd, Fine Gilleland met them. He roped at the bull but missed. Powe pulled his six-shooter and shot at the bull but missed. By this time, Gilleland was off his horse shooting at Powe to kill. He killed.

Gilleland now remounted and left the roundup in a run. In all probability he was honest in claiming the brindle maverick for his employers. Perhaps he hoped to make a reputation. There was a strong tendency on the range for little owners to "feed off" any big outfit in their country. The big spreads sometimes hired men to be hard.

The Powe boy rode immediately to Alpine to notify rangers of the killing. Meanwhile men remaining with the roundup branded-out the calves and yearlings, the **H H P** stock included.

When the brindle bull was dragged up to the branding fire, there was a short discussion. He was thrown on his right side. Then a man with a running iron burned deep into the shaggy, winter hair on his left side the letters **M U R D E R**. The letters ran across the ribs from shoulder to flank.

"Turn him over," the man said. The bull was turned over. With a fresh iron the man branded on the right side, **JAN 28 90**. The bull was not castrated or earmarked.

A few days later two rangers killed Gilleland in the mountains. What happened to the brindle maverick, with that brand that no one would claim, is not so definitely settled. R. W. Powe, the son of the man who was killed, whose account [8] of the matter has been followed in this narrative, says that the Murder Bull was eventually driven out of the country with a trail herd bound for Montana.

Whether he was or not, many stories still circulate over the wide spaces of the trans-Pecos country about "the maverick branded **M U R D E R**": How for years he wandered a lone outcast on the range, never seen with other cattle, and, for that matter, seldom seen at all. How he turned prematurely grey, the hair over the scabs of his bizarre brand showing a coarse red. How cowboys in the bunkhouse at the Dubois and Wentworth ranch one night saw the bull's head come through an open window; he was looking, they imagined, for the man responsible for that brand of horror traced on his own side. Some brands grow in size with the growth of animals; generally they do not. According to the stories, the **M U R D E R** brand grew until the elongated letters stood out in enormous dimensions, making one familiar with literature think of the pitiless Scarlet Letter that blazoned on Hester Prynne's breast and in the soul of every being who looked upon it.

The Murder Maverick became a "ghost steer." A cowboy might see him, usually about dusk; and then he "just wasn't there." There were some who did not want to see him. Eugene Cunningham, Barry Scobee and perhaps other writers have woven "the murder steer" into Wild West stories for the pulp magazines. The gray Confederate coat with slit sleeve worn by the murdered Powe of one arm is in the little college museum at Alpine, under the mountains where the roundup was held, **JAN 28 90**. That brindle bull hide with the outlandish brand on it really would be a museum piece.

"Maverick steer," a phrase often come upon in fiction, is a contradiction of terms. A bull calf or yearling is turned into a steer — a bull of some age, into a stag — by the simple process of removing his testicles. When a bull is castrated on the range,

he is invariably earmarked and branded or — in the occasional absence of iron or fire — at least marked. He is then no longer a maverick; he is a steer, though he may be wilder than he was in the maverick stage. Science does not record examples of males being born without testicles. Nevertheless, according to family tradition, John Mercer while killing wild cattle to supply beef for Sam Houston's army, during the Texas Revolution, shot a very large and fat "maverick steer."

It does not take a range man to understand why various Western states passed laws strictly defining a maverick and making mavericks and orphan calves of the open range public property to be disposed of according to law.[9]

A stockman finding an unbranded animal a year old, or older, in his fenced pasture, where only his own cattle range and breed, calls it nowadays a maverick, though there can be little question of ownership.

About the opening of this century, the Leahy family had a ranch, well fenced, of ten or twelve thousand acres along the lower Nueces River in the thickest part of the brush country of Texas. Their cattle were so wild, the brush was so thick and the river water so uncontrollable that, though they had introduced graded bulls, maverick Longhorn bulls kept the old strain going. To clean out all this outlaw stock, the Leahys finally fenced off about three thousand acres against the river, where the outlaws were concentrated. They caught what they could with dogs and ropes. Everything that was roped fought. A two-year-old heifer when she hit the end of a rope would bounce back charging man and horse with the ferocity of a bull. One such heifer — black, mealy-nosed and line-backed — jabbed her dagger-pointed horn through the heavy leather leggins worn by the brush hand who roped her, through the calf of his leg, and into the vitals of his horse, completely disemboweling him.

By 1900 steer horns of the old length and size had become

scarce. In the Leahy thickets were steers with prize horns, old mossy-heads that by day laid up in brush utterly impenetrable to horse and man. At night they would stalk forth on little openings, where they bawled long and mournfully, expressing to the stars their fierce wildness and the utter loneliness of the liberty that their aboriginal strength, their ceaseless wariness, their primitive instincts and keen senses preserved to them. No rider of moonlight or dawn could slip up within a rope's length of them on the circumscribed opening where they pawed the earth like bulls and bellowed their challenges. Age and bullets could alone remove them from the range. The Leahys were determined to clear them out. Hunters with high-powered rifles came from Kansas City and other places, to shoot them for their mighty heads. Thus ended the day of their destiny, though here and there, in the Mexican part of the great *brasada*, or brush country, a sprinkling of Longhorn mavericks and branded outlaws endured some years longer — for a similar fate.

IV · ON THE TRAIL

*To Ab Blocker, credited with more originaι sayings
and with having drunk water out of more cow tracks
than any other trail boss of America.*

ONE TIME up in Oklahoma Joe Brundette, an old trail
man and Texas ranger, told me how, along in the late
seventies, the Wiley Brothers below Red River imported fifty
grade-bulls from the north to turn loose with their native stock.

"And they all died," Joe Brundette concluded.

"Texas fever?"

"No, they were simply walked to death by them Texas
cattle."

Up to the middle of the eighteenth century, large areas of
England — the England that has furnished all the blocky, heavy

beef breeds prized by the world — were roadless, undrained low-lands in wilderness and morass. Conformable to environment, the cattle were tall, rawboned; the sheep, lean and leggy. At agricultural shows prizes were offered for the longest legs; legs were very important where miry lanes had to be traversed and sheep and cattle had to roam for miles in search of food.[1] When, towards the end of the century, Hereford cattle were becoming established as a breed, judges still made note of their "athletic" frames and fitness as "beasts of draught."[2] The object of Robert Bakewell (1726–1795), whose contribution to the advancement of animal husbandry entitles him to an enduring niche in the history of civilization, was to breed cattle that weighed most in the best joints and most quickly repaid the cost of food consumed. How well he succeeded is attested by a single pair of figures. In 1710 beeves sold in Smithfield market weighed on the average 370 pounds; in 1795, 800 pounds; the average weight of calves for the same years and market increased from 50 to 148 pounds.[3]

The men who marketed Texas Longhorns had hardly heard of the objects for which Robert Bakewell worked. They had to trail their cattle hundreds and even thousands of miles. The only cattle they could take to market were cattle with legs. It is said that the Spanish cattle on their peninsula homeland were docile. Their descendants that walked up the Long Trail probably developed leg power and length to an appreciable extent. Bovine generations are short and come fast, and physical changes in the process of adaptation to environment need not require long periods of time.

"During the last days of the buffalo," George Bird Grinnell recorded, "a remarkable change took place in its form, an example of specialization — of development in one particular direction — due to a change in the environment of the species. The buffaloes during the last years of their existence were so constantly pursued and driven from place to place that they never had time to lay on fat as in earlier years. As a consequence of this continual running, the animal's form changed and, instead of a fat, short-backed, short-legged animal, it became a long-legged, light-bodied beast, formed for running." [4]

Environment developed legs and other "athletic" features on the Longhorns. No other cattle have ever shown themselves so well adapted to herd travel. "All kinds of cattle stampede," Charles Goodnight said, "but in a run the Longhorns would hold together better than any other. They would circle and not split up as will Durhams, Herefords, and Polled Anguses. Fine-blooded cattle will run over a man or a bluff that Longhorns would dodge. They would string out and not bunch up and thus become overheated. A herd of two or three thousand head, once on the trail, seemed to space themselves by instinct." They furnished their own transportation, rustled their own forage, and asked no odds. On the way to the Pacific they crossed deserts still feared by automobile drivers. The vanguard of the northward-winding millions got almost within smelling distance of the wood bison along Peace River in Canada.

Handled properly, a trail herd, no matter how wild the individuals making it up might be on their native ranges, generally became, within a short time, a perfect traveling unit. There was always a leader, who assumed his place at the head of the herd and there kept it day after day. Behind him in the color-splotched ribbon that stretched out from a quarter of a mile to two miles or more — the length varying with the size of the herd, the nature of the ground and the boss's attitude towards keeping them "strung out" or "coupled up" — the other cattle found their positions and without much variation maintained them. The stronger, more alert and energetic animals inclined to work towards the lead, the weak and lazy towards the rear. The drags might be sound of feet, limb and wind, and in good flesh, but from the day they started they had to be pushed by the drag men, and they would have to be pushed until the end. If a forward animal became footsore, it would drop back, but after its feet healed it would take its old position.

In a beef herd, most steers had "traveling pardners," and when in any kind of mix-up these pardners became separated, they would go to bawling until they found each other. When one was hunting another, he would raise his head and try to get wind of him. In a mixed herd, nearly every cow had her following. There was generally a sprinkling of muleys in any good-sized herd, and within a week or ten days after it hit the trail these hornless animals would have found each other and would be bedding down together every night a little apart from the horns. Of course there were pariahs, and there were "lone wolves" that wanted to prowl up one side of a herd and down another, but unless they steadied down they would end up with the drags. When cattle were thrown off the trail for grazing, relative positions among them would be changed, but, back in travel formation, they would be resumed. It is said that two-year-old heifers — the capricious age — were the most difficult to get "road broke," that, indeed, a herd of them could not be depended upon to settle down at all.

Shanghai Pierce, as might have been expected, had a story to illustrate the genius of his "sea lions" for a David Crockett kind of go-aheadness.

Soon after the Civil War he drove a thousand big steers from his coast range to New Orleans. "The mud and water of the Louisiana swamps," he used to tell, "compelled us to pick every step. Why, the public roads — where there were any in that country — would have bogged a saddle blanket. My steers were nice, fat, slick critters that knew how to swim but they were used to a carpet of prairie grass. They were mighty choosey as to where they put their feet. They had a bushel of sense, and purty soon over there in Louisiana they got to balancing theirselves on logs and roots in order to keep out of that slimy mud. Yes, they got so expert that one of them would walk a cypress knee up to the stump, jump over it, land on a root and walk it out for another jump. If there was a bad bog hole between cypresses, you'd see a steer hang his horns in a mustang grapevine or maybe a wisteria and swing across like a monkey. The way they balanced and jumped and swung actually made my horse laugh."

"We were trailing up the North Platte in '83," J. L. Hill wrote,[5] "with a herd of 3000 Lytle dogies branded **S L** and bossed by Till Driscoll. Those yearlings had become better trail-broke than any other cattle I ever drove. One day we came to where the trail passed between two big rocks so close together that only one animal could walk through at a time. The cattle had to string out for miles, and a beautiful sight they made winding over that high, fresh country. The bluffs at the narrow pass stood sixty or seventy feet over the swift water below. About a third of the distance down was a steep, rocky slope; the rest of the way was straight up and down. The river bed for some distance was nothing but a canyon gorge. It took a good hour for all the cattle to walk through the pass, but finally the last drag went by.

"Now this animal was a little pot-bellied dogie that had been at the tail end of the herd all the fifteen hundred miles we had walked. The boys called him Baby Mine. Just as he got through the pass, a big yearling that had stopped on the yon side hooked him off the trail. As the drag driver saw him whirl over the bluff, he yelled out, '*Adiós*, Baby Mine!' He never expected to see him again.

"A few miles on up, the ground became smooth and open with fine grass and an easy approach to the water. We camped there for the night. The next morning Baby Mine was at his place in the drag. Nobody had seen him come in, but somehow he had escaped rocks and rapids, crawled out of the river, and followed on to the bed grounds."

If a yearling played out on the trail, Sam Glenn — who made

his reputation as a drag hand, always walking, leading his horse or letting him loose to follow the cattle — would let it drop behind without fear of losing it. After it rested a while, he knew that it would catch up that night. Yearlings "boging in" at late hours sometimes stampeded a herd.

To resume J. L. Hill's account of the trail-broke yearlings: "Till Driscoll, our boss, knew the nature of cattle down to their hoofs. He would never force a herd off the bed grounds. He let them get up in the morning just as they pleased, stretch, and then graze out in the direction we were headed. By the time the cook had got his breakfast dishes washed, his wagon loaded, and had driven around the cattle to go on ahead and camp for the next meal, the dogies were ready to trail also. They got into the habit of falling right in behind the chuck wagon, and that habit gave us a lot of trouble later on, as you will see.

"Finally we reached our destined range on the edge of the Bad Lands near the mouth of the Little Missouri River. Before we turned the dogies loose, we branded them **7 7 7**. Then most of the boys went back to Texas, but three or four of us hired ourselves to stay up in that cold country and help locate and winter our pets.

"Well, one day out between Big Beaver and the Little Missouri I rode up on a butte to take a view of the country. I saw two emigrant trains going west on the Keogh Trail and about a hundred cattle following the last wagon. I was sure the cattle were ours, and rode to overtake them. A little nearer, and sure enough I made out the **S L** yearlings, their tails rolled over their backs and their heads bobbing, seemingly mighty happy to be hitting the trail once more behind a wagon. We had to ride that emigrant route all fall to keep the cattle from following wagons out of the country. Those yearlings would graze awhile every morning and then string out over the first trail they struck."

"Cattle, like human beings, are creatures of habit," another trail driver commented, citing a herd he helped move from Oregon to Wyoming, where they were shut up for a while in a small enclosure. "Every morning at the usual time for hitting the trail, the leaders, followed by most of the bunch, would march solemnly around the fence. The same thing would happen along towards evening, only to a less extent. It took the leaders at least a week to realize that they had reached the end of their journey." [6]

Indians and blizzards occasionally left a trail outfit afoot some place far remote from aid; yet in every instance that the records tell of, the footmen managed somehow to keep their Longhorns together and to keep them moving towards their destination. One night on the Pecos, in 1872, Apaches raided down on a Chisum outfit and left only four horses — ridden by men on guard at the time — for driving four thousand steers. There was no thought of letting them go. Cowboys afoot would get away out from the cattle and scare back any animals that inclined to wander from the herd. The horses were ridden by the pointers; it wasn't difficult for men on foot to keep the drags moving. Some days the herd moved only three or four miles, up the river. Often a man would have to lie down in the grass or take refuge in rocks in order to allay the curiosity of big old steers heading out to examine that strange object — a man on foot. Gradually, however, they became more or less accustomed to the sight. One of the men wrote:

"Had it not been for the fact that the herd was used to handling by this time and was trail-weary from the many miles they had come, we would have lost them all. We made it to the Bosque Grande Ranch in New Mexico in fifteen days with the entire herd, except possibly a few that the boys afoot had to use their Colts on to keep from being run down and gored by the long, keen horns." [7]

Not just anybody could get cattle to go. Charlie Siringo [8] tells how in 1871 a Kansas "shorthorn" by the name of Black came down with an outfit of shorthorn men and horses and received eleven hundred steers "from seven to twenty-seven years old" on the Navidad River in Texas. He started north, but before he reached Red River all he had left was his chuck wagon. His men lost every single steer. Many of them came back to their old ranges, and Shanghai Pierce had the pleasure of selling them to somebody else. "Old Shang" later met Black in Kansas — sticking to his proper trade of blacksmithing. "He said Mr. Black cursed Texas shamefully and swore that he never would, even if he should live to be as old as Isaac, son of Jacob, dabble in Longhorns again."

Longhorn men themselves sometimes got hold of a herd that distinguished itself for anything but orderly trailing. In the spring of 1873 Dunn Houston and Major George W. Littlefield sent Jim Towns to Columbus on the lower Colorado River to receive 3150 steers they had bought from Shanghai Pierce and Stafford Brothers.[9] Some of the steers were old enough to vote, among them probably certain individuals that had refused to go with Mr. Black of Kansas. Towns had ten men, besides the cook and horse wrangler.

After he had received the herd, Bob Stafford said to him, "Young man, you'll never on earth get 'em out of the country. Why, by gracious, we've sold and delivered these old scalawags so many times that we are actually ashamed to look at them. They get away from everybody who tries to drive them off. You never saw such critters for running, and when they hit a thicket they are gone."

"Well," Towns answered, "I've got some mighty good men to handle them. They are contracted to the Indian Agency at Fort Sill, and I don't see anything else to do but deliver them."

"All right, young man," Stafford said, "go ahead. But you'd better have your life insured and get all you can on your men. These cattle will run over you before you have gone a hundred miles."

"As insurance companies would not risk the lives of cowboys in those days and as no cowboy wanted insurance anyhow," Towns told the story, "I did not follow Stafford's advice. We drove the cattle as hard as we could the first day, and that night we milled 'em around and around so as to tire 'em out.

"It was on a Sunday morning when we neared the Webberville crossing on the Colorado River. Webberville was just a wide place in the road. A seedy farmer riding an old plow mare wearing a blind bridle offered to pilot us through the bottom. We had to go down a lane made by picket fences that enclosed some fields, and as we got opposite one of the houses a dog rushed out barking. Hell broke loose in Georgia right there. Those steers all jumped at once, and as the lane was too narrow for the whole herd to run forward in, a lot of them broke through the fences into the fields. The old farmer was in front. He had a pair of rawhide hobbles that he was using for a quirt, and the way he quirted was a caution. He finally managed to cut off and get out of the way. When the run was over, I offered to pay him for his piloting if he would go on across the river. He said no, he ought to have been at church instead of trying to make a dollar on Sunday. He was convinced that our trouble was a kind of judgment on him and us too for breaking the Sabbath, and he sure wasn't going to invite further 'visitation.'

"About the time we got the herd milling, here came a posse of citizens with a deputy. The deputy said I had simply ruined the fields and that he was going to put me in jail and take charge of the herd. I told him that maybe he could jail me but that before he took charge of the herd he'd have to put up a big bond. He had not thought about that. I finally paid a twenty-dollar gold piece for damages.

"But I was not through with that Webberville bunch. When we counted the cattle, we were sixty or seventy short. I felt confident that some of the citizens had cut them off in the brush. With two hands I went back and struck the trail. We found our steers in a pen. Maybe it was a good thing we saw nobody around. We took the steers.

"The herd got the habit of running every night about eleven o'clock. A herd will acquire a habit that way, just like a person waking up at a certain hour. As it was a dry year and waterings were scarce, the cattle were often feverish. We could find water for the horses where there wasn't enough for the herd, but our horses suffered just the same.

"As we were approaching Red River, Dunn Houston caught up with us. He had heard about the stampede at Webberville and was mighty uneasy. I had no more than quieted his fears when the thirsty steers sniffed water. They stampeded and scattered for miles up and down the river. Finally we got them together and across into the Indian Nation. Here we struck another dry stretch. The wind was from the south, and after we had gone about twenty miles the cattle either scented the water behind or else remembered it. Anyway they turned back. We simply could not hold them.

"Some of them ran that whole twenty miles. They jumped over a bluff that the horses couldn't go down, recrossed Red River, and banked up under the opposite bluff. The men had to pull off their clothes, swim over, and scare the crazy animals back to the north side. The water was strongly impregnated with gyp, or alkali. Dunn Houston swallowed so much of it that by dark he was in agony with cramps. I thought he would die. I made a poultice out of the ashes of buffalo chips and applied it to his abdomen, but it seemed to do no good. Then I remembered a dugout several miles off that I had ridden past during the day. A squaw man lived there. I rode to this place and asked for medicine. The man said he had some paregoric and brought out a bottle about half full. I ran my horse all the way back to camp. I thought that if the directions were right about a little of the stuff doing good, all of it would do better, and Dunn was mighty bad off; so I poured the whole bottle

down his throat. Very soon he was asleep, and the next day he sent a rider to Fort Sill with word that we would deliver the cattle on time.

"Colonel Hunter of the Indian Agency was on hand to receive them. There were a number of three-year-old steers in the herd, and as these brought four dollars a head less than the aged steers, the stuff had to be classified. Colonel Hunter savied cows pretty well, and he had a pocket full of cigars that he was liberal with, but he wore a linen duster and did not look like a cowman. Also he was a Northerner.

"After we had been cutting and classifying steers nearly all day, we still had forty or fifty head to trim. It was getting close to sundown and the little bunch was hard to hold. Everybody and everybody's horse was petered out. I was trying to cut a three-year-old steer into the bunch of aged steers and get him by Colonel Hunter. I scared the whole bunch over against a feller named Wekker. His horse was absolutely played out, and when Wekker spurred him, he kicked up and two or three animals got by.

"At this, Hunter yelled out, 'There now! I've been expecting you to play hell all evening.'

"Wekker was ringy anyhow. 'God-damn you Yankee son-of-a-bitch,' he said, 'give me any more of your talk, and I'll make a sieve out of your blue belly.'

"Colonel Hunter quieted down then. He wasn't mad. He knew well enough he couldn't talk to a Texas cowboy like a nigger, and he was a good sport. After the last steer was counted, I rode up to him and said: 'Colonel, I want to tell you something about this herd. They are a bad lot. We received 'em a-running, we have driven 'em clear across Texas a-running, and you can see for yourself that we delivered 'em a-running. Unless you post your men and ring-herd them [keep them going in a circle] tonight, they will be a-running at eleven o'clock.'

" 'Young man,' Colonel Hunter replied, 'I have bought and

handled more Texas cattle than you ever saw. My men will take care of them all right. Here are a few more cigars for your good intentions.'

"That night when Dunn Houston went to bed, he said to me: 'Jim, wake me up at eleven o'clock. I want to hear those steers run at some other fellow's expense.'

"Sure enough, exactly at eleven P.M., I shook Dunn and told him that hell was popping. The last we heard of those old mossy-horns, they were still a-running."

There were times when the same mob fear that made a herd run without reason or letup would make them balk, refuse to pass. On the plains a black furrow plowed through the sea of grass has been known to turn a herd of lumbering buffaloes and to act as a wing-fence for veering mustangs towards a corral. One trail outfit spent two days trying to get their cattle across a silent railroad track. The worst obstacles were water and the lack of it.

The sunlight on a river often had to be just so, before cattle would take it. They were averse to entering water with the sun in their eyes. If it was so wide that they could not plainly see the opposite shore, they might refuse to cross under all conditions.

A good boss had his herd strung out and the lead cattle walking freely upon approaching a stream. If they were thirsty, they would wade right in to drink. The shoving in of cattle from behind forced the leaders on out deeper and across, the men working not to let the line bend too far down the river. One or two reliable lead steers could be of more help in crossing than could a hundred hands. During the Civil War, D. H. Snyder delivered thousands of Texas steers to the Confederacy for soldiers' beef. He had to swim some of the largest rivers of the South, in addition to the Mississippi; but he had two work oxen, trained swimmers, which he would unyoke at a stream and put in the lead. They never faltered, even at the Mississippi's expanse, and the herd always followed them. Too valuable to sell as beef, they pulled the Texan's wagon home after each delivery. On the other hand, Borroum and Choate, without such trained leaders, upon reaching the Mississippi with eleven hundred big Confederate beeves had to leave a hundred head on the west bank.[10]

"Deacon" Cox of the Dodge House at Dodge City had an old Jersey cow that was often borrowed by trail men, taken to the south side of the Arkansas River and used to pilot a herd across.

In 1879 Joseph P. Morris,[11] after having crossed many rivers with his herd of 3014 big steers, arrived at the wide, wide Platte to find it bank-full. The date on which he was to deliver the cattle was drawing too near to permit waiting for the river to run down. The herd was pointed in, and safely reached a sand bar about the middle of the channel. Here they stopped. They did not like the feel of the water coming down from the icy mountains. For eleven hours they refused to go on. Many of them were standing in shallow water, and it became a question of time before they would succumb to the numbing cold. Men and horses in their desperate efforts to budge the herd were about exhausted. Finally, Morris succeeded in cutting off nine big steers that had been in the lead ever since leaving the far-away flowings of the Guadalupe River in Texas. The nine steers swam to a little island towards the north bank. The other cattle saw them and were persuaded to follow. Then the leaders, trailed by the whole herd, pulled straight for shore.

A herd that attempted the same crossing the next day lost eight hundred head in a mill that could not be broken. While a mill was what wound up a stampede so tight that it could no longer move, in swimming water it resulted in pushing the inside, or center, cattle under. Against it daring cowboys might drive in vain. Pushing from the outside often tended to make the coil tighter.

It might be broken by a movement from the center. To ride into the center was impossible. Yet there was a way to get there. At Red River Station, where the old trail crossed, the water one June day in 1871 looked like the Mississippi's. Herds were banking up on the south side waiting for the flood to go down. Yet holding over in a crowded area was always risky. Despite all remonstrances, Old Man Todd decided to cross. Without any man ahead to entice the leaders to keep moving, he shoved his herd in. Midway of the stream they began swimming in the fatal circle.

"Oh, where is my boy Foster?" white-bearded Todd cried. Foster came — like most of the cowboys whom we think of as veterans now, very, very young — so young that he was ready to be generous with his life as well as with everything else. The narrative is his. "I stripped to my underclothes, mounted a big horse called Jack Moore, and went to them. I got off the horse and right on to the cattle. They were so jammed together that it was like walking on a raft of logs. When I got to the only real big steer in the bunch on the yon side, I mounted him and he pulled for the shore. When I got near the bank, I fell off and drifted down stream to the horse, who had come on across. It must have been about nine o'clock in the morning when I climbed out on land. I kept the herd together until nearly sundown — no hat, no saddle, just my underclothes — before the outfit got across to help me."

The river did not always have to be wide. J. Evetts Haley quotes Goodnight on a singular experience: "We came to the Charco, a creek probably twenty feet wide, with banks six to eight feet high, and level with flood water. We put our leaders against the creek, head on. After about three hundred had passed over, something caused the leaders to stampede, and they whirled in their tracks, right back the trail. The distance was short, and we failed to control or stop them. They simply took the water, met those in the stream behind them, actually filled the creek with cattle, and crossed the water on their own bodies.

"I put my horse in upstream, just above the mass of cattle, and crossed in dead water. I expected a heavy loss from drowning, but it happened so quickly that all came out alive, and in less than ten minutes we had them moving across the creek again in the right direction. It sounds unreasonable, but it is true just the same."

The chickens had to be not only hatched, but out of the shell, out of the nest, and in hand before you could count them at a river. Dick Withers pointed his 3500 long-legged steers into the surging North Canadian. They took the water without a bobble and were climbing out on the opposite side when the embankment, which was quite steep, gave way. The cave-in threw the leaders back, and there in deep water, jammed against a bank they could not climb and would not now willingly touch, the herd was. Before the men could get them strung back towards the south bank, 116 were drowned.

One of many easy ways to detect imposture in some man setting himself up as an experienced authority on range life is to let him string along until he mentions a herd of ten or fifteen thousand cattle. I have met many such herds in print — created by feeble and brazen pretenders. Occasionally there was a roundup of such numbers, but it was too large to be worked advantageously, much less driven. An old cowman once listened to a tenderfoot spouting about what a monstrous herd he had helped drive. The listener said nothing until asked what was the biggest herd he was ever with. "I don't remember the number exactly," he replied, "but it was so big it took us three days and nights every morning to get it off the bed grounds." It would have been impossible to water one of these fictitious herds, to say nothing of stringing it out. However, there is evidence that in 1866 over a hundred Apaches or Comanches, both of which tribes were at the time stealing in Texas for the New

Mexicans, started west from the San Saba River with ten thousand stolen cattle in one body.[12] How those Indians got across the dry divide to the Pecos — if they ever did get across — with such an enormous mixed herd of cattle unbroken to the trail has never been explained.

The largest trail herds were those massed for defense against Indians. The record — in so far as I have learned — was topped by 15,000 cattle started from the Brazos River, in lower Texas, for California, in 1869. They were owned by a number of ex-Confederate men dissatisfied with having to live under carpetbaggers who insisted on the equality of Negroes with white men. There were two hundred people with this outfit, many wagons, and 1200 horses. The cattle were driven in four divisions, but whenever there was danger of a night attack by Indians, they were bedded together in one vast herd.[13]

The trail herds before the Civil War generally contained only a few hundred head each, those made up for California being larger. When the Kansas market opened in the sixties, a thousand head made a good-sized herd. Later, as trail driving became more systematized and standardized, big operators sent their cattle up in herds numbering from 2500 to 3500 head. Occasionally two herds of cattle thoroughly trail-broken were thrown together. After Walter Billingsley, trail boss, reached Dodge City in 1884 with a big string of King Ranch cattle and had another added to it for delivery in Montana, the size of the composite herd, 5600 head, became the talk of the country.

The figures on drives out of Texas before 1866 have never been compiled, but I am convinced that the aggregate was much larger than is generally supposed.[14] Official figures on the cattle in Texas at the close of the Civil War give their number as between three and four million head. Taking many factors into account, I am confident that the number was nearer six million.[15] Considering such a stock and their increase, the estimate of 10,000,000 cattle and 1,000,000 horses for the drives that followed during the next quarter of a century seems conserva-tive,[16] even after taking account of the vast numbers of cattle killed on their own grounds for hides and tallow and other large numbers shipped by boats and cars.[17]

A million on paper has come to mean nothing. Conceived of as units of hoofs and horns, it is something different. The con-ception of ten million such units streaming up the long trails appalls the imagination.

The national convention of cattlemen at Saint Louis, in 1884, still stands out in range history.[18] The cow business was at its zenith, the crash more than a year away. The Texans could ride north on railroads now, and the cattle kings and queens and princes and princesses and heirs both apparent and unapparent were present in full force.

The Texans wanted and pulled for but one thing: a National Cattle Trail, from Red River to the Canadian border. It was to be a fenced lane, six miles wide, Congress to provide money to buy any land necessary, though the route would traverse ter-ritory mostly still in the public domain. A bill providing for this "natural highway," as the convention's memorial to Con-gress called it, was soon introduced at Washington by a Texas congressman. It failed to pass. The Long Trail was obsolete almost before the cattlemen knew it. Even had a National Cattle Trail become a fact, they were progressing towards a breed of cattle powerless to walk in the tracks of the Longhorns.

V · STOMPEDES

*To Jack (N. Howard) Thorp — first to collect and
print those songs of the range sung to quiet the cattle.
His generous heart and delightful talk were richer
than any melody.*

STOMPEDE was the old Texian word, and no other cattle known to history had such a disposition to stampede as the Longhorns. Their extraordinary wildness made them nervous, constantly expectant, habitually alert, and gave them keenness of senses to detect objects that the most nature-sensitive of outdoors men were obtuse to.

Like the cattle and much else pertaining to ranching, the word came from the Spanish, *estampida.* Greek herdsmen called the same thing "panic terror." An old-timer's definition, not in the dictionary, was: "It's one jump to their feet and another jump to hell."

A stampede was the personification of instantaneousness. In arising, the Texas cattle did not, like domestic cattle, pause on their knees to "pray." The jump from bed to feet was quicker than a cat can wink its eye. The impulse to stampede was conveyed and acted upon with the unanimity and suddenness that would be felt if every single animal in a herd of, say, thirty-five hundred head had been connected with an electric wire and a switch clicked on.

About nothing else pertaining to cattle has there been so much of song, story, reminiscent anecdote, and picture. All the Western artists from Russell and Remington to Tom Lea, and on down to the latest decorators of pulp magazine covers have painted the stampede. An anthology of range verse on the subject might be compiled.

> Lightnin' rolls in hoops and circles,
> Rain in sheets is comin' down,
> Thunder rattles through the gulches,
> As the hoof-beats shake the ground.
> Top hands ride like likkered Injuns,
> Beggin' God for the break o' day.
> A stampede beats the best camp meetin'
> When it comes to gettin' men to pray.
>
> — WALT COUSINS: "The Stampede."

> The wind commenced to blow and the rain began to fall;
> Hit looked, by grabs, like we was goin' to lose 'em all.
>
> Popped my foot in the stirrup and gave a little yell,
> The tail cattle broke and the leaders went to hell.
>
> — "The Old Chisholm Trail," *cowboy song.*

> They stampeded every night that came and did it without fail—
> Oh, you know we had a circus as we all went up the trail.
>
> — "John Garner's Trail Herd," *cowboy song.*

Ride around the little dogies, O ride around 'em slow,
For the fieries and the snuffies are a-raring to go.
            — "I'm a-Leading Old Dan," *cowboy song*.

Here was always the possibility of sudden peril and, once in a great while, though not nearly so often as is generally believed, death itself. Here was the climax of action in the drama of a great occupation.

The worst stampedes were in the night, attended by the unknown inherent in destiny-weaving darkness.

Range men dreaded them not so much because of danger as because of the likelihood of losing cattle, the time entailed in getting the stampeders back together, and the injury to the cattle themselves. A trail boss for the Matadors named John Smith, driving a herd from their Texas ranch to Montana in 1891, was required to keep a "way bill," or journal. He made entries regularly — with characteristic brevity — until July 7. Then, across the lines devoted to that and the two following days, he scrawled the one word "StomPead." To the manager for whom the diary was designed no details were needed. Though circumstances might vary, the word, no matter how lettered, spelled "unadulterated hell."

The most terrifying and the most common cause of stampedes was thunder and lightning. "It don't storm now like it used to," you'll hear old-timers say. People — ranch men included — don't live out in the weather as they used to. "I was gone nine months and seventeen days and had slept under shelter only once in the whole time," an old trail man concluded his narrative. Maybe you, in your steam-heated apartment or your snug cottage, sometimes wonder what the wild-crying geese flying through the night might tell, if they could speak, of the elements. Ask the men who went up the trail in '67 — if you can find one — and who, in the seventies and eighties, without tents, often without slickers, "circle-herded, trail-herded, night-herded and cross-herded too," following the Longhorns from where the Gulf breeze blows with salty freshness on and on up a slow trail that endlessly pointed to the North Star, and then who, when they got back home from the long drive, read sign and guarded a range stretching houseless and fenceless from moonrise beyond all sunsets. Ask them. They know as much of the elements as the honking geese or the wolf hounded out of his den.

Some of them can tell things of stampedes in electric storms that seem as foreign to this world of lights, warmth and comfortable shelters as the craters in the moon.

It was a June night of the year 1884, on the Cimarron. The air was hot, stifling, absolutely still. It had been thus all day. Now the sky became overcast, and dull sheet-lightning began to blink along the horizon to the west. Two men rode around twenty-five hundred big steers, as wild and sinewy as ever came out of the chaparral down by the Rio Grande. About two hundred yards away was camp, though the fire of cow chips had died and not a spark revealed the nine sleeping forms out from the chuck wagon, their pallets spread in patternless formation. Near each sleeping man stood a horse — his night horse, the clearest-footed and surest-sighted of his mount — saddled and tied. Somewhere out in the darkness the horse-wrangler kept drowsy guard over the remuda.

The cattle and the night were so quiet that the two herders stopped now and then on their rounds to listen. They could not help expecting something. The air grew warmer and more stifling, as the lightning flashes approached and dim thunder began to rumble up. The men could still skylight the cattle.

Presently a dun steer that had been in the lead of the herd from the beginning and had been named "Old Buck" awoke, lifted his head slowly, rose to his knees, and looked around. Evidently he did not trust the looks of things, but, being long experienced in life, he wasn't startled, and he said nothing. He got on his feet, raising his nose to smell, and gazed towards the approaching storm. The two men on guard sang as gently as they could the songs they had sung over and over to soothe the cattle down and prevent any sudden sound from breaking in and frightening them.

But Old Buck had no idea of going back to bed. He seemed to be expecting something — something as sudden as a telegram can be. Another steer got up, stood still, expectant; then others and others arose until the whole herd was on its feet, motionless. The songs were louder now, unrelenting, pleading.

The night grew blacker, the lightning brighter, the humidity of the air more intense. And then, almost at once, on every tip of the five thousand horns of the waiting steers, appeared a ball of dull phosphorescent light — the fox fire, St. Elmo's fire, will-o'-the-wisp of the folklore of the world. In the intervals of utter blackness the two guards on the lone prairie could see nothing but those eerie balls illuminating the tips of mighty antlers. But they were not thinking of ghosts or remembering ghost stories. Their voices rose high in the wild but cow-quieting notes of "The Texas Lullaby," which is not made of words and can't be conveyed by musical notation. It is made of syllables and tones conveyable only by voices trained in darkness and deep thickets. The notes come long, low and trembly. The wailers of "The Texas Lullaby" did not yell or shoot, for that would have been to scare the as yet still cattle.

The ghostly balls of fire on horns must have looked as strange to the steers as to the men. The steers began to move at a walk, their motion becoming circular, the riders around them preventing any decided movement away from the bed ground. At first the walk was slow; soon it became faster. And then out of blackness came a great flash of zigzag lightning forking down over the seething mass of animals, so close that darting tongues of flame seemed almost to lick their backs. At the same time a mighty clap, a roar, a crash of thunder shook heaven and earth, reverberating and doubling.

Its answer was the thunder of ten thousand pounding hoofs that popped and clicked, while horn clacked against horn. The stampede started with the swiftness of the lightning's leap.

The cowboys arrived from camp just in time to join the pursuit. The gigantic thunderbolt had knocked out the sluice gates of the sky. The water poured down in sheets and barrels. It rained blue snakes, pitchforks and bob-tailed heifer yearlings all at once. One minute it was darker than the dead end of a crooked tunnel a mile deep under a mountain. Then the prairie was a sea of blue and yellow light dazzling to all eyes.

No matter. Hang with the cattle. Trust your horse. Follow those balls of fire tossing in the void of blackness, too dim to illumine even the horn tips they play upon, sometimes darting across to dance with each other, again fading out altogether. Now, truly, they may be the will-o'-the-wisp that lures followers to the Black Death. When the lightning won't light, run by ear. When the lightning blinds and the thunder drowns all other sound, keep on riding hell for leather. To get around them and circle the leaders, you must run wilder and madder than the horror-lashed cattle themselves.

It would probably have been better had the two night-herders not been recruited. The object was to swing the leaders around into the tail end of the herd, thus turning it into a mill. A single man *who knew how* could do this better than a bedlam of riders. Then gradually the whole mass would be wound into a self-stopping ball, the momentum dying down like that of a spent top.

One of the two night-herders with this stampede on the Cimarron was Robert T. Hill, who in later years became a mining and oil geologist renowned over the United States and Mexico.

"Before long," he says, "I found myself and another rider

chasing a small bunch of cattle, close upon their heels. Never before nor since has thunder sounded to me so loud as on that run or have lightning crashes come so rapidly and so near.

"At a crash that was the climax my horse stopped dead in his tracks, almost throwing me over the saddle horn. The lightning showed that he was planted hardly a foot from the edge of a steep-cliffed chasm. A little off to one side, the horse of John Gifford, the other rider, was sinking on his knees, John himself slumping limp in his saddle. Just beyond him lay Old Buck, the mighty lead steer, killed by the bolt of lightning that had knocked John Gifford unconscious. The rest of our bunch of cattle were down under the cliff, some of them dead, some squirming."

When morning came, clear and calm, not a man was in sight of the cook, all of whose provisions had been drenched and who could not begin to start a fire with the soaking-wet cow chips. The twenty-five hundred steers that had been trailed and guarded a thousand miles from southern Texas towards the market at Dodge City were scattered to the four winds. Before noon, though, men by ones and twos began driving in bunches from different directions. Hours later the last man was in. Meantime the wrangler was supplying fresh mounts and the boss, going at a long lope, was leading all hands, except two or three on herd, to comb the country. The men could eat later on, and a trail hand was supposed to get his sleep in the winter.

The lightning could make its own chasm. One night while J. W. Carpenter was helping hold a great roundup herd of Long S cattle on the Staked Plains, the bombardment of eternity suddenly opened up overhead. The speed of the cattle across the open prairies was terrific. "They stretched out so that their bellies seemed to scrape the grass roots." Then a bolt of lightning hit the ground in front of the avalanche, and at the same time a crash of thunder jarred the earth. The lead cattle tried to halt or turn. There was no time. The headlong-tearing mob at their heels, propelled by their own mass-velocity, plunged over the hesitating leaders. Some fell. The herd piled up, animals on the bottom being trampled to death. Now the stampede was without direction, some cattle trying to run in a circle, bunches cutting off this way and that, out of the melee coming a bawling and moaning that added terror to the thunderclaps.

A herd milling about in a storm might seem to be trying to outdo the thunder with the noise of their bawling. W. J. Elliot of the Spur Ranch once heard "a kind of sigh" come from the expectant herd — and the next instant the thunder of hoofs. In running, cattle do not voice sounds any more than race horses do. After a stampede was checked, however, the bawling and lowing were frequently tremendous. Hal Mangum told me that one night while he was racing alongside the leaders of a stampede, the cattle running too fast to be circled, an old cow suddenly let out a bawl — probably for her calf. "It acted like an air brake, and in a minute the whole herd was stopped and every animal in it bawling."

Some trail men wanted a few cows with calves mixed in with any herd of steers. In any run a calf would become separated from its mother, she would soon stop to bawl for it, and the bawl would tend to bring the steers to their senses and a halt. On the other hand, mixed cattle would not travel uniformly and in a bad run the young and weak were liable to be mutilated.

The much-talked-about popping of horn against horn was not a regular concomitant of stampedes. More often than not, the runners were so far apart that their horns did not interfere.

Now and then, the elements seemed to paralyze a herd beyond the power of running. It was out from Ogallala, Nebraska, that one appalling storm hit about midnight, in July, 1878. One trail driver who experienced it could describe:

"First there was flash lightning, then forked lightning, then chain lightning, followed by the most peculiar blue lightning

I ever see, all playing close at hand. After this show, it developed into ball lightning rolling along the ground and all about us. Then there was spark lightning. . . . Finally the lightning settled down on us like a fog. The air smelled of burning sulphur. It turned so hot we thought we would be burned up. We had thirty-five hundred head of cattle. They kept milling all the time, bawling and moaning like they were in distress, but never made a move to stampede."

On another night when "one of those Kansas zephyrs calculated to blow hell off the range" breezed up with thunder and lightning to match, John Connor, only nineteen years old, was guarding the remuda. "The horses bunched together around me," he said, "stuck their heads between their knees and moaned and groaned till I decided the end of time had come. So I got down off my horse and lay flat on the ground and tried to die, but could not."

Occasionally lightning would strike the ground and set the grass on fire, then perhaps the rain would put it out. If no rain fell, the Indians received credit for the fire. They were less dreaded than pounding hailstones as big as hen eggs.

After the cattle got wet, their long, polished horns glistened in the flashes out of the blackness, reflecting the light like moistened mirrors. The electricity played along the horn curves "as if they were lightning rods," at the same time darting around and illuminating spurs and bridle bits. Balls of fox fire ran around the wet brim of a cowboy's hat. Then the balls danced like pairs of spook-eyes not only on each head of horns out in the distance but on the ears, always working now, of the cowboy's horse. If he popped his quirt, sparks would fly out of the cracker, and the switching of a cow's tail emitted the same sparkling. "Snakes of fire" sometimes ran over the backs of the cattle and along the manes of the horses.

In the blinding blue-white, some men cast away six-shooters, spurs, knives, thinking that steel would attract the lightning.

The sight of lightning racing around the tires of chuck-wagon wheels strengthened this idea. Heat was supposed to attract lightning also, and there were men who preferred being wet and cold to risking the effect of the dry warmth a good slicker might afford. Mexican vaqueros often wore a ball of beeswax — a nonconductor of electricity — fastened inside the high crown of their sombreros. In the great storms all profanity ceased. For a cowboy to use the name of God in vain at such a time would have been inviting the destruction threatened by the elements, would have been mocking the Almighty.

"A herd of cows has lots of heat, and that draws litenin'," "Cyclone" Denton expressed a common belief in saying. Sometimes, the faces of men riding on the leeward side of the herd would be almost blistered from the heat, as if they had been struck by a blast from a furnace. At the same time, the odor given off by the hoofs and horns was nearly overpowering. The faces of men who stayed with a stampede during an electrical storm might be burned "a brimstone blue."

Many more deaths undoubtedly came to cowboys from lightning than from stampedes themselves. In fact, the memories of living men and authentic records alike are notably deficient in instances of cowboys' being trampled to death under stampedes. Dick Withers disposed of the matter thus:

"We had a stampede in the Territory. My horse fell, and I thought the steers would run over me. But I soon learned that stampeding cattle will not run over a man when he is down underfoot. They will run all around a fellow, but I have yet to hear of a man being run over by them."

Ab Blocker says the night can't get too black for cattle to split and go around a man in front of them. He "never heard of a cowboy's being run over in a stompede." On the other hand, not many men who knew cattle would have willingly got down in front of a stampede on a dark night to test out the splitting.

A stampede might start from anything – but not, as has often been said, "from nothing." Most of the unknown causes probably lay within the realm of smell, from which civilized man, generation by generation, becomes increasingly estranged. A breeze suddenly springing up after dark carried the odor of a Negro cooking for another outfit to a herd of steers that had been driven for three months by a Mexican crew without a bobble. They ran as if to make up for lost opportunities. The whiff of an Indian started many a run. Beef-hungry Indians not infrequently tried to stampede herds, so as to get a chance at scattered animals. One of their favorite ruses was to burn a sack of buffalo hair on the windward side of a herd. A stampede that lasted all night was started by the "war whoop" of a bull that smelled the blood of a yearling just butchered for camp. A panther smelled some fresh beef hanging close to a chuck wagon. Trying to get to it, he was sensed by the cattle – and the powderhouse blew up. Here was a great herd, any antlered creature of which would have chased the biggest lobo of North America and, if able to catch him, would have gored him to death; yet the sharp smell of a coyote cub coming unexpectedly to a certain steer might startle him and the startlement be instantly translated into mob panic.

The fact that oftentimes the cause could not be sensed by men, could in no way be accounted for, and that the run seemed to be contrary to all known principles of cow psychology, gave to it something of dark mystery. It would be bright moonlight. A cowboy, halted in his rounds, perhaps smoking a pipe or cigarette, would be looking at a great herd of steers bedded down comfortably and spaciously on the rich grass of a bald open prairie, every animal absolutely quiet, some with heads north, some south, some east, some west. They had been eased to the bed grounds, after a light day's travel, full of grass and water, contented. Then, in one instant, every animal would be plunging in mad flight, all in one direction.

Such a stampede was unusual; it was the exception. It was one of the profound mysteries of nature that the Children of the Sea of Grass saw manifested, and that operated to make them, under a rough-and-ready exterior, mystics and fatalists. Many of them held that cattle dreamed and saw ghosts. Certainly they were sometimes nervous in their sleep.

Ab Blocker claims that if upon bedding down at night a majority of the cattle stretched their heads out in the same direction — then was the time to look for a run before morning. This was his "sign." Another sign was "a peculiar snort" made by some of the cattle before they ran. Yet no panic flight can ever be premeditated by the mass of participants. It became a belief with various trail men — despite the contrary experiences of others — that after a herd crossed the Arkansas River it would not stampede again.

It was a saying that if you could drive a herd for two weeks without a stampede, the danger was over. It certainly was diminished. The change from familiar to strange surroundings and from sleeping in free isolation to being bedded down with a horde of other animals guarded by the most fearsome enemy of cow liberty that the primitive cattle knew — man — was naturally conducive to nervousness and panic. On their home range, cattle are familiar with every bush, gully, and stone. Driven into a territory where nothing is familiar, they are apprehensive. After some days of trailing, however, change becomes routine.

Some cowboys went strong on premonitions. This one "felt a quiver in his spine" when he went on guard and "just knew" the stampede was coming. That one "felt the air charged with tenseness." Another "grew cold with a chill" not out of the night air. An Arizona waddie, who had learned about spirits from an Apache medicine man, said: "When cattle has got these stampede devils in 'em, anybody can tell it. As soon as the sun goes down, their eyes begin to burn like bull's-eye lanterns. And when you ride in among 'em you can just feel that crazy, locoed spirit." Cowboys not superstitious about anything else were often superstitious about stampedes.

On occasions a stampede that seemed inevitable might not eventuate at all. One stormy night in Kansas a trail boss named Lankford became strangely apprehensive. "I had been working for him for ten years," Ben Thorne told me, "and this was the first time I ever saw him disturbed.

" 'I just know something's going to happen,' Lankford kept saying. 'I just feel I'll never get out of this. I don't know what it is, but something inside me says this is my night to die in a stompede.'

"I tried to persuade him nothing unusual was up, but he wouldn't be persuaded. Meantime the lightning was coming thicker and faster, and the thunder was rolling up. Lankford had ordered all hands to the herd. I was riding beside him when we saw a ball of lightning shoot down right over where the herd was and split into a million sparks and splinters. We halted a minute to listen for the rumble of the running and to locate its direction. There was not a sound. We rode on. Still there was not a sound. The thunder had passed on. When we got a little nearer, the voice of a cowboy on guard came steady and quiet over the night air. He was singing, 'Oh, listen to the crickets.' I thought it mighty purty, and I guess those Longhorns thought the same way. They were all laying down as still as mice. I never was more surprised in my life. Lankford seemed to feel right sheepish."

Obvious trivialities started more stampedes than anything else except storms: A stray dog sneaking up and smelling around a sleeping animal on the edge of the herd; a bunch of wild hogs rooting into the bed grounds; the sight of a haystack after dark in a field into which a herd of old and leery beeves had been turned for the night — "so that the boys could get some rest"; the cough of a cow; a human sneeze; the snapping of a twig; the sinking of a circling horse's foot in a prairie dog hole. It was suddenness of a sound or movement rather than its unfamiliarity that made the drags wake up and forget all about sore feet. A polecat would come sashaying along in its nonchalant way into the edge of a herd; some steer, awake and investigative, would begin following the hopping creature. Then, noticing the approaching monster, the little hair-ball would stop, pat its forefeet against the ground and go to jerking its tail with comical swiftness. Mr. Steer had never seen this performance before — and it was "so sudden." He would wheel and snort, having no intention of starting a stampede, but a moment later he was part of the panic terror he had caused. Like people, cattle are at their best when separated from the mob.

The worst stampede I was ever in, in my limited experience, was with about a thousand head of steer yearlings on the Nueces River. We had spent the hours from before daylight until slap dark on a July day — fifteen hours at least — making fifteen miles through a country of lanes and thickets. We put the dogies to bed that night in the only place we could put them, though it was not at all to be chosen — a patch of open space with a fence on one side, the bluffs of the river on the other, and a ranch house not two hundred yards away on a third side. The country out and around was a thicket of thorns cut up with barbed wire and gullies. Camp was made close to the house. The night was dark and sultry.

About nine o'clock one of the ranch boys clicked an iron latch on the yard gate. I heard it — as plain as if a six-shooter had been clicked in my ear. The yearlings heard too. They ran into gullies; some of them piled over the bluff; they kept running intermittently all night long. After we got them home and spread them out in the pastures, a hundred or two of them would for weeks get together every few nights and run to Jericho, tearing down fences and cutting themselves up. Just the click of a gate latch.

In nearly any herd of grown cattle a professional agitator was likely to show up. He was likely to find one or more *compañeros*. They spent most of their time looking for boogers and hunting some pretext to run. They were usually slab-sided and brainless. They would prowl at night when all decent animals were in bed, sometimes hooking sleeping cattle up either to get them agitated or to take their warm places on the ground. A real cowman would after a few runs spot these troublemakers and get rid of them. Again, the stampeder might not be evil-intentioned; he might be blind in one eye or unable to see distinctly at all and would thus be stumbling and scaring at nothing, setting the other cattle off. Many a herd boss went on having stampedes without discovering the cause, baffled by the "mystery."

"Nobody nowadays," Sug Robertson said, about 1904, "knows what a stampede is. These modern high-bred cattle can't get scared or run either like the old-time Texas cattle. In 1871 I was working on the Flat Top Ranch, in Coleman County, Texas. The main trail to New Mexico and Arizona split it open. This was the Goodnight–Loving Trail, which, after leaving the headwaters of the Middle Concho River, led ninety miles over a country without a drop of water before hitting Horsehead Crossing on the Pecos. Lots of cattle were being driven west at the time, and ranchmen from sixty to a hundred miles around threw in and hired me to inspect all herds passing through and to cut out cattle in their brands. I was what was called a trail-cutter.

"That year John Chisum had several herds moving into New Mexico. He led the first herd himself — 6000 stock cattle. Too many cattle of any kind for a single herd, but he drove that way so as to concentrate his forces against the Indians. Coming behind this herd, following eight or ten miles back, were 3000 head of big steers, from four years old up to twenty. They were owned and bossed by a man named Adams, and when I inspected them he told me they had been stampeding every night — the habit most dreaded by all trail drivers. Adams didn't have to tell me they had been running on him. They were ga'nted like a roundup of starved coachwhip snakes, and all of them had the scours.

"The stampede that started this nightly running, Adams said, was away down in southern Texas when a horse being ridden into camps from the second relief stepped into the opening of a McClellan saddle lying on the ground. I don't know what this contraption was doing in a cow camp, but there it was. The horse's hoof hung. In stumbling he got rid of his rider and then he lit out a-running. Every time he struck the ground with that postage-stamp saddle fastened on his hoof he made a noise that none of those old mossy-headed steers had ever heard or dreamed of. They hit the ground with a roar that would have drowned a clap of thunder, coming straight for camp. Most of the hands cleared out, but the cattle smashed the chuck wagon into smithereens and threw the cook's hip out of joint. The next morning there wasn't anything left of the corn meal and other grub but a little color in the dirt. Running into the wagon and outfit that way must have given those scalawags a scare far worse than what started them. Adams and his men, though, were all puzzled as to what kept the steers running every night. They'll stampede that way just from habit, sometimes; but usually there's some animal or some particular thing to set them off.

"Both Chisum's and Adams' herds were moving slow, filling up for the dry time ahead of them, and I rode along with them for several days, spending most of my time with Chisum's outfit, gradually working out a few strays and enjoying the company. At Eighteen Mile Crossing on the Concho River I decided to turn back. I had no hankering to again make that dry drive ahead. John Chisum was the best all-around cowman I ever knew. When I got ready to leave, he said he'd ride back with me as far as the Adams herd and see if he couldn't locate what was making the steers run.

[103]

"We reached them about the time they were bedding down. Adams told Chisum to take charge. 'Well, bed 'em down as usual,' Chisum said, 'and after they are settled I'll ride through 'em and see what I can see.'

"It was twilight and the moon was rising full; so we had no trouble seeing. I rode around with Chisum, taking lessons. After he had looked for twenty or maybe thirty minutes, taking in individually every animal he saw, he stopped and called to Adams, who came over to where we were. He didn't let out a yell, you'll understand, just called in a quieting sort of way.

" 'There's the cause of your stampedes,' he said. He pointed to a lanky paint steer about as narrow between the eyes as a razorback hog and with corkscrew horns. Most significant of all, the steer was one-eyed. In other words, he couldn't see and didn't have any sense besides.

" 'Cut that steer out, drive him down to the river and kill him,' Chisum ordered.

"The order was put into execution at once. The steers did not make even a jump that night. I learned afterwards that there was not another stampede on the whole drive. That crazy one-eyed steer had been setting the whole three thousand off every night until a real cowman spotted him."

The discovery of the agitator might be a mere accident. In 1869, A. Branshaw was with a herd that kept stampeding and stampeding, nobody able to find out why. One bitter, cold night in the Indian Nation, a low moon and the stars giving plenty of light to see by, Branshaw, who was on guard, dismounted outside the circle of sleeping cattle and began leading his horse. The cattle were all lying down except a big white steer.

Suddenly Branshaw saw this steer leap into the air and hit the ground with a thud, his nose seeming to make a part of the impact. He gave a grunt that sounded more like that of a hog than of a cow brute. That was the signal. The whole herd was up like a shot, headed for the footman. The horse jerked loose and ran; the man climbed a tree. The next day he told the boss about the white steer. Old Whitey was traded to a Choctaw Indian, and the stampedes stopped.

"Old Bugler" was not caught in the act, but was finally suspected on general principles. He bellowed like a bugle, and hence his name. He was a big paint and was always in the lead. One evening the boss said, "Cut out Old Bugler, run him to one side, rope and tie him there." That night, to the great relief of the men, the cattle kept their beds till dawn. Every night thereafter Old Bugler was staked off from the other cattle, and stampedes were no more.

The best way to manage a stampede was to prevent it. A good herd boss would not bed his cattle on ground that sounded hollow, in a narrow valley, or on a rough point. He picked, if possible, the kind of level ground the cattle would pick for themselves for a bed. He kept the camp quiet and not too far away from the herd. He watered out the cattle thoroughly and saw that they got their fill of grass before lying down.

When I was a boy on our ranch in Live Oak County, I used to have a horse named Buck that I now think of far oftener than I think of most people I have known. On his left forefoot, which was stockinged, he had the scar of a rattlesnake bite. At the rattle of a snake or, frequently, of the somewhat similar rattle of dried thistle seed struck by a stirrup, he would jump with the suddenness of a shot. Year after year, no matter how often I passed a certain agrito (wild barberry) bush growing close to the road, a few hundred yards from home, he would shy. One time he had heard and seen a rattlesnake at that bush. In spring and summer rattlesnakes stay around the agritos way-laying birds and other small creatures that feed on the dropped berries. Buck had a very strong association of ideas.

Cattle are like horses and men in the association of ideas —

ideas of stampeding. Men and other animals that live close to the soil probably have stronger associations with places than with anything else. In that fine book of the Northwest, *Ubet*, John R. Barrows tells of driving a herd of 1400 big steers across a long dry stretch and bedding them down in the darkness about five miles out from the Yellowstone River. Before morning a breeze sprang up from the direction of the water. Instantly every animal was on his feet, and, with heads lifted, the fourteen hundred let out a chorus that said they had smelt water and were going to it. For about three hours the men managed to keep them under some kind of restraint, but at the first streak of dawn they got beyond all control. The leaders were belly deep in the Yellowstone while the drag was still two miles away.

"It took a long time for every animal to satisfy his thirst, and this operation was about concluded when from the cliffs on the opposite side of the river came the reverberating reports of a dozen blasts of dynamite, made by the Northern Pacific Railroad construction crews beginning their day's work. The whole herd left with such force that they had run two miles before riders could check them. From this point we drove one hundred miles down the river, and every day when we put the cattle into the water we were compelled to handle the inevitable stampede as soon as their thirst was satisfied and association of ideas had time to operate."

All primitive animals are expectant at waterings. There, they know by instinct, predatory animals lie in wait. The title of Frederic Remington's most famous painting, "The Fight at the Water Hole," might characterize the struggle for existence in the animal world for a million years. A good boss would send a man ahead of his herd to scare ducks off the water. If they flew up after cattle began to drink, there might be no end to the running. A wavelet tickling the nose of some old snuffy steer muzzling the water might make him jump the whole herd into panic.

VI · THE WAY THEY RAN

*To Onie J. Sheeran of the Nueces. Mighty few of the
limb-splitters could outrun him. How often have his
before-daylight coffee and yarns warmed my whole
being!*

MAN does everything best — or worst; and next to thunder
and lightning, nothing could put more terror into a
herd of man-fearing Longhorns than Man himself, either in-
tentionally or unintentionally. Many a stampede was started by
some prank of boyish innocence. That's one reason why many
trail bosses would not allow a boy along.

Along about 1900, Jim Dobie bought the Dubose cattle on
the Barbón and sent Sid Grover to receive them. After branding
them, Sid Grover decided to hold them overnight in a pen and

[107]

detailed men to ride around it, two at a time. Some bosses preferred to put a man inside the pen to keep the cattle stirred up and awake against surprise.

The night was rather cold, and when Charlie Dubose and one of the Pierce boys — both of them just kids — came in from their guard, they were delighted at the spectacle Old Mose, a Negro cowboy, presented. He was lying on his back, dead asleep, with his feet towards the fire. One great flat, splay foot had got from under the blanket and, with the big toe forked out, was spread towards the fire like a monster ham being spitted.

The boys decided to see how close they could bring a chunk of fire to Old Mose's sole before he winced. They moved a mesquite chunk up fairly close; Mose did not notice it. They brought it closer and closer. At last they began to sniff the burning horny growth that covered the old darkey's soles. Yet, apparently, he felt it no more than a cow feels the burn on the end of her horn. He was like the barefooted gal from Arkansas. "Sal, take yer foot off that thar coal," her granny called out. "Wal now, which foot?" Sal wanted to know.

Then the burn got through the horny sole and struck the quick! Mose jumped with the alacrity of a Spanish bull and at the same time let out a yell that would have done credit to sixteen Comanches. The cattle awoke as quick as he did and had knocked the fence down and were on their way to Jericho before the boys on herd knew what had happened.

"Then he hung hisself so he wouldn't stompede no more cattle." That is the way a quiet little old man, a certain Chaucerian shyness and gentleness in him and very religious, named Alonzo Mitchell, of Lampasas, Texas, tells it.

"That year, 1875," he said, "we were taking up a mixed herd to Wichita, Kansas. It was mixed sure enough — cows, bulls, steers, but no calves or yearlings. Lots of times a man couldn't tell from the looks of one of those cows that she was going to have a calf before daylight. She was wiry and ga'nt and could run, jumping bushes like a deer, even when about to bring a calf. Some of our cows begun having calves before we got across the Brazos River, and they kept on having calves all the way up. Generally they'd be dropped on the bed ground at night. The next morning we'd shoot 'em in the head with six-shooters and go on. A calf just born is too wobbly on its legs to walk up with any herd. We had an ox wagon, with the bed calked for crossing rivers, but it didn't have room for hauling the calves, and 'calf wagons' hadn't then come into use. The calves were not worth much of anything. We had to take the cows along or lose them. The shooting was just an act of mercy.

"Some people would rope the cows at night and hobble them, so's to keep them from going back to hunt their calves. I don't remember that our cows gave us much trouble. They seemed to know their calves were dead. Sometimes one would have a calf while trailing along. She'd drop back into the drag, and then we'd let her stop until she was fully delivered, shoot the calf, and drive her on.

"When we got into North Texas, a woman came to the bed ground before daylight one morning driving a wagon. She asked if we had any little calves. We said maybe so. Then she said she'd like to have them if we were going to get rid of them anyway. She got three or four and put them in her wagon. The next morning, ten or twelve miles north of that camp, she was on hand again, this time with a boy to help. She must've been raising quite a bunch of dogies. We learned she was picking up calves from all the cow herds passing her way. She had better luck than the Kansas nester who got to a steer herd after dark to await the morning crop of calves. The boss told him he could have them if he'd take a turn at standing guard. Somehow his 'trick' lasted from the first shift till it got light enough for him to see the animals in the herd. Then he rode away without even coming to camps for coffee.

[109]

"In our herd were steers that stood seventeen hands high and were as fat as mud. Talk about beef! But we didn't kill any of our stuff while on the trail. There was lots of talk about 'traveling fever' — later recognized as tick fever — and we were afraid to eat the meat of trail cattle. Some outfits butchered range cattle they sighted along the trail, but we didn't believe in that sort of business.

"Our leaders were a pair of prairie steers we named Broad and Crump. Broad was a brown with wide-spreading horns that twisted straight out; Crump was a white with horn tips that crumpled in. When they walked, their heads would sway, their horns weighed so much, but they'd walk side by side, right up at the lead, day after day, with their heads swinging in such harmony that their horns never clicked or interfered with each other. The way they got timed to each other was remarkable, and we boys used to talk about it often. When they were grazing in high grass, heads hidden, we could see their horns bobbing and balancing.

"When there was a stompede — and we had several on this trip — no matter which way the herd ran or which part of it got off first, Broad and Crump would soon be in the lead. If a man racing along towards the point got a glimpse of them by a flash of lightning or skylighted them, he'd yell across to any hand on the other side to give way, for he knew that with Broad and Crump leading, he could turn the runaways and put them in a mill.

"Chain lightning caused more stompedes than anything else, and next came lobo wolves — the smell of them. After we got up into the Indian Territory, we could depend upon nearly all the storms' coming from the northwest. We and the cattle both generally got warnings out of the sky, but the storm nearly always broke with great suddenness and fury.

"The cowboys would holler to the cattle and sing and pray. Yes, they'd pray to God loud, making all sorts of promises. Then next morning at breakfast they'd laugh, cursing and poking fun at themselves and each other.

" 'Don't you ever pray in a storm?' they'd ask me.

" 'No.'

" 'Well,' each man said to me at one time or another, 'I pray when I get scared. I don't see how anybody keeps from it.'

" 'I'll tell you,' I said more'n once, 'why I don't pray. When I was twenty-one years old I turned myself over to my Heavenly Father. I pray to him regularly, and under his care I'm no more scared when it lightnings than when it don't.'

"On one trip up the trail we got next to a herd that was stompeding every night almost, the owner said. I told him he must be packing his cattle too close on the bed ground. If cattle were bedded down so close together that a steer switching his tail hit another in the face, there was mighty apt to be a stompede. The critter hit would jump up with a beller, and then the whole herd would be off like a flash in the pan. Well, this man asked me to bed his cattle for him. I had an awful time getting his men to spread out and let the cattle take natural room and positions, just as they'd take if left to themselves. 'Good gracious,' the man kept saying, 'how much more room do they need?' And, 'We're going to have an awful big territory to ride around,' he'd say. I told him the men on guard had to keep riding anyhow and it didn't make any more work to ride around five acres than one.

"After the cattle got their positions, there was a full steer-length between many a one of them and the next animal. There wasn't a bobble that night. The trail boss was satisfied. From then on he gave his stuff plenty of room and had no trouble above the ordinary.

"Up in the Indian Nation somewhere, south of a creek that I can't remember the name of, a man who was loose-herding a small bunch of cattle met our herd one evening and told us we'd better expect trouble. Every herd that crossed that creek, he said, was stompeding. According to him, a jayhawker was waylaying the place, and, after the cattle ran and split up, was cutting off little bunches and driving them up a side canyon, where he'd hold them until the owners got out of the country and then turn them over to a gang of fellow thieves.

"This creek had a reputation up and down the trail, but the cause of the stompedes had been a mystery. The trail down to the crossing was steep and thickly timbered on both sides, with lots of underbrush besides, all cut by gullies. The average herd did not have a man riding in front of it, the two point men guiding the leaders and holding them down if they got to walking too fast.

"My brother Bob Mitchell was boss, and when we started down to the creek bottom, he took his place on the right point. He didn't show hisse'f, but as the lead cattle strung along, Broad and Crump right in front and doing their duty, he rode so's to get a look ahead. D'reckly he saw something black down in the bottom flop like two big wings. He pulled his six-shooter and shot, and a man left on his horse in a hurry. Bob just got one glimpse of him in the brush. We got across all right.

"The stompeder left his paraphernalia right where he was in the habit of using it. It consisted of a kind of scarecrow with adjustable wings that could be moved up and down. When the lead animals of a herd suddenly saw this thing working at close quarters, of course they'd tear out, those following down the hill breaking off from the narrow trail-opening and scattering from hell to breakfast.

"We made camp that night on the prairie. On the edge of it next to the creek were a lot of oak trees. A funny thing. Next morning the man that had been stompeding the herds was hanging from a limb of one of them trees — considerably off to one side of the trail so's not to scare any cattle. Right by him was hanging his scarecrow machine. He hung hisse'f so he wouldn't stompede no more cattle. That's what they said."

And here the reader may visualize a little wink and hear in

imagination a little laugh from the lean, little, lithe and bright-eyed man who told me this story when he was eighty-five years old.

That professional "stompeder" was doing his work in the day-time. Daylight runs were common, though generally easier to handle than the night ones and less dangerous to man and beast. However, they could be serious. One year a Millet herd, upon crossing the Wichita River of the Indian Territory, found all the grass burned off except that upon a tongue of land protected between two creeks. Apparently all the prairie chickens in the country had come to this unburned sod; they were there by the thousands. The three thousand steers got their fill on the grass among the prairie chickens, bedded down and spent the night sleeping. But about daybreak next morning when the birds began to whirr up, the cattle tore out over the rough country in every direction. Several were killed and about a hundred got away.

In the seventies some of the north-bound herds of Central Texas passed through Stephenville. It wasn't much of a village, and a few fenced-in fields made going around it inconvenient. There were six or seven log cabins, with shed rooms of rawhide lumber, strung along the trail and out from it. The central and largest structure served as a courthouse. It had a gallery covered with boards made of pin oak. The liveliest place in town was a saloon, where, for two-bits, a purchaser could get a "fair-sized drink" of wagon-yard whisky drawn in a tin cup from a fifty-gallon barrel. Usually a group of cowboys were congre-gated here, but the dogs of the village far outnumbered both in-habitants and visitors. Dog fights furnished the chief amuse-ment. The sheriff owned a large parrot that habitually perched on the roof of the courthouse gallery. It had picked up a con-siderable vocabulary from the cowboys, including profanity. Its favorite expression was "Ye-oh, sic 'em!" which usually started a dog fight.

One day a herd was stringing through town, shying but keeping the middle of the road, when the parrot flapped his wings, gave a cowboy yell, and screeched "Ye-oh, sic 'em!" In a second all the dogs in town charged the steers. They stampeded, knocked down all the galleries, including the one the parrot was perched on, rammed through the sheds, and even demolished some of the shacks. Stephenville looked as if a cyclone had struck it.

People not acquainted with cow nature think that shutting cattle up in a pen eliminates the danger of stampedes. Cattle used to being free are, in fact, more nervous in a pen than anywhere else. If a good-sized herd inside a big pen scares, they have a space for a run against the fence. Unless it is very strong, it is smashed; otherwise the leaders are likely to pile up, while the cattle behind, forming a gigantic battering ram, rush over them and surge on over the fence, then through it, tearing it down from the top. If the pen is small and strong and the cattle are crowded into it, they are not likely to get through the fence, but they will be unable to lie down and rest, will mill all night, will lose weight, and the next day won't drive well. Every night so spent means a loss on the cattle.

I was with a herd of Double Circle cows and heifers — 1700 head of straight-bred Herefords — trailing down to the Gila River in Arizona. The boss was J. H. Willis, and when we reached the Chiricahua Ranch on the third evening of the drive, he asked me what I thought about penning. We had spent nearly the whole day coming through a mountain pass, the cattle had eaten very little, and some were getting footsore. I did not like the idea of penning at all, but at dusk Willis shut them in an enormous plank pen. We camped maybe three hundred yards away. About two o'clock one of the Apache cowhands gave a yell. It was unnecessary, for the pounding rumble had awakened every man. In a minute we were all on our ready-saddled horses. It was light enough so that, as we approached the pens, we could see the stream of cattle pouring through two or three panels of fence they had knocked down. There was no stopping them until they were all out. The lay of the mountain land was in our favor, and before noon all the "cherrycows" we had gathered in the run were cut out, all of ours were counted in, and we were going on down to the hot Gila.

Those Hereford cattle did not tear out of the pen with anything like the power, the velocity and the mania for getting away that a penful of old Texas Longhorn steers would have demonstrated. In 1885 A. B. Harper helped drive a thousand head of steers of mixed ages from the border to Captain Charles Schreiner's ranch in the hills above Kerrville on the Guadalupe River. They got in the habit of stampeding and ran almost every night. When they finally reached their destination, Captain Schreiner ordered them put in his main pens overnight, to be branded next day. The pens were big and were made with German thoroughness and ponderosity out of logs — not rails — laid ten feet high between heavy posts sunk deep in the ground. Then heavy log buttresses braced the fence all around from the outside. It was a pen nothing could break down.

The worn-out men were eating a late supper when they heard the stampede thunder they were so used to. They ran to the fence. The steers had hit it, and already some of them, climbing upon the bodies of the advance impact, had their heads over the top logs. The men quirted, yelled, and turned the climbers back. Those steers kept running all night long, but after three or four runs the leaders learned to veer at the fence, and then there would be a grueling mill. The next morning, not counting slipped horns and cripples still able to walk, about twenty-five animals were dead or so badly injured as to make killing them necessary.

Along the routes followed by drovers before the Civil War, from the interior of Texas to Shreveport and New Orleans, "stands" were established a day's drive apart. Here the drovers could get meals and pen for the night. Night-herding was not the usual order as on the great trails to the north. The builders of the pens anticipated rushes by the mighty Texas steers, but there were disastrous runs. At a plantation "stand" near Shreveport a herd, after killing or fatally injuring many of their number, broke over the pen fence, demolished a carriage house and its fine vehicles, ran into the slave quarters, and not only flattened out cabins but killed one Negro family. The steers left alive after this stampede were not nearly sufficient to compensate for the damages.

How far would cattle run if not checked, especially when they got a good start in the night? Generally, not so far as the fiction writers take them. In 1888 Tex Crosse was standing guard on the Pecos River. The advance wind of an approaching storm blew his hat off. It went rolling over the backs of two or three steers. It would have rolled over more if there had been any backs left. After a run that lasted only a few minutes, the whole herd circled back to the exact point of starting, stopped, and bedded down for the rest of the night. This return was very unusual. Trail bosses as a rule did not, after a run, want to try the same bed ground again.

Some stampedes took such odd forms that almost any story about the subject is believable. One night, while trailing over a long, dry stretch, Charles Goodnight had half of his herd moving along in sober, orderly manner while the other half raced up one side, around the point, down the other side and through the drags, stampeding around and around until they were quieted. I have heard of a head-on collision between two stampeding herds, one running full-tilt south, the other north. There may be some connection between this event and a toast that an embarrassed cowboy was called upon to give at a city banquet. All he could think of was a poem he had learned in camp:

They met on the bridge at midnight,
They never will meet again.
One was a west-bound heifer,
The other an east-bound train.

While H. W. Anshutz was riding line one day in 1883 in No Man's Land near the Cimarron River, he heard a tinkling of bells on the Tuttle Trail, which led to Dodge City. Riding over, he saw a herd of around six hundred unusually rough mossyhorns, about half of them belled. The boss said that the old scalawags had been roped out of the brush, and that the bells were to help his men keep up with them during night stampedes.

Some days later Anshutz, riding in the same vicinity, saw about twenty-five head of the steers, several wearing bells, coming down the trail from the north. Not long afterwards the Texans, on their way home, gave an account of the stampede near Dodge City. The twenty-five runaways had covered the sixty miles back to the Cimarron in fifteen hours. That is a good record. However, at ten o'clock one Friday night in 1884 a herd of 5064 big steers, bossed by Ben Doughty, stampeded north of the Platte River, and at eleven o'clock on Sunday morning, thirty-seven hours later, thirty-five of them were seen one hundred and twenty miles south. This is the record, so far as I know. These steers had been scared on by nesters and prevented from resting or grazing. Of course they could not have run the entire distance; they had run long distances, trotted, stopped, walked. A grown steer could easily walk better than three miles an hour.

Cowboys who hung with cattle intermittently running all night long were not, as a rule, when day finally broke more than five or ten miles from camp.

There have been many discussions as to which way cattle would turn, or mill, if not forced: to the right or to the left, clockwise or counterclockwise. Goodnight and other cowmen have claimed they always milled to the right. Perhaps there is a pronounced right-handedness in the whole animal world. It is said that a tadpole in changing into a frog invariably grows his first foreleg on the right side and then, after his left foreleg, the right hind leg. Plainsmen have described how buffaloes upon being rushed into a stockade by Indian hunters always ran to the right from the entrance — though this would throw the penned-up herd into a left-handed, or counterclockwise, mill.

Probably ninety per cent of North American cattle are branded on the left side. The practice of so branding them may be based on the inclination of cattle to pull to the right, leaving the "brand side" out for a view. Yet any cow can dodge to the left as well as to the right and keep her brands on either side exasperatingly hidden. As for mills following a stampede, man's inclination to pull to the right might account for the right-handed direction of many of them.

In a way, drifts were more persistent than stampedes. A herd, more often than not in wet weather, might be impelled by something in cattle nature to drift — not running at all, but walking with solid determination. A phalanx of fifty cowboys could not turn back such a herd, if it were at all sizable. All they could do would be to drift with the cattle, somewhat checking them and keeping them from scattering.

One day about noon a cold rain began driving from the east on a herd of Laurel Leaf steers crossing the Indian Territory. The cattle refused to quarter it, to keep the trail leading due north, but turned west, moving with a solid front instead of in trail formation. After the men, all soaking wet and cold, had tried desperately but futilely for hours to check the drift, the boss said, "Let 'em drift. Just try to string 'em out and hold the leaders down."

To use the words of William O'Neal, "Dark found us in a timbered bottom, and then we struck the river. It was lightning, and we could see the water whirling down like a sea. But the cattle took it, and there was nothing to do but follow. After we crossed, we came to a big prairie. The wind lulled some, and there we held 'em up.

"Several herds had crossed ahead of us, and they were holding on the big prairie. Before long they got to running, and the roar was so great at times that we cowboys could not hear each other speak. Our own cattle were trying to run too, but we held them. The other herds had all got mixed, and when it lightened and we got a glance northward, it looked to me as if there were leagues and leagues of horns, all seething.

"With one of the herds was a boss named Perkins. He had a voice like a buffalo bull, and a mile away I heard him bellering to the men to let the cattle scatter. 'God damn it,' he yelled, 'if you don't let these cattle scatter, they'll tromp each other to death.' He was right, too, for take ten or twelve thousand big steers, mill 'em together, and the inside cattle will get down. The men let the stuff spread out, and next morning they were over that prairie for miles. We rode over carcasses of big steers as flat on the ground as if their hides had been peeled off and staked out. They had fallen or got knocked down, and then thousands of hoofs had tromped over them."

No stampede was more dreaded by men responsible for property than a running together of several herds. This mixture was possible only on the trail, at places where passage was clogged, or near destinations.

In the late spring of 1882 Red River got up so high from continuous rains that trail bosses were afraid to trust their cattle to its swift, drift-laden current. At sundown one evening eleven herds, all waiting to get over, could be counted south of Doan's Crossing, and besides these there were two or three trail herds of horses. That night all the "corn waggins" between heaven and earth rumbled across the skies, and it rained regular waterfalls over the whole country. All the herds stampeded, running into each other, milling and mixing until at daybreak not a single outfit had its property separate. The two thousand or so wild horses — mustangs with a brand on them — were keeping up the confusion and adding to it by racing back and forth through the cattle, nickering for their lost companions and trying to get together and get away. It took 120 cowboys ten days to reshape into their respective herds the 33,000 head of cattle of that mix-up.

VII · EPITAPH ON THE LONE PRAIRIE

*To Dave Donoghue. Instead of cattle, he trailed
Coronado down the Palo Duro.*

HORSES can see better at night than cattle, and probably have a finer sensitiveness to what is ahead. Many a horse on a night of pitchy darkness has suddenly halted, trembling and refusing to go an inch farther, his rider then ascertaining, by a flash of lightning or by getting down and feeling the ground, that he was at the very edge of a precipice. Some very sensitive blind people feel in an indefinable way, perhaps by vibrations in the air, the presence of an obstacle they have not touched. It may be that a void of space is thus sometimes sensed by a horse without his being able to see it, though horses have gone over the brink also. A horse can stop more quickly than a cow brute.

The lead steers in a stampede, even if they sensed a gulf and would stop, were pushed on by the running battering-ram at their tails.

In 1872, on the Smoky River near Hays City, Kansas, Mark Withers while running in the lead of a stampede saw by a flash of lightning that he was on the edge of a high bluff. His only recourse was to spur on. His horse, uninjured, landed in three or four feet of water. Instead of going on across, he pulled up at the base of the bluff. From this protected point he heard and saw by flashes the steers pouring down. A large number were killed and crippled.

A great majority of the tall jumps made by cowboys are found in tales just a little taller.

"Talk about it being dark!" Frank Mitchell of the **J A**'s used to tell. "It was darker'n the inside of a cow with her lights drilled out. The stompeders headed for a bluff that I didn't know existed and went on over like hell after a preacher. I was riding on their fetlocks when my night horse — and, God, he was a good one — went with 'em.

"He didn't make a bobble goin' down, jest kept steady, his feet straight out. I don't know how long we was making the descent. I had time for several thoughts and could have rolled a cigarette maybe. I was still a-settin' in the saddle like a reg'lar hand when Flying Machine — that's what I named him — hit on his all-fours. Jest hit and stood there like he wanted to rest a while. I sorter teched him with the spur, but he couldn't budge, it seemed. Derned if we didn't stay there till daylight, and then I see he's bogged up to his knees in solid rock. That little experience shore developed his eyesight, and after that he was a better night horse than ever."

A cowboy might have to ride something besides space. In San Antonio one day old Tom Gilroy told me this story, swearing to the truth of it.

"One time going up the trail our outfit had a cowboy named

Jack. He was sorter weak-minded like, and always slept a ways off from camps and on the south side of the herd. One night a norther hit with a bang, and the steers stompeded — south. Jack didn't have no time to get on his horse. He run a ways in the only direction he could run, away from the stompede. Before he was good winded, he stumbled into a kind of gully, rolled over a time or two, and lost his six-shooter. He didn't have no time to feel around for it. By now he could hear the steers right on his hocks. He butted into a tree and then shinned up it. After he'd got about ten feet up and thought he was safe, he heard the unearthliest growl a man ever heard. He skylighted, and there right above him was a panther, stretched out and just moving its tail like a panther does when he's about to spring.

"Jack took one look below. There wasn't anything under him but horns going by like the clatter-wheels of hell. Quicker'n I can tell, he decided he'd ruther risk riding a Longhorn than being rode by a panther. He leaped off on the back of a big white steer that made a good target to jump at. And he rode that critter till he was carried out of the main herd to a clear place where it seemed safe to drop off. He said that white steer didn't bother to look back when he turned him loose."

In 1876 Wilson Brothers of Kansas City bought a big string of mature steers in Central Texas and concentrated them in one herd, west of the Brazos River. There were about twenty-five cowboys in the outfit — too many. At ten o'clock the cattle appeared to be sleeping safely, though some of them were nervous. During the preceding afternoon an electrical storm had made them jumpy. Then they had shied at a rainbow, one end of which almost touched the pointers of the herd. The men who rode that night always insisted that the rainbow and dreams of it were back of the stampede.

The stars were out and the breeze was soft when the cattle jumped, heading for the breaks cutting into the Brazos River.

The eldest of the Wilson brothers and one cowboy got to the point of the runners first, on the left side. The stampede would soon have been in a mill had it not been for a Mexican. He had been in camp drinking forbidden whisky when the cattle tore out. He raced around them on the right side, getting to the leaders just as Wilson and the man with him were turning them from the other side. He began shooting. The running cattle straightened back.

Just ahead was a deep gully. Wilson and two or three additional men who had by now caught up with him saw the gully and jerked to one side, but the main herd was already upon them. Wilson yelled, "Shoot to kill." The riders succeeded in killing enough steers to make a kind of breastworks for splitting the oncoming mass. The gully filled with plunging animals, trampling and crushing those underneath to death. The men found a crossing and threw the herd — what was left of it — into a mill. When the count was made next day, 2700 steers were missing, the majority of that number dead. For a long time horns marked the sides of the gully and were strewn down its bed. It is known yet as Stampede Gully. The Mexican was not killed in the stampede, but something a good deal faster prevented his crossing the Brazos River next day.

Had Wilson ridden alone, or with only one man along, and had a six-shooter not been pulled from the scabbard, the stampede would have been controlled. If a man wanted to stampede a bunch of cattle, he could not find an easier or more effective way than shooting near them — as an excitable cowboy on guard one night found out when he cut loose on a Spanish dagger, thinking it was an Indian.

One time, Oscar Rush wrote, he was helping drive a string of "Southern" steers in New Mexico when one of them "busted" out of the herd and refused to be turned back. The owner of the herd gave chase, and as the runaway went over a hill, proceeded to smoke him up. Down the hill was a windmill at which about three hundred range steers were taking their noon rest. The firing and the terrified animal plunging into their midst set them off. They circled and ran into the herd being driven. Then the combination split like a covey of quail, some of them running until dark. There were fourteen hundred head of steers in the pasture where the so-called cowman experimented with his six-shooter. The next morning there were only two hundred head, and five hundred of the missing were later rounded up sixty miles away.

Six-shooters for controlling a stampede never have been popular anywhere except in fiction. You don't dash kerosene on a fire to put it out. George W. Saunders, gatherer of data for the two extraordinary volumes entitled *The Trail Drivers of Texas*, conducted a query among trail men as to the use of six-shooters in stampedes. He found only one man who had ever seen such use.

A mob of riders yelling and helling after a stampede were generally as bad as a six-shooter. Jim Dobie, if he were present during a night stampede, had every man but one stay in camp. He wanted only one man to help him. Gus Withers and Ab Blocker had the same system. Running in terror, cattle have an instinct to stay together. If crowded by numerous riders, all yelling, waving slickers, beating on their leggins and making as much noise as possible, they will cut off in bunches and scatter.

Circling the leaders and throwing the herd into a mill was not the only way to stop a stampede. A few men who knew cow psychology and who felt in themselves a power over cattle could check the wildest running herd by riding in front, quavering out "The Texas Lullaby" and gradually getting the cattle to feel that the man and his horse were the leader, the dominator of the run. It took a born cowman to do this — something entirely different from a mere expert at bronco-busting and roping and shooting off his mouth or six-shooter.

He had to ride, nevertheless, "like a drunk Indian," zigzagging across the front of the stampede and directing its course. A kind of chant that the master of a run might croon — but never yodel — to the cattle went somewhat in this wise:

> Wo-up, wo-up, wo, wo-o-o-o, wo boys, wo-o-o-o-o-o-o boys.
> Be good, be good, wo-o-o-o-o, you wall-eyed rascals. . . .
> (*Expurgated*)

So much has been written about the effect of cowboy songs on cattle that little need be said here. Singing, whistling, chanting, humming seemed to have a soothing effect on the toughest old Longhorns. Most of all, the sounds — supposed to be harmonious — prevented any sudden noise from startling the cattle. "It was cloudy in the west and a-lookin' like rain" — and the boss would say, "Boys, I reckon you'll have to sing to 'em tonight." Nearly all the old authentic cowboy tunes were slow, as slow as a horse walks around sleeping cattle at night, and the majority of them were mournful.

> Oh, beat the drum slowly and play the fife lowly.
>
> Those words came low and mournfully.

The music that hath power to soothe the savage breast is low — and, yes, on the lone prairie, in the mouth of many a cowboy who "could not sing," it was sweet. They sang "Dan Tucker" until a horse would kick up his heels, and they sang "My Lulu Gal" with additions not to be printed, but they sang also "Nearer My God to Thee," "The Old Time Religion," "Jesus Lover of My Soul," and "In the Sweet By and By." " 'Old Hundred' had a more soothing effect on wild cattle on the run than any other tune I knew," one veteran recalled. Reed Anthony, Andy Adams' cowman, tells how he and other Confederate soldiers guarding a herd of Texas steers saved the life of one because he would always walk out and stand attentive to the notes of "Rock of Ages" sung by his herders. Half of the tunes of genuine cowboy songs sound as if they had been derived from camp-meeting hymns. The tune of "Jesse James" will make a sinner want to go to the mourners' bench. And those old, slow, mournful tunes made Christians out of many a herd of devil-hardened steers. Cowboys used to say they could not sing "right" until the herd got restless — but then they could pipe them back down to rest.

Oh, say, little dogies, when are you goin' to lay down
And quit this forever siftin' around?
My horse is leg-weary and I'm awful tired,
But if you git away I'm sure to git fired —
Lay down, little dogies, lay down.

Some of the best known songs sung to prevent and to quiet stampedes were on that subject: "Little Joe the Wrangler," whose horse fell just in front of the stampede and who was "mashed to a pulp"; "Utah Carl," who gave his life to save the boss's daughter from "those cattle on a mad and fearless run"; and "When Work's All Done This Fall" — a rough-hewn classic, though it takes memories and the tune to arouse connotations.

While riding in the darkness so loudly did he shout,
Trying his best to head them and turn the herd about,
His saddle horse did stumble and on him did fall —
The poor boy won't see his mother when the work's
all done this fall.

And there was "Lasca," by Frank Desprez, which many a lad who had never read a poem knew by heart, and which a generation ago was recited on Friday afternoons in country schoolhouses from Montana to the Gulf of Mexico.

The air was heavy, the night was hot,
I sat by her side and forgot, forgot;
Forgot the herd that were taking their rest,
Forgot that the air was close oppressed,
That the Texas norther comes sudden and soon,
In the dead of the night or the blaze of noon;

That, once let the herd at its breath take fright,
Nothing on earth can stop their flight;
And woe to the rider, and woe to the steed,
That falls in front of their mad stampede!

Was that thunder? I grasped the cord
Of my swift mustang without a word.
I sprang to the saddle and she clung behind.
Away! on a hot chase down the wind. . . .

The cattle gained on us, and, just as I felt
For my old six-shooter behind in my belt,
Down came the mustang and down came we,
Clinging together — and, what was the rest?
A body that spread itself on my breast,
Two arms that shielded my dizzy head,
Two lips that hard to my lips were prest;
Then came thunder in my ears,
As over us surged the sea of steers,
Blows that beat blood into my eyes,
And when I could rise —
Lasca was dead!

I gouged out a grave a few feet deep,
And there in the earth's arms I laid her to sleep;
And there she is lying, and no one knows;
And the summer shines and the winter snows;
For many a day the flowers have spread
A pall of petals over her head;
And the little grey hawk hangs aloft in the air,
And the sly coyote trots here and there,
And the blacksnake glides and glitters and slides
Into the rift of a cottonwood tree;
And the buzzard sails on,
And comes and is gone,
Stately and still, like a ship at sea.
And I wonder why I do not care
For the things that are, like the things that were.
Does half my heart lie buried there
    In Texas, down by the Rio Grande?

One more story, and I am done with stampedes. In its fidelity to that part of the good earth that was once the open range, in its simplicity and rhythm, and in its elemental power, it is perhaps the finest story that has ever been written about cows or cowboys — "Longrope's Last Guard," by Charles M. Russell.*

"I've read of stampedes that were sure dangerous an' scary, where a herd would run through a camp, unsettin' wagons an' trompin' sleepin' cowpunchers to death. When day broke they'd be fifty or a hundred miles from where they started, leavin' a trail strewn with blood, dead cowpunchers an' hosses, that looked like the work of a Kansas cyclone. This is all right in books, but the feller that writes 'em is romancin' an' don't savvy the cow. Most stampedes is noisy, but harmless to anybody but the cattle. A herd in a bad storm might drift thirty miles in a night, but the worst run I ever see, we ain't four miles from the bed-ground when day broke.

"This was down in Kansas; we're trailin' beef an' have got about seventeen hundred head. Barrin' a few dry ones, the herd's straight steers, mostly Spanish Longhorns from down on the Cimarron. We're about fifty miles south of Dodge. Our herd's well broke an' lookin' fine, an' the cowpunchers all good-natured, thinkin' of the good time comin' in Dodge.

"That evenin' when we're ropin' our hosses for night guard, the trail boss, 'Old Spanish' we call him — he ain't no real Span-iard, but he's rode some in Old Mexico an' can talk some Spanish

* Used by arrangement with Doubleday, Doran and Company, New York, publishers of *Trails Plowed Under*, by Charles M. Russell, 1927, pages 203–210. Copyright 1927, Doubleday, Doran and Company.

— says to me: 'Them cattle ought to hold well; they ain't been off water four hours, an' we grazed 'em plumb onto the bed-ground. Every hoof of 'em's got a paunch full of grass an' water, an' that's what makes cattle lay good.'

"Me an' a feller called Longrope's on first guard. . . . When we reach the bed-ground, most of the cattle's already down, lookin' comfortable. They're bedded in open country, an' things look good for an easy night. It's been mighty hot all day, but there's a little breeze now makin' it right pleasant; but down the west I notice some nasty-lookin' clouds hangin' 'round the new moon that's got one horn hooked over the skyline. The storm's so far off that you can just hear her rumble, but she's walkin' up on us slow, an' I'm hopin' she'll go 'round. The cattle's all layin' quiet an' nice; so me an' Longrope stop to talk awhile.

" 'They're layin' quiet,' says I.

" 'Too damn quiet,' says he. 'I like cows to lay still all right, but I want some of the natural noises that goes with a herd this size. I want to hear 'em blowin' off, an' the creakin' of their joints, showin' they're easin' themselves in their beds. Listen, an' if you hear anything I'll eat that rimfire saddle of yours — grass rope an' all.'

"I didn't notice till then, but when I straighten my ears it's quiet as a grave. An' if it ain't for the lightnin' showin' the herd once in a while, I couldn't 'a' believed that seventeen hundred head of Longhorns lay within forty feet of where I'm sittin' on my hoss. It's gettin' darker every minute, an' if it wasn't for Longrope's slicker I couldn't 'a' made him out, though he's so close I could have touched him with my hand. Finally it darkens up so I can't see him at all. It's black as a nigger's pocket; you couldn't find your nose with both hands.

"I remember askin' Longrope the time.

" 'I guess I'll have to get help to find the timepiece,' says he, but gets her after feelin' over himself, an', holdin' her under his cigarette, takes a long draw, lightin' up her face.

[131]

" 'Half-past nine,' says he.

" 'Half an hour more,' I says. 'Are you goin' to wake up the next guard, or did you leave it to the hoss-wrangler?'

" 'There won't be but one guard to-night,' he answers, 'an' we'll ride it. You might as well hunt for a hoss thief in heaven as look for that camp. Well, I guess I'll mosey 'round.' An' with that he quits me.

"The lightnin' 's playin' every little while. It ain't making much noise, but lights up enough to show where you're at. There ain't no use ridin'. By the flashes I can see that every head's down. For a second it'll be like broad day, then darker than the dungeons of hell, an' I notice the little fire-balls on my hoss's ears; when I spit, there's a streak in the air like strikin' a wet match. These little fire-balls is all I can see of my hoss, an' they tell me he's listenin' always; his ears are never still.

"I tell you, there's something mighty ghostly about sittin' up on a hoss you can't see, with them two little blue sparks out in front of you wigglin' an' movin' like a pair of spook-eyes, an' it shows me the old night hoss is usin' his listeners plenty. I got my ears cocked, too, hearing nothin' but Longrope's singin'; he's easy three hundred yards across the herd from me, but I can hear every word:

> Sam Bass was born in Injiana,
>   It was his native home,
> 'Twas at the age of seventeen
>   Young Sam began to roam.
> He first went out to Texas,
>   A cowboy for to be;
> A better-hearted feller
>   You'd seldom ever see.

"It's so plain it sounds like he's singin' in my ear; I can even hear the click-clack of his spur chains against his stirrups when he moves 'round. An' the cricket in his bit — he's usin' one of them hollow conchoed half-breeds — she comes plain to me in the stillness. Once there's a steer layin' on the edge of the herd starts sniffin'. He's takin' long draws of the air; he's nosin' for something. I don't like this, it's a bad sign; it shows he's layin' for trouble, an' all he needs is some little excuse.

"Now, every steer, when he beds down, holds his breath for a few seconds, then blows off; that noise is all right an' shows he's settlin' himself for comfort. But when he curls his nose an' makes them long draws, it's a sign he's sniffin' for something, an' if anything crosses his wind that he don't like, there's liable to be trouble. I've seen dry trail herds mighty thirsty, layin' good till a breeze springs off the water, maybe ten miles away; they start sniffin', an' the minute they get the wind you could comb Texas an' wouldn't have enough punchers to turn 'em till they wet their feet an' fill their paunches.

"I get tired sittin' there starin' at nothin'; so I start ridin' 'round. Now, it's sure dark when animals can't see, but I tell you by the way my hoss moves he's feelin' his way. I don't blame him none; it's like lookin' in a black pot. Sky an' ground all the same, an' I ain't gone twenty-five yards till I hear cattle gettin' up around me; I'm in the herd, an' it's luck I'm singin' an' they don't get scared. Pullin' to the left, I work cautious an' easy till I'm clear of the bunch. Ridin's useless; so I flop my weight over on one stirrup an' go on singin'.

"The lightnin' 's quit now, an' she's darker than ever; the breeze has died down, an' it's hotter than the hubs of hell. Above my voice I can hear Longrope. He's singin' the 'Texas Ranger' now; the Ranger's a long song an' there's few punchers that knows it all, but Longrope's sprung a lot of new verses on me an' I'm interested. Seems like he's on about the twenty-fifth verse, an' there's danger of his chokin' down, when there's a whisperin' in the grass behind me; it's a breeze sneakin' up. It flaps the tail of my slicker an' goes by; in another second she hits the herd. The ground shakes, an' they're all runnin'.

"My hoss takes the scare with 'em an' 's bustin' a hole in the darkness when he throws both front feet in a badger hole, goin' to his knees an' plowin' his nose in the dirt. But he's a good night hoss an' 's hard to keep down. The minute he gets his feet under him he raises, runnin' like a scared wolf. Hearin' the roar behind him, he don't care to mix with them locoed Longhorns. I got my head turned over my shoulder listenin', tryin' to make out which way they're goin', when there's a flash of lightnin' busts a hole in the sky — it's one of these kind that puts the fear of God in a man, thunder an' all together. My hoss whirls an' stops in his tracks, spraddlin' out an' squattin' like he's hit; an' I can feel his heart beatin' agin my leg, while mine's poundin' my ribs like it'll bust through. We're both plenty scared.

"This flash lights up the whole country, givin' me a glimpse of the herd runnin' a little to my left. Big drops of rain are poundin' on my hat. The storm has broke now for sure, with the lightnin' bombardin' us at every jump. Once a flash shows me Longrope, ghostly in his wet slicker. He's so close to me that I could 'a' hit him with my quirt an' I hollers to him, 'This is hell.'

" 'Yes,' he yells back above the roar; 'I wonder what damned fool kicked the lid off.'

"I can tell by the noise that they're runnin' straight; there ain't no clickin' of horns. It's a kind of hummin' noise like a buzz-saw, only a thousand times louder. There's no use in tryin' to turn 'em in this darkness; so I'm ridin' wide — just herdin' by ear an' follerin' the noise. Pretty soon my ears tell me they're crowdin' an' comin' together; the next flash shows 'em all millin', with heads jammed together an' horns locked; some's rared up ridin' others, an' these is squirmin' like bristled snakes.

"In the same light I see Longrope, an' from the blink I get of him he's among 'em or too close for safety, an' in the dark I thought I saw a gun flash three times with no report. But with the noise these Longhorns are makin' now, I doubt if I could a-heard a six-gun bark if I pulled the trigger myself, an' the

[134]

next thing I know me an' my hoss goes over a bank, lightin' safe. I guess it ain't over four feet, but it seems like fifty in the darkness, an' if it hadn't been for my chin-string I'd a-went from under my hat. Again the light shows me we're in a 'royo with the cattle comin' over the edge, wigglin' an' squirmin' like army worms.

"It's a case of all night riding. Sometimes they'll mill an' quiet down, then start trottin' an' break into a run. Not till daybreak do they stop, an' maybe you think old day ain't welcome. My hoss is sure leg-weary, an' I ain't so rollicky myself. When she gets light enough, I begin lookin' for Longrope, with nary a sign of him; an' the herd, you wouldn't know they were the same cattle — smeared with mud an' ga'nt as greyhounds; some of 'em with their tongues still lollin' out from their night's run. But sizin' up the bunch, I guess I got 'em all. I'm kind of worried about Longrope. It's a cinch that wherever he is he's afoot, an' chances is he's layin' on the prairie with a broken leg.

"The cattle's spread out, an' they begin feedin'. There ain't much chance of losin' 'em, now it's broad daylight; so I ride up on a rise to take a look at the back trail. While I'm up there viewin' the country, my eyes run onto somethin' a mile back in a draw. I can't make it out, but get curious; so spurrin' my tired hoss into a lope, I take the back trail. 'Tain't no trouble to foller in the mud; it's plain as plowed ground. I ain't rode three hundred yard till the country raises a little an' shows me this thing's a hoss, an' by the white streak on his flank I heap savvy it's Peon — that's the hoss Longrope's ridin'. When I get close he whinners pitiful-like; he's lookin' for sympathy, an' I notice, when he turns to face me, his right foreleg's broke. He's sure a sorry sight with that fancy, full-stamped, center-fire saddle hangin' under his belly in the mud.

"While I'm lookin' him over, my hoss cocks his ears to the right, snortin' low. This scares me — I'm afeared to look. Somethin' tells me I won't see Longrope, only part of him — that part

[135]

that stays here on earth when the man's gone. Bracin' up, I foller my hoss's ears, an' there in the holler of the 'royo is a patch of yeller; it's part of a slicker. I spur up to get a better look over the bank, an' there tromped in the mud is all there is left of Longrope. Pullin' my gun, I empty her in the air. This brings the boys that are follerin' on the trail from the bed-ground. Nobody'd had to tell 'em we'd had hell; so they come in full force, every man but the cook an' hoss-wrangler.

"Nobody feels like talkin'. It don't matter how rough men are — I've known 'em that never spoke without cussin', that claimed to fear neither God, man, nor devil — but let death visit camp an' it puts 'em thinkin'. They generally take their hats off to this old boy that comes everywhere an' any time. He's always ready to pilot you — willin' or not — over the long dark trail that folks don't care to travel. He's never welcome, but you've got to respect him.

" 'It's tough — damned tough,' says Spanish, raisin' poor Long-rope's head an' wipin' the mud from his face with his neck-handkerchief, tender, like he's feared he'll hurt him. We find his hat tromped in the mud not fur from where he's layin'. His scabbard's empty, an' we never do locate his gun.

"That afternoon when we're countin' out the herd to see if we're short any, we find a steer with a broken shoulder an' another with a hole plumb through his nose. Both these is gun wounds; this accounts for them flashes I see in the night. It looks like, when Longrope gets mixed in the mill, he tries to gun his way out, but the cattle crowd him to the bank an' he goes over. The chances are he was dragged from his hoss in a tangle of horns.

"Some's for takin' him to Dodge an' gettin' a box made for him, but Old Spanish says: 'Boys, Longrope is a prairie man, an' if she was a little rough at times, she's been a good foster mother. She cared for him while he's awake; let her nurse him in his sleep.' So we wrapped him in his blankets, an' put him to bed.

"It's been twenty years or more since we tucked him in with the end-gate of the bed-wagon for a headstone, which the cattle have long since rubbed down, leavin' the spot unmarked. It sounds lonesome, but he ain't alone, 'cause these old prairies has cradled many of his kind in their long sleep."

VIII · BULLS AND THE BLOOD CALL

*To hearty Kate Stoner (Mrs. Thomas) O'Connor,
contributor to Texas civilization, who in her ranch
home gave me the idea for this chapter.*

> Way down on Sam Bonello,
>   Long time ago,
> Big black bull run down in the meader,
>   Long time ago.
> He pawed up dust and then he beller,
>   Long time ago,
> Shook his head and jarred the water,
>   Long time ago.
>   — *Negro song of a long time ago, South Texas.*

IN WINTER TIME the bulls kept apart, some individuals staying utterly alone, others ranging together in small bunches, looking upon each other with lack-luster eye, hardly looking at cows at all, not one moved by the faintest intimation of a dream from the sources of his bullhood. But by the time the grass was up high enough to afford whole mouthfuls, even the draggiest old bull had the feeling that the sun rose for his particular benefit, while at the same time the "shelliest" old cow shed her poverty-bedraggled hair and came into ambitions that made her forget the misery of suckling a calf on weak weed-tips in front of a February norther.

A seasonable spring was becoming summer in some year before 1890. Any ranch in the southern half of Texas might be taken as the setting, but to please my own memories we'll particularize one on Ramireña Creek in the county of Live Oak, about the season when the wild turkeys began chasing grasshoppers around sand-hill plums and the mustang grapes were big and hard enough for nigger-shooter bullets.

A brindle bull, six or seven years old, at the apex of his prowess, had been hanging around the Ramirez water hole for hours. His powerful neck showed a great bulge just behind the head. He had a big dewlap accenting his primeval origin. He had drunk but was by no means water-logged, for he belonged to a breed that knew what it was to drink only once every three days and then walk directly for hours back to grass. Over-eating or over-drinking would never allow those powerfully muscled foreparts and lithe flanks.

Three or four other bulls were among the cattle, perhaps a hundred and fifty head, resting in the vicinity. But Brindle paid little attention to them. They knew their places and they regarded him as impersonally as did the cows, heifers, calves and steers. A bull does not cut out a bunch of cows, herd them together and claim them for his own, as a stallion claims mares, fighting all other stallions away. His promiscuity destroys loyalty in both himself and the cows. He is free of the jealousy that goes with loyalty. He has no cohesive following. The dominion of a champion fighter of the range was territorial, the other bulls in that territory recognizing his prowess but being free to go their own ways with any cows that showed them favor.

A majority of the cattle this day at the Ramirez water hole were lying down or standing in the shade, out of sight of Brindle, chewing their cuds. Yet all, by the way they turned their heads and now and then ceased their cud-chewing to listen, indicated an interest in him — the acknowledged bull of their woods. The woods consisted of prairie land running into and islanded with thorny thickets and of noble live oaks overtopping mesquites, hackberries, granjeno, brazil and other growth along the creek bottom.

Brindle had been calling plenty of attention to himself. He seemed mad through and through, though it was not in his nature to vent his rage — a rage sullen and reserved — on just any member of society that got in his way. Utterly oblivious for the time of the world animate and inanimate, male and female, around him, he went on nursing his wrath to keep it warm against some contester worthy of his mettle that might emerge from beyond the rim of his acknowledged domain.

Having taken a position on a rise of open ground perhaps a hundred yards up from the water hole, he had for a long while been pawing dirt from an old bull-scrape in the soft soil — a sink about like a buffalo wallow. He lifted the dirt with his forefeet so that it went high up in the air and fell in part upon his own back. While pawing, he often stopped to hook one of his horns — the "master horn," as Spanish bull-fighters call it — into the ground, goring down to a kind of clayish damp that stuck to the tip. He even hooked both horns in, one at a time, and, kneeling, rubbed his shoulder against the bank of the wallow. At times the uplifted dirt from his flexible ankles came down in clumps and dust on tossing horns. The powerful lungs in his body, free from choking fat, bellowsed out streams of breath that sprayed particles of earth away from his nostrils. Now, earth daubing his horns, matting his shaggy frontlet, and covering his back from head to tail, he was a spectacle.

[141]

But pawing and dirt-hooking were nothing compared to his vocal goings-on. When he came in to water, he was talking to himself, his truculent head swaying with the rhythm of his walk and the weight of his thick horns. Hoarse and deep, like thunder on the horizon, his mumbling talk went *uh-uh-uh-uh*, four deliberate notes, the last a low-descending jerk, in four steps. This was his war march. Often he stayed the throaty *uh-uh-uh-uhing* and halted to raise his head in a loud, high, defiant challenge that might be described as a basso-scream, combining a bellow from the uttermost profundities with a shriek high and foreign. Beside the water hole a fat two-year-old calico-colored heifer craved his attention, but only by a few curls and astounding twists of his upward-pointing nose after he smelled of her did he seem aware of her existence. His mind was on other things.

Thus now, pawing up dirt, lunging his horn in as if to rip out the guts of the earth, bawling, bellowing, muttering, shattering the air, Brindle was sending his threats, his oaths of revenge, his challenge to earth and hell, too, over the hills, against the echoing caliche cliffs on the far side of the Ramireña, and up a little canyon that emptied into the creek just above the water hole. As his fury waxed, he now and then let out in quick succession a series of far-carrying bawls, agonizing — yet fascinating — to human senses, for they seemed to be tearing the very lungs out of the bawler.

Then at what seemed the zenith of this ecstasy of rage he heard something that infuriated the bottommost reserve of passion.

"He shook his head and jarred the water."

What he heard was an answer to his prayer, a response to his invitation, a defiance of his boasted power, a mockery of his challenge. The sounds were coming from the prairie divide between Ramireña and Lagarto creeks, the eager-for-battle maker of them having been lured from his trail to another watering.

He could not be seen yet, but he was drawing nearer. *Uh-uh-uh-uh*, and then mighty throatings, growling a deep and hollow roar.

At length he came into view, a glossy dunnish-brown merging into black — the *golondrino* (swallow) color — white speckles and splotches on his rump and a washed-out copper line down his back. His thick horns, like Brindle's, were set forward for tossing a lobo wolf into the air or ripping any kind of belly open as effectively as that scimitar-curved plebeian Mexican knife called *saca tripas* (gets the guts).

It was a belief that the bulls kept their horns sharpened for bloody work by rubbing them against trees and brush and whetting them in the ground. A hundred yards off, the *golondrino* bull stopped and went to pawing dirt, answering bellow for bellow. He not only gored the earth but thrust his horns into the tough stems of a cenizo bush and, jerking and twisting his head from side to side, broke the bush to stubble. He came nearer, but the preliminaries were long-drawn-out, each warrior practising his thrusts, each seeming to wait for the other to take upon himself the war-guilt of the first assault, yet neither wearing himself out with exercise. This bullying was more than sound and fury; back of it lay immense reserve.

Brindle emerged from his wallow. Then he and Golondrino began to circle one another, each fronting his antagonist and maneuvering for an opening. They halted perhaps four yards apart. Meanwhile the other cattle had congregated, keeping well out of the way, and with sympathetic bawlings were adding to the atmosphere. Yet more cattle, attracted like boys to a dogfight, came stringing in at a trot from far away. The big steers, which often seem to imagine themselves bulls and which no bull ever notices, were especially interested.

Now the time for talk by the champions was over. The object of each was to get a side entrance for a horn, but each was a master of defense. At the simultaneous lunge that brought them together, the impact of skull against skull and horn against horn made an air-shattering report like that when an iron-headed freight car is rammed into the iron of another car. Then, heads locked, the bulls stood planted in the soil, neither giving away to the other. Shoulder muscles stood out like bronze studies; massive neck thews rose almost to the height of humps on Brahma bulls; backs curved tensely, the downward sweep of line as beautiful in its grace and strength as any curve of nature that art ever revealed. One bull and then the other tried a quick side step to unbalance his opponent and get in a side thrust, but neither could win the advantage. With horns that were both weapon and shield, they parried strokes in such rapidity that the clashes could hardly have been counted. A turkey gobbler went to gobbling in his ridiculous way at each fresh impact of horns. The bulls backed and rushed again and again. The dust they raised went up into the air like a signal smoke. The ground they fought over was torn up as if giants with spikes and spades on their feet had wrestled there.

The shovings, the head-on lunges, the dodges, the impregnable stands went on and on. The heat of the strain brought slobber to mouths, and tongues lolled out. Eyes, bloodshot, bulged forth. Once Brindle's horn brought blood from a tear — which, however, he was not allowed to take advantage of — in Golondrino's brisket. The smell of blood was caught by an old blue steer among the surrounding cattle and the blood cry went up and volumed in a discordant chorus. The throng of cattle now congregated were as uneasy and excited as a million robins gathered to migrate from the cedar brakes of the Colorado River to their summer homes on the Atlantic coast two thousand miles north. A coyote came to peer from behind a prickly pear bush up the ridge.

The sun swung low. The wild turkeys disappeared. The bulls backed off from each other and pawed up dust. Then with hearts still pumping against bursting lungs, they clashed again. Darkness came.

Often the battle was a draw, ending only from sheer exhaustion on both sides. Once a bull realized he was outdone, he backed as if shot out of a catapult, wheeled with a loud snuff, and ran for life. If he ran fast enough, his opponent could at best merely hook him in the rump — a spur to added swiftness. Let the victor get a side run at him, then he might knock him down and gore the vitals out of him. Death, while not frequent, was sometimes the end of a day-long battle.

Against an old bull a young one had the advantage of endurance; cunning acquired from many experiences often gave victory to a waning bull pitted against some youngster with more strength and bravery than science. If this youngster was not killed, his day would come. He was acquiring experience. The whole activity — aside from eating — of a high grade Hereford bull, despite his big horns, is begetting calves; at least half the activity of the Longhorn range bull was in battle. Fighting was the breath of life to him.

Despite front attacks, I have never heard of a bull's hooking his opponent's eye out — a tribute to parrying powers. A vaquero of other days told me that he once saw a wild bull gore another through the top of the neck. The horn went clear through that thickest part of the bull's thick hide. It was so deeply twisted in and the hide was so unyielding that for a considerable time the bulls were fastened together not unlike bucks with interlocked antlers.

Although it is not the nature of cattle to graze and move about at night like horses, the Longhorns were much more given to night activity than domesticated varieties. When bulls fought at night, then their bellowing and roaring, the bawling of other cattle, the hoarse howls of lobo wolves aroused by hope for a victim as they restlessly circled out from the fighters, and the long-drawn-out cries of coyotes beyond the lobos gave the prairie a truly weird character.

It is impossible to convey sounds in print — the wild, raucous hair-raising sounds made by the old range bulls; their growls; their threats loud and deep that seemed to blast the earth; their uplifted notes carrying like the finest coyote bark; their expressions of pride and fury. But imagine them coming down a thicket or over the prairie grass in the deep night.

All you can do is imagine. "The Spanish bull that used to water at the seep spring at the foot of the hill no longer makes the canyon roar with the echoes of his bellowing."

When a herd of cattle was rounded up from a wide-spreading range, thus bringing into proximity bulls that were strangers to one another, each of them a big frog in his own little puddle, there was sure to be raging and roaring, and fighting was inevitable unless the opponents were separated before they actually clashed horns. "Prayer meeting" was the name an old Negro hand used to give these carryings-on of the bulls. "Jes' listen to 'um testifyin'," he'd say. A "prayer meeting" of this kind made working in a herd both difficult and dangerous. Any responsible cowman would break it up before zeal ran too high.

At one fight that started in a herd, John Rigby saw a cow get in the way just at the moment the bulls simultaneously rushed at each other. One rammed his horns into her belly from one side and one from the other. She was lifted high up and came down dying.

The worst danger of a fight was when one of the bulls decided to quit. His sole purpose then was to get away. Running from his opponent, he would have his eyes and attention on the brute behind him, trusting to his own power to get through or over any obstacle in front. Not many men had the foolhardiness to try to ride in to separate the fighters, for though a man might stop the fight, he was liable to be in the way of the flight. One man was working with some cattle a short distance off from two engaged bulls, not keeping an eye on them, when suddenly one broke away, rammed into his horse, killing it and crippling him for life.

Ask any old-time range man of the south country to name the quickest animal he has ever known. He won't say a cutting horse, a polo pony, a wild cat, a striking rattlesnake. He doesn't know the duck hawk. He will say a Longhorn bull. Some other bulls are quick; many breeds fight, even the Polled Angus. But none of them can bawl, bellow, mutter and rage like the bulls of Spanish breed and none can move with such swiftness.

I know of no contemporary photograph revealing a bull of the Texas Longhorns, on his own range, in the day of his dominion. A few American artists attempted him, but without the intimate knowledge or the power that vivify the canvases of Goya and lesser Spanish masters who glorified his forebears in multiplied attitudes and situations. The type, because it produced the greatest fighters of the taurine world, is, in its ancient and undiluted purity, still represented in the bull rings of Spain, Mexico and the Argentine.

The bullfight the range people delighted in was on the range itself. Like scattered cattle, riders were often called to the battles from afar. Boys, usually without sanction from the profit-lusting cattle owners, would drive a proven champion to where he could meet a contester. On Sunday, sometimes quite an aggregation of boys and men would gather for a prearranged combat, bringing champions from distant areas to some watering place, where other cattle could add to the show. Voices as well as fighting power were highly regarded. At branding time any fighting cow's bull-calf that demonstrated bravado, alacrity, strength and lusty lungs was likely to be branded and let loose uncastrated to make a fighting bull.

If a bull decided he would not be driven from his range, no matter for what purpose, that was an end of the matter; but the herd instinct usually made him tractable in the company of other cattle. Yet not always. On the Stoner ranch in the Victoria, Texas, country there used to be a bull named Frank

Swift. He was called after the man who raised him, an individual with the habit of swallowing at one gulp a whole handful of the fiery little red Mexican peppers. Frank Swift was in color a dark dun running into white. Every once in a while he would be put in a herd bound for the shipping pens at Victoria, but he never got there. When he was ready to turn back, he turned; and the only way to stop him would have been to shoot him. Of course his horns might have been chopped off and then he might have been necked to some powerful lead ox and dragged to the pens. After such punishment he would hardly have been worth the freight — and certainly not the trouble. Once Frank Swift traveled to within sight of the pens, and the cowboys thought he was on his way sure, this time, to make canned beef. Then he changed his mind about taking another step forward. He was the champion fighter and bellower of the country, and these virtues saved his life.

The horn of a fighting bull has the penetrating power of a spike driven by a sledgehammer. "Many times," says Ernest Hemingway in his treatise on bulls and bullfighting, *Death in the Afternoon*, "I have seen a bull attack the inch-thick wooden planks of the *barrera* with his horns, or horn rather, for he uses either the one or the other, and splinter the planks into bits. There is in the bull ring museum at Valencia a heavy iron stirrup that a bull perforated with a horn stroke to the depth of four inches."

No reader of the chapter on "The First Spanish Cattle" will have forgotten Colonel Philip Saint George Cooke's account of the charge by wild bulls on the Mormon Battalion. Hemingway cites a Spanish work called *Toros Celebres* "which chronicles the manner of dying and the feats of some three hundred and twenty-two pages of celebrated bulls" of the ring. Such a volume might be compiled on celebrated fighting bulls of the range.

Afraid of nothing on earth, their bravery was almost unearthly. They not only joyed in combat with each other but

[148]

sought combat with other beasts and with man himself. Nat Straw, grizzly hunter of New Mexico, told me that he was in the Black Range when cattle, Longhorns from Texas, were introduced in that region. Then, he said, the grizzly bear — *Ursus horribilis* — met the first living beast, the bull, it had ever known that would not give way to it.

Jack Thorp and another cowboy were chousing horses up the bed of Sacramento River, in New Mexico, one day when they came upon a red Longhorn bull, about six years old, that they both knew well; each had more than once given him the trail as he came down to water.

"As we rode around him now," Jack Thorp related, "and saw him standing so quiet, we noticed one eye was gone and a great patch of hide and hair hanging down from his back just behind the shoulders. His foreparts were badly clawed. Both horns were covered with dried blood.

"About halfway up the steep trail was a flat — a little bench — at a sharp turn. Here the horses ahead of us snorted and broke away into the brush. Jumping ahead to turn them back, we noticed how the shin-oak over a big patch of ground had been broken down and the earth turned up. Then I found a monstrous grizzly, lying across a fallen log, his entrails strung out on the ground and his hair matted with dried blood. The bull, even if he didn't come off unmarked, had very plainly horned this grizzly bear to death. Yes, that Longhorn bull got well all right, but being one-eyed kind of cramped his style."

Back in the eighties a dun line-backed bull on the Cross S range in the Brush Country of Texas achieved a wide reputation. Like a few other exceptional individuals of his stripe, he would waylay trails and attack horsemen from the rear. One time, Jake English was riding along close to a thicket when the dun bull rushed upon him and ripped the guts out of his horse almost before horse or man knew the bull was in the vicinity. Unhurt, Jake English climbed a little tree. The tree went to falling and Jake thought his time had come, but the bull at this juncture made off. He had, it is claimed, worn out four rawhide riatas strung on him by men who had to cut loose, and had killed ten horses before he finally took up with some milk cows and came to the pen of a rancher who shot him dead.

While "cleaning up" a big pasture on the King Ranch, vaqueros found that an outlaw bull, his breed signified by the "lobo stripe" down his back, habitually approached a water trough by a trail leading under a live oak tree. One evening two of them tied their horses in brush a considerable distance away from the trail and climbed up in the tree with the idea of roping the bull when he passed underneath. After waiting a good while, they heard a horse shriek and other sounds of commotion. Rushing to their horses, they saw the bull goring one to death, the other one already dead. The bull had smelled these animals and, knowing from experience that they carried his enemies, had rushed upon them. A day or two later a vaquero shot the bull.

When R. J. Kleberg decided to "clean up" and bring into subjection the brushiest part — then a veritable frontier jungle — of the great King Ranch, of which he was manager, he had a small pasture built around Tularosa Lake, leaving wide gaps open for the cattle to come in. The first night the gaps were closed, he captured four thousand head of wild cattle. The next morning his outfit lost all of them, except a few that were roped, trying to drive them away. The next trap he made caught hundreds of wild horses intermixed with the cattle. When the vaqueros started to work the stock, the wild bulls took charge of the herd like stallions trained to guard *manadas* of mares. They advanced to the front, rushed at the vaqueros, and in the melee gored to death several of the wild horses.

Some few bulls seemed to be positive man-haters. One of them might charge a campfire, the sign of man. Bob (R. D.)

Routh, who was born in Collin County, Texas, in 1854, told me about a black and white bull that was the terror of his boyhood. This bull would make for any person he saw on foot. Once he put Bob Routh up a tree and kept him there for hours. One morning before daylight a ranchman of the vicinity sent "a feller named Smith" out afoot to bring in some gentle horses. It was noon before Smith got back. He was a sight, his clothes torn and caked with blood and cow dung.

The ranchman looked at him coldly and said, "How've you spent the morning?"

"Killing that bull," Smith replied.

"By God, that's a valuable bull, and if you've killed him there's going to be trouble."

"He won't make no more trouble and he ain't valuable no more," Smith said.

While day was still dawning, he explained, he saw the bull rushing towards him on the bald open prairie, not a tree in half a mile. He knew something about bulls. At the charge, head down, the bull shut his eyes, and Smith stepped aside. The bull went by, wheeled and came again. After several such passes, Smith got out his "frog-sticker" and as the bull came by again jabbed at him. Time after time, as the sun climbed high, he cut into the tough bull-hide. Finally he got the knife into the entrails. After the bull went to stepping on them, he stopped, reeled, and sank. Smith was ready to sink too.

That encounter makes me think of knife-to-paw contests between Mountain Men and grizzlies — in which the man did not always win.

Years ago, a man-hating bull ranged in the vicinity of the Fronteriza Mine in mountains facing the Rio Grande on the Mexico side. He was a blend of gold, brown and black colors — the *hosco-golondrino*. At the base of his neck he had an enormous hump; curly thick hair from his forehead almost covered his eyes.

One day a Mexican goat herder was coming into the Tinaja de los Alamos driving a burro loaded with provisions when this bull, loitering at the water hole, saw him. Immediately he charged, killing both burro and man. As sign was afterward read, he smeared himself with the man's blood and caused a great commotion among the other cattle. During days that followed he returned several times to the water hole, trampling the remains of the man and hooking them about but paying no attention to the dead burro. Don Alberto Guajardo eventually shot the bull, using more than twenty .30-.30 bullets on him before he brought him down.

"On skinning him," Don Alberto wrote me, "I observed that he had several bullets in the hide and flesh near his left ear. I deduced that other hunters had tried to kill him. Perhaps for this reason he was so spiteful towards man."

Yet range bulls killed very few men. Even in Texas, the number of people gored by Longhorn bulls over a period of a hundred years was probably less than the number gored by Jersey bulls in recent decades. Sam Allen, who in the course of time handled hundreds of thousands of Texas cattle, is said to have offered ten thousand dollars to the widow of any man working for him killed by a bull. The offer may have added to the bravery of some of his hands. He never had to make it good.

Some cowboys would get in a pen with a fighting bull and dare him by making feints with a hat or a ducking jacket, as a matador uses his cape in the bull ring. Morris Mack, a Negro of the San Bernard, would squat down in the pen with any bull that raged. "Bull won't know what you is when you squat," Morris Mack explained. "Then he'll be scairt." Maybe so. One old rawhide I knew would get down on his all-fours and paw up dirt, mocking with bellowings the bull in front of him. He was a curiosity to man as well as to beast. A man on horseback charged by a bull couldn't squat or paw up dirt.

Ernest Hemingway discredits the popular idea that a bull

charges with eyes shut whereas a cow keeps hers open. Nevertheless, range men experienced in handling fierce cattle have always been more leery of a fighting cow in a pen than of a fighting bull.

Many a Longhorn cow would not wait for the drop of a hat to fight. She was all pluck and vinegar, as ready as a fighting cock for the chance to use her spurs. She would fight a circular saw, fight "six yoke of oxen, the hired man and a breaking plow," fight anything. The bravest bulls came from brave cows. Of course, however, no cow has the strength of a bull. Cows do not fight bulls, as the females of most species fight the males.

Jack Thorp, who told of the bull that killed a grizzly, was driving years ago with his wife from Albuquerque to Santa Fe in one of Henry Ford's earliest models, the foreparts trimmed brilliantly with brass. The car was laboring up a steep mountain, radiator boiling, hugging the bank of a road so narrow that cars could pass each other only at bends, when Jack saw, almost falling over herself as she tore down the road, an old Longhorn cow — one of several thousand from the Terrazas herds in Chihuahua that had been turned loose in that country. There was no room to get out of her way. She did not propose to get out of anybody's way. She hooked one horn into the radiator and the other under it, raised the front part of the car up and struggled until the rear end hung in the bank. Only after water boiled out on her head did she disengage herself.

In talking of bulls I have dwelt long on their wonderful utterances. No wild animal, or domestic either, that I know of has as many vocal tones as the Longhorn. In comparison, the bulls and cows of highly bred varieties of cattle are voiceless. The cow of the Longhorns has one *moo* for her newborn calf, another for it when it is older, one to tell it to come to her side and another to tell it to stay hidden in the tall grass. Moved by amatory feelings, she has a low audible breath of yearning. In anger she can run a gamut. If her calf has died or been otherwise taken from her, she seems to be turning her insides out into long, sharp, agonizing bawls. I have heard steers make similar sounds. They seemed to be in the utmost agony of expressing something so poignant to them that the utterance meant more than life and would be willingly paid for by death.

The bawling of thirsty cattle used to be all too familiar a sound on ranches before wells and tanks became plentiful and the gasoline engine was devised to pump water when the wind fails to blow. Day and night, day and night, it would go on around empty water troughs, the moans getting weaker in time, though the endurance of a cow brute in keeping up a continual bawling would make insignificant the record of any long-winded filibuster that ever held the floor of Congress. Cattle walking a fence in futile anxiety to get back to a range they have been driven from make the same distressful, relentless sounds.

There was something almost refreshing in the lusty bawl of a big bull-calf being branded. The "gosling stage" voice of a bull yearling was positively ridiculous. An old stag or bull, when wounded, would stick his tongue out a full foot and bawl so loud that cattle two miles away would turn to listen.

The mingled bawls and lowings, each of a different pitch and timbre, of a big herd of mixed cattle held forcibly while hungry and thirsty after a day of being ginned about, frantic heifers and headstrong old cows separated from their calves, calves in misery for their mothers, yearlings adding to the din in the same way that each of forty babies will go to crying if one opens up, steers bawling for their lost powers of masculinity or for the same reason that great Arctic wolves bay at the midnight sun or from some urge that only God is aware of, bulls bellowing at the memory of past combats or maybe without memory at all — all make a kind of music to many a cowman's ears, especially at a distance.

Bill Halsell was a cowman of the old Texas breed that held their ranges against Comanches and their cattle against thieves; he fought his hardest fights, though, against blizzards and drouths. At last he lay a-dying in faraway California. His friend Charles A. Jones of the **S M S** Ranch went to the hospital to see him.

"I'm not long for this country, Charlie," the old cowman said.

There was a pause. Then he added, "Before I leave there's one thing I'd like mighty well to experience again. I've been wishing for it for days. You couldn't guess what it is."

"Well, no, but I imagine it has to do with ranching."

"Yes, that's right. I'd like to be away out yonder where it's quiet and roomy and the wind is blowing over mesquite grass. Then just one more time I'd like to hear an old Texas bull beller down the canyon. Don't talk to me about a lot of taller-faced angels singing hymns."

But no cattle voicings, not even those attending a bullfight, ever had the power, the might and the terror of the massed blood call. In *The Naturalist in La Plata*, W. H. Hudson has described it well.

Out on the pampas of the Argentine, stocked with Spanish cattle in countless numbers, Hudson came one morning to a spot where thieves had butchered a cow during the night, leaving the ground soaked with blood.

"A herd of cattle numbering about three hundred head appeared, moving slowly on towards a small stream a mile away. They were traveling in a thin line, and would pass the blood-stained spot at a distance of seven or eight hundred yards, but the wind from it would blow across their track. When the tainted wind struck the leaders of the herd, they instantly stood still, raising their heads, then broke out into loud excited bellowing; and, finally turning, they started off at a fast trot, following up the scent in a straight line until they arrived at the place where one of their kind had met its death. The contagion spread, and before long all the cattle were congregated on the fatal spot, and began moving round in a dense mass, bellowing continually.

"It may be remarked here that the animal has a peculiar language on occasions like this; it emits a succession of short bellowing cries, like excited exclamations, followed by a very loud cry, alternately sinking into a hoarse murmur, and rising to a kind of scream that grates harshly on the sense. Of the ordinary 'cow music' I am a great admirer, and take as much pleasure in it as in the cries and melody of birds and the sound of the wind in the trees; but this performance of cattle excited by the smell of blood is most distressing to hear.

"The animals that had forced their way into the center of the mass to the spot where the blood was, pawed the earth, and dug it up with their horns, and trampled each other down in their frantic excitement. It was terrible to see and hear them. The action of those on the border of the living mass in perpetually moving round in a circle with dolorous bellowings was like that of the women in an Indian village when a warrior dies and all night they shriek and howl with simulated grief, going round and round the dead man's hut in an endless procession."

One of the memories I shall carry to the last is of cattle congregating around a blood-soaked cowhide that had been thrown, the flesh side up, over a pen fence. It had been flung there at the end of a summer day, after most of the cattle watering at troughs in the pen had gone out to graze in the cool of the evening. But two or three latecomers smelled the hide. They began to bellow. Cattle not yet grazed out beyond hearing came to the sounds in a trot, adding to the wild utterances. Cattle beyond them heard and came too, calling yet others from parts

of the pasture watered by another well. By dark between two and three hundred cattle were milling and carrying on, bawling their lungs out and making such a to-do that we could hardly eat our suppers in the rock house a hundred and fifty yards up the hill.

The primitive excitement produced by the strong scent of fresh gore was what enabled hunters to kill sometimes as many as a hundred buffaloes at a single stand. Utterly without sympathy for the dying or dead buffalo, its associates would become so crazed by the blood smell that they would stamp and "carry on" around the bleeding carcasses until the hunter, who began with the wind in his favor and remained hidden, had slaughtered them all.

After Mexicans had roped and waylaid outlaw cattle for generations, a cowman named Mike Carrigan conceived the idea of utilizing the blood call. He was ranging a large number of big steers in a big country where thorns are as thick as the hair on a dog's back.

One evening before he began gathering to ship, he saved a bucket of blood from a butchered beef. Early next morning he carried it to an open spot where steers bedded every night, poured it on the ground, drove a few gentle steers — gentle enough to get in sight of and hold in a herd — to where the blood had been spilled, hid his men in a thicket, and then let nature work. Those beeves set up a bellering — a word much more expressive than "bellowing" — and a bawling that soon drew five hundred of their kind to the stomping grounds. Among them were mossy-horns that for years had hardly been in a place open enough to hold their shadows. Carrigan's vaqueros now slipped out of their hiding and had a herd together before the steers knew work was started. Old Mike Carrigan used to call this method "gathering cattle de luxe."

Claude McGill could imitate the blood call and draw cattle to him. Jack Maltsberger conceived the idea of a blowing horn that would give the blood calls. I have seen him blow it and bring up a bunch of cattle that by their own agitated responses would drown out a foghorn.

Yet by no means did every hide or whiff of blood excite such demonstrations. Often the blood was almost unnoticed and mass meetings over it were comparatively rare. It was not sorrow over the death of a fellow being that excited the blood call. The feelings of pity and sympathy are unknown to bovine nature. The poorest cow staggering up to where feed has been put out is the one that all her fellow creatures will hook. The "smell of mortality" seems to have little effect on cattle. The "cow funerals" that the little McKee girls used to listen to on the Brazos prairies were not from pity or mourning.

I cannot be absolute, but all the evidence I have on the subject leads to the conclusion that, of bloods, cow blood alone has the power to awaken the terror both expressed and aroused by the blood call. Yet occasionally an old cow, sniffing the bleached bone of a disassembled skeleton, perhaps with intent of chewing on it — for cattle are cannibalistic to the extent of eating the dried bones of their kind — might suddenly let out that unearthly combination of scream and bellow that brought other cattle from all directions to join in an orgy of sounds more timber-shaking than the unrelenting tom-toms of an African jungle through the longest night that ever throbbed.

Superb as it may be, the mounting of animals in museums without representation of their voices leaves out something very characteristic and dramatic. Will nobody mount me a brindle bull and add to him the call of blood and the bellow of battle?

IX · COWS AND CURIOSITY

To my dear and delightful brother, Elrich H. Dobie.
I could get more milk from the cows, but he was
champion at riding the calves.

IN THE FEMALE of the species, responsible for rearing the young, instinct is generally stronger than in the male. It was markedly strong in the Longhorn cow. The only help the bull ever gave the young was in hooking off wolves or other predatory animals. Before entering a swift stream, the cow maneuvered to place her calf on the lower side, thus protecting it against the force of the current.

She was cunning in hiding her calf, and even though she might be a gentle milk cow, her fixed purpose was to prevent anyone's seeing her infant before it was strong enough to run.

A child or a dog coming near the concealed calf stood in danger of attack. A man might watch the cow for hours, intent on finding where her calf was hidden, but so long as she knew she was watched, she would stay away from it. Wild or gentle, she would do her best to keep from being driven far from the vicinity of the calf. She might be driven a certain distance; then the only way, as a rule, to get her a step farther was to drag her.

"General" Sears was not a cowman; he was a tenderfoot acting as a cowboy. "One day," he records, "I was driving a herd of [Texas] range cattle towards the ranch house on the Arkansas River, when suddenly a cow dodged out of the herd and ran towards the hills. I followed and tried to drive her back. I did not know at the time that she had a young calf concealed in the grass in the hills. . . . Suddenly she became enraged and quickly turned and charged, and before my pony could get out of the way, she drove her sharp, slender horns through its breast, causing its death within a few minutes. I drew my revolver, intending to shoot the cow, but she walked quietly away. I had to carry my heavy cowboy saddle about three miles." [1]

Frank Wilkeson's cows habitually went into the dense, tall grass of a certain bottom land to bring forth their young, and there they would keep their calves hidden until they were three or four days old. "Once," he says,[2] "I desired to see the young calves and rode into the grass to hunt for them. After assiduous search I found one calf lying prone upon the earth, its head and neck pressed into the thick mat of old grass that lay on the ground. The little creature lay perfectly quiet, watching my horse. It did not so much as wink its dark eyes when I dismounted and extended my hand towards it. I leaned over it. It watched me intently but did not stir. I dropped my hand upon its head. Instantly it was on its feet and calling loudly for protection, calling that the wolf . . . had come.

"I heard twenty mother cows bellow in answer. The dry grass

[161]

snapped and cracked in all directions as the maddened cows rushed to their young. I mounted my horse and rode quickly away from that spot. Each cow ran in a direct line to the place where her calf was hidden. The entire herd grazing out from the covert rushed thither. What an uproar there was! Cows, bulls, steers, all calling loudly in angry, excited tones. I had a foolish setter dog with me. . . . The first cow that saw him bellowed to the others that she saw the wolf. They all pursued him, and he, doglike, fled to me for protection. They gave me a brisk chase as I galloped over the prairie. The herd was angry and excited for hours."

As a boy I had the task of going out horseback of an evening and driving up the milk cows. There were certain cows that we milked year after year; breaking new ones was troublesome, and we had tested many to select the best milkers. Out in "the big pasture" I would occasionally find one of the gentle cows that had just calved and that I wanted to bring in. If her calf was not visible, I would hang around her for an hour or two hoping against experience that she would go to it; I would imitate the distressed bleat of a calf; she would remain utterly indifferent. Finally, my animosity aroused by her stubborn calmness, I would start her towards the ranch and then when she refused to go farther would run her, knowing that she wouldn't — but hoping that she would — go to the calf. Sometimes I would "chouse the daylights out of her." Her patience was always longer than mine, though if I found her with her calf and it could walk, she could be worried to the pens she knew so well.

I remember a pen full of these cows with affection. There was Pet, a black cow splotched with blue-white patches, that we children had ridden when she was a calf and that always raised excellent saddle calves. There was Old Paint, with a crumpled horn and undying fire in her spirit; a strain of Holstein blood made her give more milk than any other two cows we had. There was Hookey, a red with brindle marks so faint that they barely showed except when she was wet from rain; she would never allow our dog Joe in the pen, and one time she tossed my sister Fannie into the air. Muley, a little, meek, long-haired roan, could be imposed upon to raise any orphaned calf we put with her; she mothered dogies every spring and the adopted calf always got more milk than her own. Old Sabina, speckled red and white, had an excess of ticks and her horns had been sawed off in order to cure her of the "hollow horn." Clabber — a white cow, of course — was as patient as any ox and never kicked, but her tail was so long and active that it was tied to her legs during the milking operations.

I can see the cows now, chewing their cuds and licking their calves; I can see the blackbirds picking ticks off them. I can smell their strong, good, wholesome breaths. I can hear the placid but affectionate *moos* with which each calf was greeted as it came through the gate from the calf pen to suck until the teats were well moistened and the flow of milk started, then to be tied off while white streams were squeezed musically into the buckets. In blood these cows were far superior to straight Mexican cows, but the best qualities of the Longhorn were dominant in them. What mothers they and their type were!

The newborn calf of a Longhorn cow would bristle up at the presence of a shepherd dog and run; a pedigreed Durham calf will walk innocently up to any kind of dog and smell of it, hunting for milk. The Longhorn calf, if chased away from its lair during the absence of its mother, would, like a fawn or a kid antelope, go back to the spot where it last suckled, there to await its dam. Unless dead or in prison, she would meet it.

If particularly wild or cautious, she would, upon approaching the spot where she had left her calf, give only a low *moo* that carried well to its ears but not to others. However, if she became separated from her calf in a herd, then she would almost bawl her insides out. There are few sounds more distressing than the continual bawling of a cow for her calf.

The expression "cow talk" usually means talk by cowmen about cows, but cows of the Texas breed were at times as forcible in their own talk as in gestures. John Lomax tells a story that brings in this talk.

A few years ago he went to the **S M S** cowboy reunion at Stamford, Texas. He was sitting on the ground with two old waddies, Jeff Hanna and Ed Nichols, watching the performance in the arena below, when he noticed Will Rogers almost by his side. Rogers had slipped in unannounced and wanted to watch instead of being watched. However, he was glad to see Lomax and gladder still to meet the veteran cowhands that Lomax introduced.

"How long you been out in this country, Jeff?" Will Rogers asked.

"Why, Will, when I come out here, the sun was jest about as big as a saucer." Then Jeff went on to tell about Ed Nichols.

"Now, Ed here," he said, "is one of the kindest-hearted fellers you ever see. When he was riding west from Bosque County one time, he sorter found it convenient to ride in the night."

"Uh, huh," and some winks.

"Well, he was coming along way late and the moon was down and it was as dark as the inside of a cow. He was in a bottom, down clost to a running creek, when he begun to hear a cow bawling, but he couldn't locate her. He seemed to be near her, and he knew from the way she was going on she was in trouble and appealing for help. You know how one of them old-timey cows could talk."

"She shore could," Will Rogers agreed.

"Well, d'reckly Ed here got down off his horse and begun feeling along the ground. Purty soon he come to the edge of an old well, and then he realized the cow had fell in. She didn't seem to be hurt though, from the way she was talking. Ed knew he couldn't pull her up by hisself with a rope, but he jest couldn't ride off and leave her, on account of his soft heart.

"What you guess he did? Well, as I said, he was clost to a running creek. He went to the water and got a hatful of it and brought it back and poured it in the well. He kept packing water thataway till daylight, the cow sorter floating and swimming until finally the water was high enough for her to scramble out.

"Then you know how she turned around and tried to hook Ed."

"Yea, I know" — and Will Rogers was off on the way an old cow, so poor her backbones rattled when she coughed, would, when pulled out of a bog-hole, invariably make her first wobble in an attempt to hook the man who had tailed her up.

One of the most delightful pieces of natural history pertaining to the range ever recorded is found in a chapter called "A Texas Nursery," by an educated English rancher named R. B. Townshend.[3] Riding one day over his range, still unfenced, in Colorado, he came upon a cow "lowing most mournfully and looking anxiously back over the prairie.

"That unhappy voice told plainly enough that she was in dire distress over her calf, and I galloped up to see what was wrong. She was a big white American cow, a strain of shorthorn in her veins. There, sure enough, about three hundred yards behind her, lay her newly-born calf, under the scanty shadow of a soapweed. She had been brought out from the States, and came of gentle domestic stock, too domestic, perhaps, for life on the range.

"The calf was not yet strong enough to follow its mother over the three long miles to the watering place, where all the rest had gone; and when his strength gave out he had lain down in the only bit of shade he could find. His mother, tortured by thirst, had hurried on without him, and then halted, with divided mind. Thirst pulled her feverishly on towards the water; mother love plucked at her heart-strings to drag her back to her calf. And here the poor fool had stood for an hour, making the prairie echo to her distracted wails, and telling any wolf lurking within a mile of her that the bell was ringing for his dinner.

"I dismounted beside the calf, picked him up, heaved him into the saddle, and climbed back and settled myself there with him in my lap.

"Small chance should I have had of doing it, if the mother had been one of my war-like Texas cows, a fierce, wild daughter of the desert. But this gentle, idiotic creature offered no objection; she was accustomed to devolving her maternal responsibilities on man, and she shambled along behind me with docile content, only lowing at intervals to tell her son she was there, as we made straight for the water-holes.

"There I left the pair, safe in the protection of numbers, a thousand head of range cattle being strung all up and down the creek.

"I turned back to the rolling prairie, and as I went I noticed half a dozen dun and brindle Texas cows, who had already slaked their thirst, traveling steadily away from the water in the same direction as myself. A few young heifers and steers accompanied them, though the mass of the cattle, as I well knew, would stay by the water till the heat of the day was over; but this party of long-horned, long-legged Texas ladies clearly had business elsewhere. . . . An old brindle cow with rings out to the end of her horns was leading the travelers. . . . They struck into one of the innumerable cattle trails leading from the high pastures to the water and pressed up it, traveling one close behind the other at a steady walk that occasionally became a trot. I rode parallel to them, curious to see the goal they were making for so eagerly.

"Up we went into the high rolling sand-hills, and there, in the middle of them, in a little cup-like hollow, I saw a regular nursery. Eight little dun-coloured Texas calves lay there, squatted close to the sandy ground which their coats matched so well, their heads lying out flat, with the chins pressed down on the sand, just as little antelope fawns would have crouched. In this pose they were all but invisible. Beside them lay two elderly Texas cows, whose office had been to guard the crèche.

"The mothers, who had travelled till now in perfect silence, began to low loudly and lovingly when they caught sight of their offspring, and in a moment each young hopeful had jumped up and rushed to his own dam, where his wriggling tail and nuzzling head, the busy lips frothing with milk, soon showed he was getting the dinner he had waited for so patiently. Meantime the two guardian cows had risen to their feet, and lost no time in starting off in their turn to make their trip to the water, leaving their own two calves safe in the care of the rest of the band.

"The system of mutual protection was perfect. Br'er Wolf might prowl around and watch with hungry eyes till his lips watered — there was no chance for him to get veal for his dinner while the sharp horns of those fierce Texas mothers guarded their children. Broadly speaking, one might say the Texas cow, the cow of the wilderness, evolved an institution that has enabled her and her offspring to survive the dangers of savage life.

"This institution has been long superseded by the civilized life of the farm for the well-bred shorthorn cow; but take her away from her sheltered surroundings and turn her loose on the range, and she is as helpless as most duchesses would be if left on a desert island. The pedigreed daughter of fifty prize-winners must inevitably succumb to the dangers of her new life unless she has initiative enough to revert to the social system of her own primitive ancestors who fought with the wolf and bear in the woodlands of early Britain."

The most dangerous enemy that cattle of the open range

knew was the wolf — not the coyote, which seldom molests even the tiniest calf and never thinks of attacking any animal of strength, but the lobo, which in bands brought down even old buffalo bulls cut off from the herd. The Longhorns were probably more effective against lobos than were the buffaloes. John Williams, who has for many years worked on the great lobo-infested Babícora range of western Chihuahua, and who has seen Herefords there displace the best grade of Mexican cattle, told me that he once came upon three lobos pulling down a calf; about the time he arrived on the scene, seven Mexican cows arrived also and chased the wolves into the breaks. The Mexican cattle throve and increased and multiplied surrounded by lobos, but the Herefords had to be protected; man had to kill the lobos off in order for the whitefaces to maintain existence.

There are very few lobos in the United States now, but the range is infested with a worse enemy, the disgusting screwworm. Nowadays the calves of all fine-haired animals have to be doctored against this enemy. Soon after the calf is born, blowflies deposit their eggs on its navel and, also, under the cow's tail. The Longhorn cow licked the worms out of herself and out of the calf, no medical attention from man being required. For this reason alone many a ranchman of South Texas regretted giving up the breed. If a Longhorn got worms in some part of its anatomy that it could not lick, it would, like a deer, stand for long hours in water, trying to suffocate the worms. Of course, a wound in the eye or some other part of the head could hardly be self-treated. But the long, heavy tail prevented flies from blowing many vulnerable parts of the body.

In the days of the open range it was a saying — and the saying had a basis of truth, though it might have been equally applicable to Montana, the Argentine and various other regions in between [4] — that Texas had more cows and less milk than any other country in the world. Milk was considered proper only for babies and goat herders. The babies got theirs from their mothers; the

[168]

goat herders, Mexicans supposed to be lunatics, from nannies. The fact that a poor settler with thirty cows did not get enough milk to supply clabber for soda biscuits, and that a cowman with three thousand cows could not offer cream to his guests, was not always altogether the fault of the owners. "From this Longhorn cow I got my first lessons in liquid measure," Joe Cross said.[5] "I learned from her that four gills make a pint; two pints make a quart; and four cows a gallon, provided both hind legs were tied with a rawhide tug and at least one tit was left for the calf."

Yet many ranch people did milk cows, and it was a custom among ranchers to allow poor squatters to catch up range cows, provided the borrowers would not "knock the calf in the head with a churn dasher" — would leave it a fair share of the milk. The majority of families turned their cows out during the winter, not because of the invariable lack of a stable to protect them against northers both wet and dry, but because they were going dry at this time and feed was scarce. "I don't care for milk and butter out of season," was a common saying.

Nobody ever saw a Longhorn cow on the range with a spoiled bag. If she lost her offspring, her bag would dry up promptly. The flow of milk was adapted to nature's conditions. The cows were regular breeders, a calf crop of ninety or ninety-five per cent being counted on under normal conditions. Cows not infrequently brought calves at the advanced age of twenty-five years.

Steers are not as "crazy" over cows as mules are over mares, but any wild cow on the range is a Cleopatra for magnetizing steers. There was "Old Rud." [6] Her range was the six hundred sections of moisture-forsaken land controlled by the Johnson Brothers of the **W** brand for thirty miles up and down both sides of the Pecos River, in Texas. When Evans and Means bought the ten thousand cattle and the range rights of the **W** outfit in 1912, "Old Rud" had not been in a roundup for ten years. The **R U D** brand she bore, in addition to the **W**, marked her as having been born not later than 1886. She was twenty-six years old at least, and was described to the Evans and Means men as being a dark red, with black feet and nose, whitish around the eyes, and with sharp black horns curved in so that the points almost entered her own head. Some steers were always with her. On the rare occasions when sighted, she was in the *mesquitales* of the sand hills out from the river. She and her bunch watered only at night, and often they ranged more than twenty miles out from the only water — the river. There was a kind of sentiment in favor of Old Rud, her cunning in eluding man being a wonder; but she was such a demoralizer of steers that she was badly wanted. Furthermore, any cowboy who caught her would have the same kind of feather in his cap as at one time came from killing a bad man. She had worn out three or four ropes that she had broken loose with, and had been shot a time or two.

Joe Evans was on the point of a bunch of cattle headed for the roundup grounds, still several miles away, when he noticed a cow shy at something in the brush a little to one side of her path. Joe knew he was in Old Rud's territory. He edged up to investigate what the cow had shied up. He could see nothing at first, but halted his horse for closer scrutiny. Then he made out some kind of animal lying down about forty feet away, perfectly camouflaged in the brush, weeds and pear. Looking intently, he made out the animal's head flat on the ground; he saw a curved black horn, then white-with-age eyelashes over unblinking eyes. He knew he was looking at Old Rud. She was as still as a setting hen. She did not seem to be breathing. Without moving his body or head, Joe reached down with his left hand and tightened his cinch; then, working only his right wrist, he loosed the rope tied to his saddle horn. The cow did not jump until she was certain that the man had seen her and was coming after her. When she jumped, a bull and three steers, all hidden in her manner, jumped also.

"She headed for the thickest brush she could find," Joe Evans said, "but I was determined to rope her or skin myself all over trying. She crossed a little opening about as big as a bandana handkerchief, and I piled it on her. When the rope hit her, before it had tightened, she ran her tongue out about ten inches and bellered like a bull, and here she came back towards me fighting mad. I was going north as fast as my horse could run when she turned back south. As we passed each other, she got both forefeet over the slack rope. When I hit the end of it, I threw her at least five feet high and knocked all the wind out of her. The impact broke the rope right at her head. I whirled and took after her again, for she didn't pause a second in getting back on her feet. She was dodging through that brush like a jack rabbit. I was fighting limbs to keep my eyes from being punched out and was making a new loop and trying to overtake her at the same time. I had yelled and a couple of the other boys were after the steers and bull. Well, I roped her again, threw her, jumped down and cut her throat with my pocketknife before she had a chance to get up."

She was "packing plenty of tallow" even if she was growing white with age. The Evans men and the Means men had their families at the roundup, and this day everybody celebrated with a barbecue of Old Rud's best ribs. She was the most noted cow of the Pecos, a relic of the old mustang breed. Joe Evans still has her head and horns. The people who cemented the phrase "as clumsy as a cow" into the English language were not familiar with Old Rud's breed.

I have talked about fighting cows and fighting bulls; I shall talk about fighting outlaw steers. Yet the reputation of the Longhorns for being dangerous to any man on foot was based largely on a misunderstanding of admirable curiosity. The cowmen whom Philip Ashton Rollins [7] records as forbidding their employees to appear afoot within a quarter of a mile of range cattle, because of the danger to man, were really concerned over not having their cattle disturbed.

Cattle are curious in direct ratio to their alertness. The Long-horns, being all animation and aliveness, had an "intellectual curiosity" that never stirs in heavy, sluggish cattle resembling hogs in their obtuseness. They were curious in the same way that deer and antelopes are curious, and, like deer and antelopes, they were sometimes betrayed by curiosity. James Capen Adams, the bear hunter of early-day California, who was also something of a naturalist, tells how one evening about sundown he saw a huge grizzly bear rolling and tumbling in the grass and sticking up his legs, arousing the curiosity and then the fury of cattle around him until a heifer made a lunge at him, whereupon the bear leaped to his feet, killed her and went to drinking her blood and gorging on her flesh.[8]

Modern range cattle, not used to seeing human beings except on horseback, will, upon sighting a man walking out in the pasture where they have never seen a pedestrian before, either tear out or move forward to investigate. If, when they get close enough for a good look, the pedestrian makes a sudden move and adds a little yell, they run like a turkey. Many of the old-time Longhorns had never been in a pen, knew nothing of man-provided water, around which men work on foot, had never glimpsed a human being walking over their range. Observant of and distrustful of everything strange, if a herd of them out on the prairie so much as saw a man dismount and stand beside his horse, they were apt to become excited. As Charlie Russell put it, they seemed to think the animal made by a man on top of a horse had "broke in two"; they were likely to try to break in two also.

A human being showing up afoot on the ground where they grazed was, especially at a distance, far more curious than a wolf or a panther. If, when the Longhorns came in a trot to investigate, the footman ran, then he was to be chased. Maybe he was a new kind of two-legged coyote! I will not say that by standing his ground the footman could in every single instance

make the cattle retreat, but the exceptions were minor. The investigators were motivated by curiosity, not viciousness. If an old sack were dropped on their range, within a few days every animal in the vicinity would have nosed it.

Frank Reaugh never felt himself in danger while moving afoot among the Longhorns, painting them. He would go out on the prairie with his sketching materials and a big four-foot umbrella to shade himself from the sun. "No sooner," he says,[9] "would I settle down to my easel for work than all the wild steers in sight would come to investigate. Cows with calves would seek safety somewhere else, and the few old bulls were too dignified to show much interest."

One day, Mr. Reaugh spread his umbrella, put up his easel, and sat down to await the approach of some big steers grazing a half mile or more to the north. A delightful breeze from the south carried his scent to them. Presently a dozen or so of the Longhorns came on the run. At a distance of two hundred feet they suddenly stopped.

"But soon, with curiosity unsatisfied, with eyes and ears intent to catch the slightest move or sound, with working nose thrust forward to test the strange odor on the air, cautiously, slowly, a few steps and then a pause, and then a few steps more, they came closer and closer as I worked. All the little group were fine big cattle. The leader especially was fine in form and carriage and beautiful in color. I was working with my utmost speed to get him on canvas when a gust of wind pulled my umbrella loose to go up a dozen feet in the air and then light on its edge and go rolling straight towards those cattle. They stampeded at once, all but the leader. He was made of sterner stuff.

"He braced himself and lowered his head to meet the thing. Doubtless he hoped to run a bluff as he had often done before. He was prepared, and he was a powerful steer with keen, black-tipped, forward-pointing horns. Few things would have rushed in on him, but the umbrella never hesitated. It came right on with a crazy, wabbling, bouncing gait that was disconcerting. The steer had never seen anything like it before; he had no way of estimating its power or possibilities.

"He was a powerful and brave steer, prepared to fight, but at the last minute he lost his nerve. With a bawl of terror that was almost a shriek, he whirled and rushed away after the rest of the herd. They all disappeared over the horizon in a little cloud of dust; and they never came back."

X · SMELL AND THIRST

*To James R. ("Mister Jim") Dougherty, because it is
so pleasant to talk with him about nature and characters of the Texas soil.*

BUFFALOES in their native state would scent a man or
other enemy two miles, sometimes four miles, away on
the windward side. They hardly relied on their eyes for warn-
ing. But put in a pasture and fed, reduced from self-reliance,
they showed, as the most marked of all changes, a diminution
of the sense of smell. Domestication seems to have a similar effect
on all nostriled animals. I have ridden with Mexicans — virtual
Indians — who could smell javelinas and outlaw cattle almost as
surely as dogs. The difference in keenness of nose between a
parlor poodle and a bloodhound is not greater than that between

a housed, hand-fed milk cow and a Longhorn of the open range.

One summer in the late seventies, while the Texas Panhandle was yet covered with free grass, John Farrington took a cow crowd from the **J A** Ranch to join in a general roundup on the Canadian River and gather in estrayed cattle.[1] The **J A** men had two or three hundred head of cattle in their herd, which was increasing daily, when they cut into it a big black cow with a brown streak down her back, brought from New Mexico the year before.

One night she dropped a calf on the bed ground. Its legs were yet too wobbly for it to walk any distance when early next morning the herd started for the next roundup ground down the river. It was the cook's business to put the calf in the wagon, but he "failed" to take it. The herd moved ten or twelve miles, by a circuitous route, the black cow trying all the time to dodge back. After camp was made, Farrington, who had been working with the main roundup, took a look at his day-herd, noticed the bawling black cow, and discovered that the cook had not brought her calf. He felt responsible for property and he was of a sympathetic nature. He started back to get the calf.

He found it where it had been left and where, according to its instinct, it might expect the mother. Farrington lifted it from the ground and put it across the saddle in front of him. Then he made a beeline, not taking the roundabout course the herd had taken, for camp. When he got there, he found that the day-herders had let the cow go. Determined to get the two together, he saddled a fresh horse and struck back for the old bed ground, to which he knew the cow had bolted. A mile or two from it, he saw the cow coming his way in a long trot, her nose to the ground. He pulled aside. The cow did not waver. She went on trotting and smelling. Farrington fell in behind her. She was following the tracks, over thick turf, made by his horse *when he carried the calf in.* She trailed straight to the herd, lowing, as she drew near, in anxious expectation.

Range cattle are guided far more by smell than is generally realized. A cow, if not too highly bred, may look at her calf and seem to know it, but she will not claim it until she smells it. You will see her nose its body and then give a kind of *moo* that says very plainly, "My own child! Now come, dear little one, and suck."

Charlie Goodnight told me that when he began taking a "calf wagon" along, to pick up calves born on the trail, he had much difficulty in getting mother cows to accept their young after they were unloaded from the wagon in the evening. A half-dozen or twenty calves jostling together during the day would get their scents mixed, thus making each a stranger to its mother. Goodnight overcame the difficulty by putting over each calf a loose sack, so marked that it was used on the same calf day after day, being removed at evening; thus the scent proper to a calf would be retained for recognition by its mother.

If a cow lost her calf and at the same time there was a calf that had lost its mother, the bloodless hide of the dead calf fastened loosely over the orphan would influence the cow to adopt it.[2] Generally she was tied, head and hind feet, each morning and evening, until she became accustomed to a strange calf suckling. The adoption was hastened by milking her milk out on the head and body of the orphan, thus giving her scent to it. Another means of conveying the family scent was by a baptism of the orphan in the cow's urine.

At old Frio Town, which consists today of a ranch home across the road from the deserted courthouse, you can see the horns of a steer that W. A. Roberts captured in 1888. Roberts had a big trap, built of mesquite poles, around a water hole in the Frio River. The gate into this pen was perhaps ten feet wide, wide enough not to be treacherous-looking. When closed, it was barred with eight or ten long poles. On the day that Roberts took his stand, the poles lay on the ground to one side of the opening. The dews of many nights and the suns of many days had fallen on them since they had been touched by the hand of man. A live oak tree sent a limb immediately over the gap.

The weather was dry and had been dry for months; water holes in the Frio were scarce. In the hope of catching some wild cattle, Roberts rode with a vaquero to the trap, halted beside the tree, pulled out of the saddle into a fork, and then crawled into position. The eyes of cattle are not placed to see what is above them; scent seems normally to float upward instead of downward. The vaquero, who did not dismount or touch anything about the trap, led Roberts' horse away with instructions to go half a mile or so down the river and not return until he heard a yell.

After waiting in the tree for a considerable time, Roberts saw an old mossy-horn steer standing out in the brush, apparently trying to make up his mind whether he should enter to water or not. He did not know the steer, had never heard of him. He thought he knew all cattle in the country. He froze in his perch, and long before the play was over he was almost paralyzed from the cramped immobility in which he remained.

The steer was alone. He approached very, very slowly, often stopping to look behind him and to all sides — listening, alert in the nostrils. He was "snuffy" at his own shadow. He had not had water for days, though he had no doubt eaten prickly pear in that time. He was ga'nt, but thirst did not hasten him. It was about an hour from the time the steer was sighted, less than one hundred yards away from the gap, until he stood at the entrance. Every foot of advancement had aroused fresh suspicions.

With his head almost inside the gateway, he whirled and looked behind him. Then he began smelling of the poles lying on the ground. He smelled up and down each long pole. He went to the uprights at one side of the gap and smelled up and down them; then he went to the uprights on the other side of the gap and smelled up and down them. He smelled deliberately, often looking up and around, always listening. He sniffed of the ground all about the gap. "Lean sides make a long nose," the vaqueros say. At last he stood with his head inside. He stood still. No human scent had been detectable; yet something seemed to be telling him that man was stalking him. Anyhow, as he well knew, the trap was man-made. He whirled again and, standing clear of the gap, gazed for a long time into the brush whence he had come.

"Be careful," the Indians of the North Woods said to Grey Owl, "not to think too strong about the elk when you are near him. He will feel your anxiety and flee."

For maybe twenty minutes the old steer stood looking into the brush. Once more he turned, and again he smelled of the poles, the gateposts, the tree base and the ground. He walked through, looked back, walked for the water.

Just as he was about to reach it, Roberts dropped from his perch and stood in the gap. The steer saw him and ran towards him. It took nerve to stand there; Roberts had nerve. The steer halted twenty or thirty feet away, shook his head, pawed up dust. He had a fighting head, with horns twisted corkscrew-fashion clear out to the tips. As he had debated within himself whether to enter or not, now he debated whether to attack the man or not. Fear conquered. Futilely he began looking for another exit that did not exist. Roberts barred the gap and tied the bars so that they could not be rubbed or shaken loose.

The next morning he and his men killed the steer — all they could do with him. The brand he bore was **D I**. It had not been used for twenty-one years. The steer had to be at least that old, and he may have been older. He was a pale red, line-backed. All these years he had escaped cow hunts, a lone, lone wolf protected by his ever vigilant senses. His tallow was yellow and his meat strong with wild strength.

Steers can probably smell more acutely than cows or bulls. They seem to have a more objective curiosity. Free from the care of offspring and the obsession of sex, thrifty range steers four years old and up are extremely investigative, not from fear but from innate alertness. They enjoy smelling and constantly cultivate the sense of smell.

The meager accounts we have of all primitive cattle show the same wild distrust and the fierce repugnance of man-scent observable in the mustang cattle and in the Texas Longhorns. According to Boethius, the white wild bulls of the great Caledonian Wood, "informed by their acute sense of smell, fled from herbs, trees, or fruits which, within a period of many days, had been touched by the hand of man." When a domestic cow in heat was for experimental purposes introduced to a bull among the famous wild Chillingham cattle of England, "he would take no notice whatever of her. The Chillingham people ascribed this behavior to one thing only: that she had been lately handled by man, and that the wild bull could not endure the smell." [3]

As in other mammals, there is in cattle a strong connection between smell and sex. The manifestations of this connection are not so spectacular as the "scrapes" made by buck deer, the urinary responses of passing does, the investigations of returning bucks, and their running-trailing of does in heat. Yet many observations of bovine courtship at the end of the nose are possible.

One action of steers that is, I am satisfied, dependent upon scent and sex is very puzzling. The steer, like an old man, no matter how impotent, retains his interest in the female. Hence the old-time cowboy saying, applicable to many forms of conduct — "Like a steer, I can try." If a considerable number of range steers, particularly steers with "cold blood" in them, are brought together and held for a time, some of them will be observed riding others. Heat, activity and nervousness seem to stir dead desires. Some steer, usually small, will be picked upon for mounting. Half the steers that get in reach of him will rear upon him. He must emit some odor that provokes them. I have seen such an animal, the skin rubbed off his back, hip-joints and tail bone, utterly worn down, seemingly ready to fall and die.

Cattle can smell a shower far off. In arid lands, grass begins to green a few hours after a rain, and if rain falls on turf that has been burned off, green shoots will spring up almost immediately. Mason Maney told me that when he was a boy his father sent him out one day to bring in a little bunch of gentle cows that habitually ranged near the ranch house. He could not find them and so reported. "Well," said the father, "it has rained on that big burn down on the Frio River, and those cows have gone to it." The next day father and son went to the burn; it was greening and the Maney cows, with many other cattle, were on it. They were so far from the ranch that it took nearly two days to drive them home. Longhorns in the Jornada del Muerto country could smell a shower in the mountains fifteen miles away and would make for the place where it had fallen, knowing they would find fresh pasturage there.

There have been many discussions as to how far a herd of thirsty Longhorns could smell water. Perhaps not as far as a Spanish mule, which, turned loose, has led many a perishing man to water. The distance varied with the wind, elevation, temperature, moisture in the air and other factors. There are reliable records of cattle's having smelled water, on a cross or adverse wind, from four to ten miles away. Jack Potter told me that one time while he was driving over an eighty-mile dry stretch from Fort Sumner on the Pecos to Thatcher, Colorado, he saw a lead steer he had named Sid Boykin stop, lift his head, smell long, and then head east. One of the point men turned him back in. Again Old Sid sniffed and two or three other steers sniffed with him. It was forty miles back to the brackish water of the Pecos and forty miles to water ahead. The cattle were in great distress.

"We'd better keep going," the point men said.

"No, Old Sid knows," Jack Potter asserted. "I'm going to ride in the direction he's pointed. If I find water, I'll signal you all to bring the herd."

He galloped east. After riding for half an hour or so, he saw antelope and mustangs. They meant water. About seven miles from where Old Sid had sniffed, Potter sighted a solitary lake — a lake of clear, fresh water surrounded by fine grass. Up to this time none of the range men on the Pecos had known of its existence. It made a fine resting and filling-up place for the herd for two or three days. "Old Sid seemed proud of hisse'f."

Cattle, like men, go crazy from excessive thirst. Their eyes sink in, some of them going blind and hooking savagely at anything near them that moves. Their voices become moans, but as long as they can make a sound, they will, at the faintest stir of a fresh breeze, face it, lift heads and run out their tongues in a bawl of agony and hope. Their bodies have the hollow, shrunken look of their sunken eyes. If they set their heads to go in a certain direction, they are almost impossible to turn, though they may be halted. After traveling over a desert for days, and being almost within smelling distance of water ahead, a herd has been known to turn around and, in a blind doggedness that no human power could stem, take the back trail.[4]

The actions of thirst-crazed trail cattle upon approaching water were variable. At the first whiff, they might lift heads, sniff and strike a long trot forward. They might try to run and then, when checked, go to milling, adding to their own heat and thirst. They might upon reaching water lose all self-control and plunge over bluffs to death. An overdose of alkaline water like that of the Pecos could decimate a herd, but casualties at watering places were out of the ordinary.

In the drouthy summer of 1868 Reuben W. Gray gathered 1700 head of mixed cattle on the San Saba to drive to New Mexico. His route led over the long, high, dry stretch — estimated at from seventy to ninety-six miles — between the headwaters of the Concho and Horsehead Crossing on the Pecos.

For a day's ride back east from the Pecos, cattle ribs and skulls and horns, like sculpturings in chalk, extended the line of Golgotha markers that originally gave Horsehead its name.

Reuben W. Gray's thirst-maddened herd headed for a bluff below the crossing. Five hundred head rushed over and were killed by the fall and by being trampled on, or were drowned in the canyon of water.[5] More than one herd upon approaching the Pecos was deflected from the river by smell of alkali lakes and, despite all that men — desperate themselves for water — could do, were poisoned.

Castle Gap is about thirteen miles east of the Pecos. In 1872 a boss passing through the Gap with about a thousand head of westward-bound steers ordered them checked at this place. A light shower was at the very time moistening the surface of the greasewood-nurturing ground. The steers went crazy over the damp smell. They milled and bawled and could not be driven to water. Perhaps a more resourceful boss could have budged them. They all died on that alkali flat, and for years their bones marked the place.

Before arriving at Pontoon Crossing, below the Horsehead on the Pecos River, the plains pitch off abruptly to a secondary level, making the descent like that from a steep mountain. J. D. Slaughter told me that when in the eighties his west-bound herd reached the point where the trail started its plunge, he saw hundreds of dead cattle in the Long S brand that had been lost there only a short time before. Crazed with thirst, the Long S herd upon reaching the brink overlooking the hidden river refused to go farther. The men worked with them for hours and, indeed, with some of them for several days. The waters of the Concho were too far behind for the weakened cattle to reach by back-trailing; they would not go down the mountain to the water. Probably the smell did not float up to them. A high percentage perished from stupid stubbornness.

As a rule, big steers liked to wade out into water until it

came up to their sides, and then to drink long and deep. If the water was shallow, they would walk up and down in it, stirring up the mud. The test of a cowman lay in his ability to water out a herd.

How long cattle could go without water depended on their age, condition, the weather, and so forth. Animals naturally become more heated and thirsty in a herd than in solitude. Big old steers located on the Pecos River used sometimes to walk back twenty and even twenty-five miles to find good grass, coming in to the river not more than twice a week. Crowded into a herd, those same steers would have become very thirsty by the time they traveled twenty miles. Heavy, high-grade cattle of modern days seldom get more than two or three miles away from water, and ranchmen attempt to provide waterings so that grazing distance from any well or tank will not be more than a mile or two.

Numerous instances could be adduced of cattle of the Spanish breed thriving without water like mountain sheep and mule deer.[6] "One time," related a Mexican rancher of that fearfully dry country along the Texas–New Mexico line, "I kept missing a big steer of mine. The other cattle were poor. There was nothing for them to eat. They were just existing on the water at Hueco Tanks. After the big steer had been gone for several weeks, I decided to look for him. I found him twenty-five miles away, and he was rolling fat. He was in a dagger country; the daggers were in bloom, and all the moisture he had been getting was from dagger flowers. I drove him home and killed him for beef. When I cut him open and examined his bladder, I found it no bigger than a sack of Bull Durham tobacco."

Arid lands, which are still given over to grazing and are destined so to continue, are thought of nowadays as being the chief habitat of the Longhorn; actually, however, when the horns were longest, their wearers ranged in a country fairly well watered. They wanted lots of water — and could live for a long time on little feed, provided they got an abundance of water. During a drouthy summer, about 1881, before windmills had arrived, Walter Billingsley was drawing water in whisky barrels from hand-dug wells on the Texas coast and decided to test the consumption of half a dozen representative cows. The cattle would come in to water about ten o'clock in the morning and hang around until about five o'clock that afternoon. He fenced in a small trough for the test. The cows he put inside the fence drank fifty gallons of water each per day.

Certain wild cattle that Billingsley knew were not coming to the wells, where men drew water with horsepower day and night. "One moonlight night," he said, "I saw a big bunch of them out in the bay, standing in the salt water up to their hips. They were so wild that they would have died before coming to a trough that man was pouring water into. I learned that they stood in that way for hours, soaking into their systems the salt water they could not drink. Those old cold-blooded Longhorns could live as long as anything could live, and the wilder they were, the better they could take care of their own hides."

Contrary to the observation of many range men, scientists have claimed that the drinking of sulphur water will not make a cow shed ticks. Without going into that subject, it is an established fact that before fences cut the Longhorn stock off from following the dictates of instinct, and while ticks were bad, cattle in the spring of the year used to leave good water and travel twenty and thirty miles to drink from the sulphur springs in Wilson County. These springs are not forty feet away from the clear non-mineralized waters of Cibolo Creek; yet cattle would come from a long distance and fill up on the mineralized water. Milk cows around Adamsville, accustomed to coming each evening to their calves, would along in the spring lay out long enough to go twenty-five miles to drink from the sulphur springs near Lampasas, afterwards resuming their regular habit of coming to the pens at night. There were no medical advisers among these cattle to tell them that what their systems craved was what they should not have. How did they come to be guided to the tonic waters?

In the eighteenth century buffaloes made annual migrations of perhaps two hundred miles, across the Alleghenies, from their wonted range to drink of and wallow about salt springs in what is now Union County, Pennsylvania.[7]

D. Wilburn (Doc) Barton located, in 1872, a herd of Texas cattle on the Arkansas River some thirty miles above the spot where Dodge City was soon to become famous. He became one of the great cowmen of the West. He told me that his Longhorns used to drift annually — towards the first of June — from sixty to seventy-five miles to the salt waters of Crooked Creek. After satisfying their spring craving for salt, they would generally return to the home range. The cattle smelled that salt water, Doc Barton holds.

XI · VITALITY, DRIFTS AND DIE–UPS

*To Frank McGill, as good a man as he is cowman. His
interest in lands and cattle includes more than the
money they will make.*

ONE Saturday in 1870, as Frank S. Hastings tells the story,[1]
he and some other boys went to a packing plant at Leavenworth, Kansas, where a string of mossy-horned Texas steers
were being slaughtered. As the cattle passed down a chute, a
man with a long, sharp lance struck them behind the horns.
"We saw him lance one particularly big fellow," says Hastings,
"with the usual result: a quick fall, the trap door opened, and
the beef was dragged to the skinning beds. When the knife
was at his throat, he jumped with one bound to his feet, saw
daylight through a door at the rear, jumped a story and a half

to the ground, swam the Missouri River to a sand bar one quarter of a mile distant, shook himself, and turned his head to the shore — at bay."

About this same time a herd of Longhorns was being shoved into the pen of a hide and tallow factory at Fulton — a dead town now — on the Texas coast. Suddenly a big brindle steer plunged for liberty, ran from his pursuer into the bay, and swam twelve miles across to the point at Lamar.

After the Civil War, Robert Hall, a noted Indian fighter, was catching wild cattle on the Nueces. A Negro boy came in one evening and reported that he had roped a two-year-old maverick bull that morning and left him tied in a thicket. For some reason nobody went to brand the bull and release him. Exactly twenty days later Hall while hunting panthers heard his dogs baying something. Galloping up, he found them barking at the bull, which was on his feet, attempting to get loose.[2] Men who roped outlaws in the brush often left them tied for days — "so's to take some of the starch out of 'em" — before returning to lead them in. One roped by the neck at the base of the head might be choked down until its eyes showed white and the heart stopped beating, but after the rope was loosened, it would revive, in contrast to the Brahma, which may be choked to death in a surprisingly easy manner.

Longhorn hardihood was next to that of the burro. What vitality! What will to live! The period of usefulness of both cows and bulls as breeders lasted twice that of modern cattle. Only the rawhided Longhorns could have stood the exceedingly rough work on the range, where they were chased for ten or twenty miles into a great seething herd, there to be ginned about in a way that would have ruined tender-natured stock. Northern stockmen were appalled when for the first time they witnessed the rough manner in which Texans handled their cattle. Originally the method was a blend from the Spaniards, of whom the bull ring and the Inquisition are representative expressions, and from Indians that gloated in torture. Like the cattle themselves, the early-day range men and their horses were made of rawhide. There were always some gentle handlers of cattle among them, but they were in the minority. If a cow could not stand the roughness, let her perish.

The cattle were seldom bothered with any malady that a veterinary could have helped. They had almost no herd diseases. Tuberculosis among them was unheard of. Abortion was unknown. Now and then one might be seen with the "big jaw." Some were afflicted with warts. The way to get rid of them was to name the animal "Pike" and to call him or her that name upon every possible occasion.

The vulnerability of the Longhorns was as unheroical as that of Achilles. The one enemy that threw them into a panic was the heel fly. When heel flies struck them, whether loose on the range or under herd, they h'isted their tails and bolted as if highlife had been poured on their backs. If water was within reach, they ran into it and stood. The usual refuge was brush, in which they would squat, attempting to cover up their ankles. Not much is known about the heel-fly, and few people have seen it. It deposits its eggs in the tender region just above the hoof and to the rear. The sound of its buzzing seems to make cattle lift their tails straight up. You can see one tail go up, then a dozen or more, before the cattle break.

As evidence of the cattle's extraordinary adaptability to environment, I will bring up another insect. In the days before drainage construction and screen wire, people living along the Gulf Coast used in summertime, when mosquitoes are especially vicious, to go down to the shoreline, where naked sands and a breeze from the water afforded some relief. A north wind would bring the mosquitoes in from the salt grass, the marshes, lagoons and upland prairie grass far back, drifting them on out to sea. The surf would bring them back dead, and the ribbed sea sand would be black with their bodies, a strip several feet wide marking the shore. Sometimes they were in such clouds as to obscure the sunlight. A person could not move through them without covering his face. Tormented to madness almost, the Texas cattle would drift to the open shore in vast numbers and go out in the water to the second and third tiers of sand bars, there spending the night and parts of the day. They would ride the waves, raising heads and shoulders, very much as people do.

At such times human beings seeking refuge from the mosquitoes might get very near the cattle. Like wild animals driven into a stream by a great forest fire, they seemed to lose fear of enemies, the great predator Man and the Wild Bull standing side by side. If people built fires of driftwood to smoke the mosquitoes away, the cattle would crowd into the smoke.

Their adaptability was continental. From where rank banana-leaves shade water-snakes in the tropics of Mexico, far, far below the southern limit of buffalo migration, Longhorns trailed northward to locate on the bleak blizzard-swept prairies of the Dakotas, to winter beneath mountains of snow and ice overlooking Montana coulees, and even to graze at home under the rim of the Midnight Sun on the plains of Alberta. Mature cattle transplanted from the hot climate of lower Texas would grow and fill out after roughing it through a rigorous winter in the high Northwest and be a month ahead of other cattle in fattening. Statements have been made that they pawed snow and ice off grass. However, the cloven hoof on cattle is not constructed to paw with, like that of horse or mule. One never sees cattle pawing in water like horses; a fighting cow will not paw a man as will a vicious horse. Longhorns by the thousands endured deserts to reach valley grass in California; they packed their meat through the bayous and marshes of the Mississippi delta. The steaming marshy lands of Louisiana stunted the breed but did not take away their thrift. In the piney woods of East Texas and through the infertile lands of the post oak, they seemed to shrivel up so as to have less anatomy to expose to ticks and less body to seek nourishment for, but ticks did not kill them.

> The ticks were there by millions —
> I tell the very truth.
> For they covered up the cattle
> Just like shingles on a roof.
>
> They sucked the very blood of life
> From the time the calves were born,
> So bodies had no chance to grow
> And calf went all to horn.[3]

Yet no kind of cattle could live on air and sand in an overstocked or "sheeped-off" country. The Longhorns could not rustle where there was nothing to rustle. When they became poor on account of a dearth of food, they were liable to fall victims to cold, sleet and winter rain. At times they simply starved to death on their native ranges, the stomachs and intestines of some that died being found half-stuffed with sand and dirt they had taken in while chewing on stubble. Even the wild animals best accommodated to natural environment ebb and flow in population according to the unfavorableness or favorableness of seasons. At times exceptional blizzards killed even buffaloes.

Drouths, which before the advent of bored wells, windmills and tanks meant a dearth of drinking water as well as of grass, seem to belong to the history of the Texas Longhorn. From a dateless past there have been drouths in the Southwest and West. Cabeza de Vaca was asked by Indians on the Rio Grande, four hundred years ago, to tell the sky to rain so that they could plant their corn. There had been no rain for two years, they told him, and moles had eaten up all the seed in the ground.

While the "rabbit-twisters" of Kansas and Oklahoma were gathering and selling buffalo bones left by the great slaughter that almost extinguished that animal from the face of the earth, wagons and Mexican carts far to the south were hauling cattle bones for shipment by the trainload. Recently I gazed upon Pike's Peak, but it did not look so high to me as in memory will always look the mountains of dazzlingly white cattle bones piled up at Alice, Texas, then a railroad terminus, after the great die-up of 1899.

About 1910 the **W** outfit on the Pecos River contracted to deliver ten thousand head of cattle "thirty days after the first general rain." It was three years before rainfall in West Texas fulfilled the condition for delivery — and then the owners had to go out and buy a considerable number of cattle in order to fill the contract. This was one of the drouthy periods when frogs lived a lifetime without learning to swim. It was the same kind of drouth as that during which a ranchman hauled up a load of gravel to his house and threw it on the roof so that when it did rain the children would not stampede at the unprecedented noise.

Cows with sucking calves, calves, steer yearlings and bulls nearly always died first. Dry cows and grown steers survived best. Bulls, powerful and mighty with vigor in a seasonable spring and summer, drooped surprisingly under adversities. Yet, taken altogether, year in and year out, the Longhorns were beyond all doubt the thriftiest rustlers that the cattle-raisers of America have ever known. That observant Englishman, William French, thought it worthy of remark that one terribly drouthy year he slipped up on a lanky steer, five or six years old, standing on his hind legs with his forefeet resting on a cottonwood limb eight or nine feet above the ground while he hooked down and ate sparse twigs and leaves.[4]

One time out in Colorado a rider noticed the hide and bones of a cow brute caught in the limbs of a tree growing along a gulch. It had evidently been lodged there by a spring rise. The rider noted that the brand on the dry hide belonged to a famous Texas cowman. Not long after this he met the cowman in jovial company and informed him how he had found one of his tree-climbers hanging by the horns in an elm. "Great browsers, those Bar **Y** cattle of mine," the cowman expanded. "Spring of the year, and that old Longhorn clumb the elm like a squirrel to eat the buds, and jest accidentally hung himself."

These cattle would hook down the bloom stalks of the Spanish dagger, live for months on prickly pear without drinking water, and, in some grassless regions, endure for a lifetime by browsing on brush like deer. Generally, cattle, on account of their short necks, graze down and not up, but the Longhorn's neck was as limber as a goat's. He had a hard mouth for withstanding the thorns of cactus and chaparral — a mouth to match flinty hoofs and tough hide. He did not shed his teeth from old age. No man who has eaten the meat of cattle fat from browsing on guajilla, black chaparral, chapote and other brush will cease to long for its wild, strong, sinewy taste — in contrast to the pallid sweetness of "baby beef" from animals that have never exercised and have all their young blank lives been hand-stuffed like the geese that furnish *pâté de foie gras*.

Once in a long succession of years a norther bringing sleet clear to the Gulf of Mexico might freeze to death cattle in good condition as well as poor ones. Old-timers are agreed, however, that the coastal Longhorns stood up against ice and dampness better than the Brahmas now succeeding them.

If they died along the coast so that some years in some places "you could walk a mile without stepping off the carcasses," it was largely because they had drifted thither from long distances, banking up, trampling out and eating off the grass. Gentle cattle around ranches with cover and cattle in brushy country did not drift much. The great drifts were from the prairies, and after the Longhorns took over the Plains, they and their half-breed descendants afforded, a few times, a drama in drifting comparable to the migrations of the buffalo or the southward flight of the wild-crying wedges of sand-hill cranes.

In the spring of 1880, which had been preceded by a severe

winter, representatives from ranges in Nebraska, Colorado and even Wyoming, as well as Kansas, took part in the roundups on the Canadian and Red rivers in Texas in order to take their drift cattle back home.[5] Before the worst of any winter set in, Longhorns located on the high, naked plains habitually got down into the broken country under the caprock. From the plains along the Arkansas River in western Kansas, Texas cattle drifted regularly each winter clear into the breaks of the Brazos River, three hundred miles south.

Yet generally the drifts were sporadic, not seasonal in regularity. Notoriously weather-wise, the cattle, especially on the plains, often preceded a storm in their travel south, stringing out in long, thin lines. If they came to brush or broken country before the storm broke, they were likely to halt for refuge.

Whether they drifted or not, their uneasy behavior presaged a norther many hours, or even a day or two, before it struck. They would stand with heads pointed to the north, sensing expectantly; they would low and bawl and look off south; they would be bunching up or sifting down from the uplands to sheltering breaks, their routine of grazing, watering and sleeping entirely upset. "I knowed something was going to happen from the way the cattle acted," the old-timer said. How did the cattle know? They were a part of nature. They never comprehended the philosophy that God tempers the wind to the shorn lamb — a philosophy that God most certainly did not inaugurate, though only He could explain the sensitiveness to barometric pressure possessed by some wild animals.

After the storm broke, the cattle would stand with lowered heads, tails to the storm — or go with it. In contrast, buffaloes might drift against a blizzard. More than one bunch of cattle drifting in blinding sleet and snow has been known to walk over a precipice and plunge to death. Such disasters came after fences prevented the cattle from following their instincts.

The greatest cattle drift in North American history was in the

winter of 1884–1885. A vast part of the West was not yet enclosed. Cattlemen in what is now Oklahoma had, however, built a drift fence a hundred and seventy miles long from the New Mexico line east. Away south of it another drift fence paralleled the Canadian River. On south of this, line riders patrolled the new Texas and Pacific Railroad — its right-of-way unfenced — to guard against the passing of cattle.

When a terrible blizzard struck late in December, cattle from southwestern Kansas and No Man's Land went with it. The grass lay under a pavement of sleet and ice. The plains afforded no harbor or shelter. As endless strings of cattle going with the wind crowded up to the first drift fence, the leaders stopped, stiffened and went down, to be trampled on by followers until piles of the dead made overpasses. In places the posts were shoved over and cattle struggling through cut themselves to pieces on the barbed wire. At the second drift fence the operation was repeated. After the storm the fence lines were marked by tens of thousands of frozen bodies. In the spring cattle from the upper ranges were found five hundred miles south in Texas.[6]

A line rider along the Texas and Pacific Railroad left an account of his experiences with the great drift.[7] "One evening about three o'clock," he said, "a black cloud appeared in the north. We knew a howling blue norther was coming and a drift was certain. There were twenty-five of us in the line camp at Big Spring. Forty miles west was another camp of the same number of men, and forty miles east still another.

"About four o'clock the blizzard struck, but it was about midnight before the lead of the drift herd passed. By this time the ground was covered with six or seven inches of sleet. Sleet was still falling, the wind driving it like knives. Nothing alive could have faced it. The first cattle were from ranges just north of the railroad. Behind them cattle were stringing from the plains two hundred miles distant.

"It was our business to follow the cattle until they stopped and then to head them back. To try to head them before the wind laid would have been like trying to turn back the norther itself. They would keep going night and day until they fell dead or until the storm died or until they struck shelter. When they got to drifting this way, they might go right across a canyon without halting to hunt a windbreak in it. All that night and all the next day the blizzard raged and the avalanche of cattle rolled with it. A little after dark on the second night the wind lulled and the cattle quit marching. For twenty hours we cowboys had ridden with them, stopping only long enough to prepare and eat some grub we carried. We rode corn-fed horses. We had not tried to keep up with the lead cattle. About nine o'clock the next morning we sighted them.

"The sun was shining bright. Not a breath of wind was stirring. The cattle were all lying down, most of them utterly exhausted, their backs covered with sleet and snow. All of them seemed to be in a kind of stupor. Many of them would never get up. About noon we stirred the southernmost cattle up and headed them back north. We estimated that the drift herd was eighty miles long. Of course the cattle were not in a compact body, but were scattered in bunches. The seventy-five line riders from the three big camps along the Texas and Pacific Railroad were reinforced by other cowboys. Wagons and fresh horses came. We went slow, finally shoving the bigger part of the stuff into the canyons and breaks along the Colorado River [in Texas]. The losses that winter were about twenty-five per cent."

In the spring of 1885 enormous roundups were held on the Lower Pecos and in the Devil's and Concho rivers country to gather up and drive back the cattle belonging on ranges to the north and east. At the mouth of the Pecos cattle from ranges two hundred miles northeast were found wadded up. A relentless drouth was on. The cattle had nothing to eat where they were and were dying. The barren divide east of the Pecos was waterless. Cowboys representing outfits hundreds of miles apart gathered for the hopeless work. There were scores of wagons and remudas. Herds were amassed into hordes too unwieldy to manage. By arrangement with the Texas and Pacific Railroad, troughs and water were provided at two or three places, but probably not half of the original drift reached the home ranges.

The unspeakable winter of 1886–1887 will probably continue to go down as the most disastrous in range history.[8] It synchronized with a panic that ruined a majority of the cattlemen, both big and little, of America. By this time, however, more than half of Texas was fenced; the winter here was not so severe as in the Northwest, and the effects of weather and panic were not nearly so disastrous.

> I may not see a hundred
>   Before I see the Styx,
> But, coal or ember, I'll remember
>   Eighteen–eighty-six.
>
> The stiff heaps in the coulee,
>   The dead eyes in the camp,
> And the wind about, blowing fortunes out
>   As a woman blows out a lamp.

That was the winter that Charlie Russell, on a ranch in Montana, drew the picture of the lone starving cow with a wolf in front of her and — according to a tradition over which facts are powerless — labeled it "The Last of the Five Thousand." Along in the fall cowmen on the Missouri River noticed the wild animals unwontedly drifting south; nearly all birds disappeared; Granville Stuart saw arctic owls in the Judith Basin for the first time. The old Indians pointed to them, wrapped their blankets more closely about their bodies, and, predicting out of traditional memories, said, "Heap cold!"

A long drouth had desolated the ranges; yet at the same time the greatest boom the cattle industry has ever known had just reached its climax, bringing in foreign capital and spurring on rangemen to stock up, until all the public domain and most of the privately owned ranches from Alberta to the mouth of the Rio Grande were overgrazed. The stream of herds from the south had flowed into every glade and nook of the plains and mountains of the Wyoming–Montana territory. And then the bottom fell out, the dam broke, and the devil pitchforked for every pound of flesh due him. In the Land of the Chinook, where now for months no warm chinook breath would thaw the icy hinges, cattle died like sheep. Big steers went under with poor cows. Bands of starving Texas cattle that had recently been driven up and turned loose, cattle that had never smelled a wisp of man-cured hay in their lives, "gathered around ranch houses, bellowing and bawling and crowding up to the windows and looking in, in appeal for help that the appealed to were powerless to give. . . . Their instincts seemed to lead these cattle to believe that their human masters could do something for them." Longhorns that had gone through the preceding winter on these ranges and were well located stood up better than any other class of cattle, far better than the "pilgrims," or "barnyard stock" that had been shipped west from Iowa and other states. However, freshly arrived Texans, nearly all of which stock went into the winter thin, perished beyond precedent.

When the spring thaws at last came, creeks were dammed with carcasses. A ninety-per-cent loss was general over a vast territory. Some owners gave up trying to find their scattered remnants. For years bones bleached on windswept foothills against the high Rockies and wolf-gnawed fragments of rawhide lay scattered from one side of the land of buffalo grass to the other. What had a few years before been a solid carpet of grass was now a threadbare patchwork of stemless roots. A whole generation of cowmen were dead broke, the majority never to recoup their fortunes.

The high tide of the Longhorn had passed. Man had crowded the range beyond the rustling power of any cattle. The time of free and expanding ranges was at an end. Hereafter, cattle would be fed in severe climates, and feeders clamored for a stock of cattle that would convert every pound of feed into beef. Grass was getting too high for pasturing "common cattle" on it. In the Brush Country, and all along the coast, the breed held on for years. But the great day of the Longhorn was over.

KINGLY CROWN OF THE OPEN RANGE
"MINE HORN IS EXALTED"
I SAMUEL:2

XII · HORNS

To Tom East, who still raises Spanish horses, saves a
few horns, and has coyote sense as well as horse sense
and cow sense.

THEY SAID that you could pack all the roasting meat a
Texas steer carried in one of his horns. They said that when
the black prairie lands cracked from drouth, the cattle would
fall into them and be saved from going to the bottom only by
their horns hanging over the banks. Some people will horn in:

> Ole Joe Clark has got a cow —
> She was muley born.
> It takes a jaybird forty-eight hours
> To fly from horn to horn.

In County Cork a saying goes, "Cows far away have long
horns." At a meeting of the Trail Drivers of Texas in San

[203]

Antonio in 1929, I made a talk on old-time cattle, raising the question of horn length. Thereupon a little old man named W. W. Purcell jumped up and said: "When I was a boy on the Navidad, we neighbored with an old Missionary Baptist named Bill Grumbles. He was a truthful man, and Sam Houston appointed his brother John as ranger captain. He was always accurate about things. He could quote a page of Scripture and never miss a word. Well, old Bill Grumbles used to tell me over and over about a pair of wheel oxen he freighted with 'way back yonder between Port Lavaca and Austin. One of the wheel oxen had horns that measured thirteen feet and six and one-half inches from tip to tip. The other one measured eleven feet and six and one-half inches." Those cows, and old Bill Grumbles too, are far, far away now.

Where are all the big horns? A huge old steer that came to Cushman's hide and tallow factory on the Texas coast in the early seventies is said to have worn horns spreading nine feet. A patriot had them mounted and sent them to General Grant. I wonder what became of them, and also of the prize horns that Dennis M. O'Connor sent to President McKinley in 1897. They were finely mounted, a Texas star set in one horn and a buckeye in the other.[1]

According to M. S. Garretson, curator of the National Museum of Heads and Horns in the New York Zoological Park, two sets of horns of a nine-foot spread or better were to be seen at Chicago during the Columbian Exposition of 1893. Whether these horns had been steamed and straightened, I do not know. Horns contain the essence of glue. They can be steam-heated or boiled and straightened out so that a certain amount of curve is transformed into horizontal length.

The desire for spread has resulted in a violation of nature by dealers who take advantage of the ignorance of purchasers. Not all horns that go straight out like handle bars have been tampered with, but some of them have. Moreover, in mounting a pair of horns on wood — for few that are sold are on the original skull — unscrupulous dealers add several inches to the frontal piece, thus further increasing width. All that is advertised is the spread. Yet the natural twist of horns, nature's curves, give them far more character, interest and beauty than mere length. Twists were characteristic of Texas horns.

In 1881 Frederick Albert began assembling heads and horns for what came to be an extraordinary collection in his Buckhorn Saloon — now the Buckhorn Curio Shop — in San Antonio. The heaviest steer horns he was able to procure came from Africa. The widest-spreading Texas horns he could get hold of measured eight feet, one and three-eighths inches from tip to tip. Several pairs of horns with a spread of eight feet or so are scattered over the country.

The best-known steer in the world was Champion. For more than forty years his likeness on postcards has circulated from Newark to El Paso; it has been published many times in magazines, newspapers, textbooks and trade books, and has served as a model for countless drawings. It has become the standard representation of Longhorn cattle.

In the fall of 1892, Sid Grover bought the steer for my Uncle Jim (J. M.) Dobie, for whom he was working, from Nick Dunn, of Nueces County, in a bunch of two hundred other steers, at twelve dollars around. He was only "a long two," but he had a "six-year-old head." He had been calved on a little Mexican ranch down near the Rio Grande, and was comparatively gentle. He was driven to the Jim Dobie ranch near Lagarto in Live Oak County.

Later he was moved up to the Kentuck Ranch, also in Live Oak County. It was there that I had my only look at him.

I can see him yet: between a pale red and brown in color, mighty-framed but narrow, the ponderous horns, which were reaching maturity by then, weighing his head low when he stood and wobbling it when he walked. They curved outward, not upward. To scratch the root of his tail with a horn-tip, he had but to turn his head slightly. His mother was undoubtedly a plain Mexican (or Texas) cow, but on account of the texture of his hair — rather finer than the coarse, sunburned hair characteristic of the Texas-Mexican cattle — it was thought that his sire must have had a considerable amount of Devon blood in him. In his prime he weighed around twelve hundred pounds.

In 1899 Longhorns were becoming historic, and the managers of the so-called International Fair at San Antonio, held in the fall, invited entries of this class of cattle. Only two of the four Longhorns entered were considered worthy of consideration: Champion and another steer belonging to George West, also of Live Oak County. They received considerable newspaper attention,[2] but no measurement of Champion's horns seems to have been recorded at the time.

His picture was soon sold, however, on a medallion of enameled tin, advertising a horn spread of over nine feet. The next year the Fair association scattered the picture abroad on another tin medallion bearing the words: "I'll be there. Will You?" Champion was having his hair sprinkled with fish oil — to keep the flies off — for higher things, however. New York and Chicago papers in February of 1900 ran articles giving his horn spread as nine feet and seven inches.[3] In July, Will B. Eidson, a South Texas cowboy and for a short while champion roper of the world, took Champion, in the employ of Jim Dobie, to Kansas City for exhibition during the Democratic National Convention. The steer did not attract as much attention as William Jennings Bryan, but receipts were good. Will Eidson had dreams of making "a mint of money" out of Old Champion.

Plans were made to take him to the Paris Exposition, but the French Government objected, fearing "Texas fever." Champion and Will Eidson became vagrants, expenses constantly increasing over receipts. People appeared to have little curiosity about "this pair of horns with a steer hitched to the bottom of them." I have searched in vain for a leaflet giving Champion's history and measurements that was passed out to individuals who paid the admission fee of two-bits.

Along in 1901 Champion was leased to a "very tame Wild West show" operated by C. Z. Green and his wife. About a year later Will Eidson saw him in Davenport, Iowa. "The old steer mooed as if he was mighty glad I had come back," Will Eidson told me. What became of Champion in the end I am unable to say. I have heard that he was "butchered" in Michigan; that he died in Chicago, where his horns were preserved; that he was mounted and placed in a museum in St. Louis; that he passed into the hands of Miller Brothers' 101 Ranch Wild West Show. Jim Dobie never knew what his end was.

According to Will Eidson, "pole measurements" — straight across from one horn tip to the other — gave Champion's spread as eight feet, seven and three-eighths inches, while the circumference of each horn at the base was approximately seventeen and seven-eighths inches. When, in the 1920's, I used to ask Uncle Jim Dobie about the measurements, he would reply, "I am afraid to say." Like the great majority of real cowmen, he disliked the popular exaggeration of so many factors pertaining to range life and was more given to under- than over-statement. Sid Grover and Ed McWhorter both assert that the horns spread "about nine feet."

Yet all human memories are treacherous, and newspaper reports even more so. The steer was shipped north from Beeville. In April, 1900, the *Beeville Bee* reported a horn spread of seven feet, eight inches. In June, following, after the steer had walked down the main street on his way to a car that would carry him to Kansas City, the same paper reported a spread of "a little less than six feet straight across," and a length, following the curves of the horns, of seven feet, eight and one-half inches. At the same time, the *Beeville Picayune* reported a straight-across spread of six feet and three inches.[4]

Despite all conflicting reports, I believe that Champion had the longest horns of any Texas steer outside of legend. Surely they are preserved somewhere. It is of historical importance that they be located.

To revert now to the prize George West steer, exhibited with Champion in San Antonio in 1899. Born on the West ranch in Live Oak County in 1883, the steer was at the time sixteen years old. There was not a drop of improved blood in his veins, and he weighed close to 1700 pounds. His horns had an upward curvature, and when he stood at rest their tips were over eight feet above his hoofs. They measured seven feet and nine inches straight across, and about nine feet following the curves. George West considered him the noblest specimen of the type he had ever owned.[5]

He had handled many thousands, on both range and trail, and had several magnificent mounted heads. He was a steer man. When the great drouth and die-up of the middle eighties came, he had 150,000 acres stocked with mortgaged steers. After the leaves of the brush had shriveled and there was nothing at all left for cattle to eat and they went to dying in earnest, George West ordered his hands to quit skinning, to ride with hatchets, and to knock off and bring in to him the left horn of every dead steer their noses and eyes could locate. Thus he kept account of at least a part of his losses. Twenty-two hundred horns were piled in a corral at the ranch house, the pile, it is said, looking as big as the stack of mesquite wood out behind the ranch kitchen. Here on this pile of mesquite George West used to sit for hours gazing towards the horizon, hoping for a sign of rain. He was one of the cowmen who knew horns.

In a glass case on the courthouse grounds of the town of George West, in Live Oak County, another steer owned by the man for whom the town was named stands mounted — a well-intentioned piece of work, but an execrable example of taxidermy. During this steer's lifetime newspaper stories gave the spread of his horns as being all the way from nine to eighteen feet! Actually, it is a fraction over six feet.

The average spread of horns of a herd of Texas steers going up the trail in the eighties was no doubt under four feet. In the late sixties and through the seventies, at which time the steers were much older, the average spread may have been better than four feet. Steers with five-foot spreads were not uncommon. Anything over six feet was notable, and old-time cowboys still talk about examples.

For instance, John Custer remembers that while his father was cutting mesquite posts in the Artillery Thicket of Bee County in 1876, he found the skull of a steer with such long horns that he measured them with his ax handle, which was notched for measuring posts. The horns on the skull measured eight and one-half feet from tip to tip. They were left in the Artillery Thicket. Nobody in those days saved horns.

J. M. Mills remembers being at the roping of an outlaw steer on the Frio River that had a horn spread of eight feet, two inches. This steer was ten years old, as his brand told. He was a powerful brute and in running tore brush down with his horns, though he could slant them through any space wide enough for his body.

Webster Witter, who still drives oxen, remembers that as a boy in the seventies his father had a brindle ox named Old Ben with a horn spread of six feet, eleven inches. He had to turn his head in order to get through a fence gate. At the age of twenty-four years Old Ben was sold to a butcher in Lockhart. Sad at parting with him, the family did not buy any meat for a month for fear of getting a piece of Old Ben.

After railroads came and cattle began to be shipped instead of trailed, the problem of getting a steer's head through a car door was often serious. Some steers simply could not be loaded before the horns were chopped off. Sam Allen used to keep two Negroes at a car door to twist the heads of steers as they came up the chute. One horn had to be worked around the door-jamb before the other could be maneuvered inside.

Even with head twisting, some steers could not be put inside cars. The standard door of stock cars on most railroads today has a width of five feet and a height of nearly eight feet. In the days of the Longhorns the cars were lower and shorter, but the doors were generally not more than six inches narrower. It has often been claimed that the difficulty of loading was the reason for developing shorter-horned cattle, but this factor was minor. Horns worked more injury in feed pens than in cars, but it was primarily the bodies, rather than the horns, that breeders were trying to change.

Horns often prevented a shipper from packing a car with beef bodies. A steer was likely to hang a horn between the slats of a boxcar, get down, and be trampled into hamburger steak. Men accompanying shipments sometimes took saws so that if a horn got inextricably fastened, it could be sawed off and the animal thus liberated.

Neither bulls nor cows of any breed of cattle will grow the length of horn that steers will. Exploring the Far West in the 1830's the naturalist Maximilian, Prince of Wied, observed among the buffaloes certain individuals "extremely large and fat, with longer horns than the others; these, when calves, had been castrated by the Indians" [6] — or perhaps by wolves. Cow horns were slender, the longest pair I have seen spreading well over four feet.[7] Bull horns were generally thick and stubby, though some grew rather long, and many were very sharp. Stags, males castrated late in life, develop horns more like those of a bull than those of a steer. This explains in part why Mexican steers crossing the Rio Bravo by tens of thousands have seldom yielded phenomenal horns, as compared with outstanding Texas horns

The Mexican *modo* is to wait until the bull is fully conscious of his masculinity before castrating him. Yet Spanish-blooded cattle — along with Africans — are nowadays supplying the horn-dealers' market of America.[8]

The Spanish-speaking people believe in horns. A Texas cowman remarked on a muley cow he saw on a ranch in northern Mexico.

"These muleys," the Mexican *ranchero* replied, "cannot thrive."

"Why?" the Texan asked.

"Because cattle have to have *un lugar para sangrar*, and only the horn affords such *a place to bleed*, to drain."

Texans seemed to think a cow brute might drain too much inwardly in the horn — or not enough. If some animal was not doing well, they pronounced the cause as "hollow horn," and, as a remedy, either bored a hole of small diameter into each horn or sawed the horns off short. From this practice came the saying, applied to some person who appeared to be brainless, "He ought to be bored for the holler horn." As a matter of fact, the horn pith in poorly nourished cattle sometimes shrinks; the proper remedy for the animal is food, and not bloodletting from the horn. Texas steers, when driven to Colorado, Wyoming and other Western states, lengthened their horns while adding weight.

Horns might deceive. Steve Franklin was boss for the great Quien Sabe outfit, owned by an old German-Jew named M. Halff. He was a good man and made good money out of his operations, though, characteristic of his race, he was never a cowman of the soil.

One time Halff bought a big string of old, rough Mexican steers, and when he received them on the Texas side of the Rio Bravo took cognizance of a floating belief that the animals would fatten better if their horns were sawed off.

"Steve," he said to his boss, "I tink you bedder cut dem horns off. Dey is too long and dem steers is too thin."

Then he left, and Steve Franklin with his vaqueros worked for days sawing off the horns. Piled in a heap outside the corral, they "looked like a stack of cordwood."

The next spring Halff was out for the roundup preparatory to shipment. After he had looked over the cattle, he said, "Steve, vhere is de big steers?"

"Why, Mr. Halff, they are in the herd. Didn't you see them?"

"Yes, but I mean dem big, big steers, de ones we got from Mexico."

"Oh, you mean the steers with the long horns that you told me to saw off?"

"Yes, yes, dem big steers is de vones."

"Why, they are in the herd. They just don't have the horns any more, and I guess they don't look so big."

They didn't.

I asked Ab Blocker where the longest horns he ever handled came from.

"From the Blanco River brakes," he replied.

The Blanco is in central Texas, twisting through hills matted with cedar and Spanish oak, the mean altitude being probably above a thousand feet.

In the fall of 1876, the Blockers went up on the Blanco with seven lead oxen to neck to outlaw steers, and with a remarkable maverick-catching dog named Hell Bitch.

The Blocker earmark was grub the left ear — the ear cut off almost to the root — and two under-bits out of the right ear. Day or night Hell Bitch never caught anything but slick-ears. She would unerringly pick the one maverick out of any bunch of cattle, grab it by a long ear, drop between its front legs, throw it and keep it stretched out until a man came to her assistance.

The Blockers roped and branded mavericks all fall and winter. At the same time their main business was "snaring" old steers, roping them in the thickets, catching them at waterings, surpris-ing them with a dash and a tie-down on the openings where they grazed only at night. Daily the neck oxen led the catch of steers to pen camps. When a fair-sized bunch had been accumulated, they were driven down to the Lockhart prairie, where they were day-herded, until spring.

The outlaw steers, all the way from five to fifteen, and even occasionally twenty, years old, were roped irrespective of what brands they wore. Owners who could be located were paid eight or ten dollars a head for them. In the spring there were 3700 pairs of horns on the Lockhart prairie. Eighty-two days after the herd headed up the trail, it was delivered at Cheyenne, Wyoming. Those big steers would walk all day, the point men having to hold them down, and many times they ran most of the night.

"I am confident," Ab Blocker said, "that at least five hundred head of those steers had horns that would average up with the famous specimens in the Buckhorn Saloon in San Antonio."

These steers had the age necessary to produce real horns. Horns continue to grow until a steer is twelve or fifteen years old. The corkscrew curves come with maturity. It is said that wrinkles begin to grow on horns at the age of three. The older an animal, the more wrinkles show. When "the Old Cattleman" in one of Alfred Henry Lewis' *Wolfville* stories says, "He's got plenty of wrinkles on his horns," meaning age and experience, and calls a veteran cowman a "mossy-horn," the language is true to the range. The rough wrinkles probably generated the Texan word *mossy-horn*, not only descriptive of horns but also a name for any old, rough steer. Also, the horns gathered, and were at times twisted about with, the low-hanging Spanish moss from the bottoms, where wild cattle took refuge.

While the United States Government was in 1927 locating a stock of Longhorns in the Wichita Mountains Wildlife Refuge in Oklahoma for the purpose of preserving the breed, Charles Good-night wrote me: "Climatic conditions will prevent these cattle from producing horns of the old type. The horns will become shorter and thicker, the bodies of the cattle more compact, and no power on earth will defeat nature." The Government started out with twenty cows and three bulls, Will C. Barnes, the purchasing agent, having combed the Texas border and East Texas both for specimens. Several animals selected showed Brahma blood. It has virtually been bred out of the offspring, bulls from Mexico having been brought in to strengthen the breed. The herd now (1940) numbers over a hundred and sixty head. Steers eight and ten years old weigh from fifteen hundred to two thousand pounds each — magnificent beeves. Some of them have interesting heads, no spread, however, much exceeding four feet. It cannot be asserted that a spread of six or seven feet — always exceptional — will not some day show up, but so far the Goodnight prophecy has proven fairly accurate.

Many men have held that it takes low ground and moist air to develop horns; others that it takes high ground and dry air. Not enough is known concerning horn growth to warrant categorical assertions. Why did the Spanish cattle up and down a thousand miles of California coast never grow horns commensurate with Texas horns? While millions of Texas cows and heifers were driven to stock the Great Plains, they were generally crossed with graded bulls, the horns thus being bred off the resultant steers.

It takes nourishment to make horn. The "common" cattle of East Texas seldom had the horn, just as they generally lacked the frame and weight, of the same blood of cattle west of the Guadalupe River. One rancher used to claim from experience that greasing the horns of an ox would make them grow. The oxen whose horns he greased picked up shucks, nubbins and other stray food around the barn.

Of the two types of horns, the oxbow and the corkscrew, the latter seem to me more expressive of primitive wildness and variety. One of the range nicknames for Longhorns is "twist-horns." The horns, in their curves and in twists, in their comparative straightness and in their convolutions, one horn often drooping and involuting with more spirals than the other, were as various as the cattle's color combinations, as various as the veining in elm leaves. If a number of pairs of horns be examined, it will be seen that the right horn in a majority of instances points up or down or out quite distinctly from the left horn, which is, on the average, more regular. Perhaps this is partly the reason for the old-time preference for the left horn in making blowing and powder horns. Also, the left horn fits the body of a right-handed man for carrying better.

Some soils more than others seem to provide a substance especially conducive to horn growth. The most powerfully beamed and widely spreading deer antlers on the white-tailed deer of Texas grow in the fairly low brush country, where also — despite Ab Blocker's record for the Blanco River — the greatest steer horns have *generally* developed. A stock of these brush deer, transplanted to the limestone and cedars of the hill country something over a hundred miles away, will develop comparatively spindly horns.

No amount of skill in the ways of animal husbandry, plus the best of feed, can ever produce in a little pasture the horned might that characterized Texas cattle before population, fences, furrows, machinery and cement cut a range, continental in its vastness and primordial in its laws of existence, into policed paddocks, wherein bovine life is protected against the hostility of drouth and cold, as well as against the savagery of beasts. Under primitive conditions only the fittest could survive; predatory animals and the adversities of climate promoted selective breeding. Left to make their own way, the cattle developed hardihood, fleetness, self-dependence. They grew horns to fight off wolves, to hook down succulent mistletoe out of trees, to sweep out of the way thorned branches protecting sparse tufts of grass on the parched ground.

Those mighty horns seemed, like the hoarse howl of the lobo, the wide wheeling of the eagle, and the great silence on the grass, to be a natural part of the freedom, the wildness and the self-sufficiency of life belonging to the unfenced world. They were the crown of the open range, something that the Master Artist of the Fitness of Things might have put there because they belonged.

Yet any virtue carried too far turns against itself. Many wide-spreading horns were not set right for hooking. The steer might rake with his horns, but he could not gore with them as could a black bull or some slim-horned cow. True, many a cowboy tied to a steer has had to cut the rope, but the charging horns that made him cut loose almost never had an exhibition spread.

It was when cattle were massed that horns presented the most extraordinary spectacles. Grazing in tall grass, a herd sometimes appeared to be almost headless, the curved horns bobbing and jerking in the air as if separated from any fastening. The play of lightning on a sea of wet horns was a sight to be remembered forever. Crowded in a pen with their chins resting on or held over the necks and backs of neighbors, the cattle sifted about under a bizarre panoply of seething horns that almost made beholders forget there was anything else in the cattle world.

Sometimes they swam high, heads and tails well out of the water. Again, all parts but noses, faces and the surmounting horns were submerged. Then the glistening river of horns composed by their own undulating formation, surging on in curves as graceful as those of the old moon's horns, was something that not the Colorado, the San Gabriel, the Brazos, the Trinity, the Canadian, the Arkansas, the Platte or the Yellowstone ever surpassed in wonder. Remembering how he crossed the Brazos on a great rise, his herd of two thousand steers all swimming at one time in a long, wavering S in the wide, reddish waters.

Jerry Nance said, "It looked as if I had no cattle at all, for all I could see was the horns."

Horns were put to many uses by pioneer people. They furnished hand-cut buttons and spoons; they made holders for homemade soap, seeds, and other things. Painted and carved, they served as decorative wall pockets. More than one legend of the Southwest relates how Spanish doubloons were buried in a long horn. Horned skulls marked routes. Like deer antlers, the heads made racks for rifles and pegs for hanging harness and saddles on. A long blowing horn not only called hunting dogs but hung at the river bank of ferry crossings so that travelers might with it summon the ferryman; on plantations it tolled field hands in to dinner and at camp meetings announced the hour for services under brush arbors.

Often and often I have wished that I could have seen the wonderful fences of horned skulls enclosing fine homes at Buenos Aires as described by W. H. Hudson in *Far Away and Long Ago*. The walls about these *quintas*, seven, eight and nine feet high, were built entirely of cows' heads, the horns projecting outward. "Hundreds of thousands of skulls had thus been used, and some of the old, very long walls, crowned with green grass and with creepers and wild flowers growing from the cavities in the bones, had a strangely picturesque but somewhat uncanny appearance."

During mission days in California the *rancheros* and *padres* used to take skulls — which they used also for chairs — from the slaughter grounds, where they lay bleaching by the thousands, and top the adobe walls of their corrals with them as a palisade against horse thieves.

The *conquistadores*, and long after them the gold hunters of California, prospected with a great horn spoon. David Crockett used a horn cup pretty regularly in an endeavor to carry out the first part of his rule never to eat on an empty stomach or to drink on a full one. In the desert lands of the Southwest a horn, in place of canteen or gourd, sometimes carried water meaning life itself. In Mexico some of the finest carving of the Western Hemisphere has been done on horns of Spanish cattle designed for blowing, for flagons and for powder flasks. There, too, an art has developed in fashioning birds, crocodiles, armadillos and other animals out of horns.

I have made something of a collection of horn artifacts. It is on exhibition in the Texas Museum at Austin. The fitness of things demands that in Texas, some day, a great collection of horn objects and horn art be assembled, along with a varied assemblage of Longhorn heads in their natural state.

The cattle kings of the eighties and nineties had a passion for chairs made of horns — with leather or red-plush seats; and there were horn tables, stands, hat-racks and other articles of furniture.

When the Stockman's Band, later famous as the Cowboy Band, of Dodge City was organized in 1881, the ægis on which its banner rested was a set of horns from a Texas steer. A pair of horns was the symbol of the whole cow country and a sign that it never wearied of erecting. No bank was complete without one or more heads, and the picture of another head adorned its checks. Livestock commission companies used the same emblem on their letterheads. The barbershop — with the only heater in town for a hot-water bath — had its head of horns. Characteristic of saloons from Brownsville to Helena, the Cowboy's Saloon in Carlsbad, New Mexico, had hanging behind the bar a reproduction of "Custer's Last Stand," flanked on either side by a picture of a naked woman; but the whole art exhibit was dominated by a pair of longhorns said to measure close to nine feet in spread. On six-shooters with handles of bone, silver and ivory the favorite adornment was the head of a Longhorn.

That head signified not only an occupation, but a kind of honor that men not engaged, as well as those engaged, in it

would render the animal on which it rested. That head symbolized strength and power and wide-ranging freedom in the great
out-yonder. As generations are outmoded, their artifacts and
gewgaw ornaments are discarded with them, but something in
the mighty horns of the Texas steer has kept them from the
junk shop. They are more highly prized today than ever before.

XIII · RAWHIDE

*To Evetts Haley, range historian, range man, natural-
ist, storyteller. If money would back his project for a
museum of the cow country, with emphasis on rawhide art and artifacts, he would build one of the original institutions of America.*

IF, considering technique as well as interpretation of life, I
were asked to pick out the best short story dealing with any
theme of the Southwest, I should choose Stewart Edward
White's "Rawhide." Yet it is but a writing man's utilization of a
tradition that, in popular anecdotes of reality and in more popular folk yarns, has for generations been massing itself into a
cycle both grim and rollicky. Longhorn hides and men who
rode "rawhide horses," swung rawhide ropes and slept on raw-

[221]

hide beds gave the tradition its body and zest. This was during times in a parched land when thirst was supposed to be allayed by keeping either a bullet or a bit of rawhide in the mouth. Rawhide, lead and thirst seem to go together.

One blazing summer day, long ago now, Print Olive rode up on a rustler burning out the brand on one of his cows, in the San Gabriel country. He killed the cow, made the thief help skin her, wrapped him up in the hide, and left him in the sun.

The salient qualities of rawhide are durability and toughness, flexibility and power to stretch when wet, and a corresponding power to contract when dry and remain as stiff as an ax-handle.

Over and over, with multiplied variations, the story has been told of the settler who one summer day hitched a horse with rawhide traces to a "lizard" and went down to the creek a half mile away to drag a barrel of water to his house. Just after he got the barrel filled, a rain came up. With head down, walking close beside the horse so as to use its body as a shield against the driving rain, he drove back up the hill. About the time he stopped beside the kitchen door, the rain ceased and the sun came out. He looked and he saw that he had no sled or barrel of water. All he could see was a thin, long-stretched-out pair of rawhide traces.

The settler was neither startled nor perplexed. He unhitched, threw the hames — to which the forward ends of traces are attached — over a stump, sat down under the shed at the front of his house, and while he slowly chewed tobacco and fanned the gnats away, watched down the road. The sun was scorching now and the earth was steaming. After a while he saw the barrel on the sled snailing homeward. The dependable laws of heat and dryness and of rawhide were contracting the traces. Finally the sled stopped right at the stump.

One time a freighter with two wagons of eight oxen each got bogged in the black waxy San Miguel country, in the bottom of a creek. He took the oxen out of his second wagon and hitched them to the first, but still the sixteen oxen couldn't budge the wagon. They would pull, pull, all of them together, laying all their weight against the yoke, not lunging like horses or mules, but steady. Yet the wheels would not move. They seemed vised with steel in the deep, tight mud.

Then the freighter had an idea. He told his helpers to unyoke the oxen and let them graze. He had heard a range bull bellowing down in a thicket. He got the wind, crawled up, and shot him. The bull was an old-timer with hide as thick as an elephant's — almost. The men skinned him. Then the freighter cut a broad band, around and around, out of the thick hide. It was damp and pliable from animal moisture, but he let it soak an hour in the creek water. Then he tied one end of it to the wagon tongue, pulled with all his forces on the other end until the thong was taut, and tied it around a mesquite tree well up on the bank.

The sun was shining. The freighter filled his pipe, smoked, took a nap, chunked up the coals around the coffeepot, drained it, and then, after filling his pipe again, began watching the spokes of his wheels. At last he saw a minute movement. The hot sun was at work. The freighter shifted himself into better shade. Every now and then he could note a fraction of a revolution in the wheels, as slow but as inevitable as the late afternoon prolongation of the shadow of a high mountain across a valley floor.

At the end of the day the wagon was perceptibly forward. That night the freighter let the rawhide soak again. The next morning he fastened it once more to the tongue and stretched it to the mesquite. The sun shone. The rawhide pulled — pulled like raw bacon drawing a boil to a head. The freighter almost got tired of resting, smoking his pipe, and napping in the shade. His oxen were getting a fine rest and fill of grass. He wasn't an impatient man. If he had been, he would not have chosen oxen. Again the rawhide was soaked over night. On the third day it drew the wagon clean out of the mud and up on to the hard bank.

The contracting and expanding powers of rawhide gave an ingenuity to Indian torture on the desert comparable to that imagined by Edgar Allan Poe in "The Pit and the Pendulum." Vicente Gomez, a *mestizo* of northern Mexico, hated all Spaniards. He perfected the art of sewing up his *gachupín* prisoners in fresh bull hides and then leaving them on lava or sand under a blazing sun that would not fail to add to the agony of thirst the exquisite agony of slow, slow strangulation of the entire body.

Another form of rawhide torture – though I have heard of it only among the gauchos of South America – was to stake out the prisoner in four directions with green hide. Under the pitiless sun, the hide bindings would in the end quarter the wretch as effectively as wild horses hitched to his limbs and lunging in opposite directions. Pancho Villa's reputed method of binding a narrow strip of wet rawhide around a victim's head and putting him in the sun followed the principle.

It is told that the Yaqui Indians used sometimes to tie a prisoner down and then bring a captured rattlesnake near his face, staking it by a rawhide thong. They would tease the snake so that it would strike at the face of the fixed man, just missing it. Then an Indian would begin dropping water slowly and patiently, drop by drop, on the rawhide. Soon it would begin to stretch. At each lunge the maddened rattlesnake would dart his pitted head a fraction nearer until the fangs finally sank into the nose or cheek of the victim, to whom would now come an end of the many deaths he had already died while the rawhide stretched.

A prisoner held by Mexicans at Presidio on the Rio Grande was bound hand and foot by rawhide strings and left under a bush a short way out from the river. Somehow he managed to roll over and over until he got to the edge of the bank. Then with one more effort he rolled down into the water. As he had planned, his soaked bonds stretched so that he was able to free hands and feet before his captors discovered the ruse.

Texas used to be called "the Rawhide State," and the saying went that "what a Texan can't mend with rawhide ain't worth mending." Before barbed wire arrived, according to another saying, Texas was "bound together with rawhide." It was well bound. Some people called the binding "Mexican iron." It was an essential factor in the culture of the country. In the form of riatas, which took the place of chains, it had fittingly measured off the earliest Spanish grants of land. The rope-lengths stretched between two horsemen surveying in a lope resulted in boundaries well described as being "*más ó menos* (more or less)" so many leagues and varas in extent.

One of the many ranch uses of rawhide was for horse hobbles. When kept greased — with melted tallow or neat's-foot oil — they did not chafe a horse's legs. Cattle at their cheapest were never so cheap as in South America, where a rider of the Argentine pampas might at evening kill a bull in order to use his horns for a picket pin. The Texas cowhand, if he did not expect to return at night to the place where he saddled his horse in the morning, carried his rawhide hobbles either on his saddle or, more frequently, around his horse's neck — like a bell strap, which was also of rawhide.

In 1868 Jim Loving struck out from Parker County, Texas, with 2600 head of cattle and twenty cowboys, for Colorado. In the Indian Territory, a Comanche chief with about a thousand warriors halted the herd. Immediately he accused Loving and his men of being Texans — in Comanche, as in Mexican, minds a nationality apart and distinct from Americans. Loving did his best to convince the Comanche that his outfit was from Kansas. He was making out a pretty good case when a warrior noticed the pair of rawhide hobbles around the neck of a horse ridden by one of Loving's men.

"*Tejano!*" he growled, pointing to the hobbles and then giving the Texan's nose a pull.

The Indians took a lot of cattle, though the Texas men escaped with the main herd and their lives. Rawhide gave them away.

A trail outfit usually had a dry cowhide slung under the bed of the chuck wagon for carrying wood or cow chips in, for fuel on the plains. This hide was called a "cooney" (from *cuna*, cradle); movers with numerous children sometimes placed the little ones in this cowhide sling and then it was truly a *cuna*. Other names for it were "caboose" and "possum belly." It told the origin of the Texas trail drivers as plainly as a license plate tells the origin of an automobile.

In 1873 Missouri, because of the fear of "Texas fever," had a law against the entrance of any Texas cattle that had not been wintered north of Red River. During the summer of that year Shanghai Pierce sent a herd of his coastal steers from Wichita, Kansas, where they had just arrived, into Missouri. Soon after the herd got across the line, a Missouri stockman rode out to camp, looked at the cattle, looked at the men, and began to ask questions. The boss assured him that the steers, although originally from Texas, had been wintered in Kansas. But the Missourian kept looking at the "cooney" under the chuck wagon. He rode off only to return with a posse and a writ putting the whole trail crew under arrest. How Shanghai Pierce came to the rescue does not pertain to the story of rawhide.

When they got up into the Northwest, the trail men were dubbed "rawhides." Charles M. Russell's character "Rawhide" Rawlins illustrates the esteem with which the name was applied. When a dogie yearling, "just a ball of hair," was called a "rawhide," no slur was intended on the old-timer with the bark on characterized by the same name.

A class of Texans not highly respected were called "rawhiders" — at least in New Mexico, where James A. McKenna

knew them. Before setting out on any trip, McKenna asserts, the migratory rawhiders "usually killed three or four large steers, not for food, but for hides. These were stored in their wagon beds and supplied a hundred and one needs. If they had a breakdown, they soaked the hide and cut it into long strips, called whangs, which they wrapped around the broken hub, wheel, or tongue. As the whang dried, the edges of the break drew together. Their chairs, campstools, wheelbarrows and buckets were made from hide. Their oxen were shod with it, and the shoes they themselves wore were usually made from leftover pieces. All rawhiders came from West Texas years before farming and drilling for oil became common there."

The nearer to Mexico and Mexican cattle the ranch breed lived, the tighter they were "held" by rawhide. When the brush poppers from southern Texas pointed their herds north right after the Civil War, many of them rode rawhide-rigged saddles, tightened their horse-mane girths with wreathing straps of plaited rawhide, protected their feet from thorns by *tapaderos* (toe-fenders) of rawhide, and wore leggins (now generally called chaps) of the same material. If not of horsehair, their headstalls and bridle reins were of rawhide. On the trail, rawhide served them as thread, pins, nails, iron, cloth — for anything to be made or mended. Rawhide was plaited into the quirts, which when hit across leggins made a noise that would almost jump a wild steer out of his own hide.

At the close of the last century rawhide leggins were still common with Mexicans in lower Texas. One February while I — just a kid — was going with my father and some vaqueros for a herd of yearlings two or three days' drive from our ranch, a cold rain soaked us. That night everybody was drying himself out against a long mesquite fire, for wood was plentiful. An old Mexican, blacker than a black Comanche, with deep smallpox pits covering his hairless face, had a pair of rawhide leggins that he let dry too long. They had been as limber as dishrags. After they were dry, he stood them up, as stiff as two stovepipes, before the other vaqueros. Then he began to hold a conversation between himself and the *chivarros*, making up right there a little stage comedy that set everybody to roaring.

Fiber ropes in earlier days were almost unknown. The rope attached to a hackamore for use in breaking horses was of horse-hair and so was the stake rope, the *cabestro*. But the roping rope, the lariat (from *la riata*), was of rawhide, four, sometimes eight, strands plaited into a long, graceful, even and beautiful line. It was worked, stretched and oiled until it was just stiff enough and just pliant enough to sing through the air like a fiddle string and fix itself around the object to be lassoed with the deftness and sureness of a roadrunner's dart upon a grasshopper on a blade of grass.

The California vaquero put far more reliance on his ability to lasso and drag to death a horse thief Indian than on any kind of firearm. While the Texas rangers — as *cuerados* (clothed in and equipped with rawhide) as the Mexican *rurales* (mounted police) — were making Colt's six-shooter famous, they guarded as alertly against the riatas of Santa Anna's guerillas as against his cannon. After the battle of Buena Vista, orders issued from headquarters of the American troops permitted soldiers to shoot down any Mexican found within the limits of the city of Saltillo with a lariat attached to his saddle horn. The best riatas in North America today come from Sonora and Sinaloa, and many men living in those regions remember when horsemen fought duels with the riata, each dodging the other's loop, while trying to rope his opponent, jerk him off and drag him into shreds.

The one handicraft of Mexican vaqueros and American cow-boys to be classed as true native art was the art of plaiting raw-hide — along with the weaving of horsehair. When the history of native art in the Southwest comes to be written, the historian, advancing beyond Indian crafts, will go to hide, hair and horns

— hide first, in that order. No machine can ever cut long thongs like a vaquero, around and around out of a hide, widening the strip at thin places and narrowing it at thick places, so that when stretched it will be uniform in width and strength. No machine will ever be devised to take eight of these thongs, tapering from each end to the middle, plait them together half their length and then double back and plait them into the original plaiting, making a quirt of sixteen strands that for texture, symmetry, flexibility, balance of weight and gradation of diameter equals in workmanship the accomplishment of any weaving, whether of basket or blanket, of any time.

The bullwhackers of the Plains made a reputation by their ability to pick a fly off an ox's back with the popper on a long blacksnake whip. The whip might be of leather — which is cured hide — or rawhide. In California and Texas the early day cowhunters used plaited rawhide whips, fifteen feet or so long, with poppers of buckskin, fine leather, plaited horsehair, or specially prepared rawhide. On the prairies the popping of these whips brought cattle running to the roundup grounds. It could be heard much farther than a pistol shot and was more startling. There was never a braver sound than the popping of a long, well-made whip in the hand of an expert. Overton Stoner, who wore a rawhide string for a belt and never carried a gun, always said he wanted no better weapons than his riata and his rawhide cow-whip.

Sometimes a long, broad thong of hide was twisted, or curled, so that the result was round. After being dried, the twist would remain, no matter if wetted. On occasion, rawhide neither plaited nor twisted was used as a rope. That border hero of tale and ballad, Mustang Gray, acquired his name by such a use.

> He ne'er would sleep within a tent,
> No comforts would he know,
> But like a brave old Texian,
> A-ranging he would go.

Some fatality cast him afoot out on the prairies, where being horseless was next to being dead. Gray discovered a hole of water at which mustangs drank, coming down a trail under a tree. He killed a buffalo, skinned it, cut the hide into a long rough riata, hid himself in the tree, and when the mustangs passed beneath cast a loop over the head of a powerful stallion. This creature he finally subdued sufficiently to mount. Without saddle and with only a rawhide thong around the horse's under-jaw to guide him, Gray rode to a distant settlement — and to the name of "Mustang."

As the Comanches used shields of dried buffalo hide, the riata-ed Mexicans made theirs, just as tough, of cowhide. While traveling through Chihuahua in 1834 on a trading expedition, John J. Linn saw Mexicans armed against the Comanches with shields of rawhide "decorated by curious and artistically executed devices," some bearing dates "as early as 1734." It is claimed that sometimes a California vaquero would, protected by one of these rawhide shields, advance afoot to knife a grizzly bear he had roped.

Some of the early Spanish *conquistadores*, unable to get iron, shod their horses with silver; perhaps it was after finding how soft this metal is that they began shoeing with the more durable rawhide. Or it may have been the Apaches who initiated raw-hide horseshoes. A generation ago they were still not uncommon in the Southwest. Now and then they are still made, by cutting out a round piece of rawhide, punching holes along the edge of it, inserting a drawstring, and then drawing the piece, wet and soft, up around the horse's hoof. Unless carefully put on, the rawhide would chafe the horse's heel or fetlock when dry — but it served.

The use seems to have been unknown in the eastern hemi-sphere until introduced from the west. A detachment of troops in British Africa being guided by the great scout, Frederick Russell Burnham, found their horseshoes worn out and their horses too lame to travel farther. Burnham had had his training among the Apaches and the range men of Arizona. In an abandoned hut he now observed some bull-hide shields. He soaked them in water and cut the hide into patterns that were stretched tightly over each horse hoof. With their mounts thus reshod, the Britishers proceeded, greatly astonished, for they had never before heard of rawhide horseshoes.

There was another way of making horses go with rawhide. The plains Indians were proficient in the practice. Small sacks of dried rawhide containing rocks will rattle more hideously than tin cans. These were strung on a riata tied to a horse's tail and then the horse was sent pell-mell into any *caballada* the Indians thought they could steal by stampeding. A dried cowhide fastened to the tail of a runaway horse is an effective stampeder.

While John Woodhouse Audubon, son of the ornithologist, was crossing the Sierra Madre with a California-bound expedition in 1849, he experienced a variation in the methods of rawhide stampeders. "The scoundrels," he wrote, "take a strong horse, cover him with the skin of an ox that has been newly killed, putting the flesh side out, tie all the bells they have on the horse, and, fastening an enormous bunch of dry brush to his tail, set fire to it and start him off with yells and shouts through the camp to be stampeded. Horses and mules, keen of scent and hearing, receive warnings through both faculties and are so frightened they will break any ordinary fastening," and stampede, leaving their owners afoot.

At times the "Mexican iron" became steel. Comanches used it for bridle bits as well as for headstalls and reins. Apaches discovered that the riata made a good saw. One morning John Chisum's "warriors" — as he correctly called his cowboys on the Pecos —woke up to find that Apaches had by sawing a riata back and forth cut a gap in a high adobe pen wall and stolen their entire remuda.

It was the domestic use of rawhide by pioneers that made it

a component of American culture. One of the earliest school-teachers among the Texas colonists on the Brazos River was W. W. Browning. He used to tell of a certain experience he had in trying to teach one of the young Texans how to spell "bed." Finally in desperation he asked the blockhead, "What do you sleep on at night?"

"Cowhides and blankets," came the prompt reply.

The blankets were a luxury except for covering. One form of bed was made by fixing a post out from the corner of a cabin, running a rail from it to the wall on either side, and then a rail from the extreme end of each of these two rails to the corner. On the frame thus made was stretched a cowhide that served as slats, springs and mattress, the occupants not requiring "beauty rest." One time a traveler on the frontier stopped at an old-timer's ranch for the night. After supper and a smoke, the host yanked a beef hide from the corner of the cabin, threw it on the dirt floor, and, turning to his guest, said, "You sleep here. I'll rough it."

Even hats were occasionally made of rawhide, a hole more or less the size of the wearer's head being dug in the ground and then the wet hide rammed and stretched into this hole until it was head-shaped. Such a hat could never have been as comfortable as a bull-hide mattress.

On the walls of the ancient Governor's Palace at Santa Fe used to hang Spanish portraits of the sixteenth century done on rawhide. That is exactly what pictures of the *conquistadores* should have been painted on. Tom O'Connor, who during the days of the Texas Republic founded the great ranch that still flourishes under his family name, had his prayer book bound in rawhide.

The most durable and the most comfortable chairs ever fashioned have rawhide bottoms, either of solid hide or of criss-crossed thongs. Trunks, buckets, wine vats and hoppers for grain mills were made of hide.

One way of giving a hide proper flexibility for robe or rug

was to use it as a sled for hauling water barrels on, or, better still, for hauling dirt. The old Randado Ranch of Southwest Texas is famous for a big tank constructed, according to tradition, by cowhide sleds that hauled dirt out of the pit and onto the dam.

Cowhide sleds drew up Uncle Ship Carnes. He was a mighty deer hunter, but during the summer when deer ranged out on the open prairies he had difficulty in approaching near enough for a shot — until he devised a ruse. He got a large "flint hide," put a bell on his old gray horse, hitched him with a set of plow harness to a singletree tied to the tail of the hide, and set out for the prairie. While some distance away from the deer, he would hunker down on the hide, and, guiding his horse with lines made of rawhide, allow him to walk and graze near enough for a shot. High grass obscured the form of the man on the sled, and the leisurely movements of the belled horse aroused no suspicions. "Uncle Ship Carnes seldom failed to get a deer when he went out on his beef hide."

One way to shoot wolves was to stake out the head of a slaughtered beef, and then with two dry hides, which would stay in any kind of propped position, make, a little off to one side, a tent-shaped blind for concealing a man with a gun. The wolves would come to eat on the beef head.

A hide was "as handy as a shirt pocket" — for anything. In 1875 a woman who had then been in Texas for fifty-two years wrote: "After we stayed on the Brazos River a few days we thought we would go a visiting to see your Pa's people over to Coloread [the Colorado River] which I think was about fifty miles. Well we had nobody to leave ouer things with. So your Pa took all of ouer goods off in a thick part of the cain brake and hid them under a yearling beef *hide* which would protect them from the rain. Then we set out on Tormentor and rickety poly [the two horses]."

If brush was not handy, cowhides roofed a shed. Colonel

Gussett started Gussettville with nothing but a barrel of whisky and a cowhide stretched over the barrel. Rawhide laced by strings of the same material to a frame of poles doored and windowed many a cabin. Hides for such purposes were dried without salt; then they would not soften so much when damp. Wooden doors and windows were fastened to frames with rawhide hinges.

The rawhide playing-cards with which Comanches and Apaches gambled seem not to have been adopted by the frontiersmen, but they would not have been out of place in a cabin of "rawhide lumber" — boards sawed or hewn from green oak, elm or cottonwood that warped when dry until they were as crooked as a "Davy Crockett log" — a log that could never lie still in its hunt for the unfindable center of gravity. One time, they say, a carpenter who was as deliberate as a West Texas drouth in breaking and as slow as molasses in January got hold of a green cottonwood plank to be used for flooring. While he was considering how to lay it, it warped around him and held him so fast that another carpenter had to come and saw him out. The people living in the cabin of rawhide lumber up above the forks of the creek drove their wagon out over a "rawhide road" — a bridge of rough logs.

The early settlers never wore the rawhide *guaraches* (sandals) of the Mexicans, but they had rawhide shoeing of another style. Jack Hawkins told me that all the pay he drew for six months of service as a Texas ranger in 1874 was ten dollars, and that meanwhile he and his companions had been nowhere to spend even that amount. If they were low on footgear and found an old bull, they would shoot him, skin out the hocks and let the rest of the hide go.

"Our hearts were cased with buffalo hocks."

The hocks made their shoes. After they got wet and then dried, they might pinch, but pounding with rock or hammer would limber them up. One ranger who had no drawers and whose pants' seat had worn out patched the hole with rawhide. A rain came, the sun shone, the patch shrank, and the ranger was compelled to cut it out and wear his breeches in Indian style. This suggests a whole string of yarns about buckskin breeches that stretched and shriveled, making their wearers get in tune with that old fiddle breakdown "Leather Britches."

In extremity, men might turn coyote and eat rawhide. A party of Mormon emigrants, storm-besieged in a desolate part of the Rocky Mountains, were reduced to a little sugar and the flint hides taken from their starved oxen. After various experiments, they worked out a recipe for rawhide gelatine. "First, scorch the hide. This has a tendency to purify the bad taste. Then scrape the hair off and boil one hour in plenty of water. Throw away the water after it has extracted all the glue. Now, after rinsing in cold water, boil the hide to a jelly. Eat cold with a little sugar sprinkled on it." Daniel Jones, leader of the starving Mormons, adds: "We asked the Lord to bless our stomachs and adapt them to this food. We hadn't the faith to ask Him to bless the rawhide. This fare kept us alive for six weeks, without any cases of gout."

Occasionally a green cowhide made the coffin for a frontier burial. In 1877 some ranchers of Lee County, Texas, on the lookout for cattle thieves, came upon two just completing the skinning of a beef. The rustlers had prudently dug a hole in which to bury the hide so as to destroy brand evidence. It was an unusually large hole, in sandy soil. After the ranchers shot, they wrapped the bodies in the big hide, tied a rope around the bulk, rolled it into the hole, and covered it up. — "So red the rose."

During the dreadful cholera epidemic in San Antonio in the late 1840's, hides served for biers as well as winding sheets and shrouds. "We met no one in the streets," the wonder-loving French missionary Domenech related, "save those who were carrying off the dead. Coffins were scarce and corpses were strapped to dried ox-hides and thus dragged along, all livid and purple, to their graves."

Many a child of the frontier was rocked in a rawhide cradle, and the birth of Cotton Wright was in harmony with the cradle. His father, "W 6" Wright, so known on account of his brand, was returning with his wife and children to their Nueces County home, driving an ox cart. Bad weather had delayed them. Then one night a howling norther of sleet and rain whipped slits in the canvas over the cart bed, in which Mrs. Wright lay in the throes of childbirth. Faithful Mexican hands grabbed a huge beef hide from a tree where somebody had left it to dry and held it over the canvas, keeping the pallet in the cart dry and protecting it from the blast. Thus little Cotton was born.

When, in 1867, George Reynolds in a fight with Indians on Double Mountain Fork of the Brazos River was shot by an arrow that went through his stomach — the iron spike lodging in his backbone and there staying until it was removed fourteen years later by a surgeon in Kansas City — he was brought back to the Stone Ranch on a litter made of a cowhide stretched between two horses.

"As tough as rawhide," the old saying went. Probably no form of animal structure except teeth and ivory was ever tougher than the dried hide of an old Longhorn bull. The ultimate in "guying," "ragging," deviling a human being was appropriately termed "rawhiding." To cowhide man or beast in a more literal sense was to "beat the living daylights out of him."

The hides of lean animals are stronger and more durable than those of fat animals. Hence the superior toughness of hides from the lanky Longhorns. The test of toughness was in the encasement of cart, wagon and buggy wheels. In the dry climate characterizing the land of two continents over which Spanish cattle roamed, all woodwork shrinks. Within a short time the fellies of any new wagon would shrink away from the iron tires. Far from blacksmiths, the wagon operators might drive wooden wedges under the metal bands to make them stay on, but this remedy could be only temporary. Wet rawhide wrapping would in drying clamp the tires on the wooden circumference of the wheels. Except in sharp rocks, it would wear indefinitely.

Before starting on a long trip across the pampas and over the Andes, about 1820, the overseer of transportation came to Captain F. B. Head and asked "for money to purchase hides, in order to prepare the carriages in the usual way. The hides were soaked and then cut into long strips, about three-quarters of an inch broad, and the pole as well as almost all other woodwork of the carriages was firmly bound with the wet hide, which, when dry, shrunk into a band nearly as hard as iron. The spokes and fellies were similarly bound, so that the wheels traveled on hide. . . . It went perfectly sound for 700 miles and was then cut only by sharp granite rocks."

A suspension bridge across a deep river in Chile was made of rawhide. If you visit the old church in Juarez across the Rio Grande from El Paso and fall under the direction of a certain guide who is liberal with his facts, you will learn that the swagging rawhide cables from which the cracked bells swing have not been replaced since they were fixed there two centuries or so ago. I did not ask this guide how he knew. It is a fact that more than eighty years after artisans lashed rafters and beams together with green rawhide in the roof of the Mormon tabernacle at Salt Lake City, the original fastenings still hold.

The stake-and-rider fence, made of poles, was characteristic of the old South; the corral of the big Mexican hacienda was made of adobe or stone. The representative pen on a Texas ranch was made — and in mesquite and cedar country still is made — of pairs of posts set in the ground from four to eight feet apart, the space between uprights being filled lengthwise with interlacing poles. In order to keep the posts from spreading at the top and thus letting the filling tumble down, they must be tied together. The tying nowadays is usually with scraps of barbed wire; fifty years ago the hoops were of slick wire; before that they were of rawhide. Often a corral was made by digging a continuous trench, about three feet deep, planting pickets upright in it, and then lashing them together near the top with green rawhide. The result was a fence hog-tight, horse-high and bull-proof. The poles that closed the gap were tied in place with rawhide ropes.

In Mexico, where oxen push against yokes laced to their horns with rawhide, where rawhide alternates with native fiber in binding down the rafters of cabin roofs, where rawhide ropes bind loads on burros that are followed by footmen wearing rawhide sandals, fence pickets held in place with *cuero de vaca* may still be found. There also, in some places, horse power still lifts water from hand-dug wells in buckets of bull hide.

Before the Civil War great amounts of silver pesos were freighted by ox and mule wagons from Chihuahua City to San Antonio and thence to the coast for shipment. The coins were sewed up in wet bullock hides, 3000 pesos to the hide, which when dry were as hard as bone, making — except for gnawing rats — a casement as protective as it was unwieldy.

In California, before the Gold Rush, the hides themselves were coins of the realm, commonly known as "California bank notes." There, "Cheyenne" Dawson recorded, "a horseman would come galloping into town with a dry beef hide fast to his riata and springing up and down behind him — this was his money." He traded it for what he needed. If he had vegetables, chickens or some other produce to bring to town to sell, he brought the articles on a cowhide. On such a transport he might bring his own family. If he had an oxcart — the wheels made of segments of tree-trunk with holes in the center for the axle — its bed was a bull hide. A big cow-horn filled with soap afforded lubricant for the screeching wheels and axles. In his home the native Californian sat on a cowhide or an ox-skull. The dining table was a cowhide spread on a dirt floor. The meat, boiled with chili, had been dried on a line made of a rawhide riata.

In a chapter called "For Their Hides and Tallow," in *A Vaquero of the Brush Country*, I have told of the "skinning wars" and of the "hide and tallow factories" that operated in Texas during the late sixties and early seventies, when cattle were hardly worth stealing and when a cow's hide was actually worth more than a live cow. That was when old steers with horn-spreads wider than the length of a man from his feet to the tips of his fingers on upraised arm were driven by the hundreds and thousands to such plants as that above Brazoria. Here Negroes shucked the hides off, tried out the tallow, and then skidded the meat down chutes into the Brazos River, where catfish gorged themselves and grew to gigantic size. A similar establishment at Quintana at the mouth of the Brazos so attracted sharks that people were afraid to go in swimming. The operators of these hide and tallow factories would buy out whole brands of cattle and after skinning what was worth skinning sell yearlings at a dollar a head. It was a time when bands of Mexicans rode the country between the Nueces and the Rio Grande, running onto cattle, cutting their hamstrings with machetes, then stabbing them, skinning them, and leaving the carcasses for coyotes and buzzards, the hides being hauled in carts across the Rio Bravo to be bonded back for shipment to Boston.

In some areas hide rustlers burned off the grass so that cattle would starve to death. With not a drift fence or a line rider between the Gulf of Mexico and the North Pole, the blue and the wet northers of some winters would drift vast numbers of cattle southward for hundreds of miles, until along the creeks and in the coves of the coast lands they would bank up, mill about, eat off everything in reach of water, bog down and starve. Then a cold wet spell would pave the stomping grounds with carcasses, and, from towns like Corpus Christi, saloonkeepers, draymen, carpenters — everybody — turned out to skin dead cattle. Often they helped out of their misery cattle that had life as well as skins. During the early 1870's the waste of Longhorns for hides in southern Texas, from the Rio Grande to the Sabine, was equalled only by the buffalo slaughter proceeding on the Plains. In this part of the country the "range wars" were over hides rather than over sheep.

No wonder the cowmen organized, called upon rangers, hired gunmen, to prevent their cattle from being exterminated by hide thieves and to save the hides off dead cattle for themselves. With everything else vanishing in a die-up, a hide could at least furnish expense money. One hard year, long after the skinning wars had passed but drouths had not, Mexican skinners were daily bringing in hides taken from cattle owned and owed on by a philosophic cowman of the Brush Country. Every evening after the reports were all in, he used to say, "Thank God, the hides ain't mortgaged."

And now, let's go get something to cut the dust. My throat feels like a piece of old rawhide.

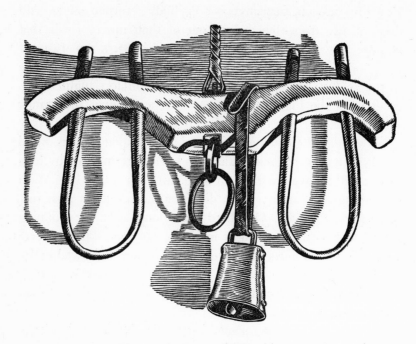

XIV · OXEN AND TAILS

To Railroad (R. R.) Smith, defender of free speech,
reservoir of folk history, and talker until the Morning
Star is up.

When the Mormons drifted southward,
He was one of a ten-span team,
The biggest young ox them Utah
Bullwhackers hed ever seen.

Tawny en' bony en' holler,
At three years full six feet tall,
En' he'd break the chain whenever he'd strain
In a heavy wagon stall.

Out of a team of twenty
Which died in the White Sands Pass,

He alone pulled through en' made his way
To the springs of San Nicolás.

Twenty Mormon women,
In all, fifty Mormon souls,
Died from the lack of water,
Paying the desert toll.

The ranchmen on hearing the story,
How everyone had died,
Let the big steer have his freedom
Through the Organ Valley wide.

In the winter he'd drift down southward
To the Franklin Mountains warm;
In the summer you'd find him grazin'
On the top of El Toro's horn.

THIS is Jack Thorp's tribute to Old North,[1] an ox of the rock-bottom breed.

The smartest ox that ever lived, according to the stories that have come down,[2] must have been a muley Texas steer named Old Brindle. He belonged to a freight outfit that made a practice of traveling empty to a railroad point and returning with heavy loads. One evening, preparatory to starting out on the long trip for freight, the wagon master gave the night-herder orders to bring in the oxen before daylight next morning. By the time they arrived, bedrolls were in the wagons, breakfast was ready, and as soon as it was bolted, each bullwhacker began to inspan his oxen.

But the nigh wheeler, Old Brindle, in Joe Goodbread's team was missing. This was strange, for Joe had just seen him; the night-herder swore he had pounded him on the rump several times while bringing him in, and the boss remembered that when the oxen came in he had noticed him walk over close to his proper wagon. Each wagon had a trailer, and all the wagons, including the trailers, were covered with wagon sheets. Being

a muley, Brindle was always conspicuous. Now, the whole outfit was delayed on account of his absence. With the first light
the boss and the night-herder were scouring the country around
on horseback. It was "so bare and level that a jack rabbit needed
to carry a fly for a shade," but Brindle was nowhere in sight.
Finally the boss told Joe Goodbread to turn Brindle's mate into
the "cavayard," yoke up another pair of oxen for wheelers, and
pull out.

The wagon train went about eight miles and stopped for a late
dinner. While the men were eating, they continued to speculate
on the strange vanishment of Old Brindle. Joe Goodbread remarked that he was going to have to grease his wagons. "Why,"
he said, "from the way my trailer is pulling, you'd think it was
loaded."

Then suddenly he jumped as if he had had a thought and went
around behind his wagon and looked into the trailer. The wagon
sheet at the front was open, though closed with the puckering-
string at the rear.

"Come here, fellers," Joe said, a smile spread over his face.

There were plenty of witnesses to what some people might
not believe. In the trail wagon, hidden by the sheet, was the missing ox. He was coiled up and sleeping like a bear in his winter
den. He was even using Joe's bedroll for a pillow. Joe Goodbread could not be mad; he was proud of having such a smart
ox. He crawled in and gave the ox a few kicks in the ribs. Old
Brindle opened his eyes, yawned, got up as deliberate as a ticket
agent, and jumped out.

It didn't do much good to bell some of these smart old oxen.
Along about daylight, when most cattle are grazing, there would
not be a sound of the bell. The ox wearing it was lying down in
the thickest clump of brush he could find or in some gully, his
head on the ground, not moving. A certain pair of oxen named
Tom and Jerry would, after being turned out at night, stay
together until towards morning. Then they would separate, go-

ing in opposite directions, to hide. When one of them was finally found and brought in, he could not be worked until his mate arrived. They acted in exasperating harmony.

Jerry Hendricks had a big old wheel ox named Sam Houston that could almost manage a wagon by himself. Hendricks always drove with a long whip fastened to a long handle; upon starting down hill he would tap the handle across the skulls of his wheel oxen to make them hold back. Sam Houston caught on, and whenever Hendricks showed his whip-handle, he would, while holding back himself, hit the other wheeler across the frontal with his inside horn. A person a hundred yards off could hear Sam Houston's horn clacking against some green ox's head.

The way a pair of great-horned oxen could work side by side without their horns' getting in the way of each other was a wonder. Bob Routh told me that during the Civil War his family had a red ox in Collin County, of northern Texas, that stood seventeen hands high and had a horn spread of seven feet and eight inches.

Never were such creatures for habit as aged oxen. "We used to have a spotted pair named Buck and Sankey," Railroad Smith remembers. "Sankey was named for an evangelist, and gentle was his nature. Buck was set in his ways — and talk about being smart! He could tell twelve o'clock on a hot summer day as accurately as the mark on the kitchen floor. Yes, we had a clock, and set it by the sun, according to the almanac, when it went down. But the mark — a kind of sundial — on the kitchen floor was handier to a woman in the kitchen than the clock in the front room. The mark was curved according to the sun's slant through varying seasons. Buck knew nothing about that mark; there was no bell or horn to tell him when the sun reached it. Something within told him that. I don't know whether it was his stomach, his heart, or his head. But one grown man and two little boys could not make Buck go farther than five steps down a row away from the house when the sun reached the meridian.

Then, if an effort was made to keep him plowing, he would drag Sankey and the plow and the man and the two little boys across the field and up to the lot gate. Yet, before noon or after noon, a little boy alone could plow him and his mate. He 'hawed' and 'hiked' to the boyish treble as accurately as soldiers respond to 'right face.' But he was set in his ways about dinner time." [3]

Crossing Death Valley in '49, as William Lewis Manly tells in his famous narrative, the perishing oxen, when released from the wagons and loaded with children and a few articles, would not travel unless the yoke was upon them. Behind the bar of the old Iron Front Saloon in Austin used to hang the mounted head of an affectionate creature of habit named Dan. He was a dun in color and was so fond of turnip greens that he would leave the best mesquite grass in Texas and break through the best garden fence in order to get a few mouthfuls of his favorite vegetable. His mate was an ox named George. One night George got into a steep gully and was drowned. After that Dan would not work with any other ox — simply would not work, and his owner finally sent him up the trail with a herd of steers, specifying that his head should come back to Austin when he was butchered.

Ab Blocker told me that when he took that herd of 3700 steers with such exceptionally long horns up to Wyoming in 1877, the cook had three yoke of oxen for the wagon. Generally he worked only two, resting one pair daily, in rotation. The most individualized of the oxen was named Bully. Whenever his turn came to rest, Bully always stayed with the wagon, his head right at the tail board. When the herd got to the Platte River, the water was high and ice cold from melting snow in the Rocky Mountains. Just as Ab Blocker was about to put the herd in, a Negro hand, who dreaded the cold, told him he had another plan.

"What is it?"

"Looky at Ole Bully follerin' dat wagin," the Negro said.

There was a Government bridge not far up the river. Why not

take the herd to it, the chuck wagon in the lead, hold Bully at the bridge entrance, the lead steers close to him, until the wagon was halfway across and then let him loose? He would bolt for the wagon and the lead steers would follow. They did. The great herd strung across the bridge like a remuda of horses — the first bridge any steer in it had ever put foot upon.

Compared with oxen, the horse-and-buggy days were as swift as a weaver's shuttle. On the old cotton road from Texas to Monterrey, during the Civil War, Mexican freighters would, upon making camp in boggy weather, walk back to their camp of the night before for a coal of fire. Seeing a pair of oxen hitched to a plow in an Arkansas field some distance off from the road, I have halted and sighted from a fencepost in order to make sure whether the team was moving or not. On Sunday afternoon, back in the forties, George Jackson and his brothers used to ride an old gentle ox from their cabin to a field only three-and-a-half miles away, in order to be on time for Monday morning plowing.

These slow, patient creatures often became the butt of jokes by vigorous young men. On one freighting trip a big, dependable ox became too sore-footed to pull. A part of the freight was bacon, and one of the whackers suggested that the rinds be cut off a couple of bacon sides and shoes fashioned out of them for the ox. The ox was accordingly thrown and shod. Another part of the freight was barreled whisky. The ingenious whacker now had the happy thought of giving the ox a dram. They drew a quart bottle full of the best brand, and while one of the boys held Old Samson by the nose and horns, another poured the bottle of whisky down his throat. "The old ox licked out his tongue and smacked his lips and got up. For a time, with his new bacon-rind slippers and morning dram, he was as frisky as a young colt. He tried to pull the whole load by himself." [4]

On cold nights many a teamster snuggled up close to the back of his favorite ox and slept "as warm as wool." According to

[247]

Ezra Meeker of Oregon Trail fame, this practice fathered the term "bedfellow to the ox." The poet who wrote "The Man with the Hoe" seemed to think that being "brother to the ox" was mighty bad. I doubt if it was as bad as being a slave to a punching machine.

The relation between a driver of oxen and the oxen themselves was much more intimate and very different in quality from the relation between a driver of wild cows and the cows. This relationship, working on the spirits of both man and beast, had an effect on man that was nearly always wholesome and kindly.

Not long after Texas joined the Confederacy, a youngster named Tim Cude went from Live Oak County to enlist in the army. Although he was only sixteen years old, his way with oxen had been noted — especially the power of his voice over them. It was a voice young and lush, but strong, without the gosling quality. He did not charm the oxen by whispering — horse-charmer style — in their ears.

At Appomattox, Tim Cude was still alive, a grown man now, strong and rangy, with a grown beard. But months, then a year, then two years went by, and still Tim did not come home, and there was no word from him. At first his father and mother talked with high hopes of his coming. Then they said little. They still nursed a hope, but the heavy conviction came down that Tim must be among the many other boys in gray who would never return. Their hope grew gray and secret, without confidence. The days went by as slow as laboring oxen walk.

And oxen had never walked slower than their two yokes inched along, pulling a load of supplies home from Powderhorn on the coast. It had taken them five days to go down, two days to buy lumber — for a new shed — a plow, calico, shoes, hat, groceries, kerosene lamp and other goods and to load them all. Now they had been a week pulling back. Mrs. Cude began to talk again about Tim. "Perhaps he came home today," she'd say at the evening camp. "I dreamed last night that he came just after dark," she'd say over the campfire before dawn. This was in the fall of 1867, two long years and a half after the end of the war. In all those dragging months, months adding themselves into years, no day had dawned, no night had fallen, that she had not made some little extra preparation for her boy's coming home. In all the period of waiting, this was the first time she had not been there to welcome him. As she approached the waiting place now, the hopes of fourteen absent days and of fourteen absent nights were all accumulated into one hope. Perhaps Tim had come. Mr. Cude shared the hope too, but it hurt him to see "Mama disappointed," and a thousand times he had reasoned that it was better that they both be resigned.

At last they were only six miles from home, when the oxen stalled in La Parra Creek. For an hour Mr. Cude struggled and worried with them, trying to make them make the supreme pull, Mrs. Cude throwing all her strength on the spokes of one wheel. He was starting the weary business of unloading some of the freight and carrying it on his back out of the creek.

Then suddenly they were aware of a man, dismounted from the horse beside him, standing on the bank just ahead. Being down in the creek, they could not have seen his approach. His frame, though lank, was well filled out, his face all bearded, his clothes nondescript. In his posture was something of the soldier. Nearly all Southern men short of extreme middle age had, in those days, been soldiers. For a second he seemed to be holding something back; then he gave a hearty greeting that was cordially responded to.

"Those look like mighty fine oxen," the young man said, coming down, as any stranger in that country at that time would come to help anybody in a tight.

"They are good oxen, but they won't pull this wagon out now," Mr. Cude answered. "I guess they're getting old like us. We been working 'em since before the war."

The stranger had moved around so that he was very near the

wheel oxen, which he faced, instead of the driver and his wife. His hand was on Old Brindle's head, between the long, rough horns. "I believe I can make these old boys haul the wagon out," he offered.

"They wouldn't do any better for a stranger than for their master," Mr. Cude answered.

"There's only one person who could get them to pull," added Mrs. Cude. "That's our boy who went to the war."

"Did he know oxen?" the young man asked out of his beard.

"Oh, yes, and they knew him. They liked him."

Then for a little while there was silence.

As Mr. Cude began drawing up his rawhide whip, again the offerer of help, pleadingly now, asked for a chance to try his hand.

"Very well," Mr. Cude agreed slowly, "but every time you try to make 'em pull and they don't budge the wagon, they're that harder to get against the yoke next time."

The young man took the long whip, not to lash the animals — for that was not the whip's function — but to pop it. He swung it lightly and tested the popper three or four times, as if getting back the feel of something long familiar that had been laid aside. Then he curved the fifteen feet of tapering plaited rawhide through the air — and the ringing crack made the sky brighter. At the same time he began calling to the oxen to come on and pull out. He talked to them harder than a crap-shooter talking to his "bones."

The oxen, without a jerk, lay slowly, steadily, mightily, into the yokes. The wheels began to turn. The whip popped again, like a crack of lightning in the sky, and the strong voice rose, pleading, encouraging, commanding, confident, dominating.

The oxen were halfway up the bank now. They pulled on out, but nobody was talking to them any longer. No welcome of feast and fatted calf ever overwhelmed a prodigal son like that, initiated by four faithful old oxen, which Tim Cude received from a mother and father, all the gray in the world suddenly wiped out by sunshine, on the banks of an insignificant creek in a wilderness of mesquite. All the mockingbirds between the San Antonio River and the Rio Grande seemed to be singing at once, and the oxen kept on pulling, silent and slow, down the road.

On occasion a lethargic bull train could stampede with all the animation of a herd of high-headed "fieries." If work steers were habitually slow, they were dependable. One of the famous bets of the West was that won, in 1858, by a bull train over mules on a race with freight between Fort Leavenworth and Fort Laramie, about seven hundred and fifty miles away.[5] The story of the tortoise was repeated.

Indians did not try to steal oxen as they did horses and mules. They were the first cattle the Plains Indians saw. These Indians, hearing the bullwhackers shouting "Whoa," "Haw" and "Gee," called the oxen, and later all other cattle, "wohaws." In crossing the Indian Territory, Texas drovers were generally met with demands for "wohaw," and many a stray was cut out of the herds to satisfy the demand. "Wohaw" was one of the few Indian words that passed into the vocabulary of the range.

The great firm of Russell, Majors and Waddell, which operated the Pony Express and the Overland Stage also, had, in the heyday of wagon freighting business during the fifties, 75,000 oxen west of the Missouri River.[6] The trails to Oregon and California were mainly ox trails.

While the majority of these freighter and emigrant oxen were not Texas Longhorns, a great many of them were. Frequently before the Civil War almost the only cattle in some parts of Texas for which there was much sale were oxen broken to work. Thousands of Texas steers were trailed to Missouri to be sold for work oxen. Their hard hoofs — harder than those on cattle from the east — walking powers and ability to endure, especially in desert regions, gave them a reputation. Outfits made

[251]

up on the Missouri often had more wild steers than gentle ones, and it would take all hands, including cook and boss, to break them in.[7]

There were ways and ways of breaking steers. With time and trouble, the snuffiest range-charger could usually be made as domestic as a schoolmaster with an ailing wife and six babies on his hands. The rollicky cowboy way explained by Jim Foster will do as a sample.[8] In 1871 Colonel Todd, in preparation for a trip up the trail, bought a fine pair of steers on the Guadalupe River to drive to the chuck wagon.

"He wanted them broke. So we drove them out on the prairie, roped and tied them down, yoked them and tied their tails together, tied the bed on the wagon frame so it wouldn't bounce off, put a rope around the horns of each steer and a half-hitch in his mouth, the ropes to be used as lines, and then hitched the steers to the wagon. Al Myers and myself got into the wagon to drive. Two boys unhobbled the legs of the steers while about half a dozen others stood mounted on either side of the team so as to keep it headed straight. Talk about kicking like a bay steer! And when we got into the hog-wallows, talk about your ocean-wave rides! A few tryouts like this, and by the time the herd was counted and pointed north, the cook was able to handle that yoke of oxen, provided the horse wrangler and maybe an extra hand helped him. The farther we went, the gentler Samson and Goliath — that's what we called them — became."

On occasion the Longhorn could be ridden. According to Indian tradition, the first Spanish priests to cross the Sierra Madre of northern Mexico rode black bulls. They had the example of Chinese philosophers for precedent. Riding oxen descended from Spanish blood is a common practice in Bolivia today.

"I was working for the Quien Sabe outfit on the Pecos," Horace Wilson used to relate,[9] "while Barnes Tillus was boss. One night we made what we called a 'moonshine' — that is, a

night ride and a dry camp — with the intention of starting at daybreak on a fifteen- or twenty-mile drive back to the roundup ground. Next morning Barnes Tillus woke up to find that a coyote had chewed his stake rope in two during the night.

" 'Boys,' he said while we were saddling up, 'just rope me a big old steer and bring him close to my saddle. Then after I'm on him, throw him into the drive and I'll ride to camps.' "

"It didn't take long for a couple of us to stretch out a big old moss-horn. Tillus saddled him and, just as we let him up, went aboard. The way that steer bawled and bellered was a caution. We headed him in the right direction, and every once in a while that morning I got a glimpse of Tillus a quarter of a mile or so ahead, riding off some pinnacle in a run, whooping and hollering and whipping the old ox with his hat. At the roundup ground, within two hundred yards of the chuck wagon, Tillus loosed his cinch and fell off, saddle and all."

The greatest ox ride in the annals of the cow country was made and will keep on being made by the cowboy-outlaw-cavalier Ross McEwen, in Eugene Manlove Rhodes's heart-clinching story called *Pasó Por Aquí*. McEwen is hitting the flats and making for the tules, the dust of his trailing pursuers barely rising into visibility far behind, when at an abandoned ranch his horse plays slap out. There's a likely-looking steer in the pen, watering. McEwen ropes him, saddles, and then, bawling and spurring, the pair go on. They go far. There's one thing wrong with this steer, however, and Eugene Manlove Rhodes, finely true to the range, caught it after the story was printed. The steer is a red roan Durham — too fine-haired, short-winded and liable to be overheated for what he had to endure. But the episode was based on a piece of personal history.

"I rode that steer myself," Rhodes inscribed on the flyleaf of a copy of the story that he gave away, — "a brindle steer with big horns. Seven miles I made on him before he sulled on me. I wasn't particular where he went, you see, or he might have sulled sooner. Where I wanted to go was away."

A brindle steer with big horns. That was the breed for oxen to work or ride.

According to the old saying, the tail goes with the hide. Here it goes with something else. It is almost surprising that in the arena of horn-worshipers not a single exhibitor of long tails has emerged. The Longhorns certainly had long tails, and in coloration, curls and contour they were every whit as interesting as any assortment of foxtails ever hung up over a hunting-lodge fireplace. Like other parts of the animal's anatomy, they have been the subject of yarns.

"One time up on Pease River," Horace Wilson related, "I made a long throw at a vanishing outlaw, but missed his head and caught a big ball of cockleburrs matted into the switch of his tail. My pony squatted like a rabbit, and when the steer hit the end of the rope we jerked the whole end of his tail off, the knot of cockleburs whizzing back past my head like a shot out of a cannon. You could have heard that bull beller for five miles."

R. B. Pumphrey used to tell of the awful time he had when a herd bogged by their tails. It was rainy weather and for days the cattle had been dragging through soggy ground, their long tails gathering mud that made bigger and bigger and harder and harder balls. Some steers walked as if they were each dragging a ball and chain. The quicksands of the Canadian River caught a lot of the steers hard and fast by the tail. They were strong enough to pull their feet out, but were powerless to pull their tails out. Pumphrey and his men had to bob the tails before the brutes could be extricated.

Cow people have always been strong on joshing each other about their stock. They used to tell how a Kansas City beef-buyer offered the mighty Dillard R. Fant two dollars and six bits per hundredweight for his Santa Rosa steers provided he would bob their tails before they were weighed.

According to another yarn, Shanghai Pierce had shipped a

long string of "sea lions," as he called his coast cattle, to the Indian Territory. After seeing them located, he had barely reached Matagorda County when he received a telegram as follows: "COME AT ONCE THEY ARE STEALING YOU BLIND. BILL BUTLER."

Shanghai caught the first train north and hunted up Bill Butler.

"I got your telegram all right," he roared. "Who's doing the stealing?"

"Don't talk so loud, Shang, they'll hear you," Bill Butler drawled.

Shanghai's ranch house was a mile away from his stock pens, and he used to stand on the front gallery and give orders to his niggers in the pens. Now, trying to lower his voice, he begged Bill Butler to go ahead.

"Well, they're shore stealing 'em all right," Butler divulged, "and not having much trouble doing it neither."

"Who, who?" Shanghai bellowed. "I've come back to make hell pop."

"We can't pop it yit," Butler mildly replied. "We got to let it sizzle fer a while. But I'll tell you what I seen with my own eyes, and I can bring up other witnesses to the same doings."

"Go on, damn it, and tell," Shanghai exploded.

"Well, the other evening I was riding down a trail across a section of the country where your sea lions located thickest, and I met a man on a little Osage pony with great big saddle pockets. I noticed he acted sorter like he didn't want to stop and speak. I looked closter, and, bless me, I seen a cow's tail sticking out of each saddle pocket. They looked just like your cows' tails. Then I begun cutting for sign and found this feller was actually making three trips a day and saddle-pocketing a couple of cows each trip. It's . . ."

But Shanghai Pierce had heard enough. Maybe you have too. Heads, I win; tails, you lose.

XV · SANCHO AND OTHER RETURNERS

To John Rigby, trail boss, horse man, brand inspector.
He told me the best range story I have ever listened
to — the story of Old Sancho.

NO OLD fogy farmer was ever more regular in his habits than cattle are in theirs. Under herd they get up regularly about midnight, ease themselves, maybe take a few bites of grass, step to a fresh bed and lie down again on the other side — for a cow brute can't lie flat on his back or belly. When the average cow comes to water, usually at a regular hour, she likes to drink out of the trough at a particular spot and will either hook away any other animal occupying that spot or endure her thirst until it is vacated. After drinking and resting, she will each day walk to a certain patch of ground to begin grazing, her

[257]

regularity of habits, if left alone, being shifted by the shift of seasons.

He was a drifter at times; he ranged far and could walk to the end of the world; but the Longhorn was also a home lover and a persistent returner to his *querencia*, as the vaquero language calls the place where an animal is born or to which he shows a strong attachment. (The noun comes from *querer*, to like, to love.) If a cow was missed out of a trail herd, she might be depended upon to return to the last bed ground and linger there a while.

Day after day, week after week, month after month, a sparrow hawk can be seen looking out from a certain stretch of telephone wire. A pair of wrens will build their nest year after year in a certain box. A she-wolf, unless molested, will litter time after time in one particular cave. Like these and many other creatures, all kinds of cattle, some individuals much more pronouncedly than others, have strong attachments to their accustomed home. In the spring of 1845 John McMillan, in company with about fifteen other families, left Decatur County, Georgia, moving West. They drove their wagons to the Mississippi River, were ferried over, and that fall settled in Jasper County, Texas. Before long a yoke of oxen belonging to McMillan "came up missing." The next year sometime he received a letter saying that along in the spring the oxen had appeared at their old home in Georgia.[1]

Before the trails were barred by fences, some steer driven from far down in Texas to Louisiana, Kansas or elsewhere would not infrequently distinguish himself by showing up months later on his home range.[2] Gentle animals seem to have been the most persistent returners. Chief of all such was Sancho. I put the story of his travels in *On the Open Range*,[3] but he seems to belong here also, with so many others of his breed, though he never was much of a mixer. He is entitled to be remembered alongside Old Blue, who led Goodnight's herds, Alamo in Emerson

Hough's *North of 36*, "The Blue Roan Outlaw" in Will C. Barnes's *Tales from the X-Bar Horse Camp*, and the Poker Steer in Andy Adams' *Cattle Brands*. John Rigby, who told me about Sancho, helped drive him to Wyoming.

To begin with, a man by the name of Kerr had a little ranch on Esperanza Creek in Frio County, in the mesquite lands south of San Antonio. He owned several good cow ponies, a few cattle, and a little bunch of goats that a dog guarded by day. At night they were shut up in a brush corral near the house. Three or four acres of land, fenced in with brush and poles, grew corn, watermelons and "kershaws" — except when the season was too drouthy. A hand-dug well equipped with pulley wheel, rope and bucket furnished water for the establishment.

Kerr's wife was a partridge-built Mexican named María. They had no children. She was clean, thrifty, cheerful, always making pets of animals. She usually milked three or four cows and sometimes made cheese out of goat's milk.

Late in the winter of 1877, Kerr while riding over on the San Miguel found one of his cows dead in a bog-hole. Beside the cow was a mud-plastered little black-and-white paint bull calf less than a week old. It was too weak to run; perhaps other cattle had saved it from the coyotes. Kerr pitched his rope over its head, drew it up across the saddle in front of him, carried it home, and turned it over to María.

She had raised many dogie calves and numerous colts captured from mustang mares. The first thing she did now was to pour milk from a bottle down the orphan's throat. With warm water she washed the caked mud off its body. But hand-raising a calf is no end of trouble. The next day Kerr rode around until he found a thrifty brown cow with a young calf. He drove them to the pen. By tying this cow's head up close to a post and hobbling her hind legs, Kerr and María forced her to let the orphan suckle. She did not give a cup of milk at this first sucking.

Her calf was kept in the pen next day, and the poor thing bawled herself hoarse. María began feeding her some prickly pear with the thorns singed off. After being tied up twice daily for a month, she adopted the orphan as a twin to her own offspring.

Now she was one of the household cows. Spring weeds came up plentifully and the guajilla brush put out in full leaf. When the brown cow came in about sundown and her two calves were released for their supper, it was a cheering sight to see them wiggle their tails while they guzzled milk.

The dogie was a vigorous little brute, and before long he was getting more milk than the brown cow's own calf. María called him Sancho, a Mexican name meaning "pet." She was especially fond of Sancho, and he grew to be especially fond of her.

She would give him the shucks wrapped around tamales. Then she began treating him to whole tamales, which are made of ground corn rolled around a core of chopped-up meat, this banana-shaped roll, done up in a shuck, then being steam-boiled. Sancho seemed not to mind the meat. As everybody who has eaten them knows, Mexican tamales are highly seasoned with pepper. Sancho seemed to like the seasoning.

In southern Texas the little chiltipiquin peppers, red when ripe, grow wild in low, shaded places. Cattle never eat them, leaving them for the wild turkeys, mockingbirds and blue quail to pick off. Sometimes in the early fall wild turkeys used to gorge on them so avidly that their flesh became too peppery for human consumption. By eating tamales Sancho developed a taste for the little red peppers growing in the thickets along Esperanza Creek. In fact, he became a kind of chiltipiquin addict. He would hunt for the peppers.

Furthermore, the tamales gave him a tooth for corn in the ear. The summer after he became a yearling he began breaking through the brush fence that enclosed Kerr's corn patch. A forked stick had to be tied around his neck to prevent his getting through the fence. He had been branded and turned into a steer, but he was as strong as any young bull. Like many other pets, he was something of a nuisance. When he could not steal corn or was not humored with tamales, he was enormously contented with grass, mixed in summer time with the sweet mesquite beans. Now and then María gave him a lump of the brown *piloncillo* sugar, from Mexico, that all the border country used.

Every night Sancho came to the ranch pen to sleep. His bed ground was near a certain mesquite tree just outside the gate. He spent hours every summer day in the shade of this mesquite. When it rained and other cattle drifted off, hunting fresh pasturage, Sancho stayed at home and drank at the well. He was strictly a home creature.

In the spring of 1880 Sancho was three years old and past, white of horn and as blocky of build as a long-legged Texas steer ever grew. Kerr's ranch lay in a big unfenced range grazed by the Shiner brothers. That spring they had a contract to deliver three herds of steers, each to number 2500 head, in Wyoming. Kerr was helping the Shiners gather cattle, and, along with various other ranchers, sold them what steers he had.

Sancho was included. One day late in March the Shiner men road-branded him **7 Z** and put him in the first herd headed north. The other herds were to follow two or three days apart.

It was late in the afternoon when the "shaping up" of the herd was completed. It was watered and thrown out on open prairie ground to be bedded down. But Sancho had no disposition to lie down — there. He wanted to go back to that mesquite just outside the pen gate at the Kerr place on the Esperanza where he had without variation slept every night since he had been weaned. Perhaps he had in mind an evening tamale. He stood and roamed about on the south side of the herd. A dozen times during the night the men on guard had to drive him back. As reliefs were changed, word passed to keep an eye on that paint steer on the lower side.

When the herd started on next morning, Sancho was at the tail end of it, often stopping and looking back. It took constant attention from one of the drag drivers to keep him moving. By the time the second night arrived, every hand in the outfit knew Sancho, by name and sight, as being the stubbornest and gentlest steer of the lot. About dark one of them pitched a loop over his horns and staked him to a bush. This saved bothering with his persistent efforts to walk off.

Daily when the herd was halted to graze, spreading out like a fan, the steers all eating their way northward, Sancho invariably pointed himself south. In his lazy way he grabbed many a mouthful of grass while the herd was moving. Finally, in some brush up on the Llano, after ten days of trailing, he dodged into freedom. On the second day following, one of the point men of the second Shiner herd saw him walking south, saw his **7 Z** road brand, rounded him in, and set him traveling north again. He became the chief drag animal of this herd. Somewhere north of the Colorado there was a run one night, and when morning came Sancho was missing. The other steers had held together; probably Sancho had not run at all. But he was picked up again, by the third Shiner herd coming on behind.

He took his accustomed place in the drag and continued to require special driving. He picked up in weight. He chewed his cud peacefully and slept soundly, but whenever he looked southward, which was often, he raised his head as if memory and expectation were stirring. The boys were all personally acquainted with him, and every night one of them would stake him.

One day the cattle balked and milled at a bank-full river. "Rope Old Sancho and lead him in," the boss ordered, "and we'll point the other cattle after him." Sancho led like a horse. The herd followed. As soon as he was released, he dropped back to the rear. After this, however, he was always led to the front when there was high water to cross.

[262]

By the time the herd got into No Man's Land, beyond Red River, the sand-hill plums and the low-running possum grapes were turning ripe. Pausing now and then to pick a little of the fruit, Sancho's driver saw the pet steer following his example.

Meantime the cattle were trailing, trailing, always north. For five hundred miles across Texas, counting the windings to find water and keep out of breaks, they had come. After getting into the Indian Territory, they snailed on across the Wichita, the South Canadian, the North Canadian, and the Cimarron. On into Kansas they trailed and across the Arkansas, around Dodge City, cowboy capital of the world, out of Kansas into Nebraska, over the wide, wide Platte, past the roaring cow town of Ogallala, up the North Platte, under the Black Hills, and then against the Big Horn Mountains. For two thousand miles, making ten or twelve miles a day, the Shiner herds trailed. They "walked with the grass." Slow, slow, they moved. "Oh, it was a long and lonesome go" — as slow as the long drawn-out notes of "The Texas Lullaby," as slow as the night herder's song on a slow-walking horse:

> It's a whoop and a yea, get along my little dogies,
> For camp is far away.
> It's a whoop and a yea and a-driving the dogies,
> For Wyoming may be your new home.

When, finally, after listening for months, day and night, to the slow song of their motion, the "dogies" reached their "new home," Sancho was still halting every now and then to sniff southward for a whiff of the Mexican Gulf. The farther he got away from home, the less he seemed to like the change. He had never felt frost in September before. The Mexican peppers on the Esperanza were red ripe now.

The Wyoming outfit received the cattle. Then for a week the Texas men helped brand **C R** on their long sides before turning them loose on the new range. When Sancho's time came to be branded in the chute, one of the Texans yelled out, "There goes my pet. Stamp that **C R** brand on him good and deep." Another one said, "The line riders had better watch for his tracks."

And now the Shiner men turned south, taking back with them their saddle horses and chuck wagons — and leaving Sancho behind. They made good time, but a blue norther was whistling at their backs when they turned the remuda loose on the Frio River. After the "Cowboys' Christmas Ball" most of them settled down for a few weeks of winter sleep. They could rub tobacco juice in their eyes during the summer when they needed something in addition to night rides and runs to keep them awake.

Spring comes early down on the Esperanza. The mesquites were all in new leaf with that green so fresh and tender that the color seems to emanate into the sky. The bluebonnets and the pink phlox were sprinkling every hill and draw. The prickly pear was studded with waxy blossoms, and the glades were heavy with the perfume of white brush. It was a good season, and tallow weed and grass were coming together. It was time for the spring cow hunts and the putting up of herds for the annual drive north. The Shiners were at work.

"We were close to Kerr's cabin on Esperanza Creek," John Rigby told me, "when I looked across a pear flat and saw something that made me rub my eyes. I was riding with Joe Shiner, and we both stopped our horses."

"Do you see what I see?" John Rigby asked.

"Yes, but before I say, I'm going to read the brand," Joe Shiner answered.

They rode over. "You can hang me for a horse thief," John Rigby will tell, "if it wasn't that Sancho paint steer, four years old now, the Shiner **7 Z** road brand and the Wyoming **C R** range brand both showing on him as plain as boxcar letters."

The men rode on down to Kerr's.

"Yes," Kerr said, "Old Sancho got in about six weeks ago. His hoofs were worn mighty nigh down to the hair, but he

wasn't lame. I thought María was going out of her senses, she was so glad to see him. She actually hugged him and she cried and then she begun feeding him hot tamales. She's made a batch of them nearly every day since, just to pet that steer. When she's not feeding him tamales, she's giving him *piloncillo*."

Sancho was slicking off and certainly did seem contented. He was coming up every night and sleeping at the gate, María said. She was nervous over the prospect of losing her pet, but Joe Shiner said that if that steer loved his home enough to walk back to it all the way from Wyoming, he wasn't going to drive him off again, even if he was putting up another herd for the **C R** owners.

As far as I can find out, Old Sancho lived right there on the Esperanza, now and then getting a tamale, tickling his palate with chili peppers in season, and generally staying fat on mesquite grass, until he died a natural death. He was one of the "walking Texas Longhorns."

XVI · LEAD STEERS AND NECK OXEN

To Jack Potter, the old "Lead Steer," cow psychologist, one trail man to put down in writing the character of the Longhorn.

ALWAYS in any group of animals, whether men or beasts, certain individuals emerge. The emergers on the trail were mostly lead steers. Trail men talked about them as they talked about cutting horses back home or sure-footed night horses in last night's run. Now and then a steer became so distinguished that his owner would not let him go with the cattle he led but would keep him for leading others. Old Blue, sometimes called Blue the Bell Ox, was known from the Pecos to the Arkansas, in Colorado as well as in Texas. He knew the trail to Dodge City better than hundreds of cowboys who galloped up its Front Street.[1]

Blue was calved down on the Nueces River, near the Texas coast, in the spring of 1870. His mother may have been wild, but, judging by Blue's nature, she was never "snaky." He was four years old before anybody took sufficient notice of him to give him a name, which came from the color the vaqueros call *moro*, or "mulberry."

At the age of three he was put in a herd of other brush cattle bound for New Mexico. Its route was over the Goodnight–Loving Trail. Above Horsehead Crossing on the Pecos, the Apache Indians swooped down one night, stampeded the cattle, and got away with six hundred. In a sharp brush next day six or seven warriors paid for these cattle with their lives, and there was one more cowboy grave on the lone prairie. The remainder of the herd, something over 1500 head, went on ten days farther and were sold to John Chisum at his Bosque Redondo ranch. That fall the Apaches were fierce, and one morning a hand found Blue with an arrow in his rump. It was cut out and the wound healed rapidly. Blue had learned the smell of Indians.

The next spring Charlie Goodnight bought Blue in a "string" of five thousand steers from John Chisum, cut them into two herds, and trailed them on northward to the Arkansas River above Pueblo, Colorado. Blue went in the first herd. He was a mature beef now, four years old. He had seen a lot of the world and from the day the herd trailed out he asserted his natural leadership. Every morning he took his place at the point and there he held it. Powerful, sober and steady, he understood the least motion of the point men, and in guiding the herd showed himself worth a dozen extra hands. The cowboys all noted him. One youngster from Oxford named Hughes, son of the author of *Tom Brown's School Days,* wanted to call him Sir Walter Raleigh, but Blue was the name that stuck.

Instead of sending Blue on up to feed Indians at an agency in Wyoming, as he sent so many steers, Goodnight kept him

on his Colorado range. Cattle thieves were bad, and, one morning while trailing a little bunch of cattle through the snow, Blue's
owner discovered him and a dozen other steers in a picket corral
snugly hidden in the middle of a thicket. Near by was a pile of
hides. Blue had escaped having his shucked off, and for reasons
that a certain cottonwood limb was drawn into — or drawn
from — this particular gang of cow thieves never butchered
another animal on the Arkansas.

Goodnight had one of his hands break Blue to the yoke. A
man driving an ox wagon to California wanted to buy him, but
he was not for sale. The Goodnight herd moved down on the
Canadian River to winter.

In the summer of '76 the restless Goodnight decided to pull
up stakes in Colorado and return to Texas. So Blue led the herd
that stocked the first ranch in the vast Texas Panhandle of the
Staked Plains. There were 1600 head of cattle in that first herd,
and as they filed down the bluffs, rising nearly a thousand feet
above the floor of the Palo Duro Canyon, they must have smelled
buffalo. The disassembled wagon and its freight were carried
down on mules. Below the pass the canyon opens out ten miles
wide, the bluffs on either side making a natural fence. Out of
this enclosure Goodnight and his men routed ten thousand buffaloes. Then they blocked up the few trails that led from the
plains into the mighty Palo Duro cut, and rode line daily to keep
the buffaloes out. The cattle wintered "in clover." Goodnight
found a Scotchman, Adair by name, with money. Within ten
years their **J A** brand was showing on the sides of 75,000 cattle
and the **J A** range embraced a million acres of land up and down
the waters of the Palo Duro. Meanwhile, other outfits had
stocked the whole plains country — and Blue had become the
outstanding animal in it.

The outlet for the Palo Duro was Dodge City, two hundred
and fifty miles north. It was October 26, 1878, that a herd of

[269]

1000 **J A** steers headed in that direction to trample down the grass over a route thenceforth known as the Palo Duro–Dodge City Trail. Old Blue was in front.

This trip was different from any other he had made. It was customary to bell the mare leading a horse herd. Away back in the sixties some young men belled an old cow to lead a thousand head of maverick yearlings they had caught on the forks of the Llano River — and after a maverick got used to that bell, he would, if cut off, make haste to get to it.[2] But when Blue's owner decided to bell the leader of a trail herd of steers, he was making an innovation. The leaders were often the wildest old steers of the herd and could never have been managed as Blue was.

His bell was brand new, with green stain and red label fresh upon the brass. The collar was clean and shiny and had the wholesome smell of fresh leather. When Blue got that collar around his neck and heard the ling-ling-ling of his bell, he was as proud as a ranch boy stepping out in his first pair of red-topped boots.

The steers soon learned to follow the sound of Blue's bell. Attached to it was a little strap for tying up the clapper. Before the herd was to be bedded down for the night or halted for grazing during the day, one of the cowboys would pitch a rope over Blue's horns, walk up to him and strap the clapper into silence.

After leading a thousand steers all day, Blue believed in exercising the privileges of individuality. He considered himself always as apart from the masses. He would walk right into camp among the pots and pans and eat pieces of bread, meat, dried apples — anything the cook would give him or the boys could steal from the cook. He became a great pet. Often he was hobbled and left to graze with the saddle horses. Sometimes he was staked out at the end of a long rope. He preferred to bed down away from his inferiors — and he had no peer.

[270]

The trail work followed a well-established routine. When it was time to travel after the early morning's grazing, Blue nosed out toward one of the point men to have his bell clapper loosened. Then he would give a toss of the head and a switch of the tail, often throwing in a low chuckling bellow to emphasize his pleasure, and stride north. Some waddie with the voice of a bugle horn would sing-song out the old Texas call, "Ho, cattle, ho, ho, ho, ho," and the big steers would soon be strung into line. Blue must have known the North Star, he coursed so unswervingly. He was always "raring to go," and, unless checked, he was apt to walk too fast.

One evening up in the Indian Nation, just beyond Beaver Creek, Blue came near walking right into an unfenced squatter's field, but the point man veered him around it. The squatter came out of his dugout to sell some of the pumpkins he had grown. The **J A** foreman bought a few and then ordered his men to bed down "away over yonder."

"No, no," pled the squatter, "bed nigh here. I need cow chips for fuel." Blue was just one among many manufacturers of "prairie coal."

When this pioneer herd from the Palo Duro reached the Cimarron River, they found it on a rampage, but Blue shouldered straight into the waters, and after him strung the thousand **J A**'s. After all were across, six of the cowboys swam back to the south bank. Four of them hitched their ropes to the tongue of the chuck wagon; two of them, one on either side, hitched ropes to the stays on the bed. Thus pulling and guying the wagon, they helped the cook's team bring it across. It was time to camp, and Old Blue had worked around the herd and was at the bank to meet them when they emerged.

At the Arkansas River, just south of Dodge City, a cold wind was blowing and the north was black. December was at hand. "Every man saddle and tie up," the foreman ordered. "We'll have hell before daylight." About midnight a storm of sleet and snow hit the herd. Every hand went to it. The steers wanted to drift, but the boys held them like a solid wall.

At daylight there was a yell: "Untie Old Blue's clapper and take the river." The water was frozen out from the bank, but plunging into the icy current, the big steers "made the riffle." When they reached the north bank, they felt like running, and harder and faster they crowded Old Blue. Two thousand horns clacked and four thousand feet roared. The frozen ground fairly shook. But if Blue was gentle, he had the speed of a race horse. Still at the lead of his herd, he headed straight for the twenty-foot gate that opened into the big shipping pens. With one bunch of cowboys to cut, another to count, and a third to run the cattle up the chute into the cars, they were loaded long before noon and on their way to Chicago — all but Old Blue.

He had proved himself far too valuable to be sold for steaks. He stayed with the remuda and ate hay while the cowboys warmed their stomachs at a bar and their feet on the floor of a dance hall. After a day and a night of celebration, they had spent themselves empty and were ready to leave. So at Wright and Beverley's store next morning the wagon was loaded with chuck and sacks of shelled corn. The grains in those sacks were colored red, white and blue, and on the road home Blue learned to eat corn; in fact, he loved it, and the colored grains seemed to add to his spirits.

The weather was freezing cold, and as the outfit headed southward, men and horses alike felt like making time. Blue was ready to travel also. He had the stride of seven-league boots and could walk up with any horse. Sometimes the thirty-miles-a-day clip made him trot, but he never tired or lagged. Down on Wolf Creek one night a hungry band of Kiowas rode into camp and, pointing at the big steer, demanded "wohaw" (beef), but Chief Lone Wolf and all his warriors could not have taken Blue away from those Palo Duro cowpunchers.

[273]

After this trip up the trail as bell ox, Blue's occupation for life was settled, but besides leading herds to Dodge City, he was put to various uses. When the chuck wagon was out in the spring and summer, Blue would generally follow it, taking choice food the boys would hand him. If an outlaw steer was roped in the cedar brakes and had to be led in, he was necked to Old Blue, the pair was turned loose, and, straight as a crow flies, the bell ox would bring him to camp.

If a wild herd of cattle was to be penned, Blue was put with them to show the way in. Wild cattle upon approaching a pen often circle and try to break away; but the wild ones could not break ahead of Blue, and his course was right into the gate. Upon entering a pen, range cattle will rush for the opposite side, pushing, hooking, milling. Blue never got into such jams. As soon as he had brought the lead cattle inside the pen, he would step aside and impatiently wait beside the gate until the last animal entered; then he would bolt out.

Once John Taylor and another cowboy took him up on the Canadian River to bring back a pair of young buffaloes. They necked the two to him, both on one side, and, of course, they were contrariness personified. "Old Blue was the maddest steer a man ever saw." He shook his head and bellowed, worked around until he had one of the green buffaloes on each side of himself, and then struck a course. When he wanted to go to water with them, he went; when he wanted to stop and graze, he grazed. He knew every camping place on the route, and when he got to one would stop, whether the men with him wanted to stop or not, and he would not move until his free will motivated him. He tamed the buffaloes thoroughly and in good time brought them into the Palo Duro, where they were turned loose to help make the famous Goodnight herd.

For eight years Old Blue kept at his occupation of leading herds. Some years he went up to Dodge City twice. The horns and legs of the steers he led were growing shorter and shorter, and often the cowboys had to shoe the fine, big shorthorns that the **J A**'s were coming to raise, but never once did Blue limp. His hoofs were as hard and bright as polished steel. All told, ten thousand head or more of the **J A** cattle followed Blue and his bell into the shipping pens of the "Cowboy Capital."

The older he grew, the more philosophical he became. It sometimes made a Spanish cow horse almost laugh, they say, to see him step aside in a night stampede and go to bawling. No slipping of horns, knocking down of hips and running until his tongue lolled out and his rump was chafed green from entrail-emptying for him. "To step aside is human," and Blue was mighty human when a stampede started. If the boys could get the stampeders to milling, Old Blue's bawl had a powerful effect in quieting them. At the head of a herd he never "buggered" when a jack rabbit suddenly jumped up from under a sage-bush at his nose, or something like that happened, and thus day and night he was a steadying influence.

When he was twenty years old, he died. For a long time his horns remained in the office of **J A** headquarters, over the door leading into the vault. They may be seen today in the fine little museum maintained by the Panhandle–Plains Historical Society and the West Texas State Teachers College at Canyon. Like his trail-breaking owner, Old Blue of the Texas Longhorns belongs to history.

Bill Blocker — brother to Ab and John R. — was nineteen years old when he quit school against parental will, borrowed some money on his own hook, and in partnership with two older men put up a trail herd. He went along as a hand with the understanding that he was to have no say-so in the directing of affairs. This was in 1870, and Abilene, Kansas, was the destination.

On the Pedernales River they struck a bunch of wild cattle containing an **A P B** (Blocker) steer that young Bill immediately decided he had to take along. He was a big bay with black spots, lithe, in fine condition. But it was not his value as a mere bovine that drew young Blocker. "He looked so proud and free," Blocker used to tell long afterwards, "that he reminded me of the way I felt. I wanted him for company." Accordingly he roped the steer, ran the Backwards Seven road brand on him, and turned him loose in the herd.

Before the day was over the big bay was in the lead. Blocker's place was on the northeast corner, the right point. Somehow the bay seemed also to sense something in the free-riding young point man that was kin to his nature. Within ten days this steer, which ran with the wildest bunch in the roughs of his home range, which would still have stampeded at the drop of a hat, and which carried himself so "proud and free," was walking up with Blocker's horse, never quite even with him, but with his noble head so near that the rider could put out his left hand and grasp the right horn. Blocker liked to ride along resting his hand on the powerful horn, and the steer seemed to like to have the hand there. He walked in rhythm with the horse. Blocker called him "Pardner."

No matter where he was after the cattle had watered or had grazed a while, when the yell arose to hit the trail and string out, Pardner would in a long walk — sometimes a trot — pass or go around everything until he was at the point. Plainly he enjoyed the feeling of power and self assurance that leadership gives and felt himself a kind of peer to the high-headed leader on horseback.

When the outfit got near Red River, they learned that it was on a rampage. Herds were being held out from it, waiting for the water to go down. Several attempts to swim over had failed. Most of the trail bosses considered it useless to try further. Two or three rainy days went by and still the expanse of waters raged. Holding an idle herd is tedious business. Bill Blocker said to his partners, "If you men will let me take charge of this herd,

I'll cross." There were responses of half-admiration, half-irony. The herd was turned over to the kid.

His first order was to drive it back, south of the river, three or four miles. Then he swung it around and soon it was strung out in customary formation, headed towards faraway Abilene. Young Blocker rode at his customary place on the northeast corner. The proud and free bay steer stepped up with him in the customary manner, and hand rested on horn.

At the brink of the water neither hesitated. Centaur and steer plunged in together and were soon swimming, the herd coming on like mules strung out behind the bell mare. Other herds had prepared to follow, should the first take the water all right. and now they came on, each on the tail of the other.

That was a rainy year. At the Salt Fork of the Arkansas, the herd got into a mill, out in the middle of deep water. While Blocker was trying to break the mill and save the cattle from drowning each other, a plunging steer pawed his exhausted horse under. Weighed down with boots and leggins, he was making a desperate but losing struggle when the bay leader cut out of the mill and came by him, headed for the north bank. Blocker grabbed his tail and was towed out, the herd following.

After this the proud and free pair seemed to keep step with each other more constantly than before. However, had the man tried to approach the steer afoot, a chasm between them would have opened wider than the Mississippi. It was a great pity to deliver the bay leader along with the herd at Abilene. But what else could be done?

There was a last grasp of hand on horn, and then, "*Adiós,* Pardner, I hope you break loose and come back to Texas." But Pardner never got back.

Jack Potter usually named his lead steers after noted characters.[3] Buckshot Roberts exhibited the stubborn insolence of that victim of Billy the Kid's gang whose name he took. During a blizzard out in New Mexico, Lew Wallace tried one night to get inside Potter's dugout and the next morning demanded a share of the corn meant only for favored horses. A sourdough biscuit filled with black pepper did not break him of hanging around camp. Then one hot afternoon, after having been without water for seventy-six hours, Lew Wallace led the herd down to the Blue Holes of the Pajarito. "Before I realized the long drouth was over," Jack Potter says, "we were in water up to my horse's shoulder. I crawled off and stooped over and tried to drink. I could not swallow. When Lew Wallace had filled up, he looked around at me, and he must have suspicioned something was wrong. He stood there and stuck his tongue out to tell me what to do. So, with my mouth full of tongue, I started throwing water on it with my hand. Finally I got so I could drink. When Lew Wallace thought I had enough, he pushed me with his horn. We went up the bank and cooled off, and after a while we went down and finished our drink."

But I guess Jack Potter's gratitude is strongest towards a rangy steer of the Pecos named after John Chisum. "Ten herds bound for Clayton, New Mexico, were caught by the blizzard of '89," old Jack recalls, "and mine was the only one that got through. The credit goes to John Chisum. We had just finished the fall roundups and nobody was prepared for or expecting such cold weather so early. It proved to be the worst blizzard in the history of that country. Thousands and thousands of sheep and cattle were frozen to death. Several men died. Clayton was without train service for thirteen days and during that time ran about out of food and coal and all out of whisky.

"When the blizzard struck us, we were traveling north. The cattle, which had been thrown off the trail, began to drift south. After we'd fought them a while, John Chisum gave up resisting, turned his head into the blizzard, held it down between his legs, and, with the other cattle following, kept the direction.

"I knew that if we could get over into the Tremperos Canyon

we'd find shelter for the cattle in some protected pens and for ourselves in an old ranch house. Never in my life have I seen such snowflakes as we made into. They were as big as your finger and were driven by a gale blowing sixty miles an hour. We were going up El Muerto Creek, and I kept wondering what traveling would be like when we left it and got out on the naked divide.

"By the time we reached the place to top out, the prairie was covered with snow. The red sand-hill grass was a foot high here. I was piloting the herd, following a newly beat-out road. It wasn't graded or anything like that — just some twisting wagon ruts. The only way I could distinguish it was by noting that the snow was smooth in the ruts and uneven in the grass. I had to pull my hat down over my eyes to protect them from the cutting storm. I could not see ten yards ahead, but I kept the road. I had never been over it, and knew the country only in a general way.

"Then we came to a prong. I figgered one branch led off into the breaks of the Pierdenal — towards shelter. I took it. But old John Chisum, close to my horse's tail, refused to follow. He ducked into the one that seemed to keep on going over the bleak prairie. I was puzzled and commenced to talk to that steer.

" 'You don't seem to realize I am piloting this herd,' I said to him. 'I know a horse has more sense than a man. If you give a horse with any sense at all his reins on a dark night or in a snowstorm, he will take you to camp; but you've never been where you are headed, so far as I know. What right has an old, cold-blooded, scalawag steer to be making decisions for a trail boss? If we don't find shelter before night, God knows what will become of all of us. Nevertheless, I'm just guessing too, and now I'm going to let you have your way.'

"John Chisum was right. In twenty minutes we reached a ridge with canyons covered with big pines running off on each side. The trail led down one of these into the Tremperos. As we entered it, four riders from the ranch came out to help us pen and to welcome us to their shelter.

"The storm lulled for a few days, and we floundered on, but if Clayton had been a mile farther off I don't believe my horse would ever have got me there or that John Chisum would ever have led the cattle into the shipping pens. We were holed up for two weeks. All the other herds trying to get to Clayton were drifting and dying. Several men that persisted in hanging with their cattle perished. There seemed to be only one John Chisum on the trails that time — but I do take a little credit to myself for having had sense enough to pay attention to what a good lead steer says."

In the parlance of the range, a lead steer or a lead ox often means a neckin', or neck, animal — one to which wild cattle roped in rough or brushy country are necked and led in. Every ranch of any size in the brush country once had one or more lead oxen. On an occasional ranch where the only cattle, including wild ones, now to be found are of improved blood, one may still find an old Mexican ox for leading in the outlaws. Spanish-blooded steers make the best neck oxen; one well trained has always sold at a premium, though generally he is not for sale.

A good many years ago a cowman who had the "Mustang Pasture" leased, down in the brush country, gave it up. After his brush poppers had worked for weeks driving out what cattle could be handled in a civilized way and roping scores of others, he still had a "considerable sprinkling of snakes" left. He had no idea how many. He contracted with Onie Sheeran to clean the pasture up. Onie took in as partner another noted brush hand named Atlee Weston. His main help, however, was a five-year-old brindle stag named Pavo. The partners were to get five dollars a head for every animal they could deliver alive, and were to turn in the hides of whatever they ran to death. In the course of time they roped one hundred and twenty-five outlaws, tying each one in the brush where it was roped. Pavo by himself led every one of the "snakes" to a pen where a windmill furnished water and the two ropers pitched in prickly pear for the cattle to eat until they were driven away. Without Pavo or some other good lead animal, the men would have been almost as handicapped as without horses to ride.

In Frio County along in the eighties the Martins had two lead oxen named Geronimo and Camino. Geronimo had been a work ox, and scars on both his sides showed how Mexicans had prodded him with burning chunks of wood. An outlaw would be roped somewhere in the brush and tied to a tree — no matter how far from the strongly built trap pasture in which the wild cattle, after being captured, were kept. A vaquero would toss his rope over the horns of Camino or Geronimo and strike out for the tied animal, the ox leading like a horse. After he was necked to the outlaw, he would make straight for the trap, not following the trail he had made in coming, but taking an airline, in so far as brush and gullies would permit. He might have to worry with the outlaw considerably, hooking him, going around and around him until the unwilling animal set off in the right direction. Then he would butt ahead with full force, the pair tearing a hole through the brush, running over pear and bushes, knocking down or bending over good-sized mesquites. Usually by next morning the pair would be at the trap gate, the ox impatient to be unnecked and have a treat of burned prickly pear or of cottonseed. If they failed to show up, it was because the outlaw had sulled and died. Then a man must go to where the pair had been turned loose, take their trail, and follow it until they were found, untie the necking rope, and free the lead ox.

Ab Blocker told me that while he was working in the Blanco breaks in 1876–1877, catching old outlaw steers, he had a brown lead ox that did not have to be fed. His inducement for coming in was to be released from his bothersome burden. The Blockers were camping sometimes at one pen and sometimes at another, holding their bunch of wild cattle in a pen at night, herding them by day. This old brown ox would strike the trail of the cattle being kept under herd and follow them to camp, no matter if it had been moved several miles from where he had spent the preceding night.

Old Ben always went to bawling when he got to headquarters with his outlaw. It might be midnight in freezing weather. No matter, a man would go out and free him. If nobody came promptly, he'd bawl louder. Certainly the reward of freedom was his due.

All neck oxen become gentle. They are a part of the story of the outlaws of the brush, about which a long chapter follows.

XVII · OUTLAWS OF THE BRUSH

*To eager Rocky Reagan, top brush hand, refined
gentleman, cowman. I learned about outlaws from him.*

THE WORD "outlaw," however legitimized by common
usage, is a betrayal. The cattle I am thinking of made their
reputations in fierce, hardy, persistent, resourceful, daring efforts
to maintain freedom. They refused to be "dumb driven cattle."
Unlike the orthodox ox, they knew not their masters and would
not be led to the slaughter block. Instead of being outside the
law, they followed the law of the wild, the stark give-me-liberty-
or-give-me-death law against tyranny. They were not outlaws
any more than a deer or a wild cat in evading man is an outlaw.
Like antelopes, many of them would not go to man-erected windmills to drink, even when there was no other water. Some of them

[283]

were wilder than any other animal that eats grass. Yet, because the American language does not have any such accurate, convenient and readily understood word as the Mexican *ladino* or *cimarrón*, I must use the inaccurate and man-smug term *outlaws*.

Among these outlaws revealing the law of the wild that the Longhorn blood coursed to fulfill was one owned by Marcus Snyder, a Texan now ranching in Wyoming.

"About 1913," he wrote me, "I bought five thousand steers, four-year-old and up, from William Randolph Hearst's Babícora Ranch in the State of Chihuahua, Mexico. At that time the Babícora stock were bred up just enough to make them better than common 'Mexicans.' They were good Longhorns. I placed these steers on about 150,000 acres of land leased from the University of Texas in that high country north of Sierra Blanca, some of it very rough.

"As we approached this range, a big snow-white steer with the widest spread of horns I had ever seen outside of a house kept lifting his head and looking away off towards the Diablo Mountains. He must have been ten or eleven years old. As soon as we turned him loose, he pulled out for the Diablos. He got in the roughest part of them. Those roughs were his natural home. Water was scarce, and from where he ranged there wasn't a drop for twelve miles. He would water about twice a week, as we discovered, and then only at night. A round trip of twenty-five miles over rocks did not bother his feet in the least.

"I wintered the steers and the next fall began shipping. We got the white steer in a roundup, but failed to hold him. So he went back to the Diablos for another year. He was as wild as any blacktail deer I ever saw but more cunning in keeping out of sight. Lack of timber prevented his staying permanently hidden. Shipping time came again. We rounded in Old Whitey once more, took extra precautions, and this time held him. When he saw no chance for a break, he'd get in the middle of the herd, as far away from man as possible.

"One evening we shut him up, along with several hundred other steers, in the shipping pens at Sierra Blanca. We had to hold over until next morning before loading out. As men familiar with stock pens know, the big railroads build theirs high and strong. I stayed in the little Sierra Blanca hotel that night, and the next morning before going to the pens met a man who had just driven in from the north in a car. He said that about fifty miles out he had seen our white steer going in a long lope towards the Diablo Mountains.

"During the next two or three months we got about that many glimpses of him and saw that he was getting very fat. The range was good, and that run back home must have put Old Whitey's glands to functioning. One day after cold weather came, I took a long-range rifle, a couple of pack mules and a cowpuncher and went to the Diablo roughs. I shot the steer. We dressed him and brought him in. He must have weighed around fifteen hundred pounds. That night the beef froze where it was hanging outside. It was as tender as calf when cooked and at the same time tasted like big beef ought to taste. I believe it was the best I have ever eaten."

After the ranges were all claimed and fenced, the outlaws that escaped ropes and bullets were comparatively few. Gid Graham's story of one escaper gives me particular satisfaction and pleasure.[1]

His mother was a keen-horned, dun "Spanish" cow driven up from the south to the great Shoe Sole Ranch bordering the Snake River in Idaho. Despite panthers and wolves that prowled the broken country she chose to range in, she always raised a calf, and she became a marked animal. One year her calf — a bull — escaped branding. She kept it in solitude, and when it was a yearling she charged a man riding to throw her into the roundup and hooked his horse in the hip. But the yearling was branded and castrated. Upon being turned loose, he butted down one

[285]

brander and sent the others tearing out. His mother smelled with solicitude the blood and burned hair on his body, and as soon as she was let out, took him back to the "tall timbers."

He had a name now — Table Cloth, from his checkered blue, yellow and white color. The next year he was not in the roundup. He still ranged alone with his mother. The pair were seen occasionally, but by fleetness and constant alertness, and by taking cunning advantage of cedar-studded roughs, they escaped roundup after roundup until the cow was no longer seen. In the prime of life now, Table Cloth kept in fine condition and kept his figure too. He often led younger steers into wildness, but they could be cut off and rounded in while he vanished.

When he was ten years old, three punchers with special orders to get Table Cloth sighted him farther off from the canyon cedars than they had ever seen him before. They hazed him, along with his little bunch, into a herd being trimmed for the market.

Table Cloth became one among two thousand grown steers bound for the shipping pens. He walked up with the leaders. The first night on the trail, watchful guards saw that he remained standing while the other cattle bedded down. While the Dipper swung around the North Star and one relief after the other circled the cattle, he roamed about, horning sleepers out of his way in a most domineering manner, until the Morning Star began to pale. Perhaps he was accustomed to little sleep. He was full of the pride and energy of life.

About the middle of the next night, storm clouds blew up and the herd arose on restless feet. All hands were called out. They prevented a break or a drift, but when daylight came, Table Cloth was gone. Tracks showed that he had left in a lope. The herd had to go on.

Two years later, organized riders made a special hunt. One man sighted Table Cloth, fired his six-shooter as a signal, and fell in behind him up an open arroyo. The hoofs of both steer and horse were making a fine clatter, and maybe the puncher was gaining a little, when he saw an enormous bear raise up on his hind legs just ahead of Table Cloth, to investigate. Table Cloth never swerved an inch. He hit the bear, bowled him over, and tore on. He had to cross some open ground, and here two punchers "twined" him about the same time. They snubbed him to a tree until the lead ox could be brought.

Table Cloth tried his best to gore the yoke mate, but he was necked up too close for horn action. After getting to the beef herd, he was kept necked. At night he made life miserable for the gentle ox, constantly shifting round, looking for escape. Escape was never for a minute out of his mind. But he was on his way to a packing plant, and the boss had promised treats to the whole outfit if they could shut the gates behind the outlaw in the shipping pens.

They had traveled two or three days and Table Cloth was still secure and was actually lying down like the other cattle, apparently asleep, when in the quietness of night a coyote let out a sudden, piercing yell at the edge of the herd. Instantly it was pounding the ground. Riding to circle it, a puncher heard a steer moaning as if in great agony. He paused and saw Table Cloth standing on one side of a tree and the lead ox down on the other, choking to death. He had no time for anything but to cut the necking rope from the gentle animal's throat. Table Cloth was long gone before the ox could get to his feet. The stampede was not serious, and once more the cattle train pulled away from the shipping pens — without Table Cloth.

Three years went by. He was still free. He had ridded himself of the necking rope and looked to be in the prime of condition. After returning from marketing the last fall shipment, the boss proposed that certain men take their Winchesters and bring in Table Cloth's hide and carcass. He thought he was offering an opportunity for big sport. He was surprised at the opposition that rolled up.

Hadn't Table Cloth fairly won life and liberty? For fifteen years now the whole Shoe Sole outfit had been after him — and he was still free. He was getting old. He had never really tried to kill a man. He had simply outplayed his opponents. He could not be called mean. Among his kind he was rarer than a cowman out of debt, as outstanding as Bugger Red among riders of pitching horses. By God, he deserved to live among the cedars and canyons he loved so well — and the boss agreed. Table Cloth continued to enjoy his liberty for several years. Then, like his mother, he was no longer seen. No man ever came across his skull.

Any kind of cattle turned loose in a big country will revert to wildness. Among the "spookiest" cattle I have ever known were the well-bred Herefords on the Double Circle Ranch in Arizona. Until a few years ago "the Circles" stocked something over six hundred sections of Apache Indian reservation land — all in one pasture, without cross fences, taking in a big plateau called "Rustlers' Flats" and a world of wooded mountains and canyons, all watered by nature and so inaccessible that no wheel print showed on it. Here open range conditions existed, and despite the fact that men were roping and branding "long-ears" the year round, there were at times hundreds of mavericks on the range. The maverickers, both legitimate and illegitimate, did not make the cattle any gentler. Left for a hundred years in such a country to breed and fend for themselves, with bears, panthers and lobos allowed to thrive and help nature select her survivors, the shortest-legged Herefords would become highly potent in maintaining their wildness. Yet in the end they would resemble only distantly the prize-ring white-faces. The Double Circle cattle were wild, but they lacked the roughness, endurance and keen senses characteristic of the old-time outlaws of the brush.

In the brush country of Texas there are today many wild cattle, most of them having a mixture of the Hereford, Durham,

Brahma and Longhorn strains. They are so wild and wily, and the brush in which they squat and dodge has become so much thicker, that the methods employed seventy-five years ago in catching their predecessors are still practised. Yet men who have handled all kinds of cattle incline to the opinion that the nervous-natured Brahma is not so well adapted to leading a life of primitive wildness as the Longhorn was.

In this brush the Longhorns ran wilder for a longer time than in any other region. The outlaws that came out of it and that died of old age in it, uncaptured, were magnificent preservers of their freedom. Sam Blalock caught steers around twenty-five years old. He saw one thirty years old.

I cannot tell of these outlaws properly without telling of the brush itself and of the men and horses that the brush and the brush cattle molded. Scientific methods have so developed milk production in cows, and meat down to the hock on beeves, that some modern cattle, as compared with their progenitors, look as if they belonged to a different species. By giving scientific thought men have added more than a cubit to the stature and stride of race horses. The Longhorns of the brush, instead of being modified by men, bent men to their own ways.

Roughly speaking, the brush country of Texas lies between the San Antonio River and the Rio Grande, the Gulf coast and an irregular line running west from San Antonio to the Rio Grande making its other boundaries. The most concentrated brush, except some great thickets in Refugio County, is between the Nueces and the Rio Grande. Into this area several hundred thousand people have of late years been brought by citrus fruits, vegetables and other products of irrigated lands of the lower Rio Grande valley. Yet the brush country is still essentially a ranch country, only a low fraction of the land having been plowed up.

In many regions the brush is continuous for miles, its loneliness and immensity suggesting the pampas of the Argentine; in places there are natural clearings. Year by year these clearings are growing smaller, what were once vast prairies of grass now being tight mats of thicket. Dense mesquite is stabbing to death the grass of millions of acres that seventy-five and fifty years ago were bald open. There are millions of acres of black chaparral, in some places so low that a man on horseback with eyes trained to the brush can distinguish a buck's antlers raised above it a half mile away; in other places from ten to twenty feet high. The shy and delightful verdin weaves its winter roosting-nest, so soft inside, mouth so cunningly hidden, on the ends of the thorny branches of this *chaparro prieto*. Along with the black chaparral grows guajilla, a member of the catclaw family, but having only minor spines; its fernlike leaves afford fine browsing and from its flowers bees make a honey superior to that from alfalfa, better even than the honey of Hybla. Catclaw, which the Mexicans call "wait-a-minute," is not lacking. A half-brother to it, the colima, grows into little trees; how cattle eat the leaves between its claws is a marvel. Granjeno, seeds from the yellow berries of which the birds plant along fences, can match claws with anything. Down towards Brownsville the compact ebony, hard of wood and evergreen, is beautiful to look at, its thorn as sickening to a knuckle-joint as an adder's tooth. The stubborn coma, with dirklike thorns, pushes farther north; about Christmastime its minute white flowers begin scatteringly to tantalize an enquiring nose with a fragrance as cloying as the cape jasmine's; doves coo over its fruit.

In many places the huisache, golden and aromatic-flowered in spring, its spined branches sweeping almost to the ground, has run out the mesquite. No vaunted "dogwood trail," however beautiful its turnings, ever led to a more gorgeous sight than huisaches in full bloom. If massed and arranged properly, a great highway-lining of them would at blooming time vie with the cherry blossom drive of Washington. The graceful retama,

which blooms its "shower of gold" all summer long and hides its thorns under waving fronds, strives with the huisache to occupy the land. The palo verde, its green-black thorns more apparent than the negligible leaves, does not have to strive.

There are flats and draws set thick with brittle white brush and similar vara dulce ("sweetbriar," or "bee brush"). Like them, the grey cenizo — a name that means "ashes" — which bursts into a magic of solid lavender after each rain, is thornless. The iron-fibered guayacan depends on rough stobs instead of thorns to ward off intruders. The rubber-stemmed leather plant is alone delightful to touch — and the Mexicans call it "blood of the dragon." The leaves of the agrito are themselves thorns, each with from three to seven lobes; its currant-like fruit makes a jelly with a tang of the wild in its taste and a wine-ruby light in its color that no other jelly can equal.

The devil's head, the nopal — multi-colored with waxy flowers and then studded with red and purple "prickly pear apples," the tasajillo, the pitahaya and other varieties of cactus assert with stiletto points their claim to room, and they crowd up through root, branch and leaf of the brush. The hardy Spanish dagger will not retreat one inch for animal or plant, but sends up its flower-stalk like a flag of victory overtopping the plain of thorn and leaf. There are other yucca plants; and in some places the maguey, each leaf an iron spike and a steel saw, grows. Here and there like a pariah stands the "accursed jonco," the leafless all-thorn, which Mexicans say furnished Christ's crown and on which, they claim, only the butcher bird will to this day alight. However, I have seen mockingbird nests in jonco bushes. Coyotes pick berries from the brazil. There are many other bushes with thorn and bitter leaf.

The deserts of the West, like Death Valley, forbid, defy, terrify. The Great Plains challenge, but their monotony starves the sense of expectation which a country of woods and streams, however populated, arouses; the mirages that glisten on their carpet are a mockery to hope. The brush country, though often more than semi-arid, is not a desert. It stretches away as illimitable as the open plains, but it hides secrets of human life and secretes an abundance and variety of wild life, including rattlesnakes and sharp-tusked javelinas. The variety of its texture and color, the irregular interspersion of openings and, above all, the possibility of something that it hides being revealed, combine to sharpen expectation.

Yet there is nothing generous about it. Its flowers are barricaded by thorns; and its leaves, shortened and sharpened so that they will not evaporate precious moisture, give a shade shallow and checkered. If a man in the long summer lies down to shade his head under a bush in a thicket, he finds the ground so hot and the air so close from surrounding bushes that he generally prefers to stand or to stay on his horse with his head in space where the air circulates, even though the heat devils pulsate through it up to the skies.

Covered as it is by brush, this country emanates a certain sense of barrenness, especially during customary drouths. Even in bottom lands, where mesquites grow large enough for big anchor posts, and hackberries make thick shades, the brush lacks that graciousness inherent in timber. Until one has known it long, the brush country withholds and withholds. Not many white people could regard its trees with that loving intimacy felt by Wordsworth for the "four fraternal yews of Barrowdale," or by Lanier for the "glooming live oaks" of the Marshes of Glynn. It is unceasingly defiant. Only God can make a tree, but this is the land that God gave to the devil "for his own special sway."

Those who know the brush best, know it to fight it. Nevertheless, fighting it, they are enthralled. They may curse it, but they belong to it. "The *monte* has been my mother. The *monte* has been my school. All I know I have learned from the *monte*," said a thorn-knotted old Mexican vaquero not too ignorant to

[293]

have a gleaning of the world beyond. The closer they are tied to it, the more of its secrets the men of the brush know: how the prickly pear provides a healing poultice against the stabs of its own and all other thorns; how the poison of the Spanish dagger jabbed into flesh about a rattlesnake bite counteracts the venom; how mockingbirds battlement their nests against snakes with thorns of mesquite twigs; how tea from huisache bark eases the internal bruises of a man knocked senseless by a limb he has failed to dodge; how thorns lie horizontal along the inner side of a hide skinned from a brush deer. Above all, they know the secret way of wild horses and wilder cattle beside the rare water holes in the chaparral. This brush has secured many men whose own ways were secret. Looking upon it in the spring, when the pristine leaves of the mesquites give off a delicate green light that pervades the whole sky, I have thought it as beautiful as "waters on a starry night." Shrouded in darkness, thickets of guajilla and vara dulce all a-bloom have intoxicated me like magnolias in some soft Southern garden. The brush has thorned me, but it has nurtured me. I belong to it, and though I have been away from it for long years, seeking only God knows what, I am often homesick for it. Yet I can well understand how to strangers coming into it for the first time, and how to many people living with it for years without ever comprehending its spell, it may bear a sinister and fearful aspect.

"In this part of the country, near the Nueces, both on the eastern and western banks," wrote an intelligent young man who accompanied the Texan forces in pursuit of invading Mexicans, in December, 1842, "I for the first time beheld vast ramparts and towers of prickly pear that seemed to form walls and mountains in their terrible array. From the midst of many of these banks of prickly pear, young trees or saplings of the same [thorny] nature were to be seen from twenty to thirty feet in height. The whole country had a peculiar appearance, presenting a view of boundless extent and unbroken grandeur. Yet there was no beauty — it was a profound and cheerless desolation, . . . a wilderness covered thick with chaparral and presenting an appearance more dismal than anything I ever beheld." [2]

Three years before this,[3] Andrew Sowell and other rangers under "Paint" Caldwell in pursuit of marauding Mexicans had to turn back after entering Prickly Pear Prairie, north of the Nueces River, because their horses had given out. From the time they entered the "prairie" — or flat — until they left it — and what a prairie to skirt the brush! — they were not out of the sound of rattlesnakes; men on foot leading their mounts had to pick their way to avoid being bitten. Some of the Mexicans afterward captured told how several of their band were bitten while going through this barrier and how, at the very time the Texians gave up the chase, victims of poison were being buried on the Nueces. While Andrew Sowell was near this great pear thicket on another occasion, he and his companions, having seen a *manada* of mustangs run out of a motte, went to it, hunting water. Upon approaching it they were struck by a terrible stench. At the same time they heard the blood-curdling whirr made by great rattlesnake rattles. They beheld a rattler "about nine feet long and as big around as the thigh of a common man." The mustangs had run over him, and he was in his anger emitting that sickening stench that men of the brush have smelled many times.

Sidney Porter came, in time, to live in the brush country, and to derive material that, under the name of O. Henry, he later wove into short stories. "The Caballero's Way" contains his interpretation: "More weird and lonesome than the journey of an Amazonian explorer is the ride of one through a Texas pear flat. With dismal monotony and startling variety, the uncanny and multiform shapes of the cacti lift their twisted trunks and fat, bristly hands to encumber the way. The demon plant, appearing to live without soil or rain, seems to taunt the parched traveler with its lush grey greenness. It warps itself a thousand times about what look to be open and inviting paths, only to lure the rider into blind and impassable spine-defended 'bottoms of the bag.' "

Brush country . . .

The worry and work of driving poor cows and calves through this brush in hot weather could be dwelt on. Sometimes they simply would not drive. Men would get down afoot and try to push them along. It might take all day to move a herd two or three miles. But our subject is the wild outlaws of the brush.

When I was a boy in Live Oak County, about the turn of the century, my uncle Jim Dobie kept a cow outfit hunting cattle the year round in the brush of his Kentuck Ranch and a big leased country joining it. He was a "steer man" mostly, and he seldom moved out anything before it was four years old and up. Many of his cattle must have gone for years without casting a shadow, except by moonlight. They stayed on ground that the sunlight merely flecked.

The outfit, made up principally of Mexican vaqueros, was under Sid Grover and then his brother George. Both of them were noted brush hands. People used to say that Sid could pull off his boots, leather leggins and ducking jacket, and dress up in low-quartered shoes, a pair of cotton pants and a silk shirt and then run the worst outlaw through the worst thicket and rope him and tie him without getting a single slit in his shirt. Of course he never exchanged his leather for silk, but he was so lithe, so expert, so cunning in the brush and the ways of brush animals that he might have stood the test.

Our ranch was about fifteen miles from the Kentuck. On a sandy prairie, about half way between the ranches, bordering the wide and deep jungles of thorn that grew along Ramireña Creek, I used to watch those A Dot — the Jim Dobie brand — steers and those A Dot horses, ridden by A Dot hands, emerge from the expanse of thicket. The lead cattle as they walked out on the opening would be shying at their own shadows; the horses would be noticing the unfamiliar shadows too, and some of the brush poppers looked as wild and expectant as the cattle. The open ground seemed to be as strange and unfamiliar to the cattle as bright sunshine would be to a man emerging on the surface of the earth after spending years in a mining tunnel.

You can tie a wild cow in the brush and bring a bunch of tractable cattle to her, and she upon being released will keep with the bunch so long as it remains in the brush. But let it walk out into a clearing, and you'll see her break to keep in cover. The brush gives such an animal a feeling of safety, even when man is within sight or hearing.

Before he would leave the brush of liberty — the only liberty known to him or possible to his expectation — many an outlaw has lain down and died. Often, animals that have felt the hard hand of man and known confinement as well as freedom are more alert against man and flee his approach sooner than those ignorant of him. Mustangers used to say that the wariest animal in a band of wild horses was some mule that had escaped captivity.

One time the McGill Brothers caught a blue outlaw steer in the tall black chaparral on the Soledad Ranch in Duval County. They tied him to a tree and left him all night. The next morning they drove a gentle bunch to him, necked him to a lead ox, and started back for the pens. The blue outlaw appeared to be thoroughly "cooled off." He went along tractably enough for several miles until he reached a high hill overlooking the pens, house and two windmills of the old Soledad Ranch, which, true to its name, personifies solitude — a dot in the vast *brasada*.

There, overlooking the pens of gray and brown mesquite poles, the blue outlaw stopped. That prison cell was burned in his memory more deeply than on his side. The lead ox could not budge him. A vaquero beat on him with the double of his rope, spurred him on the loins. He lay down. The vaquero jabbed him, twisted his tail until the bone broke. He ground his teeth and would not budge. He showed no sign of being over-heated; he appeared to be comfortable. The vaquero rubbed sand in his eyes. He shook his head and lay still. The ox was unyoked, and with a loose rope looped around his horns, the outlaw was staked to a stout clump of brush. Then the men went on, leaving him there in plain sight of the Soledad pens.

They came back in the evening. He still lay where he had been left, facing the pens. Thus he remained for two days. Then, without having risen once, he died. The vaqueros said that he was *acalambrao*, that he "died of *sentimiento*" — of a broken heart.

Back in the seventies, old outlaw steers that yelling riders rushed with other cattle out of the great *brasada* along the lower Nueces River would sometimes stay with a herd while it was being worked, pawing, bellering, trembling with rage, occa-sionally making futile charges towards a horseman who neg-lected to give them plenty of room, until they dropped dead from sheer emotional exhaustion.

The propensity among wild cattle to hook is probably deter-mined as much by the shape of their horns as by internal urge. The steer I am going to tell about now had horns so turned that he could have ripped the guts out of an elephant. He knew his power.

Rocky Reagan was working in the famous Jack West pasture in Live Oak County. One morning his cow crowd — a half-dozen men — held up a little bunch of cattle in an opening. A Mexican roped a six-months-old bull calf, and the calf went to bawling.

"Suddenly," related Rocky Reagan, "I heard a noise in the brush, almost back of me. I looked. There charging out of it, his head raised like a buck deer's and the coarse hair on his back standing up, came a big old red-roan steer. He had been tolled out of the bushes and out of his wariness by the calf's bawling. He had heard nothing else. When he saw men, he wheeled back into cover. He had long been wanted. The horse I was riding was about run down. It happened that our cook had come out with us that day, and his horse was fresh. It didn't take a minute for us to change saddles. I had an idea where the old roan had gone, and I hit his trail on the run.

"Before long I got a glimpse of him tearing over some low chaparral. He was moving! He was fresh, and he was not the kind to lie down as soon as he came to a heavy thicket. I heard some bob wire snap. I went over the broken fence too. The roan led across this pasture for a couple of miles and jumped another fence. I let down the wire and followed.

"In a thicket of *quebradora* (white brush) I got close enough to throw my rope and caught him by only one horn. At the feel of the rope, instead of breaking loose, as he could have done very easily, he wheeled like a cutting horse and rammed one of his sharp horns into the breast of my mount. The horn went in six or eight inches. The horse stood there trembling. Maybe I was trembling too. For what seemed a good while the steer remained in his tracks, working – gouging – his horn deeper into the horse. Then he gave a jerk, turned, and left. I was helpless, without any sort of gun. The horse died.

"Six months later we jumped that same steer about eight miles from where he had hooked my horse. I roped him and the rope broke. A Mexican then roped him and we tied him to a tree. The next day I sent this Mexican and another hand with a lead ox to bring the outlaw in. When they got to the tree, they found the steer had broken the *peal* (tying rope) and gone *pa' 'lla.*

"This was in the fall. Winter is the best time to run wild cattle in. The leaves are then shedding so that a man can see farther through the brush; horses can run longer in the cool weather without becoming windbroken, and cattle are not so likely to die from getting overheated. That winter four of my men jumped the old roan and took after him. Right at the Nueces

[299]

River one of them roped him. He went to fighting, and while the rider was unfastening the rope from his saddlehorn, the steer killed his horse. Meantime the other three boys had come up and were roping at him. One of them caught him, but when Old Roan raked his horse, he turned him loose. The steer made for a third man and snagged his horse's hip.

"Old Roan now had one dead horse and two wounded ones to his credit, all in a pile. And he had two ropes dragging from his head. He swam the river and on the other side stopped in some drift. He stood there a while, shaking his head, trembling with rage, and then he stepped back into the deep water and swam out by the four men who had chased him. The man on the one untouched horse did not have the nerve to tie into him. I did not blame him. I would not have tackled that steer on a tired horse for a carload of polo ponies.

"The winter passed and spring came and nobody had seen hoof or hair of the roan outlaw. Then one day, back in the Jack West pasture, a Mexican and I jumped him in a thicket. He was no longer dragging the ropes that had been left on him. We twined him, threw him down, and tied him doubly fast to a strong mesquite. We went to camp, brought out the best lead ox we had, necked the two together, and put the pair in a bunch of steers to be shipped.

"The roan came along until he was within sight of the railroad pens. Then he stopped, refused to budge an inch farther. For half an hour or so the ox worked him around — or, rather, worked around him — trying to coax and drag him on in. Finally the ox decided to rest a while himself and lay down. The roan stood there in a clearing looking at the pens. Directly he dropped dead. I think he was dead before his body hit the ground."

Cattle like this knew when work began in their pasture. They were wise to the movements of men. Having sensed danger, they frequently jumped a fence into another pasture, sometimes several fences, returning to their accustomed range only after the cow hunt was over.

One time while a neighbor of ours was branding some Mexican steers in our pens, a big rusty-colored fellow jumped over the fence and was away in the brush before anybody could get on a horse. He stayed in one pasture two or three years, making himself scarce whenever cattle were worked, nobody trying very hard to get him. Then I bought him range delivery. We roped him and tied him to a tree, and overnight he broke off one of his long, twisted horns and slipped out of the rope. He ranged on the west side of the ranch, and he got so that if he heard a yell or saw two men riding at the same time, he would jump a fence and go on west.

Finally he decided that the brush was better to the east, and I heard of him ten miles away. A year later I learned that he was twenty-five miles to the south. He had become a regular rambler. I sold him by letter to the owner of the pasture in which he was temporarily stopping. I suppose he killed him. I have heard of gentle horses' virtually starving to death because of an allegiance to a certain barren plot of ground. The allegiance of a genuine outlaw is to whatever covert he can find anywhere that will preserve his liberty.

XVIII · HIDDEN IN THE THICKETS

*To Jack Maltsberger, a kind of Indian in the ways of
the brush. I like the* carne seca *in his camp.*

MANY outlaw cattle would not run any distance to speak of. They were not so wild as wily. They knew the exact location of the thickest clump in every thicket. There they had their "houses," as the Mexicans say, and, when disturbed, they would make for another hiding place, maybe not a hundred yards off, and squat. Such cattle were called "squatters."

There are cunning *ladinos* today that, having learned how they are sought for in big thickets, take refuge in small islands of brush surrounded by prairie. They seem to know that riders incline to go merely to the edge of a patch of brush and peer in without entering. Tiburcio, *caporal* of the San Antonio Viejo Ranch, found five outlaws in such a *mogote*. The signs showed that, having entered the little thicket, for two weeks they did not emerge to make tracks. They had eaten the brush and pear off up to the line of visibility for a man riding around the edge of the covert — no farther. The ground used over was picked as clean as a patio floor. When caught, they had all the hair rubbed off their knees, showing that they had been crawling instead of walking. Their horns were as scarred by years of contact with stubborn thorns as though they had been raked with knives and jabbed with awls.

The prickly pear leaves, on which Longhorns could go indefinitely without drinking water, analyze up to eighty per cent fluid, though in drouths the percentage shrinks to a much lower figure. Sid Grover told me that in 1896 he roped many outlaws in a pasture of thirty thousand acres where it had not rained to speak of for more than a year and where there was not a drop of water out. The outlaws were in good condition. I have seen thorns hanging all over the head of a pear-eater, as thick as quills on "the fretful porcupine." But this would be on poor cattle incapable of adapting themselves to the pear. Strong, thrifty cattle that belong to the brush do not gather so many thorns. The part of a pear thorn imbedded in flesh soon decays and festers out.

No lobo wolf was ever more wary of enemy scent about a baited steel trap than a wild Texas steer at a gate between him and water. The sight of domestic cattle wading out in water, drinking long and deep, and then standing placidly to soak in the blessings of nature is balm to a man's soul. But there is nothing placid or ruminative about the outlaws as they drink. They drink deep and then disappear immediately. If three or four of them come to water where domestic cattle are standing around, the domestics may smell of them as if they were something foreign. They are foreign to anything but the wild.

One of the great Apache dodgers bore the name of Delgadito, which means Slender. All hounded evaders who live to keep on evading are Delgaditos. Aaron Moss of the Llano claims that eighty years ago, in his boyhood, when deer were preyed on constantly by panthers and then later when men shot them the year around, does, fawns and yearlings as well as bucks, chasing them with dogs, head-lighting them by night, so that they were never free from the threat of lethal enemies — in those times he seldom saw a deer as fat as many bucks become in these times when, all predatory animals having been destroyed, stock deer are protected every month of the year and bucks are the objects of bullets for only six weeks annually.

Although the old mossy-horns, guarding without surcease their freedom, did not grow lethargic with tallow — always the enemy of wakefulness and speed — they were exceedingly thrifty and were wonderfully muscled. One of the range sayings was: "If you want beef to kill, go to the shinnery."

A man whose experiences have been limited to prairie lands and gentle cattle can hardly conceive of the difficulties involved in clearing a big brushy country of a stock of old-time wild Texas cattle. In 1902 Dennis O'Connor decided to sell off the cattle on his 58,000 acre ranch in Frio and McMullen counties. They were graded up, but the old blood in them told strong, and they had been badly spoiled. Dennis O'Connor's home ranch was a hundred miles to the east, and he had not given this western country personal supervision. He knew that a long drouth had killed all his "gentle cattle." He hired a new boss named Dave Vastbinder and together they rode for two days to see what they could see. They saw very few cattle, the land being mostly level as well as brushy. But they saw plenty of sign, and O'Connor figured that he had between three and four thousand head on the ranch.

He contracted them to Bill Jones with the understanding that Jones was to gather them and pay for what he caught, Vastbinder to count them. Jones sent a "crowd" with instructions to "work them easy." They rode for two days and did not catch a single animal. Then the trade was amended, and Vastbinder took charge of the gathering. For three days he and his men tried holding up bunches of the cattle and putting them in a trap. They did not drive even one brute through a gate. All hope of working the cattle in bunches and getting them to the shipping pens in good condition now vanished. The outfit went to roping. It took them a year of steady, horse-killing work to catch three thousand head.

The "snakes" by that time were hard to find, but Vastbinder knew that plenty of them were still left. O'Connor now sold the remnant, range delivery, "sight unseen," cash down, for $900 to a man who was willing to bet on what the brush hid. This man took a bunch of Mexican limb-splitters, roped for several months, and at the end of that time had caught around nine hundred head of cattle. When he quit, a few *ladinos* were still making tracks in the big pasture.

In the days of the open range, buying cattle, range delivery, by alleged "book account," was a frequent form of gambling. After the country was fenced, there was no reason for "range delivery" trades in the plains country. But they continued until recent years in the brush country. For example, in 1895 Jim Dobie bought the cattle, range delivery, on the Guidan Ranch of McMullen county. He estimated that there were at least two thousand head, and he paid for that many at seven dollars and a half around. He was to gather them, and without further payment he was to have everything caught above that number; if he caught less than two thousand, he would pay for that many anyhow. He put Sid Grover and his brush poppers to work. They hunted cattle for two years, first gathering what could be driven out, and then roping. They caught around thirty-five hundred head, among them old cows and bulls that had never felt a rope and steers that had been turned loose in the pasture

[305]

twelve years before. The days of such hauls as that are gone forever.

Some hunters of brush outlaws had "remudas" of more or less gentle cattle — usually a bunch of from twenty to fifty head, among them one or several lead oxen — that they drove from place to place, working easy, often just waiting, again riding wildly, the object being to decoy the *ladinos*. Night was the best time for the wild ones to mix in with the gentle stock; however, most of the work had to be done in daylight. The decoy method required patience, caution and soft movement. Not many hands of skill and vinegar would employ it if given license to run and rope.

Soon after the Civil War, a lad named James H. Cook came from Michigan to work for Ben Slaughter, on the Frio River — which frequently has no water in it. The *corrida* of ten rawhide-equipped Mexicans was bossed by John Longworth. A few days after Cook joined it, this cow crowd entered a pasture, fenced in with mesquite and live oak poles, and rounded up fifty or seventy-five head of cattle and drove them to camp. The young cow-hand's account of decoy work — written more than a half century later — is a singular record:

"These cattle were not what would have been called 'gentle' in any part of the United States save Texas. They had been separated from the wild herds, and were 'gentle' to just the extent of having become accustomed to the sight of a man on horseback, so that they could be controlled to a certain extent by riders. It required but little to frighten them into a rage that knew no bounds when they were brought to bay. This was to be our decoy herd. . . .

"We went about five miles from the home ranch and camped near an old corral. The following morning about sunrise we left, taking with us the decoy herd, Longworth leading the way through the thick growth of chaparral and mesquite. After traveling a mile or more, he led the herd into a dense clump of brush and motioned us to stop. Then, telling two men to stay with the cattle, he rode off, signalling the other men and myself to follow. We rode in single file for probably a couple of miles, I last in line.

"Suddenly I heard a crash ahead, and in less than two seconds every rider in advance of me was riding as if the devil were after him. My horse knew the work, and plunged after the riders ahead. I held up for a moment; then the thought struck me that, if I did not keep those ahead of me in sight, I might never get back to camp. I did not know in what direction we had been riding, and one acre of ground looked like all the rest — everywhere brush, timber, cactus. I gave my horse the reins, trailing the ones ahead by the crashing of limbs and dead brush. . . .

"All at once I came in sight of one of my Mexican co-laborers. His horse was standing still. He put up his hand for me to stop, and I did so willingly. He pointed into the brush ahead, and I caught a glimpse of some cattle. A few minutes later I heard voices singing a peculiar melody without words. The sounds of those voices indicated that the singers were scattered in the form of a circle about the cattle. In a few moments some of the cattle came towards me, and I recognized a few of them as belonging to the herd we had brought from camp. I saw that we had some wild ones too. They whirled back when they saw me, only to find a rider wherever they might turn. The decoy cattle were fairly quiet, simply milling around through the thicket, and the wild ones were soon thoroughly mingled with them.

"Every man now began to ride, very carefully and slowly, in circles around and around them, all except myself singing the peculiar melody known as 'the Texas Lullaby.' For all I know, I may have tackled that singing trick with wild cattle for the first time right there, for I was about as excited as the wild cattle were."

Oh, for a reproduction of that "Texas Lullaby"! But it belongs in the brush, quavering low and quavering high, soothing, harmonizing with the heart throbs of an old brush horse, who knows that in a split second the cow brutes he is watching may break in two and he will be tearing a hole through the thicket after them. "The Texas Lullaby" belongs, too, in the night, around cattle that have stampeded or are about to stampede, the notes drifting as soft as the light falling from the stars, or rising as wild and elemental as the crashes of thunder they try to drown. But let Captain Cook tell on.

"After we had ridden around the cattle for an hour or more, I saw Longworth ride out of sight of the herd, dismount, and tighten the cinch of his saddle. He then returned to the herd, and one by one the other riders followed his example. Our horses, having had a badly needed breathing spell, were now in shape for another run. After a few moments Longworth rode away into the chaparral, singing as he went. The Mexicans closed in on the cattle, starting to drive them after him, pointing the herd in the direction of his voice when the brush was too thick for him to be seen. I brought up the rear. We all kept quite a little distance from the cattle, and each man tried to keep from making any sudden move or sound. At last Longworth led the herd into the wings of the corral, and the wild ones followed the decoys in. The heavy bar poles were soon lashed.

"We had caught some wild cattle, and I had enjoyed a most thrilling experience. My clothing was pretty well torn off; also a goodly portion of my skin. About nine kinds of thorns were imbedded in my anatomy. I was ready for camp. So were our horses. Such work was hard on both horses and man, but horse-flesh was cheap, and men could be hired, at $8 a month, who enjoyed the work.

"The *caporal*, in leading a string of riders out to circle wild cattle into the decoy herd, would not only keep a sharp lookout but listen for the breaking of brush or the sound of running hoofs. He would keep an eye on the ground for fresh tracks. To go 'away round' one of these bunches of cattle after locating them, and then to circle them into the thicket containing our decoy herd, meant that the rider must not consider his future prospects as very bright. It was a case of trusting in Providence and riding as fast as horseflesh could carry one, regardless of all obstacles. It was a clear case of 'go' from the second the cattle saw, heard or smelled a human being.

"Not all cow hunts terminated in the manner of my first one. Many times we not only failed to make a catch but also lost the decoys. Some rider, not being able to tell the exact spot where the decoy herd was located, and becoming confused by the many turns the wild cattle had made him take, would dash suddenly right into the decoys at the heels of a bunch of fleeing wild cattle. Then it was the devil take the hindmost. . . . Sometimes our running scared up a bunch of javelines (peccaries). If they dashed into the nervously waiting decoy herd, then it was *adiós* to every animal in it except such as we were able to rope and tie down.

"Those brush cattle did not mind running from a man ten or twenty miles. If one was tailed down, the rider had better jump off and hog-tie it quickly. If it got up, it would charge with a rage against which a man would have to act with great and sudden care if he valued his life. If at this moment he was dismounted and unable to get back into his saddle, it would be horns versus pistol." [1]

"Catch dogs" were often used — and to an extent still are — to trail and bay wild cattle, holding them until a roper appeared. These dogs are a story in themselves.

A jack, and less often a mule or a horse, was sometimes substituted for the neck ox to lead in outlaws. Necking, which has been treated of in a preceding chapter, came, like many other ranch institutions, from Mexico. In the coastal brush away east of the Nueces, where Mexican vaqueros give way to Negro cow-hands, the ropers themselves commonly lead out what they rope, without help from a neck animal. The toughest kind of outlaw should, after struggling for several days against a rope tied around the base of his horns, become tender-headed enough to lead, when released, one man pulling ahead and another restraining and guiding from behind. With the rope around his horns supplemented by one pulling on his cod-bag, a bull would lead freely.

Jim Coward told me that while he was cleaning the Tom O'Connor brush of outlaws during the tick-eradication campaign, shooting many of them, he once left a bad steer tied for four days before returning to lead him out. The steer still wanted to do nothing but fight, and so was left to cool off a while longer. Two days later he was still "highly on the prod." He was given four more days of solitary confinement. At the end of the ten days, "he led like a dogie. He looked like somebody had reached up in him and pulled out all his insides, but he was still a steer."

Sometimes the eyelids of the outlaws were sewed up so that they would blindly follow other cattle, trying to avoid all limbs. Again, to prevent running, the head was tied down to the front foot; a hind foot was tied to the end of the tail; a hamstring or a knee tendon was cut; a thong was bound tightly around the leg just above the hock. To take the fight out of the worst scalawags and to make them more drivable, horns were chopped off with axes or knocked off with heavy sticks, were shot into with bullets from six-shooters. Another way to make a bad critter come a-walking was to slit the cartilage of the nose, tie one end of a rope through the hole, and pull on the other with a saddle horn. The hole *could* pull through, however.

Cattle thus bruised and gaunted were worth comparatively little after they were brought in. A present-day federal inspector of meat would have allowed only a small percentage of the carcass of such an animal to go even into a tin can. Ranch people, many of whom used to almost "live out of tin cans," have always distrusted canned beef. Tough cattle, tough men. As iron sharpeneth iron, they toughened each other.

The horseback world, whether of the gauchos of the pampas, the bedouins of Arabia, or the Tartars of Asiatic steppes, has never known any activity more exciting than roping wild cattle at night. The practice is about past, but I will describe it as present.

While the moon is light or long before dawn, men ride out to some opening bordering the brush. Perhaps the outlaws will be crossing it on their way back from water; perhaps they will be out on it grazing — for where they stay in daylight the brush has starved out the grass. In the dimness the men wait, some taut upon horses, listening, some on the ground trying to skylight across the opening. They have selected positions so as to have the wind on the expected cattle. The horses have their ears pointed too. It is not alone the chill of night that makes a leg now and then tremble a spur into faintest jingle. Nobody is smoking, for the odor of tobacco would betray the smoker. The only speech is in a whisper. After a while a horse suddenly stiffens. He is sure. His heart goes to pounding so heavily that the saddle leather creaks.

There the wild cattle are! Nobody can tell how many, but they never run in big bunches. Now it is every man for what he can get, and, if at all, he must get it quick. If he misses, he will be lucky if he gets a second throw. The brush is not far away. There is a wild, piercing yell — the kind that releases nerves. It is the Texas yell, a combination of the Comanche war whoop and the wild shout that the Johnny Rebs made when they charged. Ropes are down. Each man runs, casts, and looks afterward to find out what he has caught.

Some strange things have been caught in the darkness down in the brush country. I know one Mexican who claims that he thought he was roping a black muley heifer and discovered that he had caught a bear.

Old Jacinto de los Santos — Hyacinth of the Saints — is more than half Comanche. His skin looks weathered like old leather that, once red, has been rubbed with tallow, sweated against and beat upon by the winds and suns of many drouths. His voice seems to rumble up out of the earth. His hair is as thick, heavy, and coarse as the tail of a Spanish mare. He used to work for John Blocker. In some ways John Blocker was the best all-around cowman that ever rode the trails out of Texas. People speak of the "Blocker loop." It was named for John Blocker, who threw it.

"*Una vez* — one time," Jacinto de los Santos rumbled, "I was helping Mr. Johnnie Blocker catch wild cattle out of the brush. We were roping them by night on the prairie. When all was still and the world was dark, they came there to graze.

"Well, one morning we went out very early. It was before the coyotes began to sing, and it was very dark. We were all planted where we thought the cattle would pass. We heard them before we could see them. Then each of us made for the sound. When we got close, we saw only *bultos* — objects. We could not tell what they were. I leaned over almost to the ground so as to skylight the *bulto* in front of me. The way to see in the night is to look up from the ground instead of down towards it. The thing I was after appeared to me as a dun calf. I made the loop small so that the calf could not run through it. I cast the loop. My horse squatted like a jack rabbit, as if to receive the jerk of a *toro*. The jerk was sharp, but not hard. Nevertheless, I knew that the animal at the end of the rope was thrown.

"I jumped down to tie it. Before my foot was out of the stirrup, I felt the rope slacken. I mounted quickly to run on the rope and jerk the calf down again. I ran and jerked, and ran and jerked again. The thing would not stay down. Never in all my life did I feel such another animal on the end of the rope. It could bounce like a rubber ball. At the same time my horse was snorting and trying to pitch. The other three vaqueros were scattered off and were busy with their catches. I thought, 'What can be the matter with this little animal?' I thought, 'The

devil must be in that animal and I can't smell his sulphur but my horse can.' A horse often has more intelligence than a man.

"Well, after a while the light of morning began to promise itself. As soon as the dawn showed ever so dim, I saw clearly what was the matter. I had roped *un león*, yes, a lion, a panther. It was the biggest I ever saw. It was the biggest that any man in all this brush ever saw. We did not neck it to an ox."

This is the brush of the outlaws — the brush which, hiding what is within it, opens the imaginations of men — the brush which, repelling with talon and claw, yet fascinates with the unknown it may harbor. That strange denizen of the thickets, old Jack Hargis, used to tell this story.

"You know, one time when we were catching wild cattle over on the Arroyo Prieto we kept seeing barefoot tracks. Sometimes they were up on the rocky hills and sometimes in the pear flats. They were often right along with a cow's tracks. We knew from a hair left where she lay down that she was a brindle cow. We wondered about the man. We saw where he had eaten prickly pear apples, snared a cottontail with twine made out of Spanish dagger fiber, and chewed mesquite beans. One vaquero said the man was dogging a badger to catch the rats the badger ran out of holes. Another said he was following a bunch of javelinas and eating the roots they dug up. I never did believe everything I heard, but this man was sure *ladino*.

"Well, late one evening — it was in the summer — a Mexican hit the wild man's trail while the dust was still a-settling in the tracks. He followed it at a long lope, and d'reckly caught sight of the man. All he had on was a piece of deerhide. I guess he had took it from a deer killed by a panther. The feller dodged and laid down in a *mogote* and played all the tricks the cunningest *ladino* might play, but it wa'n't no use. That vaquero was a regular bloodhound. About dark he roped the wild man and necked him up short to a mesquite tree to spend the night.

"Next morning we all rode out to lead him in. Well, sir, when

[314]

we got clost to the tree, we heard the dernedest bawling and lowing and cow carrying-on you ever listened to. We went easy, and when I got up to where I could see, there, right next to the man, still necked hard and fast to the mesquite, was an old brindle cow. She was carrying on over that wild man like he was her own calf. As soon as she saw us, she lit a shuck like a buck deer, and we let her go. Her bag looked like she was giving milk.

"We took the man in and fed him frijoles and other civilized food. For quite a spell we kept his head tied down to his front foot and sorter hobbled him to the camp. Gradually he gentled down, and in time he made a purty good cow-hand. The vaqueros named him Gato del Monte — Wild Cat — and then called him just Monte. He wan't no hand to air his paunch, and I never did learn where he come from. He wouldn't talk about that old brindle cow at all. A Mexican come in one night and said he'd left her tied over on a certain holler, but next morning she was loose. Monte had been out that night. One spring I took him up the trail with me. When we struck the Cimarron, it was up big enough to float a steamboat. We hit it anyhow. Monte's hoss got mixed up with a treetop and he drownded. It wa'n't no fault of his. I often think he was about the wildest critter I ever saw roped out of the brush."

José Beltrán was the most astute of all trappers of wild cattle on the great O'Connor ranch back in the days' when cattle and horses ran wild by the thousands and a man could see as many as a hundred deer together, running one after the other, "like mules." He began trapping not long after windmills were built on the ranch. At the Mexican Water Hole was a big pen of slick wire doubled around high posts closely set together and enclosing the mill and troughs. Nothing could jump it or knock it down. At one corner a gate opened into a small, equally strong holding pen. The gate from the pasture into the trap was, except when the wild ones were to be caught, always left open so that cattle could enter and drink at will. A wire, ordinary telephone wire, led from the gate to the platform of the wind-mill, about thirty-five feet above the ground. The trapper sat on the platform and watched. When animals came in that he wanted to catch, he pulled the wire and closed the gate.

Beltrán is little and black and bowlegged and *muy alerto*, with eyes that gleam and peer everywhere. When he is telling a story, he cannot sit. He stands, kneels, bends over on all fours, squats, lies down, jumps up, looks out yonder, seeing whatever it is he is talking about, imitates the sound of hoofbeats, the bark of a coyote, the bleat of a calf, the scuttling of an armadillo. I found myself jumping up and down, looking and listening with him.

"*Bueno*, when Don Patricio Lambert told me to go to the Mexican Water Hole, he sent another vaquero with me. We hide our horses way off, way off, out of the wind. We do not walk through the gates. No, we climb over the wires at a place where the cattle do not come.

"It is hot summer. We take off our clothes and bury them in sand. The body of a man, just in his own skin, does not give out scent like the clothes he has sweat in. We rub dirt and cow manure all over our bodies and in our hair. Now we do not stink like a man at all. We go to the windmill tower. There is a bucket. I take water in it out of the trough and pour water on our tracks. We touch nothing. Then we climb up.

"On top we take off our shoes, so a step will not make one sound. We sit down. I face the gate, and the other vaquero is watching too. The wire is ready to pull. The moon is bright like day. We wait and wait. There is nothing. I see a coyote that wants some water. He makes no sound. We wait and wait. I hear maybeso one armadillo in the sticks, outside the pen. It is getting about eleven o'clock. I think nothing is coming tonight. The wild cattle do not come in after midnight, until about five o'clock in the morning.

"My *compañero* and I do not speak all this time, except with a finger and *ssh*, like that. I am nearly asleep. Then I hear from the trail in the brush one bull. *Bru-uh-uh,* he says, not loud, low down in himself. *Shh.*

"Good, I think. He is bringing some cattle with him. In the summer the bulls do not stay by themselves as in the cold time. He makes that talk again, *Bru-uh-uh,* low, quiet, like the night. He is closer. Then in that bright moonlight I see him at the gate. He is black, black, *puro negro.* He stops and smells the ground and the posts. I am looking for the other cattle.

"He comes in, all alone. He walks straight to the trough. I can hear him drinking, *hillkk, hillkk.* He drinks until he is full. He stands one little minute with his head towards the gate. He belches — that way. I am looking for the other cattle. Still they do not come. I can see the unmarked ears on the black bull. Now he starts for the gate.

"I pull the wire. I hear the gate slam. Then I hear *psh-hh-hh.* I tell this vaquero to go to the gate at the little pen in the corner and when I scare the bull through it, to shut it. I go easy to the fence and climb over and go on the outside to the big gate in front of the bull. I will scare the bull and make him run to the corner and go into the little pen. He will fight with me if I am inside with him. But outside I can play with him.

"But the bull is not at the gate. I look and look. I go all around the pen, looking through the wire, looking in the bright moonlight. The pen is not too big, and there is no brush in it, just one huisache and six, eight mesquites. The other *vaquero* he looks too. There is no black bull in the pen. No, do not deceive yourself into thinking any bull could jump that fence, that gate.

"Listen. This bull is not one bull. He is *el diablo.* I do not wish to stay at the Mexican Water Hole longer that night. Maybe so it is the Devil's Water Hole. We put on our clothes and ride to the ranch. Nobody ever saw that maverick black bull again. Nobody ever saw him before that night. What does this seem to you?"

[317]

XIX · MOLDED BY HORN AND THORN

To Ed McWhorter, who went up the trail with the
Dobie men and is one of my people.

TO understand any element of the brush country, the literary conception of a cowboy riding so free and careless over the plains must be forgotten. One time, an old story goes, a top hand from the prairie country joined a brush outfit on a cow hunt. He was all eagerness to rope something.

"All right," said the boss, "we're going to make a sashay this morning through some switches where we are sure to jump skittish cattle. You'll have your chance."

True to the promise, the prairie hand had his chance, but though he was minus some of his clothes and a great deal of skin when he came back out of "the switches," the tie rope was still on his saddle.

"Why, I thought you wanted to rope something," exclaimed the boss.

"Well, I'll tell you," replied the prairie hand. "I saw that speckled steer when we jumped him and I took after him. But the farther we went, the thicker the brush seemed to get. Finally I met one of your seven-foot rattlesnakes backing out. When the brush got so thick that a rattlesnake had to back out of it, I thought I'd just as well back out too."

Roping wild cattle anywhere has its dangers, but nowhere are they so serious as in the brush. Although surprisingly few men have been killed in this work, I know of no other in which a man can more often come near to being killed and yet keep on living and running. Occasionally you will see one with an eye out. Some of them have one leg shorter than the other; many suffer for years from internal bruises that are never cured and nearly all die with strange lumps on their limbs and trunks.

Once I asked Rocky Reagan what was the narrowest escape he had ever had, for I knew he had been in "lots of fixes."

"It was on my first night work," he replied. "I was sixteen years old. We were snaring *ladinos* out of the Artillery Thicket, and had gone out before daylight to waylay them on an opening. About dawn we sighted a little bunch moving back towards the brush. I took after what proved to be a bull five or six years old. A jump or two before my horse started going down a hill, I threw the loop. The horse squatted, the bull went out of sight, the rope tightened, and my cinch broke.

"When the saddle left, I was still straddling it and I kept right on straddling it. It hit the ground straight, and I rode that saddle for what seemed to me a quarter of a mile, though it turned out to be only about a hundred yards. It was moving too. Soon the bull, the saddle, and I all got tangled up in the brush. I got off. The saddlehorn and rope held. The bull was a fighter. We sewed his eyes up with four stitches of buckskin to each pair of lids and took him out with a bunch of gentle cattle.

"No, I wasn't hurt — just scratched up a little and bruised in a few places. I wasn't in as tight a place as Sam Cook was. One night back in the days of six-shooters he roped a wild cow in the Nueces bottom. The cinch broke, and Sam went with the saddle. He rode at a rapid gait for some distance. Then the cow changed ends and charged him. He drew his six-shooter and shot her."

Of course, such chances were never confined to the brush. It was of a similar episode on the open plains that the song called "Windy Bill" was made up and sung.

> Windy Bill was a Texas man,
>   And he could rope, you bet;
> Why, the steer he couldn't tie down
>   Hadn't sorter been born yet.

But one time Windy Bill found "a slim black steer" that had stood his ground "with punchers from everywhere."

> His old cowhorse flew at him
>   Like he'd been eating corn,
> And Bill he landed his new maguey
>   Around Old Blackie's horns.

> The horse he squatted like a rabbit,
>   The cinch it broke like straw;
> Both Sam Stack saddle and new maguey
>   Went drifting down the draw.

I have seen dogs brought from a distance that within five minutes after being turned loose to run in the spines were writhing in pain and blindness. I have seen cattle imported from the east halt in this brush in a helpless daze. But dogs and cattle learn to adapt themselves like the coyotes and deer. The men and horses that run most effectively in the brush have as a rule been born to it. The best brush horses are of the old Spanish strain.

The leather leggins the brush hand wears never have ornamental wool or hair on them. They are not for looks. His feet, whether booted or shoed, are protected by *tapaderos* (toe-fenders) that hood the stirrups but do not flap down, to be snagged and to offer more surface resistance to the brush they must drag through. A ducking jacket that fits snugly has no superfluous tail to be torn. A ten-gallon hat would be as convenient in those thickets as an umbrella. If the brush hand can afford gloves and can stand being choked by them, he wears them. If not, his own skin will pay. He is sometimes called a "limb-skinner," but it is the limbs that do the skinning.

He is "on horseback," but in tearing into the brush he is more under his horse, stretched out alongside him, lying against his neck, dodging into his flank, squirming down first one shoulder and then the other, than sitting upright in the saddle. He rides all over, along and under his horse. He must keep his eyes open, too, or have them gouged out. He has to look to dodge and he has to dodge as swiftly almost as the eye can glimpse in order to keep on looking. As a shield he uses his hands, arms, shoulders, legs and body more than his head. If he goes to dodging too much with his head, he will shut his eyes, and when he shuts his eyes, even for a second, he loses control. If, shut-eyed, he dodges one limb now, he will not be able to see another limb that a fraction of a second later he must inevitably either dodge or head into. The horse he is riding is not going to pause or stop; if he is a well-trained horse hot after a cow, his rider can only with great difficulty stop him at all.

While there are many clumps of brush too thick and low for a cow to enter, there are not many cows that a good brush hand can't follow. Early in his experience he learned that he could no more find a soft entrance into a thicket than a shivering swimmer can find a warm spot in a lake of winter water to dive into. So the brush hand hits the brush center, hits it on the run, and "tears a hole" through it. A listener may hear the popping of limbs, the raking against leather, but there can be no spectator to this run. The "hole" closes up immediately.

The brush hand carries a short rope, and he does not expect room in which to swing it. If he finds an opening "about as big as a saddle blanket" he will rope the outlaw by the head. He reaches over and casts his loop up; for the nearer the ground, the more open space there is. He catches often by one or both hind feet. Many a time he comes out of a thicket carrying enough wood in the fork of his saddle to satisfy a prairie cook. Often after a horse has made a hard run, his legs are so thorned and bruised by knocks that he can barely walk.

The brush hand is a brute for punishment. Cool-headed in directing his own skill, at the same time, once he hits a hot trail, he becomes oblivious of all else.

One time while Doc Turk and some other brush poppers were in swimming, their saddled horses standing on the bank, they glimpsed an outlaw steer crossing the open creek bed just below the water hole. Without hesitating a moment, Doc Turk leaped out of the water and, stark naked as he was, mounted his snorting horse and tore through the bushes after the steer. He roped him and tied him down. Scratches and bruises meant no more to him than a gash to a dog smelling the breath of his prey. They say that on many a cold morning his comrades have literally lifted Doc Turk into the saddle, stiff and "stove up" from punishment administered by the brush. He knew and his comrades knew that, once the chase was started, he would limber up.

The work in the brush after wild cattle fostered a tradition of hard living that belongs with rawhide and Longhorns. "I often laugh with old trail men from South Texas about the beds and clothing we had and the grub we got," Teddy Blue, of the Three Deuce Ranch, Gilt Edge, Montana, once wrote me. "Old E. S. Newman used to say, 'Horses and cattle cost money; cowboys are cheap.' One time up here he said to some Montana cowboys:

'You all have got a picnic. In Texas you would work for thirty dollars a month, ride four horses, and eat what you got. Here you get forty dollars a month, eat pie three times a day, have ten horses in your string and want to sleep with the boss.' "

Chub Poole, like a few other old-time sheriffs left in Texas, is a cowman. His stamping ground is down the Nueces. Some of his experiences will illustrate the elemental ways of life in the brush.

"Along about 1892," he told me, "I bought out a brand of cattle, range delivery, located in a pasture so big that the country might as well have been unfenced. Mavericks and strays of all kinds lay up in the thickets. The only way to catch what I had bought — and also a good sprinkling of mavericks — was to rope 'em.

"My little cow crowd consisted of myself and three Mexicans. I paid them from five to seven-and-a-half pesos — not dollars — each per month. We had no chuck wagon; we could not have taken a wagon where we wanted it even if we had had one. We didn't need a wagon. I carried a blanket and a quilt and our grub on a pack horse. The grub consisted of some meal and salt. We had no coffee, no sugar, no lard, soda, baking powder, or anything like that. Just salt and meal. The only utensils we had were a frying pan and a jug. The jug was for putting tallow in. I knocked the top off it so that it would be more handy. We would kill a fat animal when we wanted meat, dry what we couldn't use fresh, and save the tallow. That tallow, mixed up with meal, water and salt, made good corn bread, which was cooked in the skillet and was nourishing. The meat was cooked on the open fire. Fresh ribs could be spitted on a mesquite stick, and dried meat is good raw or just thrown on the coals. Occasionally we might fry steak in melted tallow in the skillet. For seasoning we gathered the little chilipiquines (red peppers) growing wild in many places. As we had no coffee, we had no use for cups. We scooped up the water to our mouths in hat-brims or by hand, or got down on our bellies and sucked it in.

"We didn't have but three or four horses apiece. They were as tough as rawhide. It was not unusual to start out from camp before daylight some morning to be gone two or three days. We took no extra horses along; we took no bedding along. The only food we took would be some corn bread and dried beef, carried in saddle pockets or a *morral*. The most important thing we had to take was a good rope and eight or ten *peales* apiece. A *peal* is a short rope for hog-tying an animal after it is roped. We stayed out until the *peales* were all used up. Then we came back to camp, got lead oxen, and went to bring in what we had caught."

Henry Beckwith passed for a Negro, but mixed in him were strains of Indian, Mexican, and white blood. He was stubby, round-shouldered, his chest built like a panther's. Until he died, about 1935, he was always up long before daylight. Anybody in camp with him noticed that he always bedded down some distance away from other men — out in the brush — alone. When he talked — and he used to say that the reason he had lived so long was that he never talked much — he was continually turning his head this way and that, looking, watching, expecting. He reminded me of a wild eagle put in a cage. The brush hides few secrets that old Henry did not know; most of them died with him. The animals that live in the brush have no instincts that Henry did not share. What I know about Henry Beckwith I learned from men who worked with him. If I can picture him as he lived and as he ran in the brush, I shall give some conception of the bleak, stark, wary life the brush fosters.

Years ago Henry used to work for a man whom for the sake of convenience we shall call Bob Kingling, who ran the **S O** brand. Henry used to gather old Bob's stuff out of the thickets far away from the Kingling ranch. He gathered and brought in

[324]

cattle wearing the brands of other men also, along with mavericks to which he was not entitled. During his most active time he had two young Mexicans as helpers.

"I worked with Henry for eight years," one of those Mexicans named Segovia told me. "In all that time, winter or summer, I never saw him with any bedding. I guess he had learned how to be a coyote from his master. I remember one time when it was bitter cold and some of us stopped to make a little fire, Mr. Kingling would not get off his horse. He had once been in a Kansas blizzard, he said, that froze thirty-six horses to death out of a remuda of forty, and could stand any weather in Texas after that. As we put our hands over that fire, we could see icicles on our horses, but Mr. Bob Kingling just sat there in his saddle without seeming to notice the fire.

"If the night was very cold, this coyote Henry Beckwith would not lie down but would build a very small fire, like the Indians build, and would sit there hunkered over it all night, dozing and sipping coffee. *Señor*, I will tell you one thing you will not believe. In the morning after breakfast — and this was always long before dawn — this coyote Henry Beckwith would mash some of those little red peppers up and stir them in with the coffee grounds left in the pot. Then when we came back, maybe not until two days later, he'd heat this liquid and drink it. I am a Mexican and I like chili, but I do not like coffee made out of chili juice.

"The Coyote always told us that the best place to make down our beds was in low ground where cattle had walked while it was muddy and then the tracks had dried. Such rough ground would keep us from being dead to sleep. He said that a man must remain always alert, even in his sleep. He would not let us make down our pallets in soft grass. I have seen him put sticks under his saddle blanket at night so that his bed would not be too soft."

He did not need much sleep. They say that lots of nights he

did not sleep at all. He could just "wallow a couple of times" and get up ready for another day.

"One time," this Mexican Segovia told me, "the Coyote and I struck a maverick cow and a wild steer running together. I took after the steer and he took after the cow. As soon as I tied the steer, I followed the Coyote's tracks, for I had not heard him yell. Soon I saw his saddle. It was on the ground, empty. I yelled. I heard his answer. I galloped on. I found him riding bareback, one end of his rope twisted around his waist and the other end on the cow's head. Just as I rode up, he jumped off his horse and let the cow drag him until he got the rope around a tree. He said the cow had turned on him in some thick brush where he could not cast the rope and had hooked a horn under his cinch, breaking it. He went off with his saddle and the cow went on. He held the bridle reins, of course, and still had his horse. He took the rope from his saddle horn and followed the cow."

One time Henry sent his Mexicans to catch a wild cow followed by two maverick heifers. The Mexicans located the *ladinas*, but somehow could not come upon them. After making several fruitless "razoos," they left. A few nights later Henry Beckwith rode into Ed McCoy's camp, which was near the haunt of the *ladinas*. He asked McCoy to indicate where the cow and heifers used.

"All right," said McCoy, "I'll show you in the morning."

"No, tonight."

There was a dim moon. Ed McCoy saddled his horse and led Henry to the edge of a big *quebradora* (white brush) thicket. Henry was riding one of his two noted dun horses. For a few moments the two men sat there in their saddles, motionless, silent. Then a stick popped. McCoy said he could feel his own horse's heart pounding against his legs. The ears of both horses were working. But these were Henry Beckwith's snakes, and, as the old saying goes, "Every man must kill his own snakes" — especially in the dark. Another noise, ever so slight, came from the sleeping thicket. It might have been made by an armadillo, but it wasn't.

Like a flash, Henry left on his dun horse. McCoy said the way they tore through the brittle *quebradora* sounded like a runaway threshing machine. That dun horse could trail by smell like a dog.[1] In no time almost McCoy heard Henry yell and knew he had roped the cow. Henry tied her, took the trail of one of the maverick heifers and tied her; then he trailed the other heifer down and tied her. Henry had picked the two dun horses he most relied on out of a big remuda and trained them to scent tracks.

In the brush, where men, horses and cattle cannot see, their faculties of smell and hearing are sharpened like those of blind people. Like many another brush hand, Henry often smelled a cow brute squatting in the bushes before he saw her. Always he watched the ears of his horse. They could point like a setter dog.

Henry Beckwith's ways were in darkness and solitude. "One time about midnight," Chub Poole said, "I was riding along a trail to a camp when I suddenly heard brush crackling ahead of me. I stopped still. The sounds told me a man was after a cow brute. Soon I heard a voice saying, 'Damn your wild soul, I've got you now.' I recognized the voice as being Henry's. I said nothing, and after a while rode on quietly. I never mentioned the matter to Henry and never learned what he had caught."

If an animal got away from him he would sulk like an old bull for two or three days, not speaking to anybody. His silences, however, did not come primarily from misses. He could be brutal, but he never was to his horses or to a catch dog he called Slacker. He was harder on nothing than on himself.

He came to work for Chub Poole for a spell, wearing new boots. Rainy weather set in, and the men worked all day, soaking wet. The next morning, long before daylight, Chub Poole heard Henry out in the bushes talking to his boots. When the stiffening in the heels of new boots gets wet and soft, they are next to impossible to get on.

"Damn you," Henry was saying, "if I ever gits you on agin, you'll stay on this foot till you rots."

Finally Henry came limping up to the fire and the coffeepot.

"To my certain knowledge," Chub Poole will tell you, "Henry Beckwith did not pull those boots off again for three months. It is my belief that he wore them until they rotted off."

One time after Henry and his Mexicans had been roping for weeks and putting their catches in a strong pen built away out in the brush, giving them food and water in the form of prickly pear, a stranger rode into camp about dark. Ed McCoy "happened" to be working with Henry this time. About midnight, he said, he detected Henry awakening the two Mexicans. All three stole away to the pens. McCoy pulled on his boots and followed softly. Looking through the cracks in the pen he saw the Coyote and his cubs mug and tail seven or eight big old steers that Henry had decided he did not want the stranger to read brands on next morning. The steers were led out into the thicket and tied securely. McCoy said the noiseless way in which Henry got them out was a marvel.

I have dwelt on the old Coyote because he represents so intensely what brush and brush cattle could and did make of men. There is no English word to denote accurately these men of the brush country. "Brush men" suggests too much the savage bushmen of Australia. "Plainsmen" and "woodsmen" are patent misnomers. They are *hombres del campo* — men of the *campo*, *campo* meaning both camp and untamed country.

I doubt if any Apache or Comanche ever surpassed some of these *hombres del campo* as trailers. Like all other arts, that of trailing is "long" — long, especially, in being acquired. As a boy, Manuel Tom, whose fame as a trailer spread far beyond the brush country, would go to a water hole, pick out a certain cow brute, note its individual tracks as distinguished from the tracks of all other cattle and then, after the animal left, trail it. To him the tracks of that individual animal grew to possess characteristics as distinct from all other hoof marks as any thumb print is to a Bertillon expert.

Tiburcio, of the San Antonio Viejo Ranch, can tell whether any track he sees is made by a cow, a bull, or a steer. All four hoofs of a cow are sharper than a steer's; a steer's front toes are sharper than a bull's, which are pronouncedly blunt. Tiburcio has been known to see an animal, note its tracks, and then two years later, without so much as having crossed its trail during all that time, point out a track as belonging to the animal in question, follow it, and prove his claim.

Late one afternoon Tiburcio rode into camp and directed a vaquero to take a rifle, go to a certain thicket and kill two outlaw steers hidden there. The vaquero killed one of the outlaws but merely flesh-wounded the other. The dead steer was hauled in for meat, and next morning the vaquero took the trail of the other.

He was gone all day. When the second morning came and he had not yet come in, Tiburcio sent two other vaqueros to trail him and see if he had been hurt. Late that day they found him. He had just finished tying the steer. He had trailed it about thirty-five miles, over more than a dozen fences. During the two days of his trailing he had not once glimpsed the steer until at the end. It was dry weather and most of the distance was through brush. He had crossed and twisted through the tracks of many other steers. Hot on the trail, he had camped for the night so as to go on without delay the next morning. This steer was what the Mexicans call a *chongo* — a steer with a drooped horn. A horn drooped down over a steer's eye may not make him any wilder, but it makes him look wilder.

Ignacio Flores had been captured by Comanches as a boy

and taught by them to trail. If he wanted to determine how old a trail not fresh was, he would spend a long time at certain places. He would look to see if a dewdrop had dried in the track; he would at a sandy place calculate on the age of a doodle-bug hole. He would scrutinize the fine little marks made on bare ground by insects, some nocturnal and some diurnal. These fairy-light tracings that a hoofprint had broken into or that were over the hoofprint told him much. The glazed track of a snail on a twig might for him be as accurately dated as the stamping on a letter. He said that blades of live grass trodden on by a hoofed animal of weight would not only start immediately to spring back into normal position but would keep on raising up for three days. He might stand or bend over some well-turfed spot for a long time, just looking at the grass-blades. If he found the leaf of a bush knocked off by the track-maker, its freshness or shriveled condition told him something. Any leaf will begin shriveling within twenty-four hours after it has been detached. Ignacio Flores would look at a leaf fallen in a dampish, shaded spot and at another fallen in a sun-lighted spot; he would con-sider the factors of light, darkness, cloudiness, sunshine, heat, cold, wind, and from those two little leaves make a pretty ac-curate estimate as to when they had been displaced.

One September day, about thirty years ago, I was preparing to leave our ranch for college. The family had moved to town. The morning before I was to leave — I always lingered as long as I could — I rode out into a pasture of about four thousand acres to look through a band of stock horses. None of them had ever been broken, and they were sometimes about as difficult to pen as a bunch of mustangs. There were about twenty of them. I found them on the back side of the pasture and, in riding around them, saw that a big colt had a bad case of screwworms. They must be taken to the pen so that the colt could be doctored and kept up until the wound healed.

As I started the mares, they, as usual, began running. I kept them coursed pretty straight until we were within a half-mile of the pen. Then, at a snaggle of brushy hollows, they circled on me and turned back. For hours we circled, crisscrossed, dodged, and maneuvered, in the brush and across the openings. The weather had been dry for months, but we made some pretty fresh trails. Finally, along in the afternoon, I penned the brutes.

After I closed the gate, I rode my horse Buck under the shade of a big live oak, loosened the girth, pulled some thorns out of his knees, and stood there waiting for him to cool off a bit before watering him. While waiting, I reached down for my watch and found it gone. As a rule I did not carry it with me while riding. Ranch people mostly go by the sun, their stomachs, and whatever they have to do. Time waits on them — in a way; not they on time. But I had taken the watch that morning. It had a fob that dangled loose from the watch pocket and that was — when worn — always kept under the leggins belt. But everything I wore had undergone various adjustments during the run. Probably a limb had raked the fob hard enough to jerk the watch out of my pocket.

A Mexican named Genardo del Bosque who had worked for us many years came to the pen. I told him about the watch.

"Where have you been?" he asked.

"Genardo," I replied, "I have been everywhere in that pasture, and I have been over several places several times. Out about those dry lakes there is not any ground left that we did not plow up."

"Well, I will take your trail and find the watch."

"Can you tell Buck's tracks from the tracks of all the other horses?"

"*Sí, señor.*"

Within an hour I was gone. When I came back at Christmastime, Genardo handed me my watch.

Like a criminal, like an often-coursed fox, many a Longhorn

outlaw of the brush has been made more wily and alert by a comprehension of the skill and persistence of his trackers.

Don Victoriano Chapa was of *gente decente* — which means something more than "decent people" — with land rights and stock, on the Rio Bravo. The stone over his grave out in illimitable brush says that when he died in 1901 he was eighty-nine years old. At the age of fifteen, in 1827, he and another Mexican boy were captured by the Comanches. They remained captive for four or five years, long enough to learn whatever coyotes know of nature, long enough for Victoriano to acquire an appetite for horse meat that he kept until he died, together with a way of gorging on raw liver and raw *huevos de toros* — but not long enough to make him and his fellow captive forget home.

They learned the lay of an enormous land. Once or twice they were taken to San Antonio on a raid for horses. In those times the Comanches called San Antonio their *rancho*, saying that the only reason they allowed the Spaniards to remain there was to raise horses for them. When a band came into the town, they would order Mexicans to guard their horses, holding the city responsible for their safekeeping. Frequently some of them contrived to steal their own horses from the guards, and then demanded pay for the alleged loss.[2] They required rations of beef and corn during prolonged visits, and the peons brought wood in for them to cook with.[3]

One time while the band holding Victoriano were camped away up on the Guadalupe River, most of the warriors left for a buffalo hunt. A night or two later the two boy captives slipped out and struck south in the little dog trot that only Indians and Mexicans can travel in. For three nights and two days, never stopping except to lap water, they dog-trotted. Then after the sun of the third day was half up to the meridian, they came to the Villita by the banks of the San Antonio River. They stopped

[333]

at the first *jacal* they came to. The woman called them *"pobre-citos"* and told them to enter. She began to prepare corn for them. In a minute, she lifted her head and hand with a quick jerk.

"Listen! . . . Galloping!" She went to the door and looked. *"Madre de Dios,"* she cried, *"los Comanches!"* Quickly she hid the youths under some deerskins and a Saltillo blanket in one corner of the room. Then she was at the door.

"We have come for the boys," one of the four Comanches said.

"What boys?"

"The ones that ran off from us."

"I know nothing of such boys."

"Yes, they came just now to your little house."

"No, they did not come, unless as ghosts. I did not see them. They did not enter. They are not here."

"You lie, you she-dog of mixed blood. They left our camp three sleeps ago. One sleep was passed and the sun was yonder when we started on their trail. It has led straight. The tracks have been plain. Look," and the Comanche pointed to the ground, "there they are coming into this *jacal*. They are so fresh that the sand is still settling in them."

Comanche visitors in San Antonio were not rare, and the entrance of three or four lone riders was not calculated to raise an alarm, though they were always to be watched with distrust. At this moment the woman saw a soldier from the fort across the river, at the bank, looking her way. The Comanches saw him also.

One said, "These boys are our property. Hurry yourself or — "

The woman said, "Get gone, or I'll give the alarm and every soldier in the *presidio* will rise."

The four Comanches left. There were not enough of them to make an attack.

In time Victoriano Chapa and his fellow returned to the Rio Grande. Very soon after this he must have married, but he and his son Prisciliano both lived to be so old that people forgot he had ever had a wife or that Prisciliano, who married also but lost his wife and was childless, had ever had a mother. Don Victoriano used to tell how some lancers scouting between the Rio Grande and the Nueces caught him with a bunch of captured mustangs and made him bring them to Santa Anna's army, on its way to the siege of the Alamo. He was a mustanger for many years, and Prisciliano became a *mesteñero* also. During the Civil War they made real money hauling cotton in ox carts from the interior of Texas to be delivered at the Rio Grande — the only escape from the Federal blockade that the Confederacy had.

Along in the seventies the Chapas were handling cattle with T. J. Lyne on Padre Island. Here Lyne and the Grace Company had a hide and tallow factory at which the best parts of slaughtered animals were pickled in brine for export to the south. Padre Island is a long sliver of land paralleling the Texas coast from the mouth of the Rio Grande northward to Corpus Christi Bay. North of it, with a narrow pass between, runs Mustang Island. One incident will reveal how Lyne and the Chapas handled their Longhorns.

They had five hundred head of big steers on Mustang Island. Lyne took his men over, got the steers all in a herd, and started them to swimming the pass for Padre and the slaughter pens. Halfway across there was a bobble, and the cattle turned back. The men worked two or three days without being able to make them take the water again. Then Lyne ordered butcher-knives, salt and ammunition brought over. The long-horned steers were kept under herd on the point nearest Padre Island until every single one had been shot down and skinned. The meat was piled out on the sand, salt by the ton poured on it, layer after layer. There was a "regular mountain of meat." Months later the receivers of it in Panama sent back word that if another consignment of beef as gritty with sand as this arrived, there would be a revolution.

In 1876 Lyne went up into Live Oak County, where there was plenty of land to be located. Don Victoriano Chapa and Don Prisciliano followed. They acquired about ten thousand acres of land. There were prairies on it then, though *ramaderos* of dense brush and *montes* of chaparral bordered and cut into the openings. In time they fenced the land. It is all — absolutely all — brush now. The Chapas raised Spanish horses and Longhorn cattle. They were quiet men, almost timid, quaintly honest in the way of simple people, and loyal to their own ways, people and land.

At the ranch house, on a hollow that makes the upper drainage of Ramireña Creek, they built a big tank. Don Victoriano laid off plots of ground for peon Mexicans, who carried the dirt out in rawhide bags, building a dam that holds to this day. To strengthen it against the rush of waters he butchered a heifer and mixed the blood into the earth at the center of the dam and at each end. This was the only permanent watering of any value on the whole ten thousand acres. In a terrible drouth of the nineties, Don Victoriano had all the old Spanish mares that came to water corralled, and there he stabbed them, so that they would eat no more grass and drink no more water. They had no sales value.

Don Victoriano was the last ranchero in a big scope of country to use a cowhide for a table, squatting by it on the floor to eat. However, he was converted to table and chairs long before he died. Martín Silvas, who used to work for him, is the only vaquero I have ever heard admit failure in finding his way back to an animal left tied in the brush. Martín told me that one time in the Chapa *monte* he accidentally rode up on some pieces of rope and bones at a mesquite tree to which he had tied a *ladino* twenty years before.

The Chapa ranch is about twenty miles up the Ramireña

Creek from our old ranch. In 1896 my father bought the steers. Martín Silvas, the vaquero I have spoken of, came down with word when they were at last gathered and ready for delivery. I remember that we stayed at the big tank several hours, the corrals being just below it. A brown cow stood in the water all that time with the lower part of her neck immersed, drowning out screwworms that had eaten a big hole in her flesh. The Chapas never doctored anything. They made no effort to improve their cattle. As long as they ranched, there were grown maverick bulls and cows in their pasture.

The steers we received were of all ages and colors. When we got home and were branding them in a chute, my father told me to guard the chute-pen gate. It was a heavy gate, but lower than the log fence through which it made an opening. I stood beside it, outside, beating my quirt against it and yelling. Directly an old, rough, pale-red steer that refused to be crowded into the chute wheeled, gave one snuff at the gate, and then jumped over it and me too, clearing us both as clean as a whistle.

The Chapas had cattle that never came to the big tank for water, drinking only when it rained, the rest of the time getting their moisture from prickly pear. When he was something over eighty years old, Don Victoriano became too stiff in the legs to mount a horse at all, and Don Prisciliano was at the same time becoming too old to run in the brush. They could no longer handle the wild cattle in the only way they knew, and the vaqueros working for them had absolutely no sense of management.

When Don Victoriano was eighty-nine years old, his son persuaded him to sell out the stock, lease the land and agree to move from the old ranch at the tank to a little corner of ground two or three miles away. The cattle were to be caught by the purchaser.

As the time approached for delivering the ranch, Don Victoriano became very morose. "When we are gone," he kept saying, "and everything in our brand has been cleaned out of the pasture, I can no longer sit and listen to the brindle bull *hablando* — talking — as he comes to water. I can no longer hear the bell on the dun mare telling me that the remuda is coming down the trail. God will never again bless me as I stand in the shelter of the *ramada* when it rains and watch the water come up in the tank inch by inch. When next spring comes, I will not see the quail pecking up berries with worms in them fallen from the agrito bushes growing under my oaks.

"Why have we been talked into this evil trade? We belong here. My roots go deeper than those of any mesquite growing up and down this long arroyo. We do not need money. When a man belongs to a place and lives there, all the money in all the world cannot buy him anything else so good. *Válgame Dios*, why, why, why?"

Bent far over on his two walking sticks of Spanish dagger stalks, Don Victoriano would disappear, muttering, into the brush under the motte of oaks. Two days before the date of delivery, on June 14, 1901, he hobbled out into a little barn with a dirt floor, got up on a box, tied a strangle knot around his neck, and fastened the rope over a rafter. Then he kicked the box out from under his feet. When he was found, his toes were not six inches from the ground and his legs were doubled up, showing that his will to die could not be thwarted by a step on to the earth he would be buried in rather than be dragged from.

One by one the Chapa Longhorns were roped out of the *monte*. Some of them ran and fought until they died. In a few years Don Prisciliano sold his ranch, except a half-section of land he kept to live on and one acre on which he had buried Don Victoriano, beside whom he expected to be laid. He sold to Tom Lyne, son of the Padre Island Lyne, at a dollar an acre, the notes being made out for forty years, at three per cent interest. He could have got more, but he wanted to trade only with a man who belonged to the land. He wanted "Tomasito" to have the land anyhow.

He willed his property — the land notes and the half-section homestead — to two old women. One of them was the grand-daughter of the woman in San Antonio who had saved the boy Victoriano from the Comanches. For a third of a century his own bones have been a-mouldering out in the brush alongside his father's. The one acre of earth reserved for those bones has never been transferred to anybody.

If, in the Great Perhaps, souls have a consciousness of this world, Don Victoriano and Don Prisciliano must often ex-perience satisfaction in knowing that their land is still "un-improved" and that the thorns on it multiply year by year, that the soil has not been "poisoned" by cold steel plowing into it or so entombed by remorseless cement that it cannot breathe or retain the tracks made by generations of living beings over it.

But no brindle bull comes talking now to the big tank for water. Like the Chapas, the last of the Longhorns in their part of the *monte* belonged to a time utterly past long ago.

XX · SUNDOWN

To whoever will preserve the Longhorn, mounted magnificently in range museum, modeled in bronze, painted in color, alive on his proper stamping grounds.

The cowboys and the Longhorns
Who pardnered in Eighty-four
Have gone to their last roundup
Over on the other shore.

They answered well their purpose,
But their glory must fade and go,
Because men say there's better things
In the modern cattle show.

— N. HOWARD THORP: *Songs of the Cowboys*

NO people of the chase ever voluntarily became caretakers of herds and flocks. No people of pastoral backgrounds in an expanse of pastoral opportunities ever willingly became delvers in the soil. No graziers on free grass, ranging at will over a great land of nomadic freedom, ever voluntarily fenced themselves in — though they might feel compelled to fence other people out. Range men did not in their hearts choose to exchange free-running Longhorns, capable of rustling their own living, for fine-haired stock requiring endless attention; did not gladly go from the self-sufficient breed to the care-requiring breed, turning from animals that existed for them to that form of slavery enforced by all dependent possessions.

"In 1888 I married and settled down on my farm," wrote one trail driver, "but could never quite give up the cattle business. The Jersey or any other breed of milk cow has never appealed to me as the Longhorn did. After thirty years of settled life, the call of the trail and the open range is with me still, and there is not a day that I do not long to mount my horse and be out among the cattle."

Circumstances forced the changes from open to fenced ranges, from common to blooded stock. The buyer controls the seller; the producer is always the seller. The buyer demand that in the end brought the Texans to destroy the animal that had made them was early represented by laws in Colorado and elsewhere making it a misdemeanor to turn a Texas, Mexican or Cherokee bull loose on the open range and permitting any man so disposed to kill such a bull found at large.[1]

Push of population and economic popularity of the ranching industry drove every man who would maintain a range to get individual title to it and wall off all contenders. Land and taxes went up so that a cowman could no longer keep a steer until he was "aged" to market him. He had to have a quick-maturing animal that would convert pasturage into choice cuts of meat instead of into locomotory energy. With the trails to walk up all cut off, the cattle, instead of providing their own freight, now had cars to ride in. They became worth so much that an owner could no longer allow them to die if they were unable to rustle their own living. Cowmen quickly learned what mush-minded philanthropy has yet to comprehend: If you are going to the expense of feeding and nursing animals, practise on the kind worth saving and, by stopping the breed, get rid of the other kind.

The Longhorn did not vanish like the wild pigeon, perishing from the deadly hand of civilization and some other cause never to be satisfactorily explained. He did not vanish, as the buffalo almost vanished, in an astounding slaughter. He disappeared in the same way that strictly Negroid features are disappearing from millions of Negroes in America. He was bred away, not only in horn but in other characteristics. Before the close of the last century all the livestock papers and magazines and all the talkers to cattle raisers harped without ceasing on the necessity of breeding up herds and getting rid of "scrub cattle." Every section of the range had its "bull men." The most outstanding of these in Texas was "Bull" (O. H.) Nelson, who during the years 1881–1888 imported over ten thousand pure-bred bulls into the Texas Panhandle.

The Longhorn breed came to be outlawed not only by economy but by a rage for standardized, uniform stock. Durhams, followed by Polled Anguses and Devons, were at first the principal importations. Then the Hereford was settled upon as the breed best adapted to the range. The time came when, to bring a price justifiable to the raiser, a crop of calves had to look as nearly alike as possible, be as uniform in age, color and conformity as a flock of lambs.

The blend in which the most Longhorn blood remains potent is that with Brahma cattle. The first Brahmas in America were landed in South Carolina in 1848; next they reached Louisiana; in the early eighties they began to enter Texas and have become increasingly popular along the coast.² Next to the Longhorns they are the wildest-natured cattle the ranges have known. They differ in many ways from the Longhorns; yet the two breeds have many common characteristics. The Longhorns, indeed, had many characteristics common to many kinds of cattle, though in no other were the elements so mixed.

The pesky fever ticks did more to extirpate the lingering remnants of Longhorns than any other agency. Compulsory dipping of cattle against ticks began in southern Texas in 1922. By law every owner had to dip all of his cattle every fourteen days. There was one alternative for cleaning a pasture: to take every hoof out of it and keep it vacant for from seven to eighteen months. Without hosts to feed upon, the ticks dropped from animals onto the ground would during that time die without issue. The tick laws forced the big ranches to cut up and cross-fence their pastures and brought every animal in the land under control and frequent inspection. Cattle that could not be worked were shot as nuisances. Many a "Texan" that had long defied man was killed. "Cold-blooded" breeders were got rid of in one way or another.

What the Longhorn might have developed into by intensive, prolonged selective breeding on a well-controlled area of land is not altogether a matter of conjecture. The magnificent herd in the Wichita Mountains Wildlife Refuge of Oklahoma produces quite easily steers that weigh over a ton. Given time and grass and water, the Texas steer, like an oak, would develop.

He was like an oak. Nearly a hundred years ago, urbane Ashbel Smith, Surgeon General of the Texas Army, Minister to England and France, and then Secretary of State, speaking with the perspective that travel, education on two continents and natural wit had given him, said: "A perfect race of cattle would, I conceive, result from the cross of the Durham and the Texan, giving to the great size of the latter the finish of form belonging to the former." ³ Charles Goodnight, who as a breeder made himself a secure place in the history of Western ranges, regretted as long as he lived that ranchmen in improving their herds diluted the blood of the original stock until the thrift, hardihood and vitality belonging to it were lost, and that the rage for uniformity in flesh marks prevented keeping enough of the Longhorn for developing "the great American cow."

Not a great while ago a cowman who had "pardnered with the Longhorn in eighty-four" got off the train at Monterrey, Mexico, and went to a hotel not cluttered up with tourists. There he met a younger man who appeared to be a cow-buyer also and who could understand. The older man said: "I am from Fort Worth and this is my first trip into Mexico. As we came along today, I saw an old blue dun, long-horned cow out to one side of the track. I hunted up the conductor right then and told him if he would stop the train, I would go out and put my arms around that old cow's neck and tell her how glad I was to see her. I'll bet she was never sick a day in her life, never had any help from a human being except something to make her run a little faster, and has raised a calf every year since Pancho Villa went on the warpath."

In Amarillo I was sitting in a hotel lobby overhearing the talk between two cowmen. The face of one of them looked as if it had never felt moisture. Yet sand and wind and sun are the finest cleansers and purifiers in the world, you know. "Rain, hell," this man snorted at something the other said about a shower. "It's rained just enough to make the wood-ants plaster dirt around what grass stems are left. It ain't going to rain. I've bought feed until I am blind. The only thing to do is to go to breeding 'em back into brutes that thrive on air and scenery."

But the Moving Finger has writ. The Longhorn is of the past — a past so remote and irrevocable that sometimes it seems as if it might never have been, though in years it was only yesterday. It is easy for the ignorant, the superficial and the self-adulating to regard that vanquished dominator of annihilated

ranges as a monstrous joke on cattle-kind, a kind of phantas-magoria of vacancy now populated and machine-modernized. But I have an immense respect for the breed. They possessed an adamantine strength, an aboriginal vitality, a Spartan endurance, and a fierce nobility that somehow makes one associate them with Roman legions and Sioux warriors. The winds of memory still shift the dust that their millions of steel hoofs raised, over trails guided by the unvarying swing of the Great Dipper or the sinking sun's infallible direction — trails across a world that then seemed as vast as the Milky Way when it canopied a lone man on the lone prairie. Truly, they prefigured the men that took their name — the Longhorns.

PHOTOGRAPHIC RECORD
OF THE LONGHORNS

Actual photographs of Longhorns before 1900 are exceedingly scarce. However, by going to many places over a wide land for the purpose of getting pictures, and through the generosity of many individuals, the author has assembled a fairly full representation of the various types, colors, sizes and ages of Longhorn cattle, of the past as well as the present.

Elwood Payne, Austin, Texas, has so exercised his skill and art in photographing and has been so helpful in planning the entire layout that follows that he deserves especial mention.

KNOTTED, HORNED AND THORNED

On a little ranch down in the brush of Live Oak County, Texas, "Uncle John" Webster raises Longhorn cattle "because they are the true Texas breed." He sells off the progeny only with reluctance and keeps the skulls of old ones that die. He has a shed-room half full of them. His weathered and thorned body, the gnarled horns, the knotty mesquite log on which he sits, the old picket fence, and the brush behind the fence all belong together.

Picture by Elwood Payne, Austin, Texas.

CHAMPION, AND ANOTHER VANISHED ANTIQUITY

Champion was calved in Texas down by the Rio Grande in 1900, in 1899 was exhibited at the "International Fair" in San Antonio, and then was shipped North for exhibition. Where he died, or what became of his immense horns, is unknown. Those horns are said to have had a spread, straight across from tip to tip, of close to nine feet. Through pictures and drawings that have been circulated all over America during the past forty years, this steer has become the symbol of the breed he represented. Chapter XII ("Horns") contains a detailed account of his history.

Photograph, 1899, by Brack (now dead), of San Marcos, Texas.

This type of animal has become so scarce that in 1931 Louis A. Schreiner, of Kerrville, Texas, who was then assembling a small herd of Longhorns, paid $1000 for the white-and-red roan steer here pictured. The steer was born in Southern Texas in 1916 and died in 1936. His horns, although horizontal, show various curves. Horns that grew straight out like handle bars from the skull were very rare on live animals.

Photograph by John R. Blocker, Austin, Texas.

LINE-BACKS

Line-backs were very characteristic of the old "mustang" cattle of Spanish origin that ran wild with the deer when English-speaking settlers began taking up land in Texas early in the nineteenth century. (See accounts of these cattle in Chapter I, "The First Spanish Cattle.")

The steer at the top was a coal-black, with white markings above and black-and-blue speckled markings beneath. Notice the black horn-tips. The dark color of the other steer was a mixture of black mud, mustard and mouse.

Photographs by Frank Reeves and Holland Magendie, both of Fort Worth, Texas.

PRIZE STEER OF THE UNITED STATES GOVERNMENT LONG-HORN HERD, AND HIS MOTHER

In 1927 agents of the United States Government combed Texas for twenty-odd specimens of Longhorns with which to start a herd in the Wichita National Forest (now designated as the Wichita Mountains Wildlife Refuge) near Cache, Oklahoma. The herd at present numbers over 150 head. (See Chapter XII, "Horns.")

The steer here shown is the prize of the herd. His horns, while not phenomenally long, are very characteristic. He was born in 1928 and weighs 2045 pounds, showing how high altitude and an abundance of nutritious grass will develop the lanky Longhorns into beef — though not into beefiness.

The cow, last survivor of the Texas cattle taken to Oklahoma in 1927, died in 1939, when she was between twenty-two and twenty-five years old. Her skull is now preserved in the Texas Memorial Museum at Austin.

The brindle bull, a young one, owned by E. H. Marks on the Gulf Coast, is one of the very, very few of his kind left in Texas.

Photographs of steer and bull by Elwood Payne, Austin; of cow by the United States Bureau of Biological Survey, Cache, Oklahoma.

BULLS

Longhorn bulls were essentially of the type seen today in bull rings of Mexico, Spain and other Spanish-speaking countries. The two individuals here pictured were brought from Mexico, not far below the Texas border, to breed with cows in the Longhorn herd of the Wichita Mountains Wildlife Refuge, Cache, Oklahoma. The bull at the top, a smudgy red, is an excellent example of tens of thousands of bulls that once ran and fought on the ranges of the Southwest. (See Chapter VIII, "Bulls and the Blood Call," also Chapter II, "The Texas Breed.") Notice his light flanks.

Photographs by J. Frank Dobie.

TEXAS COWS

Like the bulls, the cows did not grow such lengthy horns as the steers. The dun cow — shipped, with the smoky-colored one, from the border country to the San Antonio stockyards in the late 1920's — is strictly "on the prod." The other two cows, one of them an excellent example of brindle color, belong to E. H. Marks, Barker, Texas, who is growing a small bunch of Longhorns for sentimental reasons. (See Chapter IX, "Cows and Curiosity.")

Top picture from George W. Saunders (deceased), San Antonio; other pictures by Elwood Payne, Austin.

COWS AND CALVES

Never was there such a bovine mother as the Longhorn cow. She nearly always brought a calf and she
kept it safe against enemies ranging from lobo wolves
to screwworms. (See Chapter IX, "Cows and Curiosity," and Chapter XI, "Vitality, Drifts and Die-
ups.")

The cows and calves here shown are all in the
United States Government herd on the Wichita
Mountains Wildlife Refuge, Oklahoma. The young
cows in the upper and lower pictures may have a
little too much improved blood in them; anyway,
they do not look so "shelly" as the Texas cows shown
on the preceding page.

Photographs by Elwood Payne, Austin, Texas.

SWAY–BACKED AND HUMP–SHOULDERED

The top steer, a young one on the Wichita Mountains Wildlife Refuge, looks too fat to be a *lanky* Longhorn, but he has the sway-back characteristic of the long bodies of his breed. The steer at the bottom, a true Texan in every respect, rough, shaggy, rangy and lanky, shows a characteristic back, with the exaggerated shoulder-hump. The form of some of the Longhorns gave rise to a theory — not provable — that some of the wild Spanish cattle had crossed with buffaloes. The Longhorn was close to aboriginal blood, and the raised frontal bone and shoulder blades of the steer in the center illustrate aboriginal features.

The Last of the Longhorns
Owned by Sterling Bros.
Monte Cristo, Tex.

GROUP OF REPRESENTATIVE STEERS

Of this group, two white steers — one clean and slick and the other dirty and ragged — show characteristic variations in the same color. Neither of the two whitefaces has any Hereford blood; one of them, "shot" at long range, has just walked out of the brush to graze on open grass and is about to return to his security. (See Chapter XVII, "Outlaws of the Brush.") Notice the "mealy mouth" on the twisty-horn steer.

Photographs by Elwood Payne, Howard Magendie and others.

ON TRAIL AND RANGE

A herd of Chihuahua steers and cows going down a California mountainside. These cattle were shipped to California in 1897, in which year R. S. Baldwin took the picture, presented through the courtesy of R. P. Strathearn, Moorpark, California. (For traveling powers of the Longhorns, see Chapter IV, "On the Trail.")

A little bunch of present-day Longhorns being preserved by the Federal Government, Wichita Mountains Wildlife Refuge, Oklahoma. Photograph by Elwood Payne, Austin, Texas.

TWO OLD–TIMERS

Two old-timers built to run. The log fence is characteristic of Southwest Texas, though not so strongly built as the average. If the steer standing by this fence were turned around, he would probably show more brands on his left side than he shows on his right.

Pictures loaned by *The Cattleman,* Fort Worth, Texas.

A WILDERNESS OF HORNS

A canopy of horns over range cattle in the Fort
Worth stockyards. The time is said to be 1878, but
was probably later. The cattle show improved blood,
but the Longhorn strain is still strong in their veins.

Picture given to the author by the late Will C.
Barnes.

In 1907 Arthur East bought around 3000 Longhorn steers from two big Mexican ranches in the
extreme southern part of the Texas — the brush country. He placed them on the great Kenedy Ranch,
now comprising a large portion of Kenedy County.
The next year when he went to ship the steers,
Mr. John Kenedy asked him to cut out about thirty
with the biggest horns, to keep. As, later on, the
selected specimens died of old age, one by one, their
skulls were brought into a barn. This collection of
Longhorn skulls, the horns untouched by polishers, is
undoubtedly the best within the United States. The
picture, by Elwood Payne, was made through the
courtesy of Mr. and Mrs. Arthur East, she being a
daughter of the late John Kenedy.

THE HEAD THAT SYMBOLIZES A
LAND AND FREE LIFE

In homes on the range and in offices of men who have ranged and who remember the freedom of a "big country," the steer-head symbolizes not only what was, but power and vitality and the most romantic occupation of America. Moreover, some of the heads are truly decorative.

1. Head over mantel in library of Kenedy Ranch, in which a large part of Kenedy County, Texas, is located.

2. In the eighties and nineties, cattle kings sat on plush-bottomed thrones constructed of horns such as tossed over their own kingdoms. This chair is in the Museum of the Panhandle-Plains Historical Society, Canyon, Texas.

3. Steer-head in lodge of Amon G. Carter, Fort Worth, Texas newspaper publisher and owner of several Longhorn steers.

4. A noble head in office of Raymond Pearson, businessman of Houston.

5. The artist who designed bills for the Republic of Texas lacked a realistic conception of cowboy, cow horse and range cow, but he knew what symbolized the nation.

6. Office of M. S. Garretson, once a cowboy, now Curator of the Museum of Heads and Horns, New York.

BATTLE OF THE BULLS

The attack of wild bulls on a battalion just below the Arizona line in 1846 (See Chapter I, "The First Spanish Cattle") is pictured in a remarkable diorama in the Los Angeles Museum of History, Science and Art. Photographed by Edward Cobb.

In East Texas oxen still pull loads. Oxen here of mixed Brahma and Longhorn blood are pulling a wagon of wood into the Clemens State Prison Farm, on the Brazos River.

1. Head of a noted outlaw cow, Old Rud of the Pecos River. (See Chapter IX, "Cows and Curiosity.")

2. Thick, heavy horns, designed to fight with, from a black steer that went up the trail from Texas in 1876. The horns are in the Kansas State Historical Society Museum, Topeka.

3. Head of a steer with very sharp horns, of the long ago, owned by the late George W. West, Live Oak County, Texas. Now in Witte Museum, San Antonio.

4, 5, 6. The most remarkable collection of Longhorn horns in the world perhaps is in the Buckhorn Curio Shop — formerly the famous Buckhorn Saloon — at San Antonio. These three heads show oddly twisted horns.

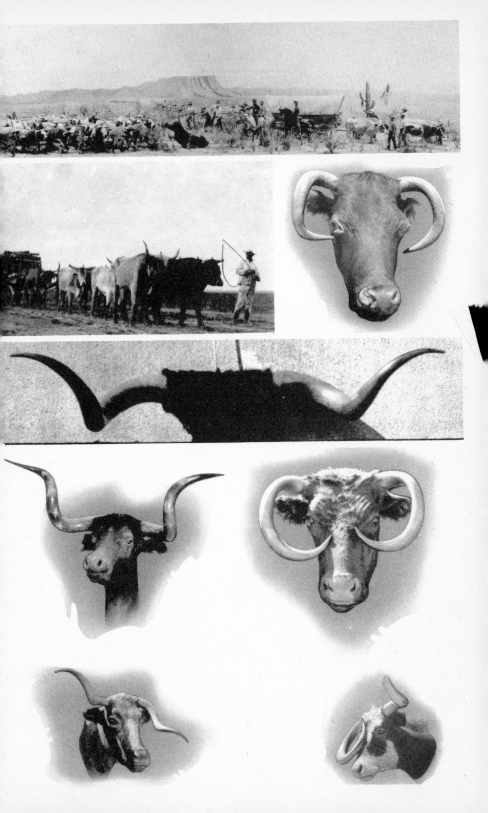

SCRUBBY AND COLD-BLOODED

These pictures say why the Longhorns have been bred virtually out of existence. In a way the three animals are representative, but they certainly do not represent the whole breed and tradition. They would have been among the cutbacks from almost any range herd.

The upper picture is of a steer twelve years old, calved in Mexico, raised on dust and prickly pear, and brought finally into the Pecos country, where his picture was made in 1936.

The poor old spiritless critter in the center used to ignore the crowds glancing at him in Breckenridge Park, San Antonio.
Picture by Helen Dumont, Waco, Texas.

The cow at the bottom could raise a better calf than her anatomy suggests.
Picture from *The Cattleman*, Fort Worth.

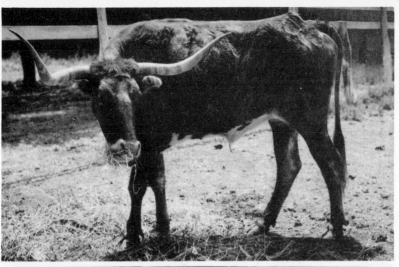

LORD OF THE WORLD

This lordly animal, and not the scrubs shown on the preceding page, made Longhorn history.

Picture of a steer on Wichita Mountains Wildlife Refuge, by Elwood Payne, Austin.

NOTES

In the beginning, it is fit that I make acknowledgment to the primary sources for information on Longhorn cattle — the men who lived and worked with them, tellers of their experiences, answerers of questions that no printed source will throw light on. I began hunting out these men so long ago that it is impossible now for me to make a complete list of all to whom I talked. Many a man would give only a disconnected fragment of a fact, and frequently in the process of composition I have welded — without explanation — this fragment onto some other. The names that follow represent probably less than a majority of the individuals who have given me something — some more, some less — on the subject of Texas cattle.

(An asterisk indicates that the person named is dead. Unless otherwise given, the state of residence is Texas.)

* Teddy Blue Abbott, Three Duce Ranch, Gilt Edge, Montana. * Fisher Atkins, San Antonio. M. W. Aushutz, Nye, Kansas. * Will C. Barnes, Arizona. * John R. Barrows, San Diego, California. W. D. (Doc) Barton, Ingalls, Kansas. Walter Billingsley, San Antonio. Sam Blalock, Eagle Pass. Ab Blocker, Big Wells. Miss Ada Blocker, Austin. J. E. Boog-Scott, Cresson. E. E. Brown, Walnut Springs. Luther Clark, Vernon. Theodore Coker, George West. James H. Cook, Agate, Nebraska. Jim Coward, Refugio. * John R. Craddock, Spur. J. B. Cranfill, Dallas. Tex (L. S.) Crosse, Los Angeles, California. John Custer, San Antonio. * Albert Dinn, Beeville. John Dinn, Hebbronville. * J. M. Dobie, Cotulla. John Doak, Del Rio. Ruth Dodson, Mathis. Charles M. Dubose, Alice. John W. Dunn, Cheyenne, Oklahoma.

D. C. Earnest, Edinburg. Tom East, Hebbronville. Will B. Eidson, Kansas City, Missouri. * Jake English, Carrizo Springs. Joe Evans, El Paso. * Steve Franklin, Starr County. Lamar Gill, Raymondville. * Tom Gilroy, San Antonio. Sam Glenn, Kerrville. * Charles Goodnight, Goodnight. Harold F. Graves, Brazoria. Alberto Guajardo, Piedras Negras, Coahuila, Mexico. J. Evetts Haley, Houston. Howard Hampton, Clarksville. A. B. Harper, Eagle Pass. L. T. Harmon, Live Oak County. James Hatch, San Antonio. * Jack Hawkins, Dillon, Montana. Rob Hinnant, Hebbronville. Adolph Huffmeyer, San Antonio. * W. S. Ikard, Henrietta. Frank James, Eagle Pass. Farmer Jennings, San Antonio. Asa Jones, Alpine. Clifford B. Jones, Lubbock. J. D. Jones, San Antonio. Jack Kennedy, Fort Worth. Caesar Kleberg, Kingsville.

Bob Lauderdale, Pleasanton. Bob Lemmons, Carrizo Springs. Stokely Ligon, Carlsbad, New Mexico. Tom Lyne, Beeville. * Claude McGill, Alice. Frank McGill, Alice. D. S. McKellar, Musquiz, Coahuila, Mexico. Jack Maltsberger, Cotulla. John T. Maltsberger, Cotulla. * Mason Maney, Pearsall. Hal Mangum, Eagle Pass. Andy Martin, Pearsall. * Tom Mercer, San Angelo. Maxie Michaelis, Musquiz, Coahuila, Mexico. J. M. Mills, San Antonio. Alonzo Mitchell, Lampasas. Frank Mitchell, Clarendon. Aaron Moss, Llano. Kate Stoner O'Connor, Victoria. * William O'Neal, Beeville. Chub Poole, Cotulla. Jack Potter, Clayton, New Mexico. * Ike Pryor, San Antonio. * W. W. Purcell, Bastrop County. Dolph Quinn, Beeville. Cole Railston, Magdalena, New Mexico. Rocky Reagan, Beeville. Frank Reaugh, Dallas. Tom C. Richardson, Dallas. John Rigby, Beeville. Mrs. W. A. Roberts, Frio Town. * Clabe Robinson, Live Oak County. Bob (R. D.) Routh, Brownwood. Will Rutledge, Kenedy.

* George W. Saunders, San Antonio. Onie J. Sheeran, Cotulla. Bruce Siberts, Henryetta, Oklahoma. * J. D. Slaughter, Llano. R. R. Smith, Jourdanton. Marcus Snyder, Sheridan, Wyoming. Captain Bill Sterling, Corpus Christi. C. A. Studer, Canadian. J. D. Tally, Austin. Henry W. Taylor, Clarendon. A. W. Thompson, Denver, Colorado. Ben Thorne, Hennessey, Oklahoma. * N. Howard (Jack) Thorp, Alameda, New Mexico. * James Philip Towns, Nixon. Beulah B. Van Deman,

San Antonio. Dave Vastbinder, San Antonio. Lloyd Wade, Marathon. George Watkins, Llano. John Williams, Babícora Ranch, Chihuahua, Mexico. * Mark Withers, Lockhart. Webster Witter, Gardendale.

Many individuals have helped me with pictures or otherwise than with range information. First among these I would name Holland Magendie, of Fort Worth, who has furnished fine pictures of many heads and of the steers owned by Amon G. Carter. Other collaborators of the kind have been: Stanley C. Arthur, New Orleans. L. D. Bertillion, Mineola. E. A. Brininstool, Hollywood, California. W. E. Caldwell, Kilgore. H. Coquat, Three Rivers. Juan Villasana Haggard, Austin. Mattie Austin Hatcher, Austin. Gabe Lewis, Stephenville. Tad Moses, of *The Cattleman,* Fort Worth. Zeke Nance, Kyle. M. Nowotny, San Antonio. Raymond Pearson, Houston. Charles Ramsdell, Jr., Austin. Frank Reeves, Fort Worth. L. J. Schreiner, Kerrville. L. F. Sheffy, Canyon. Tom Stell, Cuero and Dallas. L. J. Struhall, Austin. Philip C. Tucker, Bradenton, Florida. C. C. Walsh, Dallas. Stewart Edward White, Burlingame, California. J. R. ("Out Our Way") Williams, Nogales, Arizona. Dee Woods, Corpus Christi. Mrs. Fannie Wright, Mathis.

I · *THE FIRST SPANISH CATTLE*

[1] Hackett, Charles W., *Historical Documents Relating to New Mexico, Nueva Vizcaya, and Approaches Thereto,* Washington, D. C., 1923, I, 41.

[2] Mecham, J. Lloyd, *Francisco de Ibarra and Nueva Vizcaya,* Durham, N. C., 1927, 208–209.

[3] Mecham, *op. cit.,* 29, 158.

[4] Rangel, Nicolás, *Historia del Toreo en Mexico,* Mexico, D. F., 1924, 11; Bolton and Marshall, *The Colonization of North America,* New York, 1921, 58.

[5] Rangel, Nicolás, *op. cit.,* 14–15.

[6] Bullock, W., *Six Months' Residence and Travels in Mexico*, London, 1824, 254.

[7] Haskett, Bert, "Early History of the Cattle Industry in Arizona," *Arizona Historical Review*, Oct., 1935, reprinted in *The Cattleman*, Fort Worth, Texas, March, 1936.

[8] Cleland, Robert G., and Hardy, Osgood, *March of Industry*, Los Angeles, 1928. See also figures and estimates by William Heath Davis, *Seventy-Five Years in California*, San Francisco, 1929, 389–395.

[9] Davis, William Heath, *Seventy-Five Years in California*, San Francisco, 1929, 408–409.

[10] The substance of this and the preceding paragraph is based on Davis, *op. cit.*, 35–36, 40–41, 80–82, 224. See also *Narrative* of Nicholas "Cheyenne" Dawson, San Francisco, 1933, 38–40.

[11] Castañeda, C. E., *Our Catholic Heritage in Texas*, Austin, Texas, 1936, I, 348, 352. The expedition of 1689 may have had some cattle. See *The Alarcón Expedition*, edited by Fritz L. Hoffmann, Los Angeles, Calif., 1935, 52. It has not been proven that La Salle brought cattle to Texas, though he did bring hogs.

[12] "Diary of a Visit of Inspection of the Texas Missions Made by Fray Gaspar José de Solís in the Year 1767–1768," translated by Margaret Kenney Kress, *Southwestern Historical Quarterly*, Austin, XXXV, 56; *Pichardo's Treatise on the Limits of Louisiana and Texas*, by C. W. Hackett, Austin, Texas, 1934, II, 525–526.

[13] Castañeda, *op. cit.*, 373; Buckley, "The Aguayo Expedition," Texas Historical Association *Quarterly*, XV, 2.

[14] Testimony of the Frenchmen San Denis and Jalot, 1715, in *Documentos para la Historia Eclesiástica y Civil de la Provincia de Texas*, Tomo XXVII, Libro I, 123–124.

[15] "Captain Diego Ramón's Diary of His Expedition into Texas in 1716," translated by Paul J. Foik, Austin, Texas, 1935, 17.

[16] See *The Alarcón Expedition*, translated and edited by Fritz L. Hoffmann, Los Angeles, 1935, 52; "The Mezquía Diary of the Alarcón Expedition," by Hoffmann, *Southwestern Historical Quarterly*, XLI, 321; "Peña's Diary of the Aguayo Expedition," translated by Peter P. Forrestal, Austin, 1935, 57; Castañeda, C. E., *Morfi's History of Texas*, Albuquerque, N. M., 1935, 220.

[17] Castañeda, C. E., *Our Catholic Heritage in Texas*, II, 299.

[18] The only treatment of any consequence of Spanish ranching in Texas is a study entitled "Spanish Goliad," by Charles M. Rams-

dell, Jr., of Austin. It was written after prolonged examination of archives in Mexico City and at The University of Texas, under direction of the United States Park Service, which has done extended work at Goliad. This readable and illuminating study is still (1940) in manuscript form. I am indebted to it for all that is said concerning ranching down the San Antonio River. However, see also Dabbs, J. Autrey, "The Texas Missions in 1785," *Preliminary Studies of the Texas Catholic Historical Society*, Austin, Texas, Vol. III, No. 6, 12–15, 18–24.

[19] *Memoirs*, by Antonio Menchaca, issued by the Yanaguana Society, San Antonio, 1937, 14, 19–20.

[20] For trade with Louisiana see document cited in Footnote No. 21; also Mattie Austin Hatcher, *Opening of Texas to Foreign Settlement*, Austin, Texas, 1927, 53; Hackett's *Pichardo*, Bolton's *De Mézières*, and any full treatment of St. Denis. This contraband trade probably at times exceeded the slight volume accounted for in documents. See John G. Belisle, *History of Sabine Parish, Louisiana*, 1912, 63.

[21] "Memorial, Explanation and Defense presented by the Citizens of the Villa de San Fernando and the Royal Presidio of San Antonio de Bexar to Rafael Mrnz. Pacheco, Acting Governor of Texas, 1787." Translated from the original in the Bexar Archives by Mattie Austin Hatcher, 1930. 102 pages typewritten manuscript, Archives in the Library of The University of Texas. This bulky document goes at length into the origin of the stray cattle and reviews, entirely from a partisan point of view, the ups and downs of the live stock industry in Texas.

[22] De Pages, *Travels Round the World*, London, 1791, I, 82–83; Bolton, H. E., *Athanase de Mézières and the Louisiana–Texas Frontier*, 1768–1780, Cleveland, Ohio, 1914, I, 276; II, 187, 279, 281.

[23] Linn, John J., *Reminiscences of Fifty Years in Texas*, New York, 1883, 338.

[24] Sowell, A. J., *Early Settlers and Indian Fighters of Southwest Texas*, Austin, 1900, 284–285.

[25] Bolton, H. E., *Texas in the Middle Eighteenth Century*, Berkeley, Calif., 1915, 85; Castañeda, *Our Catholic Heritage*, III, 396–397.

[26] Bolton, *op. cit.*, 6, 57–59.

[27] Ex. Doc. No. 52, 1st Session, 36th Congress (1859–1860),

"Difficulties on the Southwestern Frontier," 25. (Serial Vol. No. 1050.)

[28] *Report of the United States and Mexican Boundary Survey*, by William H. Emory, Washington, D. C., 1857, I, 56, 67. Interesting corroborative reports on the wild cattle are found in "The Somervell Expedition to the Rio Grande, 1842," by Sterling Brown Hendricks, *Southwestern Historical Quarterly*, XXIII, 123, and the reminiscences of Jesse Sumpter, of Eagle Pass, as dictated to Harry Warren in 1902: private manuscript.

[29] At many places in the course of this chapter authority is cited for the statement. Besides the additional authorities listed chronologically below, I have in my notes the testimony of various old-timers.

Shipman, Daniel, *Frontier Life*, 56. When Shipman came to Oyster Creek, east of the Brazos River, in 1822, he found "hundreds of wild cattle, horses and hogs [peccaries]. The two former are exactly like our cattle and horses, only they are wild."

Notes made about 1828 by Elias R. Wightman, one of Austin's surveyors, in Mary S. Helm, *Scraps from Texas History*, Austin, Texas, 1884, 141, 147, 150, 183, 193. Wightman saw wild ("black") cattle in many parts of Texas.

1830's, on the Brazos, Colorado and Nueces rivers. *Lamar Papers*, Vol. IV, Part I, 39; Vol. V, 378.

Almonte, Juan N., "Statistical Report on Texas," 1835, translated by Carlos Castañeda, *Southwestern Historical Quarterly*, XXVIII, 190.

Woodman, David, Jr., *Guide to Texas Emigrants*, Boston, 1835, 62–63.

Holley, Mary Austin, *Texas*, Lexington, Ky., 1836, 69–70.

Pease, L. T., in *History of South America and Mexico*, etc., by John M. Niles, Hartford, Conn., 1837, 248–249.

Fannin County, 1837: Hill, J. L., *The End of the Cattle Trail*, Long Beach, Calif., 1924, 15.

On the Blanco River in 1838: "As we returned home" (from an Indian hunt) "we killed a Spanish cow." Brazos (pseudonym), *Life of Robert Hall; also Sketch of Big Foot Wallace*, Austin, Texas, 1898, 41.

In treating of the country as he first saw it up the Brazos River in 1840 and lived on it for decades that followed, John Washington Lockhart wrote: "There were herds of wild cattle, very much different from our domestic animals, being trimly made, with legs and feet built for speed. It would take a good horse to outrun one of them. They were different from domestic cattle in that they ran to one color, being black with brown backs and bellies. In time, however, they became mixed with domestic cattle, and their calves took on mixed colors. When harried or wounded, they were very vicious and would fight any living thing. Their sharp horns made them a very formidable foe. I saw two of them killed in 1861. They were male and female, and I think were the last to be seen in the bottom lands of Washington County." (Wallis, Mrs. Jonnie Lockhart, *Sixty Years on the Brazos*, Los Angeles, Calif., 1930, 328.)

Lawrence, A. B., *History of Texas, or the Emigrant's Guide*, New York, 1844, 78. On the upper Brazos in 1839, "innumerable herds of buffalo, deer, antelopes, horses and wild cattle."

Wild cattle out of the Cherokee Indian herds abandoned on the Neches River in 1839: Wentworth Manning, *Some History of Van Zandt County*, Des Moines, Iowa, 1919, 178–179.

Wild cattle on Red River: a bull killed weighing between seven and eight hundred pounds, 1841. T. A. Morris, *Miscellany*, Cincinnati, 1854, 311–312. *Prose and Poetry of the Live Stock Industry of the United States*, Kansas City, Mo., 1905, 191, 235.

Wild cattle on the Rio Grande beefed by men of the Mier Expedition, 1842: Sterling Brown Hendricks, "The Somervell Expedition," *Southwestern Historical Quarterly*, XXIII, 123, 136–137.

Texas: 1844–1845, by Carl, Prince of Solms-Braunfels. Translation of the original German, Houston, Texas, 1936, 29. "The wild cattle in the river bottoms" are listed as big game, along with buffaloes.

While the Castro colony was settling on the Medina River in the forties "there was a breed of cattle running along the Medina which were perfectly wild like buffalo or deer. These cattle were all of uniform color, being solid brown, only known as 'wild cattle.'" Briggs, B. F., "Elisha A. Briggs Was a Real Pioneer," in *Frontier Times*, Bandera, Texas, XVI (1939), 518.

Prairiedom, by "a Suthron" (Page), New York, 1845, 77.

McClintock, William A., "Journal of a Trip through Texas and Northern Mexico in 1846–1847," *Southwestern Historical Quarterly*, XXXIV, 23, 238.

In 1847 the supply of wild cattle and wild horses along the lower Rio Grande seemed "so abundant as to be inexhaustible." Many Mexicans supported themselves by catching them. Dwyer, Thomas A., in *A Brief Description of Western Texas*, San Antonio, 1872, 44.

Texas in 1848, by Viktor Bracht. Translation from the original German by Charles F. Schmidt, San Antonio, 1931, 120.

Wild cattle in Burnet County, about 1850: William Banta, *Twenty-seven Years on the Frontier, or Fifty Years in Texas*, Austin, 1893, 124–126.

Wild cattle in Live Oak County, 1851: A. J. Sowell, *Early Settlers and Indian Fighters of Southwest Texas*, Austin, 1900. 821–822; *Frontier Times*, Bandera, Texas, June, 1927, 26.

In 1856 and the years following, on the San Miguel in Atascosa County, there was "wild game of every kind, even wild mustang cattle and mustang horses. We killed the native wild cattle for their hides and tallow and the meat we could save." Hindes, George F., in *The Trail Drivers of Texas*, compiled by J. Marvin Hunter, Bandera, Texas, 1923, 268–269.

Immense numbers of wild cattle in thickets on lower Nueces River: *Galveston Daily News*, March 14, 1878.

[80] McConnell, H. H., *Five Years a Cavalryman*, Jacksboro, Texas, 1889, 307; see also 32.

[81] "Reminiscences" of James Buckner Barry, Ms. in Archives of the University of Texas. Dewees, W. B., *Letters from an Early Settler of Texas*, compiled by Cara Cardelle, Louisville, Ky., 1852, 22, 26.

[82] Linn, John J., *Reminiscences of Fifty Years in Texas*, New York, 1883, 75–76. For an account of the Louisiana cattle, derived principally from Spanish stock, see David Wilson, *Twelve Years a Slave*, Whitehall, New York, 1853; reprint, undated, by International Co., N. Y., 173–174; also H. E. Chambers, *A History of Louisiana*, Chicago and New York, 1925, I, 270. Spanish mustangs were also in Louisiana, which was constantly getting stock from the West: Chambers, *op. cit.*, I, 465.

[33] Flack, Captain, *The Texan Ranger, or Real Life in the Backwoods*, London, 1866, 10–11, 14–16, 64, 307–313. Another book issued by Captain Flack, London, 1866, *A Hunter's Experiences in the Southern States of America*, devotes a chapter to "Wild Cattle." Here, in addition to a repetition of his Texas experiences, he adds the details of a hunt after wild cattle on an abandoned plantation in Florida. He may have been the author of an unsigned article, "Wild Cattle Hunting in Texas," that appeared in an English magazine, *The Leisure Hour*, 1864, the experiences detailed going back to 1857. For an excellent account of the hired wild-meat hunter, see Mary Austin Holley, *Texas . . . in a Series of Letters* (written in 1831), in Mattie Austin Hatcher, *Letters of an Early American Traveler*, Dallas, Texas, 1933, 119–120; also Fiske, *A Visit to Texas*, New York, 1836, 35–36.

[34] Cooke, Philip Saint George, *The Conquest of New Mexico and California*, N. Y., 1878, 139–146. See also, for cursory details only, *Report of Lieut. Col. P. St. George Cooke of His March from Santa Fe, New Mexico, to San Diego, California*, Ex. Doc. No. 41, 13th Congress, 1st Session, Washington, D. C., 1848. (Serial No. 517.)

Bartlett, John R., *Personal Narrative of Explorations and Incidents*, N. Y., 1854, I, 255–262, 396–397, 413–418, corroborates Cooke and adds details about the wild cattle.

Dawson, Nicholas "Cheyenne," *Narrative* (first published about 1901), San Francisco, 1933, 66–67, gives further account.

[35] *José Policarpo Rodriguez*, his life as dictated to D. W. Carter, Nashville, Tenn. (c. 1897), 11.

[36] Smithwick, Noah, *The Evolution of a State, or Recollections of Old Texas Days*, Austin, Texas, 1900, 289–291.

The San Gabriel River (once called San Xavier), adjacent to Brushy Creek, was noted as far back as 1779 for "the incredible number" of wild cattle and horses in its vicinity. Hackett, *Pichardo's Treatise on the Limits of Louisiana and Texas*, II, 106, 343; Bolton, *De Mézières*, II, 281.

[37] Fiske, ——, *A Visit to Texas*, New York, 1836, 39–40.

[38] Lockhart, John Washington, *Sixty Years on the Brazos*, privately published by Mrs. Jonnie Lockhart Wallis, Los Angeles, Calif., 1930, 328.

[39] In addition to authorities already cited, see for figures Juan N. Almonte, "Statistical Report on Texas," 1835, translated by

Carlos Castañeda, *Southwestern Historical Quarterly*, XXVIII; "Texas in 1820," by Juan Antonio Padilla, translated by Mattie Austin Hatcher, *Southwestern Historical Quarterly*, XXIII, 61, 65. All figures are incomplete, and some are contradictory. The Almonte report gives Texas, east of the Nueces, 100,000 cattle — cattle owned — for 1806. Yet in 1803 the governor of the province reported "a notable scarcity of cattle." (Mattie Austin Hatcher, *The Opening of Texas to Foreign Settlement, 1801–1821*, Austin, Texas, 1927, 303.)

[40] Brewer, Wm. H., *Up and Down California in 1860–1864*, New Haven, 1930, 95; Bidwell, John, "Life in California before the Gold Discovery," *Century Magazine*, XLI (1890), 164. Wild cattle in California were also hunted for their meat. See Wistar, Isaac Jones, *Autobiography*, New York, 1937, 126–128.

[41] Hackett, Charles W., *Historical Documents Relating to New Mexico*, etc., Washington, D. C., 1923, I, 227–229, 281, 307.

[42] Bullock, W., *Six Months' Residence and Travel in Mexico*, London, 1824, 253. Holley, Mary Austin, *Texas . . . in a Series of Letters*, Baltimore, 1833, reprinted with introduction by Mattie Austin Hatcher, Dallas, Texas, 1933, pp. 133, 173, 174. Green, Thomas J., *Journal of the Mier Expedition*, New York, 1845, 179. Smith, S. Compton, *Chile Con Carne*, New York, 1857, 122. Falconer, Thomas, *Letters and Notes on the Texan Santa Fe Expedition*, New York, 1930, 117. Cleland, Robert G., *A History of California: The American Period*, New York, 1922, 37–38.

[43] The diary is still in manuscript. I am indebted for the entry to that liberal scholar and delightful gentleman, Stanley C. Arthur, of New Orleans.

[44] Hittell, Theodore H., *The Adventures of James Capen Adams* (first published in 1860), New York, 1912, 332.

[45] Joaquin Miller, less noted for veracity than as a poet, describes lines of the Spanish cattle converging on a wolf and leaping upon him with hoofs, not using horns at all. *True Bear Stories*, Chicago, 1900, 86–88.

[46] "Primitive Cattle of Corsica," by Ernst Schwarz, *Nature Magazine*, Jan., 1939, 14. For an extended discussion of various breeds of the world and of their relation to primordial bovines, see "The Taurine World," by Alvin H. Sanders, *The National Geographic Magazine*, Dec., 1925.

[1] All authorities agree on the time and circumstances of the initial use of the word "cowboy" in Texas. Following are some testimonials:

Brown, John Henry, *History of Texas*, St. Louis, 1892, II, 138–139.

De Shields, James T., *Border Wars of Texas*, Tioga, Texas, 1912, 211.

Dougherty, E., *The Rio Grande Valley*, Brownsville, Texas, 1867.

Ford, John S., *Memoirs*. Ms. in Archives, the University of Texas, III, 531.

Lamar, Mirabeau B., *Papers*, Vol. III, 106–110, 350, 424; IV, Pt. I, 211–212; VI, 99–100, 114–117, 136.

Linn, John J., *Reminiscences*, New York, 1883, 310, 322–324.

Rose, Victor M., *The Life and Services of General Ben McCulloch*, Philadelphia, 1888, 44.

Starr, James H., "Private Memoranda: Journey to Austin, 1839," entries for Sept. 21 and 22. Archives, the University of Texas.

Texas Almanac, 1860, 148–149.

U. S. Census for 1880, III, 965.

Webber, Charles W., *Tales of the Southern Border*, Philadelphia, 1868 (1887 edition consulted), 124.

[2] *Texas Almanac*, 1860, 148–150.

[3] Taylor White's ranch, being on the road to New Orleans from lower Texas, was commented on by various early travelers. See Fiske, *A Visit to Texas*, New York, 1836, 99–108; Woodman, David, *Guide to Texas Emigrants*, Boston, 1835, 62–63; Gray, William F., *From Virginia to Texas, 1835, Diary*, Houston, Texas, 1909, 171 and entry for April 17, 1836; an early letter by Dr. D. C. Hardee, reprinted in *Frontier Times*, Bandera, Texas, March, 1936, 304–308.

[4] Wortham, L. J., *A History of Texas*, Fort Worth, Texas, 1924, V, 137–138.

[5] Among the bills of sale of the year 1832 that Stephen F. Austin kept, "a black steer," a "black cow," a "brindle steer," a "white yearling," a "white and black speckled bull," and a "red cow with wide horns" are easily identified as Spanish-Mexican cattle. Barker,

E. C., *The Austin Papers*, Washington, D. C., 1928, II, 878, 894.

[6] Hunter, J. Marvin (compiler), *The Trail Drivers of Texas*, Bandera, Texas, 1920, I, 161.

[7] *Galveston Daily News* (taken from the *Atascosa Journal*), April 11, 1878.

[8] Cox, James, *The Cattle Industry of Texas and Adjacent Territory*, St. Louis, 1895, 35; Kuykendaal, J. H., "Reminiscences of Early Texans," *Quarterly* of the Texas State Historical Association, VII, 29–30.

[9] Winkler, E. W., "The Cherokee Indians in Texas," *Quarterly* of the Texas State Historical Association, VII, 96, 97, 159; Manning, Wentworth, *Some History of Van Zandt County*, Des Moines, Iowa, 1919, 178–179.

[10] *Texas Almanac*, 1860, 149; *Texas Siftings* (from *New Orleans Democrat*), June 18, 1881.

[11] Davis, Mollie E. Moore, *Under Six Flags*, 1897, 54.

[12] Cox, James, *The Cattle Industry of Texas and Adjacent Territory*, St. Louis, 1895, 35.

[13] *Lamar Papers*, III, 515–516.

[14] Parker, E. J., "Col. Shannon, Last of Famed Family," in the *Dallas News*, March 14, 1926, Section I, p. 7.

[15] U. S. Census Report for 1880, III, 965. "Almonte's Statistical Report on Texas," for 1835, translated by Carlos Castañeda, *Southwestern Historical Quarterly*, Vol. XXVIII, says that as early as 1806 there were "over 100,000 head of cattle" in Texas but that Indian invasions of the year 1810 "destroyed the greater part" of them. Almonte carelessly sets down the number of cattle in the Department of Brazos for the year 1835 as 25,000 head and for the Department of Nacogdoches as 50,000 head. The number in the Department of Bexar is not given, but they are said to "abound."

[16] McCoy, Joseph G., *Historic Sketches of the Cattle Trade of the West and Southwest*, Kansas City, Missouri, 1874, 147.

[17] *Southwestern Historical Quarterly*, XLIII (1939–1940), 212, 218; 488. For March 5, 1840, James Huckins, a Baptist missionary, made this entry in his journal: "Have today passed through two settlements on the San Bernard and West Bernard rivers. . . . In a short ride this morning I counted no less than 180 deer, and there are eminences in this vicinity from which the traveler may count

1,000 head of cattle. These low country prairies afford an almost unlimited range for stock. . . . I have never seen cattle superior to those which I find in this region. They are large and in good condition, presenting horns of very great size." (Carroll, J. M., *A History of Texas Baptists*, Dallas, 1923, 155.)

[18] For a thorough description of the breed from the point of view of technical expertness, see MacDonald, James, *Food from the Far West*, New York, 1878, 30–31, 49, 80, 92–93, 96, 268–270.

Joseph Nimmo's *Report*, House Executive Document 7, Part III, 2nd Session, 48th Congress, gives full statistics on weights, percentage killed out, etc.

See also, Allen, Lewis F., *American Cattle*, New York, 1884, 176–179.

[19] Bracht, Viktor, *Texas in 1848;* translation by C. F. Schmidt, San Antonio, Texas, 1931, 120.

[20] Woodman, David, Jr., *Guide to Texas Emigrants*, Boston, 1835, 62–63.

[21] Specific examples of uses of "cow and calf" legal tender and of other uses of cattle in barter will be found in:

Austin Papers, The, edited by Barker, I, 1113; II, 830–831, 854, 900.

Beckham, W. A., "Life Story of a Pioneer of Texas," *Yorktown News*, installment No. 11, 1924. Archives, the University of Texas.

Bowman, Hazel Oatman, "The Cattle Industry of Llano County," *The Cattleman*, Nov., 1938 (Vol. XXV), 15.

Cox, James, *The Cattle Industry of Texas and Adjacent Territory*, Kansas City, Mo., 1895, 558–559.

[Hammett, Samuel A.], *Piney Woods Tavern; or, Sam Slick in Texas*, Philadelphia, 1858, 22, 286.

Helm, Mary S., *Scraps of Texas History*, Austin, Texas, 1884, 47.

Linn, John J., *Reminiscences*, New York, 1883, 23.

Lubbock, F. R., *Memoirs*, edited by Raines, Austin, 1900, 568.

Roberts, Dan W., *Rangers and Sovereignty*, San Antonio, 1914, 143.

Smithwick, Noah, *The Evolution of a State*, Austin, 1900, 234–235.

²² Sowell, A. J., *Rangers and Pioneers of Texas*, San Antonio, Texas, 1884, 218.

²³ See Jack Potter's account of Isom Like in *Lead Steer*, Clayton, New Mexico, 1939, 71–79.

²⁴ Fenley, Florence, *Oldtimers*, Uvalde, Texas, 1939, 123.

²⁵ Davis, William Heath, *Seventy-Five Years in California*, San Francisco, 1929, 42.

²⁶ Edmonds, Joseph A., "Diary," in *Chronicles of Oklahoma*, XVII (1939), 310.

²⁷ *Prose and Poetry of the Live Stock Industry*, Kansas City, Mo., 1905, 438; McCoy, J. G., *Historic Sketches of the Cattle Trade*, Kansas City, 1874, 148–163.

III · *MAVERICKS AND MAVERICKERS*

¹ The facts about Samuel A. Maverick, his experience with cattle and the resultant word *maverick*, are found in a letter written by George M. Maverick to the *St. Louis Republic*, Nov. 16, 1889, reprinted in the *Memoirs* of Mary A. Maverick (wife of Samuel), San Antonio, 1921, 123–124; in *Ye Mavericks* (letters from George M. Maverick and John Henry Brown printed in the *St. Louis Republic*, November, 1889) — a pamphlet, San Antonio, Texas, undated but apparently issued in 1905; in *The Mavericks* (pamphlet), by Frederick C. Chabot, San Antonio, 1934; in *A Maverick American*, by Maury Maverick, New York, 1937, 73–79. See also the Maverick Papers in the Archives of the University of Texas. The George M. Maverick letter has been reproduced in various places. With interesting explanatory material it appears, in altered form, in Frank M. King's *Wranglin' the Past*, Los Angeles, California, 1935, 102–105. In *Cattle Kings of Texas*, Dallas, 1939, C. L. Douglas devotes a chapter to Maverick.

As for the legend in its various forms, see:

Baillie-Grohman, Wm. A., *Camps in the Rockies*, New York, 1905, 359–360.

Borein, Edward, *Etchings in the Far West*, a descriptive catalogue, undated, issued by that fine artist of the West, at Santa Barbara, California. One of his best etchings is entitled "The Maverick."

Branch, E. Douglas, *The Cowboy and His Interpreters*, N. Y., 1926, 127.

Bratt, John, *Trails of Yesterday*, Chicago, 1921, 195.

Burt, Struthers, *Powder River: Let 'er Buck*, N. Y., 1938, 206–207.

Cranfill, J. B., *Dallas News*, Oct. 29, 1933, "Letters from Readers."

Huffmeyer, A., *The Pioneer* magazine, San Antonio, February, 1924.

James, W. S., *Cow-Boy Life in Texas, or 27 Years a Maverick*, Chicago, 1893, 63–64.

Kingsbury, W. G., in *A Brief Description of Western Texas, together with a Report of the Third Annual Fair . . . Held in San Antonio*, San Antonio, 1872, 36.

Lawhon, Luther A., in *Trail Drivers of Texas*, compiled by J. Marvin Hunter [Bandera, Texas], 1920, I, 174–175.

Lewis, A. H., *Wolfville Days*, New York, 1902, 206–207.

McCoy, J. G., *Historic Sketches of the Cattle Trade of the West and Southwest*, Kansas City, Mo., 1874, 9.

Mills, Anson, *My Story*, Washington, D. C., 1918, 58.

Potter, Jack, *New Mexico Magazine*, Albuquerque, N. M., July, 1935.

Prose and Poetry of the Live Stock Industry of the United States, Kansas City, Mo., 1905, I, 629.

Reaugh, Frank, *Paintings of the Southwest*, privately printed at Dallas about 1937, 18. Reaugh has a noble picture of "The Maverick."

Rollins, Philip Ashton, *The Cowboy*, N. Y., 1924, 243.

Shepherd, Major W., *Prairie Experiences in Handling Cattle and Sheep*, London, 1884, 3.

Siringo, Chas. A., *A Texas Cowboy*, N. Y., 1886, 50–51.

Townshend, R. B., *A Tenderfoot in Colorado*, London, 1923, 235–236.

Twentieth Century History of Southwest Texas, A, Chicago, 1907, I, 262.

Wellman, Paul I., *The Trampling Herd*, New York, 1939, 54–56.

Wheeler, H. W., *Buffalo Days*, Indianapolis, 1925, 59–60.

Wright, Robert M., *Dodge City, Cowboy Capital*, Wichita, Kans., 1913, 284.

[2] James, Vinton Lee, *Frontier and Pioneer Recollections of Early Days in San Antonio and West Texas*, San Antonio, 1938, 68–69.

[3] Babb, T. A., *In the Bosom of the Comanches*, Dallas, Texas, 1923, 76–77.

[4] Cochran, W. C., *Story of the Early Days Indian Troubles and Cattle Business of Palo Pinto and Adjoining Counties*. Manuscript, Archives of the University of Texas.

[5] Ewell, Thomas T., *History of Hood County*, Granbury, Texas, 1895, 62. See also Elkins, John M., *Indian Fighting on the Texas Frontier*, Amarillo, Texas, 1929, 52–53.

[6] Moore, Lee, in *Letters from Old Friends and Members of the Wyoming Stock Growers Association*, Cheyenne, Wyoming, 1923, 33–34.

[7] Sowell, A. J., *Early Settlers and Indian Fighters of Southwest Texas*, Austin, Texas, 1900, 477–479.

[8] Scobee, Barry, "Brindle Bull Branded Murder," *The Cattleman*, Fort Worth, Texas, March, 1936; variant article by Scobee, *San Antonio Express*, March 29, 1936; Raht, Carl, *Romance of the Big Bend and Davis Mountains*, El Paso, Texas, 1919, 306; *Frontier Times*, Bandera, Texas, May, 1931, 372.

[9] Lotto, F., *Fayette County*, Schulenburg, Texas, 1902, 131–134; Osgood, E. S., *The Day of the Cattleman*, Minneapolis, Minn., 1929, 134–136; Von Richthofen, Walter, *Cattle-Raising on the Plains of North America*, New York, 1885, 33–41.

IV · *ON THE TRAIL*

[1] Hulme, T. Ferrier, *John Wesley and His Horse*, London, 1933, 10–11.

[2] Sanders, Alvin H., *The Story of the Herefords*, Chicago, 1914, 46.

[3] Traill's *Social History of England*, Vol. V, Chaps. 17, 18 and 19.

[4] Grinnell, George Bird, "In Buffalo Days," *American Big Game Hunting*, edited by Theodore Roosevelt and George Bird Grinnell, New York, 1893, 194–195.

[5] Hill, J. L., *The End of the Trail*, Long Beach, Calif., 1924, 66–75. I have rearranged paragraphs and some sentences.

[6] Steedman, Charles J., *Bucking the Sagebrush*, New York, 1904, 267.

[7] Fridge, Ike, *History of the Chisum War, or Life of Ike Fridge*, Electra, Texas, n.d., 14. Also from reminiscences of Charles Taylor, Borden County, Texas, oral and in *Fort Worth Star Telegram*, April 20, 1930.

[8] Siringo, Charles A., *A Texas Cowboy*, New York, 1886, 52–53.

[9] This account, given me by that fine old Texian, James Philip Towns, was published, in Chapter XVI, in my book *The Flavor of Texas*, Dallas, 1936.

[10] *Trail Drivers of Texas*, I, 240; II, 162; Marcus Snyder's memory of his father's talk.

[11] *Prose and Poetry of the Live Stock Industry of the United States*, Kansas City, Mo., 1905, 715–716.

[12] *West Texas Historical Association Year Book*, Abilene, Texas, 1939, XV, 81.

[13] McDonald, W. G., in a series of articles in *The Kiowa Herald*, New Kiowa, Barber County, Kansas, June 17, July 22 and July 29, 1886.

[14] It is estimated that the drives to California that began in 1850 aggregated 100,000 head. The "Report on Cattle, Sheep and Swine," by Clarence Gordon, in Vol. III of the *Tenth Census of the United States* (1880), is replete with figures. I have a mass of records on drives before the Civil War that show a much livelier movement than chroniclers of the cattle trade seem to have been aware of. The Texas cattle-raisers had to sell a good many cattle somewhere to keep going. Their sales had to be out of the state.

[15] The figures are conflicting. The *Texas Almanac* (p. 180) for 1858, listing tax returns — always incomplete — enumerates 1,635,-507 cattle for the year 1856, and 1,899,555 for the year 1857. By 1858, according to the *Texas Almanac* for 1860 (p. 217), the number had increased to 2,220,433. The *Texas Almanac* for 1861, without making an addition of the tax returns from various counties, lists numbers that aggregate 2,466,621.

But the U. S. Census Report of 1880 (III, 965) says that "the returns for assessment of the live-stock in Texas in 1860 showed 3,535,768 cattle. . . . If those returns were in the same proportion to the actual number as the returns for 1880, we may calculate that there were really 4,785,400 cattle in 1860." The U. S. Census for

1860 enumerates, actually, 3,535,768 cattle, but this number was not based on "returns for assessment." The figures used by the *Texas Almanac* seem to have been compiled annually from tax reports in Austin, but too early for these reports to be complete.

The assessment for 1870 shows, according to the *Texas Almanac* of 1872 (p. 115) 3,651,316 cattle. According to the Report of the U. S. Commissioner of Agriculture for 1870 (p. 47), there were 3,220,000 "oxen and other cattle" in Texas that year. The U. S. Census Report for 1870 gives 3,990,158.

Despite a ravaging drouth during the years of the Civil War, there were probably more cattle in Texas in 1865 than in 1860. Despite an unloading through drivers to Kansas from 1866 on, there should have been as many cattle in Texas in 1870 as in 1860 or 1865. The early drives were made up generally of mature steers. Not until after 1870 were large numbers of stock cattle put on the trails. Under normal conditions, with the range open for unlimited expansion and with grown steers being sold off annually, the cow population would double about every five years.

It was an old range custom — on which it took barbed wire a long time to make an impression and which, indeed, survived until the Federal Income Tax laws of 1913 and 1917 took effect, along with the exacting inquisitiveness of banks — for a cowman to report anywhere from a tenth to four-fifths of the number of cattle he owned. In some Texas counties to this day the rancher by common consent renders considerably less than the actual number of his livestock.

During the sixties no ranchman could know what he owned. Even after the country was pretty well fenced-up, a cowman "could not be sure" that a large number of what he hoped he owned were not dead, dying or otherwise gone with the wind. The cowman was constitutionally conservative. One that did not, in rendering livestock for taxes, give himself the benefit of the doubt was as rare as a white cow with a black face. The average cowman had two sets of figures: one "for taxable purposes," and one for the privacy of his head. A stranger with any sense of propriety would no more ask a ranchman how many cattle he owned than he would ask an outlaw how many men he had killed or what his name was before he came to Texas. For many years after the Civil War the country people of Texas considered all federal agents as rank outsiders. Some cowmen lived with many cattle in unorganized counties where no official interrogator ever came. Never were there such people for keeping their own business to themselves, and they lived such independent, uncomplicated lives that there was no necessity for putting down their assets in black and white.

If any official report or calculation places the number of cattle in Texas in 1860 as over 4,000,000 head, we may be assured that there were a million or two more not accounted for. I repeat that there were fully as many in 1865 — among them perhaps 2,000,000 mavericks that nobody assessed.

[16] According to the U. S. Census for 1880, III, pp. 966 and 975, the Northern drives out of Texas for the years 1866–1880 inclusive totaled 4,223,497, with perhaps 200,000 additional driven to New Mexico, Arizona and California — no account being taken of drives to the Mississippi.

Joseph Nimmo's figures on the Texas Cattle Drive for the years 1866–1884, inclusive, total 5,201,132. (Nimmo's Report in Ex. Doc. No. 267, 48th Congress, 2nd Session.)

Ernest S. Osgood, in his excellent *The Day of the Cattleman* (Minneapolis, 1929, 32) cites figures through the year 1885 totaling 5,713,976.

E. E. Dale, who has gone into economics more extensively than any other range historian, says that all these numbers are "but rough approximations" and quotes Colonel Ike T. Pryor, who was a businessman as well as a cowman, as estimating that between 1870 and 1890 the annual drive averaged half a million head. (Dale, E. E., *The Range Cattle Industry*, Norman, Oklahoma, 1930, 59–60.)

The Nimmo and U. S. Census reports show a drive of 405,000 head for 1873. The *Galveston News*, Nov. 29, 1873, said, "No less than half a million head of Texas cattle" went to Kansas in 1873. Other conflicting reports are adducible.

1871 was perhaps the peak year, 600,000 trail cattle being reported for that year. As the years advanced, perhaps a majority of the drives were stockers, destined for the new ranges.

George W. Saunders, who organized the Trail Drivers of Texas into an association and gathered from them first-hand narratives that he had printed in two volumes, knew more trail men and had more detailed information about the trail business than any other individual who has lived, I suppose. He was an extraordinary man and had an extraordinary mind. Several times I heard him tell about how he and Charles Goodnight got together, and, by various figures, came to estimate that up to 1895, 9,800,000 cattle and 1,000,000 horses went out of Texas over the trails. See *The Trail Drivers of Texas*, compiled by J. Marvin Hunter, Bandera, Texas, 1920, I, 23. These figures are repeated but garbled by atrocious printing in Volume II of *The Trail Drivers of Texas*, Bandera, Texas, 1923, page 409.

[17] The figures on shipments by rail and sea previous to 1880 as given in the *Tenth Census Report* (1880), III, 966, are not satisfactory to me. Perhaps the shipping reports by sea could be ferreted out. I doubt if the early railroad records have been preserved. Various officials of the Missouri, Kansas and Texas Railroad, though disposed to be co-operative, have been unable to furnish me figures desired.

This was the first trunk line to enter Texas and for years it hauled the bulk of north-bound freight. In 1872, according to the *Galveston News*, the M. K. & T., which entered Denison late that year, shipped over 120,000 cattle north — at the same time bringing in over 200 carloads of blooded cattle for Texas ranges. — *Galveston Daily News*, Jan. 24, 1873; June 27, 1873.

After the trails from southern and eastern Texas were closed, large numbers of cattle and horses were shipped to Vernon and other points near Red River, unloaded and thence trailed north. As long as range was free and trails were open, Texas drovers generally found driving much more economical than shipping.

[18] Cox, James, *Historical and Biographical Record of the Cattle Industry of Texas and Adjacent Territory*, St. Louis, 1895, 103–118; Dale, E. E., *The Range Cattle Industry*, University of Oklahoma Press, Norman, 1930, 69–70.

V, VI and VII · *STOMPEDES*

All of these chapters are on the subject of stampedes. Instead of making particular references, I provide a bibliography.

Adair, W. S., article on A. Branshaw in *Dallas News*, Magazine Section, June 22, 1924; on George P. Jackson, *Dallas News*, Aug. 9, 1925.

Anderson, J. W., *From the Plains to the Pulpit*, Houston, Texas, 1907, 33–37; 186.

Barnes, Will C., manuscripts with Arizona Pioneer Historical Society, Tucson: description of electrical storm from E. Richard Shipp, Casper, Wyoming.

Barnes, Will C., *Tales from the X-Bar Horse Camp*, Chicago, 1920, 58–73.

Barrows, John R., *Ubet*, Caldwell, Idaho, 1934, 140–141.

Bayliss, John Fletcher, manuscript recollections of a trail drive in 1879.

Carroll, Bess, "The Story of San Antonio" (daily feature), *San Antonio Light*, Aug. 31, 1931.

Cattleman, The, Fort Worth, March, 1934, 5.

Coolidge, Dane, chapter on "Stompedes" in *Arizona Cowboys*, New York, 1938.

Craddock, John R., "The Legend of Stampede Mesa," *Legends of Texas*, ed. by J. Frank Dobie, Austin, Texas, 1924; reprinted also, with introductory consideration of stampedes, in *On the Open Range*, by Dobie, Dallas, Texas, 1931.

Cranfill, J. B., *Chronicle*, New York, 1916, 155–158.

Cureton, John C., *The Pioneer Magazine of Texas*, San Antonio, Feb., 1926, 11.

Daily Herald, Big Spring, Texas, April 26, 1936: "Here's One Man Who Experienced a Stampede" (J. W. Carpenter).

Daily Oklahoman, Oklahoma City, Oklahoma; "Pioneer Tells of Early Drive," Sept. 21, 1924; "When 8,000 Hoof-Beats Drummed Death," July 18, 1926.

Denton, B. E. (Cyclone), *A Two-Gun Cyclone*, Dallas, 1927, 12.

Dobie, J. Frank, *A Vaquero of the Brush Country*, Dallas, 1929, 101–104, 137.

Elliot, W. J., *The Spurs*, Spur, Texas, 1939, 41–44.

Fenley, Florence, *Oldtimers*, Uvalde, Texas, 1939, 40, 137, 195.

Fridge, Ike, *History of the Chisum War, or Life of Ike Fridge*, Electra, Texas, n.d., 56.

Glover, B. J., *The Cattleman*, July, 1930, 40.

Guyer, James S., *Pioneer Life in West Texas*, Brownwood, Texas, 1938, 89.

Haley, J. Evetts, *Charles Goodnight, Cowman and Plainsman*, Boston, 1936, 145, 162–168, 229, 249–253.

Halsell, H. H., *Cowboys and Cattleland*, Nashville, Tenn., 1937, 41.

Hill, Robert T., "Cowboy Days on the Trail in Texas," *Semi-Weekly Farm News*, Dallas, Texas, June 26, 1931 — probably taken from the *Dallas News* of the Sunday preceding.

[Lewis, Gabe], "Erath County Pioneer Tells How Parrot Started Stampede," *Dallas News*, Feb. 12, 1939.

Mercer, J. W., "Memories of a Stampede," *Semi-Weekly Farm News*, Dallas, Texas, May 19, 1931.

Mosebach, Fred, "Veteran Trail Driver," *San Antonio Express*, Feb. 2, 1936.

Potter, Jack, "Stampedes," *Union County Leader*, Clayton, New Mexico, July 14, 1932.

Prose and Poetry of the Live Stock Industry of the United States, Kansas City, Mo., 1905, 502–503, 533–534, 584, 595–596.

Raine, Wm. McLeod, and Barnes, Will C., *Cattle*, Garden City, N. Y., 1930, 89, 91.

Rush, Oscar, *The Open Range*, Caldwell, Idaho, 1936, 145–154.

Russell, Charles M., *Trails Plowed Under*, Garden City, N. Y., 1927, 199–210: "Longrope's Last Guard," the finest as well as the most informing essay-story that has ever been written about stampedes.

Saunders, George W., *Texasland, The Pioneer Magazine*, San Antonio, April, 1926.

Scobee, Barry, "What Causes Stampedes of Cattle?" *Fort Worth Star Telegram*, April 3, 1938.

Sears, W. H., *Notes from a Cowboy's Diary*, Lawrence, Kansas, n.d., 6.

Shipp, E. Richard, Casper, Wyoming. Letter in Will C. Barnes Manuscripts, Arizona Historical Society, Tucson, Arizona.

Steedman, Charles J., *Bucking the Sagebrush*, N. Y., 1904, 203.

Streeter, Floyd B., *Prairie Trails and Cow Towns*, Boston, 1936, 71.

Taylor, D. K., *Taylor's Thrilling Tales of Texas*, Austin, Texas, 1926, 37, 78.

Trail Drivers of Texas, The, compiled by J. Marvin Hunter, Vol. I, 1920, and Vol. II, 1923. Printed at Bandera, Texas. The two volumes were subsequently issued in one tome by the Cokesbury Press, Nashville and Dallas. The work is made up of around 300 sketches by and about trail drivers. On every fourth page, almost, will be found some description of, or reference to, stampedes. They left an indelible impression on all men who experienced them.

Vail, Edward L., "The Diary of a Desert Trail," *Texasland, The Pioneer Magazine,* San Antonio, Texas, May, 1926.

Williams, Harry W., "Texas Trails," *San Antonio Light,* Sept. 25, 1927.

Williams, James W., signed contribution in *Semi-Weekly Farm News,* Dallas, Texas, March 26, 1937.

IX · *COWS AND CURIOSITY*

[1] Sears, W. H., *Notes from a Cowboy's Diary,* Lawrence, Kansas, n.d., 4.

[2] Wilkeson, Frank, "The Texas Steer . . . The Semi-Wild Cattle of the Lone Star State," *Galveston Daily News,* June 21, 1885, reprinted from the *Pittsburgh Dispatch.*

[3] Townshend, R. B., *A Tenderfoot in Colorado,* London, 1923, 204–207.

[4] "For long, Montana was distinguished as the state exporting the most cattle and importing the most milk products. In those days one could start a shooting match by asking a cowboy if he ever milked.

"One of the incidents of Reservation days I treasure most happened when a roundup took place near our Agency. One of the cowboys was brought in desperately ill. The Agency doctor looked him over, then turned to the patient's companion and remarked that about the only thing to pull him through would be fresh milk. The cowboys looked sheepishly from one to another and asked where it was to be had. The rejoinder was, 'Milk a cow.'

" 'Won't canned milk do?' asked one.

" 'No,' said the doctor, 'he will die if you can't get him fresh milk.'

"The cowboys withdrew into a huddle and discussed with emphasis on the latter syllable. Finally they rode out toward the corral, rounded up a cow with a calf, and drove her into the enclosure. Of course, by this time she was in a fighting mood, but was roped in good cowboy style, thrown and tied. One cowboy took a tin cup, squatted beside the cow and seized a teat. Now, if you recall your first attempt at milking, you understand. You may know, also, that a cow must be in a friendly mood, otherwise, as the farmers say, 'she will not let her milk down.' Anyhow, after long labor and much profanity, about a spoonful of milk was in the cup. Then another cowboy took a turn, but with no better luck. Once around they accumulated three or four spoonfuls; then all stood up and swore most emphatically that not another drop would they milk. Jim could just die if he was so stubborn as all that. The terrified cow was released, and with a snort or two, tail in air, she 'streaked for the blue.'" (Wissler, Clark, "The Indian and the White Man's Buffalo," *Natural History* magazine, November, 1937. XL, 627.)

The same sort of prejudice against milk and milking was common among the gauchos of South America, as brought out by W. H. Hudson in his doubly and quintuply delightful *The Purple Land*.

⁵ Cross, Joe, *Cattle Clatter*, Kansas City, Mo., 1938, 27.

⁶ Joe M. Evans told me about this cow; then he put her in his little book, *A Corral Full of Stories*, El Paso, Texas, 1939, 38–41.

⁷ Rollins, Philip Ashton, *The Cowboy*, New York, 1924, 283.

⁸ Hittell, Theodore H., *The Adventures of James Capen Adams*, New York, 1912 (reprint edition), 315–316.

⁹ Reaugh, Frank, *Paintings of the Southwest*, privately printed at Dallas, Texas, n.d., 11–16.

X · SMELL AND THIRST

¹ Told me by Charles Goodnight. The account is also in *Charles Goodnight, Cowman and Plainsman*, by J. Evetts Haley, Boston, 1936, 430–431.

² "There was no milk at the outside camps and no one to care for the poor abandoned lambs whose frivolous young mothers re-

fused to own them, leaving them to starve. Occasionally an old ewe of truly maternal instinct could be fooled into adopting one of these little 'dogies' or 'bums.' The skin of her dead lamb was taken off and slipped over the orphan, which was joyfully accepted because of its smell." (Clarice E. Richards, *A Tenderfoot Bride*, Garden City, New York, 1920, 124–125.)

³ Houseman, William, *Cattle: Breeds and Management*, London, 1897, 7.

⁴ The best descriptions of thirst in cattle that I know of are in Chapter V of Andy Adams' *The Log of a Cowboy* and in *The Days That Are Done*, by William Perry Sanders, Los Angeles, California, 1918, 84–88.

⁵ A page feature article, by N. G. Ozment and Henry L. Farrell, *San Antonio Express*, May 28, 1922. "Rancher Dies at San Saba," *Fort Worth Star Telegram*, January 10, 1938. Fred S. Millard's original pamphlet, *A Cow Puncher of the Pecos*, Bandera, Texas, 1928, 23, 36, affords some curious examples of behaviour at water.

⁶ See, for example, "Some Animals of Pioneer Days in Pecos County," by O. W. Williams, *West Texas Historical and Scientific Society Publications*, No. 3 (1930), 22. Lumholtz, Carl, *New Trails in Mexico*, New York, 1912, 153, 244, 245, 249.

⁷ Allen, J. A., *History of the American Bison*, in 9th Annual Report of the U. S. Geological and Geographical Survey, by F. V. Hayden, Washington, D. C., 1877, 503–504.

XI · *VITALITY DRIFTS AND DIE-UPS*

¹ Hastings, Frank S., *A Ranchman's Recollections*, Chicago, 1921, 6.

² "Brazos" (pseudonym), *Life of Robert Hall, also Sketch of Big Foot Wallace*, Austin, Texas, 1898, 87.

³ Jackson, George, *Sixty Years in Texas*, Dallas, 1908, 171.

⁴ French, William, *Some Recollections of a Western Ranchman*, London, 1927, 132.

⁵ Haley, J. Evetts, *Charles Goodnight, Cowman and Plainsman*, Boston, 1936, 320.

⁶ Rainey, George, *No Man's Land*, Enid, Oklahoma, 1937, 99–101.

⁷ The nameless line rider's diary is quoted by Don Biggers in *From Cattle Range to Cotton Patch* (n.d. and n.p.), 103ff. Biggers evidently took liberties with the line rider's words. I have taken further liberties. Biggers' chapter on "Awful Drifts and Die-ups," pp. 102–110, though inaccurate in spots, is a remarkable treatise on this phase of open-range cattle life. Other sources on the subject are:

Aldridge, Reginald, *Ranch Notes*, London, 1884, 157.

Haley, J. Evetts, *Charles Goodnight, Cowman and Plainsman*, Boston, 1936, 320–322.

Lauderdale, R. J. (and John Doak), *Life on the Range and on the Trail*, San Antonio, 1936, 148.

Livingston, Carl, "Cattle on the Drift," *New Mexico Magazine*, October, 1933.

O'Keefe, Rufe, *Cowboy Life*, San Antonio, 1936, 95–102.

Prose and Poetry of the Live Stock Industry of the United States, Kansas City, 1905, 704–710.

Ridings, Sam P., *The Chisholm Trail*, Guthrie, Oklahoma, 1936, 245, 267–268.

Robinson, G. C., "The Longhorn Cattle of Texas," manuscript in my possession.

⁸ See accounts in Abbott, E. C. (and Helena Huntington Smith), *We Pointed Them North*, New York, 1939, 200–218; Hagedorn, Hermann, *Roosevelt in the Bad Lands*, Boston, 1921, Chapters XXV and XXVI; Lang, Lincoln A., *Ranching with Roosevelt*, Philadelphia, 1926, 240–258; Osgood, Ernest Staples, *The Day of the Cattleman*, Minneapolis, 1929, 216–244; *Prose and Poetry of the Live Stock Industry of the United States*, Kansas City, 1905, I, 708; Reynolds, Phin, reminiscences, in the Abilene, Texas, *Reporter-News*, February 9, 1939; Stuart, Granville, *Forty Years on the Frontier*, Cleveland, Ohio, 1925, II, 227–239; Thompson, W. H., "Fire, Then Snow, Wrought Destruction on Llano Estacado," *Amarillo Sunday News and Globe*, Anniversary Edition, 1938; Wilkeson, Frank, "Cattle Raising on the Plains," *Harper's Magazine*, April, 1886.

XII · HORNS

¹ *Victoria Advocate*, Victoria, Texas, 88th Anniversary Edition, Sept. 28, 1934, 84.

[2] *San Antonio Express*, Oct. 31, 1899; Nov. 2, 3, 8, 27, 1899. The *Express* was not reproducing photographs at this time, but on Nov. 3 it printed a pen-and-ink sketch of the head of the West steer; and on Nov. 8, a pen-and-ink sketch of the Dobie steer.

[3] *Chicago Tribune*, Feb. 6, 1900; *New York World*, ——, 1900. M. S. Garretson, who knew the range while Longhorns still roamed over it, now of the New York Zoological Park, kindly furnished me the contents of clippings from these papers. Contrary to fact, the *New York World* reported that the steer had left on a boat for Paris.

[4] *Beeville Bee*, Beeville, Texas, April 20, 1900, and June 29, 1900; *Beeville Picayune*, Beeville, Texas, June 28, 1900.

[5] *San Antonio Express*, Nov. 3, 1899.

[6] *Travels*, by Maximilian, Prince of Wied, *Early Western Travels*, edited by Thwaites, Cleveland, Ohio, 1906, XXIII, 175. See, also, Shoemaker, Henry W., *A Pennsylvania Bison Hunt*, Middleburg, Pa., 1915, 18. Yet M. S. Garretson measured various mature heads of male buffaloes that had been castrated as calves in the Yellowstone National Park and found their horns no longer than those of grown buffalo bulls.

[7] I own them. Before he was killed in 1882, they belonged to Lee Pope, of Fort Ewell on the Nueces River, La Salle County. A few years ago they were given me by Mr. and Mrs. Jim Bell, of La Mota Ranch, La Salle County.

[8] The mightiest horns offered for sale in Texas during the Centennial Year, 1936, were from Panama. They have a nine-foot spread, although the curves towards the tips seem to have been tampered with. They belong to the Tate Medicine Show, of Waco, Texas, which carries two or three truckloads of heads and horns for exhibition.

XIII · RAWHIDE

Instead of making particular references, I have provided a bibliography, as follows.

Audubon, John W., *Audubon's Western Journal: 1849–1850*, Cleveland, Ohio, 1906, 95–96.

Barrows, John R., *Ubet*, Caldwell, Idaho, 1934, 221–223.

Bates, Ed F., *History and Reminiscences of Denton County*, Denton, Texas, 1918, 12.

Beckham, W. A., "Life Story of a Pioneer of Texas," *Yorktown (Texas) News*, 1924.

Bell County, Texas, Proceedings of Old Settlers' Association of, Belton, Texas, 1904, 42–43.

Bidwell, John, *Echoes of the Past about California*, Lakeside Press, Chicago, 1928 (reprint), 85–86.

Boatright, Mody C., *Tall Tales from Texas Cow Camps*, Dallas, 1934, 74–76.

Burnham, Frederick Russell, *Scouting on Two Continents*, Garden City, New York, 1927, 155, 289.

Burns, Walter Noble, *The Robin Hood of El Dorado*, New York, 1932, 49, 60, 124.

Bush, I. J., *Gringo Doctor*, Caldwell, Idaho, 1939, 230, 259.

Cheshire, Joseph B., *Nonnulla*, Chapel Hill, North Carolina, 1930, 113–114.

Cook, James H., *Fifty Years on the Old Frontier*, New Haven, Connecticut, 1923, 15.

Coolidge, Dane, *Fighting Men of the West*, New York, 1932, 44; *Old California Cowboys*, New York, 1939, 14, 157.

Cotulla (Texas) *Record*, February 5, 1937 (article by O. W. Nolen).

Craig, C. W. T., *Paraguayan Interlude*, New York, 1935, 317.

Cross, F. M., *Early Days in Central Texas*, n.p., 1910, 18–19, 71–72.

Davis, W. W. H., *El Gringo, or New Mexico and Her People* (first published 1856), The Rydal Press, Santa Fe, New Mexico, 1938, 81, 162, 164, 187, 192.

Dawson, Nicholas "Cheyenne," *Narrative*, San Francisco, 1933 (reprint), 34, 39–43.

Dobie, J. Frank, *A Vaquero of the Brush Country*, Dallas, Texas, 1929, 20–29; "A Question of Hides," *The Cattleman*, Fort Worth, March, 1935, 65ff.

Domenech, Abbe, *Missionary Adventures in Texas and Mexico*, London, 1858, 96.

Dunn, P. F., Corpus Christi, Texas, letter of, April 27, 1928.

Erskine, Gladys Shaw, *Broncho Charlie*, New York, 1934, 7–8.

Fenley, Florence, *Oldtimers*, Uvalde, Texas, 1939, 32.

Fisher, O. C., *It Occurred in Kimble*, Houston, 1937, 26.

Flandrau, C. M., *Viva Mexico*, New York, 1909, 270–271.

Froebel, Julius, *Seven Years' Travel in Central America, Northern Mexico and the Far West*, London, 1859, 404–405, 442–443.

Frontier Times, Bandera, Texas, October, 1932, Vol. 10, 13–15; May, 1939, Vol. 16 (article by T. U. Taylor on "Old McDade"), 344–345.

Galveston News for 1873, January 28 and 31, Feb. 14, 15 and 18, March 14, April 25; for 1877, January 28 and March 3; for 1878, January 8.

Graham, R. B. Cunninghame, the story "San Jose" in *Thirty Tales and Sketches*, New York, 1929.

Graves, H. F., Brazoria, Texas, letter of, October 4, 1938.

Grey Owl, *The Men of the Last Frontier*, New York, 1932, 224.

Haley, J. Evetts, *Charles Goodnight, Cowman and Plainsman*, Boston, 1936, 214.

Hall, Basil, *Extracts from a Journal*, etc., Edinburgh, 1824, 135.

Hanscom, Otho Anne, *Parade of the Pioneers*, Dallas, 1935, 24.

Hastings, Lansford W., *The Emigrant's Guide to Oregon and California*, Princeton University Press, 1932 (reprint), 125–126.

Head, F. B., *Rough Notes . . . across the Pampas and among the Andes*, London, 1828, 44.

Henry, Stuart, *Conquering the Great Plains*, New York, 1930, 69.

Johnson, Overton, and Winter, W. H., *Route across the Rocky Mountains*, Princeton University Press, 1932 (reprint), 108.

Jones, Daniel W., *Forty Years among the Indians*, Salt Lake City, Utah, 1890, 81–82.

Kelly, Luther S., *Yellowstone Kelly*, New Haven, 1926, 20.

Kruger, M., *Pioneer Life in Texas*, privately printed at San Antonio, 1930, 33–34, 62.

Linn, John J., *Reminiscences of Fifty Years in Texas*, New York, 1833, 33.

Lockhart, J. W., *Sixty Years on the Brazos*, Los Angeles, California (privately printed), 1930, 22, 91.

McCampbell, Coleman, *Saga of a Frontier Seaport*, Dallas, Texas, 1934, 157.

McKenna, James A., *Black Range Tales*, New York, 1936, 159, 177.

McReynolds, Robert, *Thirty Years on the Frontier*, Colorado Springs, Colorado, 1906, 211.

Nance, Berta Hart, "Cattle," used by permission of the author. The poem won the Texan Prize of the Poetry Society of Texas in 1931 and was printed in the *Anthology Year Book of the Poetry Society of Texas*, Dallas, 1931. It is also included in Miss Nance's *Flute in the Distance*, Dallas, 1935.

O'Neil, James B., *They Die but Once*, New York, 1935, 172.

Patterson, C. L., *The Two Conspiracies*, Boston, 1928, 79.

Rabb, Mrs., Reminiscences of, in Archives, The University of Texas.

Raine, W. MacLeod, and Barnes, Will C., *Cattle*, Garden City, New York, 1930, 17, 220, 309–313.

Reynolds, Phin, reminiscences, in the *Abilene* (Texas) *Reporter-News*, January 1, 1939.

Richardson, Rupert N., in *West Texas Historical Association Year Book*, XI (1935), 54.

Ridings, Sam P., *The Chisholm Trail*, Guthrie, Oklahoma, 1936, 558–560.

Smith, S. Compton, *Chile con Carne*, New York, 1857, 194–195.

Smithwick, Noah, *The Evolution of a State*, Austin, 1900, 47, 143, 147.

Steele, James W., *The Sons of the Border*, Topeka, Kansas, 1873, 42–43.

Stratton, Florence, *The Story of Beaumont*, Houston, Texas, 1925, 186.

Summerhayes, Martha, *Vanished Arizona: Recollections of My Army Life* (first printed in Philadelphia, 1908), edited by Milo M. Quaife, The Lakeside Press, Chicago, 1939, 296.

Trail Drivers of Texas, The (J. M. Hunter, compiler), Bandera, Texas, 1923, II, 233–234.

Ward, H. G., *Mexico in 1827*, London, 1828, II, 405.

White, Stewart Edward, "Rawhide," in *Arizona Nights*, any edition.

XIV · OXEN AND TAILS

[1] Thorp, N. Howard, *Songs of the Cowboys*, Boston, 1931, 117–118.

[2] This folk anecdote is told in *The Log of a Cowboy*, by Andy Adams, Boston, 1903, 129–132, and in *The Chisholm Trail*, by Sam

P. Ridings, published by the author at Guthrie, Oklahoma, 1936, 399–402. Ridings has a bully lot of ox lore.

³ In his *Autobiography and Reminiscences*, Chicago, 1904, 16–17, Theophilus Noel tells of a pair of oxen with the same sort of headstrong will to go to dinner when the horn blew.

⁴ Jackson, George, *Sixty Years in Texas*, Dallas, 1908, 27–28.

⁵ Rolt-Wheeler, Francis, *The Book of Cowboys*, Boston, 1921, 130–142. For exposition on the superiority of oxen to mules, see Johnson, Overton, and Winter, W. H., *Route across the Rocky Mountains*, Lafayette, Indiana, 1846, reprinted by Princeton University Press, 1932, 180–181; "Letters of Peter H. Burnett" in *Quarterly* of Oregon Historical Society, III, 418; Hastings, L. W., *The Emigrants' Guide to Oregon and California*, Princeton University Press reprint, 1932, 145; Marcy, R. B., *The Prairie Traveller*, New York, 1859, 28.

⁶ Root, Frank A., and Connelley, W. E., *The Overland Stage to California*, Topeka, Kansas, 1901, 308. See also Majors, Alexander, *Seventy Years on the Frontier*, Chicago, 1893, 143.

⁷ Bratt, John, *Trails of Yesterday*, Chicago, 1921, 50–53; Jackson, Wm. H., and Driggs, Howard R., *The Pioneer Photographer*, Yonkers-on-the-Hudson, New York, 1929, 19–20; James, Jason W., *Memories and Viewpoints*, Roswell, New Mexico, 1926, 18–22; McReynolds, Robert, *Thirty Years on the Frontier*, Colorado Springs, Colorado, 1906, 225.

⁸ Jim Foster in *Trail Drivers of Texas*, compiled by J. Marvin Hunter, Bandera, Texas, 1923, II, 101 — with some Dobie amendations.

⁹ Hampton, Howard, "The Palmy Days of the Texas Cowpuncher," in *Dallas News*, January 30, 1927.

XV · SANCHO AND OTHER RETURNERS

¹ Adair, W. S., interview with J. F. Williams, *Dallas News*, November 27, 1927. Another account of oxen driven from Mississippi to Texas that went back home was furnished me by R. R. ("Railroad") Smith, Jourdanton, Texas.

² Cochran, W. C., "A Trip to Montana in 1869." Manuscript in Archives, The University of Texas Library.

³ I have corrected a name or two. Wyoming, not Montana, as in the original story, was Sancho's destination. See the chapter on Longhorns in my book, *On the Open Range*, Dallas, 1931. I must confess to making the Mexican peppers pretty strong in the story, but it is essentially true, all of it.

XVI · *LEAD STEERS AND NECK OXEN*

¹ Goodnight was very anxious to have Old Blue "remembered," though, as he told me bluntly when I visited him in 1926 for the purpose of writing a magazine article on him, he "did not give a damn" about any article on himself. My account of Blue appeared first in *Frontier Stories*, New York, May, 1928. With some changes, I incorporated it in *On the Open Range*, Dallas, 1931. Other changes have been made in the present version. In *Charles Goodnight, Cowman and Plainsman* (Boston, 1936), J. Evetts Haley has a full account of Old Blue. Another account of him, by Vance Johnson, appeared in the *Amarillo Daily News*, January 7, 1938.

² John James Haynes in *The Trail Drivers of Texas*, I, 220–221.

³ His book, a pamphlet, *Cattle Trails of the Old West*, Clayton, New Mexico, 1935, contains accounts of the steers named Lew Wallace, Buckshot Roberts and Randao. His *Lead Steer and Other Tales*, Clayton, New Mexico, 1939, celebrates the steers named Bob Wright, John Chisum, and others. Most of the contents of these excellent books appeared originally in the *Union County Leader*, Clayton, New Mexico, and were somewhat edited for book form. I have drawn from the newspaper articles and from conversation with Jack Potter, as well as from his books.

XVII · *OUTLAWS OF THE BRUSH*

¹ I owe the history of this steer to a not well enough known book entitled *Animal Outlaws*, published by the author Gid Graham, Collinsville, Oklahoma, 1938 (157–166). The book contains the story of another notable steer named Three Stripes.

² Hendricks, Sterling Brown, "The Somervell Expedition to the

Rio Grande," *Southwestern Historical Quarterly*, Austin, Texas, 1919, XXIII, 122, 129.

³ Sowell, A. J., *Rangers and Pioneers of Texas*, San Antonio, Texas, 1884, 189–190.

XVIII · *HIDDEN IN THE THICKETS*

¹ Cook, James H., *Fifty Years on the Old Frontier*, Yale University Press, New Haven, Connecticut, 1923, 14–26. Thanks are expressed to Captain Cook for permission to quote extracts.

XIX · *MOLDED BY HORN AND THORN*

¹ About 1830, Gideon Lincecum, then living in the wilderness of Mississippi, owned a small black Indian pony, worth fifteen dollars. "He was an excellent hunting horse, for he could track a deer equal to the best trained dog." — *Autobiography* of Gideon Lincecum, Publications of Mississippi Historical Society, VIII, 1904, 487.

² *Lamar Papers*, Vol. IV, Part I, 229.

³ During the year 1807 San Antonio "entertained" 3224 Indians, mostly Comanches, many of them, no doubt, repeaters, and fed them over 200 head of cattle. *Spanish Archives Translations, January 1–31, 1807*, by J. Villasana Haggard, The University of Texas Archives.

XX · *SUNDOWN*

¹ Peake, Ora Brooks, *The Colorado Range Cattle Industry*, Glendale, California, 1937, 209–210, 221, 224, 248. Osgood, Ernest Staples, *The Day of the Cattleman*, University of Minnesota Press, Minneapolis, 1929, 140.

² Sartwelle, J. W., in *The Coastal Cattleman*, Beaumont, Texas, December, 1939.

³ Foote, Henry Stuart, *Texas and The Texans*, Philadelphia, 1841, II, 383.

INDEX

This index is intended primarily as a reference guide to the subject of the book — the Texas Longhorns; it is an index to subject matter more than to proper names, though the names of men and places associated with the Longhorns appear in it. The Notes, however, a number of which contain information beyond citations, have not been indexed.

Brush hands (*continued*)
cowboys, 318–319; 321–333. *See*
Cowboys.
Brush horses, 320–329. *See* Cow horses.
Brush poppers. *See* Brush hands.
Buckhorn Saloon, 205, 213
Buffaloes, xv, xxii–xxiii, 12, 23, 39,
70–71, 81, 98, 119, 188, 193, 196, 210,
274
Bulls, behavior of on range, 139–141;
fighting of on range, 140–146; fierce-
ness of, 146–153; ghost bull, 315–317;
4, 6, 8, 9, 15–17, 18, 20, 23, 33, 46,
51, 60–61, 180, 190, 194, 210, 214,
223, 252, 310, 319, 338, 339, 341
Bullwhackers, 223, 230. *See* Oxen.
Burnham, Frederick Russell, 231–232
Burton, W. W., 18
Butler, Bill, 256
Byler, Rufus, 39

CALDWELL, "PAINT," 295
Calf wagon, 109, 178
Calves, on trail, 109, 177, 178; on range
and in pen, 49, 154, 160–164, 165–
168, 194
Canadian River, 84, 177, 196, 198, 255,
269, 274
Carnes, Ship, 234
Carpenter, J. W., 94
Carrigan, Mike, 158–159
Caylor, Harvey Wallace, xxii
Champion, famous steer, 205–208
Champion, Jake, 61
Chapa, Don Victoriano, 333–339
Chapa, Prisciliano, 335–339
Cherokee cattle, 32, 341
Chillingham, wild cattle of, 7, 181
Chisholm Trail, xv–xvi
Chisum, John, 75, 102–104, 232, 268
Cibolo Creek, 187
Cimarron River, 90, 118, 130, 272, 315
Cimarrones, 4, 9, 43. *See* Mustang
cattle.
Cochran, W. C., 55
Colorado River, 10, 11, 18, 76, 77, 199,
234
Concho River, 102, 103, 183, 199
Connor, John, 96
Cook, James H., 306–309
Cook, Sam, 320
Cooke, Philip St. George, 16–17, 148

Coronado, brings cattle into Texas, 4,
7
Corrals, 57–59, 115–117, 232, 238–239.
See Pens.
Cousins, Walt, 88
"Cow and calf" money, 37–38
Cow horses, 122–123, 149, 199, 221,
229, 232, 273, 324, 327–328, 331–332.
See Brush horses.
Cow thieves, 49, 222, 236, 269, 329. *See*
Rustlers.
Cowboy singing and songs, 88–89, 91,
100, 110, 126–129, 132, 133, 263, 272,
320. *See* "Texas Lullaby."
Cowboys, origin of in Texas, xiv, 27–
28. *See* Brush hands.
Cowden, Jeff, and brothers, 59–60
Cows, Longhorn, as fighters, 152–153,
161, 163, 165, 344; as milkers, 162–
163, 168–169; as mothers, 160–168,
177–178; 17, 21, 30, 31, 37, 38, 49,
108–109, 153–155, 180, 190, 194, 210,
270, 315
Cox, "Deacon," 82
Coyote, 6, 98, 145, 287. *See* Wolves.
Crockett, David, as drover, 29; 217,
235
Crooked Creek, 188
Cross, Joe, 169
Crosse, Tex, 117
Cude, Tim, 248–250
Custer, John, 209

DAWSON, "CHEYENNE," 239
Deer, 168, 294, 304; hunting of, 234
Delgadito, 304
Denton, "Cyclone," 97
Desprez, Frank, 128
Devil's River, 199
Devon cattle, 206, 342
Diablo Mountains, 284
Dixon, Maynard, xxii
Doan's Crossing, 120
Dobie, Bertha McKee, xxi
Dobie, Elrich H., 160
Dobie, J. M., 107, 126, 205–207, 296,
305
Dodge, R. I., 12–13, 15, 17
Dodge City, 82, 85, 94, 118, 130, 136,
188, 218, 269–275
Dogies, 73, 109, 226, 260, 310
Dogs, "catch" (or cow), 60, 212, 309

[382]

prices of, xv, xvii, 37, 50; riding of, 252–255; sense of smell, 98, 144, 155–159, 174, 176–184, 303, 316, 328; shipping of, xvii, 209–210; smartness of, 72, 160–162, 165–168, 243–245, 300–301, 303; Spanish progenitors of, 3–25, 147; in stampedes, 71, 87–138; as swimmers, 190, 216–217; their tails, 33, 255–256; their teeth, 195; on trail, xiv–xviii, 29, 50, 69–86; as travelers, 69–86, 257–266, 284–285; their vitality, 189–196; their voices, 105, 141–143, 145–146, 147, 153–159, 164, 175, 178, 315; weights of, 34–36, 285; their aboriginal wildness, 283–289, 297–301, 303–304. *See* Bedding down, Bulls, Calves, Drouths, Hide wars, Hides, Horns, Lead steers, Maverick cattle in Texas, Mustang cattle, Outlaws, Oxen, Spanish cattle in America, Stampedes, Steers, Thirst, Trailing cattle.
"Longrope's Last Guard," by Charles M. Russell, 130–138
Longworth, John, 306–309
Loving, Jim, 225
Loving, Joe, 54
Lyne, T. J., 335
Lyne, Tom, 338

McCoy, Ed, 327–328
McCulloch, Ben, 28
McGill, Claude, 158, 297
McGill, Frank, 189, 297
McHenry, Robert, 13
McKenna, James A., 226–227
McMillan, John, 258
McWhorter, Ed, 40, 207, 318
Mack, Morris, 152
Maltsberger, Jack, 158, 302
Maney, Mason, 182
Mangum, Hal, 95
Matador Ranch, 89
Matagorda Island, 46–47
Maverick, Maury, 48
Maverick, Samuel A., 44–48
Maverick brand, 49
Maverick (cattle), origin and meaning of word, 44–49
Maverick cattle in Texas: origin of, numbers of, days and ways of catching them, the whole subject treated

historically, 43–68; 190, 212, 270, 288, 323, 327. *See Cimarrones,* Longears, Mustang cattle, Orejanos.
Maverickers, their ways with maverick cattle, 46–68, 288
Maximilian, Prince of Wied, 210
Mercer, John, 66
Mesquite, 290
Mexican cattle, 42, 168, 210, 228, 284, 301, 341
Mexican vaqueros, xiv, 93, 98, 125, 176, 180, 228, 229, 293, 296, 298, 303, 306–317, 323–339
Mexican Water Hole, 315–317
Mexican ways on range, 33, 190, 211, 224, 231, 238–240, 281, 335–339. *See* Spanish cattle in America.
Milk, 168–169, 315
Mill, cattle, 82–83, 95, 118, 126, 277. *See* Stampedes.
Miller Brothers' 101 Ranch Wild West Show, 207
Mills, J. M., 209
Mineral waters, 187–188
Missouri River, 74, 190, 200
Mitchell, Alonzo, 108–114
Mitchell, Bob, 112
Mitchell, Frank, 123
Moore, Lon, 59
Morris, Joseph P., 82–83
Mosquitoes, 191–192
Moss, Aaron, 304
Muerto, El, Creek, 279
Muleys, 72, 163, 211, 244
MURDER brand, 63
Mustang cattle, origin, nature, numbers, etc. of, 8–25; 30, 32. *See* Maverick cattle in Texas.
Mustang Gray, 230–231
Mustang Island, 335
Myers, Al, 252

NAMES of Longhorn brutes: Baby Mine, 73; Ben, 282; Blue, 267–275; Brindle, 243; Broad, 110; Buck, 90–91, 245–246; Buckshot Roberts, 277; Bugler, 105; Bully, 246–247; Camino, 281; Champion, 205–208; Cherry, 30; Clabber, 163; Crump, 110; Dan, 246; Frank Swift, 147–148; George, 246; Geronimo, 281; Goliath, 252; Hookey, 163; Jerry, 244; John